T0330385

The Euro Crisis and Constitutional Pluralism

ELGAR STUDIES IN EUROPEAN LAW AND POLICY

Series Editor: Herwig C.H. Hofmann, *Professor of European and Transnational Public Law, Faculty of Law, Economics and Finance and Robert Schuman Institute for European Affairs, University of Luxembourg*

Elgar Studies in European Law and Policy is a forum for books that demonstrate cutting-edge legal and politico-legal analysis of the pertinent policies in a multi-jurisdictional Europe. The series is as relevant for academic reflection as for practical development of the matters addressed therein, such as policy relevance, its origins and the possibilities of future development. Books in the series take a multidisciplinary or multi-jurisdictional approach to the topics at their centers, with an aim to facilitating understanding of European law and policy matters and demonstrating their connectedness throughout jurisdictional levels. The series will provide coverage and analysis of various regulatory areas at the forefront of EU law and policy, including: the development of new European policy fields, issues of market regulation, economic and monetary matters and social dimensions of EU Law.

Titles in the series include:

The Metamorphosis of the European Economic Constitution
Edited by Herwig C.H. Hofmann, Katerina Pantazatou and Giovanni Zaccaroni

Citizenship in the European Union
Constitutionalism, Rights and Norms
Anne Wesemann

Equality and Non-Discrimination in the EU
The Foundations of the EU Constitutional Legal Order
Giovanni Zaccaroni

The Euro Crisis and Constitutional Pluralism
Financial Stability but Constitutional Inequality
Tomi Tuominen

The Euro Crisis and Constitutional Pluralism

Financial Stability but Constitutional Inequality

Tomi Tuominen

University Lecturer in Law, University of Lapland, Finland

ELGAR STUDIES IN EUROPEAN LAW AND POLICY

Edward Elgar
PUBLISHING

Cheltenham, UK • Northampton, MA, USA

© Tomi Tuominen 2021

Cover image: Tomi Tuominen

Published by
Edward Elgar Publishing Limited
The Lypiatts
15 Lansdown Road
Cheltenham
Glos GL50 2JA
UK

Edward Elgar Publishing, Inc.
William Pratt House
9 Dewey Court
Northampton
Massachusetts 01060
USA

A catalogue record for this book
is available from the British Library

Library of Congress Control Number: 2021936629

This book is available electronically in the **Elgar**online
Law subject collection
http://dx.doi.org/10.4337/9781800371590

MIX
Paper from
responsible sources
FSC
www.fsc.org FSC® C013604

ISBN 978 1 80037 158 3 (cased)
ISBN 978 1 80037 159 0 (eBook)

Printed and bound by CPI Group (UK) Ltd, Croydon, CR0 4YY

Contents

Preface

The purpose of this book is to bring together perhaps the two most prevalent discussions in European constitutionalism during the previous decade: the substantive discussion on the Eurozone financial and debt crisis and the theoretical discussion on constitutional pluralism. The idea to study these two topics together grew out of two somewhat different interests. First, since newspapers and legal journals were saturated with articles discussing the Eurozone crisis, I thought that as someone working with EU law, I too must follow these events and try to understand the crisis. The crisis seemed to be especially pressing due to the way in which economic, political and legal concerns intertwined with it. Second, I have always had a keen interest in all things 'theoretical'. Thus, the theory of constitutional pluralism drew my attention, although at first I did not quite understand what it was actually about. Upon further studying the literature, my initially enthusiastic attitude changed to a more critical stance towards the main theses expounded in the constitutional pluralist literature. I then figured that the theory of constitutional pluralism should be put to the test by using the Eurozone crisis as a case study. If the crisis was truly an existential crisis for the European Union, and if constitutional pluralism is the theory that both explains and prescribes the European Union's constitutional nature, then what better context than the Eurozone crisis to study the theory of constitutional pluralism? This book attempts to do just that. While the Eurozone crisis is already an event of the past, the German Federal Constitutional Court's ruling in May 2020 on the European Central Bank's Public Sector Purchase Programme (PSPP) reinvigorates the topic in a new way, as the judgment is a paramount example of why the current pluralist constellation seems dysfunctional.

Acknowledgements

I have had the pleasure of being hosted as a visiting researcher in a number of stimulating environments whilst working towards the completion of this book. First, at the Amsterdam Centre for European Law and Governance, then at the European University Institute in Florence, next at the Europa Institute at Leiden University, and finally at the Max Planck Institute for Comparative Public Law and International Law at Heidelberg (which was unfortunately cut short due to the COVID-19 pandemic). Furthermore, the Faculty of Law at the University of Lapland must also be recognised, as it has provided me with stable funding throughout my career. Several people have helped me throughout the years. I gratefully acknowledge the valuable comments, encouragement or inspiration of Leonard Besselink, Federico Fabbrini, Nik de Boer, Massimo Fichera, Gábor Halmai, Jaakko Husa, Juha Karhu, Alison McDonnell, Juha Raitio, Jo Shaw, Kaarlo Tuori, Neil Walker and Napoleon Xanthoulis.

Tomi Tuominen
Rovaniemi, 31 October 2020

Abbreviations

BRRD	Bank Recovery and Resolution Directive
CJEU	Court of Justice of the European Union
CRD IV	Capital Requirements Directive IV
CRR	Capital Requirements Regulation
DGSD	Deposit Guarantee Scheme Directive
DIF	Deposit Insurance Fund
EBA	European Banking Authority
ECB	European Central Bank
EDIS	European Deposit Insurance Scheme
EFSF	European Financial Stability Facility
EFSM	European Financial Stabilisation Mechanism
EMU	Economic and Monetary Union
ESCB	European System of Central Banks
ESFS	European System of Financial Supervision
ESM	European Stability Mechanism
EU	European Union
GDP	Gross domestic product
GLF	Greek Loan Facility
IMF	International Monetary Fund
MoU	Memorandum of Understanding
MTBO	Medium-Term Budgetary Objective
NCA	National Competent Authority
NEC	National Emissions Ceilings
OMT	Outright Monetary Transactions
PSPP	Public Sector Purchase Programme
SGP	Stability and Growth Pact
SMP	Securities Markets Programme

SRB	Single Resolution Board
SRF	Single Resolution Fund
SRM	Single Resolution Mechanism
SSM	Single Supervisory Mechanism
TEU	Treaty on the European Union
TFEU	Treaty on the Functioning of the European Union
TSCG	The Treaty on Stability, Coordination and Governance in the Economic and Monetary Union
UK	United Kingdom
USA	United States of America

1. Introduction: constitutional pluralism as inequality and the asymmetry of the EMU

1.1 INTRODUCTION

1.1.1 Introducing the Two Themes of the Book

Who would have thought that the German Federal Constitutional Court (*Bundesverfassungsgericht*) would eventually declare an act by the European Union as *ultra vires* and order the German Federal Government and Federal Parliament to act in order to redress this state of affairs. This is exactly what the German court did in its ruling on 5 May 2020 in a case concerning the European Central Bank's (ECB) Public Sector Purchase Programme (PSPP).[1] This was despite the fact that the Court of Justice of the European Union (CJEU) had already concluded in *Weiss* that the PSPP was within the ECB's mandate.[2] This case represents a culmination of a long process and serves as the best example to introduce the topic of this book.

In the early 2010s the Eurozone faced an economic crisis that then evolved into a political and constitutional crisis. As a result of this crisis, the EU and the Member States adopted a host of legal measures that aimed to combat the crisis and to prevent future crises. From a constitutional perspective, the measures were both novel and controversial. They changed the nature and functioning of the Economic and Monetary Union (EMU) and had severe consequences for both Member States and citizens alike. Thus, it was not surprising that the measures generated a wealth of case law concerning their legality under both EU law and national law.

Such cases – just like the above-mentioned recent ruling by the German Federal Constitutional Court – are expressions of clashes between national constitutions and the EU's constitutional order as effectuated by courts acting as the guardians of the very constitutions establishing their competences. Since

---

[1] 2 BvR 859/15, 05 May 2020 (*PSPP judgment*).
[2] C-493/17 *Weiss* EU:C:2018:1000.

the adoption of the Treaty of Maastricht and the inception of the EMU, the role of courts as central participants in the European multi-level constitutional and political discourse has increased considerably. This is mainly due to a phenomenon called constitutional pluralism; namely, the fact that the national constitutions and the EU's constitutional norms are both in force in the Member States yet without a settled hierarchy between the two. Since the 1990s, constitutional pluralism has become the central theory of European constitutionalism that is used to describe the current constitutional constellation, but also, at least by some, to argue for the normative acceptance of the current constellation.

The euro crisis and constitutional pluralism seem to have been the dominant themes within EU constitutional law scholarship during the past decade. In fact, one could argue that the euro crisis has been the main substantive topic whereas the main theoretical premise has been offered by constitutional pluralism. A substantial amount of literature has been written within both broad fields.

The literature on the constitutional aspects of the euro crisis has focused on how the reactions to the crisis have affected the dynamics of political decision-making within the EU,[3] and what the adopted mechanisms mean in light of political and legal accountability.[4] A central conclusion has been that despite no formal amendments to the EU Treaties, the fundamental principles underlying the EMU have been transformed.[5] This transformation has centred around the objective of securing financial stability within the Eurozone[6] and is visible in most of the legal mechanisms adopted pursuant to the crisis.[7] Furthermore, constitutional analysis has focused on how the various economic and political assumptions on which the EMU has been established have contributed to the crisis[8] and how this constitutional framework seems paradoxical

---

[3]   A. Hinarejos, *The Euro Area Crisis in Constitutional Perspective* (Oxford University Press 2015).

[4]   M. Markakis, *Accountability in the Economic and Monetary Union: Foundations, Policy, and Governance* (Oxford University Press 2020).

[5]   K. Tuori and K. Tuori, *The Eurozone Crisis: A Constitutional Analysis* (Cambridge University Press 2014).

[6]   V. Borger, *The Currency of Solidarity: Constitutional Transformation during the Euro Crisis* (Cambridge University Press 2020).

[7]   G. Lo Schiavo, *The Role of Financial Stability in EU Law and Policy* (Wolters Kluwer 2017).

[8]   D. Adamski, *Redefining European Economic Integration* (Cambridge University Press 2018).

when compared to the federal system of the USA.[9] Moreover, the effects that the measures have had at the national level have been closely documented.[10]

The theory of constitutional pluralism has attracted attention from most scholars working with European constitutionalism, as is visible in the number of edited compilations on the topic,[11] although book-length treatments on it are still scarce. Some have used constitutional pluralism as a descriptive and conceptual starting point for broader theoretical discussions on European constitutionalism.[12] Several scholars have argued that constitutional pluralism offers the key to solving some of the persistent problems in the EU's constitutional design. These have included, for example, a substantive version of pluralism building on constitutional dialectics[13] and arguing against the constitutionalisation of post-national law, opting instead for a pluralist vision.[14] Broadening the scope from the EU's internal constitutional discussion to its relations with transnational actors, a theory of principled legal pluralism has been proposed as the way to understand and develop the EU's constitutional order.[15] Furthermore, attention has also been paid to the plurality of socio-economic ideologies found in the EU Treaties.[16]

However, the euro crisis and constitutional pluralism have seldom been studied together. The events and consequences of the crisis have not been analysed within the framework of constitutional pluralism, nor has the theory of constitutional pluralism been reconfigured as a response to the events of the euro crisis. Notable exceptions seem to be the work of Goldmann and Kelemen, who represent opposite ends in the debate. Based on the exchange between the CJEU and the German Federal Constitutional Court in *Gauweiler*,[17] Goldmann

---

[9]   F. Fabbrini, *Economic Governance in Europe: Comparative Paradoxes and Constitutional Challenges* (Oxford University Press 2016).

[10]   See e.g. M. Adams, F. Fabbrini and P. Larouche (eds), *The Constitutionalization of European Budgetary Constraints* (Hart Publishing 2014); T. Beukers, B. de Witte and C. Kilpatrick (eds), *Constitutional Change through Euro-Crisis Law* (Cambridge University Press 2017).

[11]   See e.g. M. Avbelj and J. Komárek (eds), *Constitutional Pluralism in the European Union and Beyond* (Hart Publishing 2012); G. Davies and M. Avbelj (eds), *Research Handbook on Legal Pluralism and EU Law* (Edward Elgar Publishing 2018).

[12]   K. Tuori, *European Constitutionalism* (Cambridge University Press 2015).

[13]   K. Jaklič, *Constitutional Pluralism in the EU* (Oxford University Press 2014).

[14]   N. Krisch, *Beyond Constitutionalism: The Pluralist Structure of Postnational Law* (Oxford University Press 2010).

[15]   M. Avbelj, *The European Union under Transnational Law: A Pluralist Appraisal* (Hart Publishing 2018).

[16]   C. Kaupa, *The Pluralist Character of the European Economic Constitution* (Hart Publishing 2016).

[17]   C-62/14 *Gauweiler* EU:C:2015:400; 2 BvR 2728/13, 21 June 2016 (*OMT final judgment*).

has argued that such reactions by national constitutional courts result in 'mutually assured discretion', meaning that the imminent conflict between the national courts and the CJEU is kept at bay by the somewhat relative vagueness of the CJEU's rationality and proportionality checks.[18] Kelemen, on the other hand, has argued that such cases bring to the fore the unsustainability of constitutional pluralism as the issue of *Kompetenz-Kompetenz* remains to be settled.[19] Avbelj has used the euro crisis as one example when developing his theory of principle legal pluralism; however, the objective of this theory is not the relationship between the EU and the Member States but rather that between the EU and the wider world.[20] Similarly, Fichera has also used the euro crisis as an example whilst developing his argument of security as the meta-rational of European integration, which he contrasts with the theory of constitutional pluralism, but his main focus is not on the euro crisis and constitutional pluralism.[21] The aforementioned scholarship represent the most novel accounts in further developing the theory of constitutional pluralism, but their scope and main argument differ from the one presented in this book.

This distinguished shortcoming in the pluralist literature is interesting for at least two reasons. First, the theoretical study of EU law has long been criticised for being reactive and event-driven, and thus only capable of 'middle-range theorizing'.[22] However, although the discussion on constitutional pluralism is in no way novel – it was sparked by the German Federal Constitutional Court's judgments as early as the 1990s[23] – it seems that the events of the euro crisis have not given rise to a re-evaluation of the leading theory of European constitutionalism. Should one thus conclude that theory building has not met

---

[18]   M. Goldmann, 'Constitutional Pluralism as Mutually Assured Discretion: The Court of Justice, the German Federal Constitutional Court, and the ECB' (2016) *Maastricht Journal of European and Comparative Law* 23(1), 119–35; M. Goldmann, 'Discretion, Not Rules: Postunitary Constitutional Pluralism in the Economic and Monetary Union' in G. Davies and M. Avbelj (eds), *Research Handbook on Legal Pluralism and EU Law* (Edward Elgar Publishing 2018).

[19]   R. D. Kelemen, 'On the Unsustainability of Constitutional Pluralism: European Supremacy and the Survival of the Eurozone' (2016) *Maastricht Journal of European and Comparative Law* 23(1), 136–50; R. D. Kelemen, 'The Dangers of Constitutional Pluralism' in G. Davies and M. Avbelj (eds), *Research Handbook on Legal Pluralism and EU Law* (Edward Elgar Publishing 2018).

[20]   Avbelj (n 15), pp. 88–98.

[21]   M. Fichera, *The Foundations of the EU as a Polity* (Edward Elgar Publishing 2018), Chapter 4.

[22]   See N. Walker, 'Legal Theory and the European Union: A 25th Anniversary Essay' (2005) *Oxford Journal of Legal Studies* 25(4), 581–601.

[23]   See J. Baquero Cruz, 'The Legacy of the Maastricht-Urteil and the Pluralist Movement' (2008) *European Law Journal* 14(4), 389–422.

polity building?[24] Still, there are good reasons for concluding that 'constitutional *theory* must always be about constitutional *practice*',[25] or otherwise it is useless.[26] This leads to the second reason, which is practical: the normative attractiveness and validity of the theory of constitutional pluralism is deeply questioned by the German Federal Constitutional Court's *PSPP judgment.*

If constitutional pluralism is the defining theoretical discussion on European constitutionalism, and if the euro crisis has been the main substantive topic recently – amounting to an 'existential crisis' for the EU[27] – then combining these two is highly relevant and as such offers the perfect laboratory for an analysis of the current state of European constitutionalism. This book sets out to do just that.

The argument put forth in this book is rather simple, but it goes to the very heart of European constitutionalism: differences in the Member States' constitutional orders result in their constitutional courts, or other institutions with similar constitutional review functions, being able to affect the EU's political process to varying degrees. It is the national constitutional orders as such – not EU law or the size and relative political importance of the Member State – that dictates their ability to interact with the CJEU and to affect the European-level political process. These differences mean that some national courts are in a privileged position vis-à-vis other courts when it comes to their ability to influence the course of European integration. Thus, by definition, the rest are in an unequal position. This is called the inequality thesis.

Although the inequality thesis begins as a merely descriptive argument, when connected to larger underlying debates it also gathers normative force and academic significance. As is evident, relations between national courts and EU law also have political implications. The privileged courts can essentially end up hijacking the European-level political process, while the disadvantaged courts face the ungrateful task of finding a way to accommodate their constitutional orders to the chosen path. This questions the legitimacy of such interventions into the European-level political process by national constitutional courts – and thus constitutional pluralism's capacity as a normative theory of European constitutionalism. A normative theory of European constitutional-

---

[24] See J. Shaw, 'The European Union – Discipline Building Meets Polity Building' in P. Cane and M. Tushnet (eds), *The Oxford Handbook of Legal Studies* (Oxford University Press 2003).

[25] R. Schütze, *From Dual to Cooperative Federalism: The Changing Structure of European Law* (Oxford University Press 2013), p. x.

[26] See R. van Gestel and H.-W. Micklitz, 'Why Methods Matter in European Legal Scholarship' (2014) *European Law Journal* 20(3), 292–316, p. 300.

[27] See A. J. Menéndez, 'The Existential Crisis of the European Union' (2013) *German Law Journal* 14(5), 453–526.

ism ought to tell us how conflicts between national law and EU law should be settled and what the constitutional relationship between the two respective constitutional orders should be like.

In a constitutional order comprising over 20 sovereign states, such confrontations and inequality seem inevitable. The plurality of interacting constitutions makes such confrontations unavoidable. This is true the more intricate and far-reaching the symbiosis between these constitutions becomes due to European integration being continually deepened. Constitutional pluralists argue that such plurality and the ensuing confrontations are actually beneficial for the whole constitutional constellation, since interaction necessitates taking into consideration the other and finding the best means of conciliation through dialogue.

This book argues the opposite: constitutional pluralism is not a valid normative theory of European constitutionalism. The EU's current constitutional order is undoubtedly beset by plurality, but an appraisal of pluralism cannot be based on this. On the contrary, observing constitutional practice points to just the opposite. Stricter adherence to the prescribed constitutional roles and functions is needed. In fact, from the perspective of the EU Treaties, this issue is clear, as EU law has primacy over national law and the CJEU is the ultimate arbiter of constitutional conflicts – what creates the problems are the national courts that contest this.

1.1.2   Research Questions and the Argument of the Book

The primary purpose of this book is to assess the theory of constitutional pluralism, especially the claim that the national judicial review of EU law somehow induces legitimacy into the EU's constitutional order and is therefore inherently beneficial.[28] This assessment is done by utilising the events of the euro crisis as a case study. This analysis focuses on how national courts and the CJEU reviewed the various legal measures enacted as a response to the crisis. While the substance of the studied legal mechanisms concerns the EMU, this is a legal study on European constitutionalism. Thus, the various economic reasons and explanations relating to the crisis and the functioning of the EMU in general are only discussed to the extent necessary for appreciating the studied legal events.

---

[28]   The terms 'judicial review' and 'constitutional review' are used interchangeably in this study, although historically they have a different meaning. Alternatively, what this study focuses on could be called 'judicial constitutional review', that is the review of political and legislative decisions against the constitution by a judicial organ, a court. See R. Grote, 'Judicial Review' in *Max Planck Encyclopedia of Comparative Constitutional Law* (Oxford University Press Online).

The primary interest of this study is in the constitutional practice that amounts to the phenomenon called constitutional pluralism. How did the national courts and the CJEU participate in the European-level political process during the euro crisis? What effects did this have? Answering such descriptive questions results in the thesis that constitutional pluralism is not an adequate normative theory of European constitutionalism because of the problems that the eminent plurality creates. This is, in essence, the inequality thesis.

The secondary interest of this study is in the asymmetrical structure of the EMU and the consequences it has for European constitutionalism. How did the asymmetrical structure of the EMU affect the formation and adoption of the crisis response measures? What consequences did this have on European constitutionalism? Answering such descriptive questions results in the thesis that the EMU's asymmetrical structure is unsustainable. The asymmetrical structure is the primary substantive reason for why national courts contested the crisis response measures and why the rulings of the CJEU in cases such as *Gauweiler* are open to criticism from a constitutional perspective.

Although both theses express a strong resentment against the current constitutional structure of EU Treaties, the purpose of this study is not to engage in the debate on the future constitutional and political nature of the EU. In this respect, this study does not ask questions such as: What is the best or preferable constitutional structure for the European Union? Answering this type of a question would require creating some sort of a blueprint for a federal Europe, which would broaden the scope of this study too much. Although politicians and academics have made various proposals to this effect,[29] these will be left unaddressed in this study notwithstanding a few general remarks in the final conclusions.

What type of argument is the inequality thesis? What does this book actually argue? The inequality thesis begins as a descriptive account that can be assessed through three factors.[30] The first factor is at which stage of the European-level political process a national court can participate. Chronological reconstructions of the events of the euro crisis are used to assess this aspect. The crucial point here is the distinction to courts that have delivered their ruling at such a point of the political process that their ruling has had the possibility to affect the outcome of politics at the European level, and to courts that have delivered their ruling at a later point in time and have thus only had the possibility to affect domestic politics. A closer look at the individual judgments reveals

---

[29] See e.g. Fabbrini (n 9), Chapters 4–6; Hinarejos (n 3), Chapters 9–10; Tuori and Tuori (n 5), Chapter 8; Markakis (n 4), Chapter 9.

[30] See T. Tuominen, 'Aspects of Constitutional Pluralism in Light of the Gauweiler Saga' (2018) *European Law Review* 43(2), 186–204, pp. 190–94.

that – prior to the German Federal Constitutional Court's *PSPP judgment* – no national court rejected any of the crisis response measures adopted. This indicates that the courts acting at a later stage of the political process faced a predicament to accept the European measures at whatever cost. Simply put, if a national court can no longer alter the course of European politics, it faces strong political pressure to deem the measure as constitutional. It needs to be stressed that this first aspect is not about whether national courts actually did affect the content of the European-level politics, but rather whether they had the possibility to do so. This does not, however, mean that decisions given at a later stage of the political process would be meaningless altogether. Indeed, as has been pointed out by previous research, such judgments can affect the course of politics later on through a process called autolimitation.[31] This effect is also observed in the case studies, but it is a different type of effect as the one described here.

The second factor is how a national court can interact with the CJEU or European-level politics. This refers to the jurisdiction and the rules of procedure of national courts, which define how they can review EU law or send preliminary references to the CJEU. Vast differences exist between the national institutions charged with constitutional review in the Member States.[32] In particular, the jurisdiction of the German Federal Constitutional Court has been seen to enable the intense juridification of politics, as it enables politicians and individual citizens to subject political decisions to review by the Federal Constitutional Court in an abstract manner.[33] Here, the point is that due to differences in national constitutions, some courts are better placed to interact with the CJEU. The Federal Constitutional Court especially stands out.

The third and final factor is why national courts want to review EU law, i.e., what are the substantive issues (i.e. rights) in their constitutions that they claim to protect by such a review. As the content of the Member States' constitutions differs, it is understandable that national courts, acting as the guardians of these constitutions, pay attention to different aspects of EU law. This raises the question of whether the legality of EU law should be assessed in light of the EU's own 'constitution', the EU Treaties, or in light of the different and differing national constitutions. It seems logical to favour the first, since that is the only way that the primacy, unity and effectiveness of EU law can be

---

[31]   See A. Stone Sweet, *Governing with Judges. Constitutional Politics in Europe* (Oxford University Press 2000), p.75.

[32]   See M. de Visser, *Constitutional Review in Europe: A Comparative Analysis* (Hart Publishing 2014).

[33]   See M. Shapiro and A. Stone Sweet, *On Law, Politics, and Judicialization* (Oxford University Press 2002), p. 368.

guaranteed.[34] Moreover, there are mechanisms in the EU Treaties – namely Articles 4(2) and 6(3) TEU – that facilitate taking into consideration diverging national interests.

These descriptive accounts lead to a normative question, namely whether review by national courts is actually able to induce legitimacy into the EU's constitutional order. Traditionally, judicial review is seen to increase the legitimacy of government actions, as it allows the checking of political decisions against the constitution, which embodies higher objectives, principles and rights, particularly fundamental rights.[35] The legitimacy of judicial review is usually questioned by asking why countermajoritarian institutions such as courts should be given the possibility to overrule decisions made by democratically accountable institutions.[36] The purpose of the inequality thesis is not to engage with this traditional debate; rather, the inequality thesis gives this debate a new twist by showing how, in a state of constitutional plurality, it is not a court and a legislator from the same constitutional system that are pitted against each other, but rather a single court from a group of courts (all Member States' courts) against the European legislator or political executive. Furthermore, in some instances it is not that a court is checking the decisions of a legislator, but that a court is pitted against other technocratic institutions, such as the German Federal Constitutional Court and the ECB in *Gauweiler*.[37]

Lastly, it needs to be stressed that the point of the inequality thesis is not to 'defeat' constitutional pluralism as a practice. Rather, the point is to show how constitutional plurality is not an optimal state of affairs, and therefore that one cannot derive a normative claim from it; in other words, that the 'ought' cannot be derived from the 'is'.

---

[34] See C-399/11 *Melloni* EU:C:2013:107, para. 60.
[35] See e.g. K. Tuori, *Ratio and Voluntas: The Tension between Reason and Will in Law* (Ashgate 2010), Chapter 8.
[36] See R. Bellamy, *Political Constitutionalism: A Republican Defence of the Constitutionality of Democracy* (Cambridge University Press 2007); J. Waldron, 'The Core of the Case Against Judicial Review' (2006) *Yale Law Journal* 115(6), 1346–406. In the context of the European Union, see N. de Boer, 'The False Promise of Constitutional Pluralism' in Davies and Avbelj (n 11).
[37] See M. Wilkinson, 'Economic Messianism and Constitutional Power in a "German Europe": All Courts are Equal, but Some Courts are More Equal than Others', *LSE Law, Society and Economy Working Papers* 26/2014 (2014), p. 25.

1.1.3   Selection of Case Studies and their Methodology

This book contains four case studies on different legal mechanisms adopted as a reaction to the euro crisis. These mechanisms are:

- the Treaty on Stability, Coordination and Governance in the Economic and Monetary Union (the Fiscal Compact);
- the European Stability Mechanism (ESM);
- the European Banking Union;
- the European Central Bank's Outright Monetary Transactions programme (OMT programme).

The functioning of these four mechanisms is heavily interwoven. The common denominator is that they all aim to safeguard the financial stability of the euro area as a whole in one way or the other, and behind each of them we can observe the asymmetrical structure of the EMU. Their content and the EMU's legal framework will be briefly explained in the following section.

The studied mechanisms represent all of the four main types of reactions taken as a result of the euro crisis. In this sense the selection of case studies is all-encompassing. Furthermore, the selected cases represent three different regulatory approaches: international law-based measures (the Fiscal Compact and the ESM), EU secondary law measures (the Banking Union), and decisions by an EU institution (the OMT programme). For each of these three categories, the dynamics of how national courts and the CJEU participate in the European-level political process are different. Thus, this makes it possible to engage with both of the research questions of this study in a meaningful manner: the case studies enable assessment of both the suitability of constitutional pluralism as a normative theory of European constitutionalism and also the consequences of the asymmetrical structure of the EMU.

Fabbrini has argued that recourse to international law, namely the adoption of the Fiscal Compact and the ESM, was the main cause for the intense participation of national courts, as EU secondary law does not facilitate judicial review before national courts in a similar manner. He calls this the 'paradox of judicialization'.[38] While the case studies on the Fiscal Compact and the ESM corroborate Fabbrini's argument, the case studies on the Banking Union and the OMT programme further develop this line of argument. First, the case study on the Banking Union shows, conversely, how the use of EU secondary law meant that national courts did not have similar possibilities to participate. Second, the case study on the OMT programme highlights the fact that the national constitutions truly define how national courts can interact with the

---

[38]   See Fabbrini (n 9), Chapter 2.

CJEU, as it is questionable whether *Gauweiler* could have originated from any other Member State than Germany.

As a caveat towards possible criticism concerning the delimitation of the case studies, one issue still needs to be addressed. Why is the vast array of national cases concerning the application of the austerity measures, incumbent due to accepting assistance from the ESM, not discussed at all?[39] Indeed, several of such cases have reached the CJEU,[40] and the austerity measures as such have posed relevant fundamental rights concerns.[41] The reason for excluding such cases is simple: this study focuses on the adoption of the crisis response mechanisms, not their use. Including also the latter would broaden the scope of this study impracticably. However, it is conceded that from a substantive perspective, for example the Portuguese Constitutional Court's (*Tribunal Constitucional*) judgments on the implementation of austerity measures stemming from ESM assistance seem interesting. The court has overruled many such measures due to their breaching the national constitution, and whilst doing so the court has even invoked the principle of national constitutional identity and Article 4(2) TEU.[42]

All of the case studies contain a chronological reconstruction of the adoption of the respective mechanism. These reconstructions address issues that took place at both the national and the European levels. The reconstructions explain the main political and legal events relating to the adoption of the mechanisms. The purpose of these reconstructions is to show what types of events affected, could have affected, or did not affect the adoption of the four mechanisms. The national judgments mentioned in the reconstructions are not analysed from a comparative constitutional law perspective. This study does not aim to understand why national courts reached certain outcomes. The chosen perspective is European, with an attempt to understand the consequences of these cases for the European-level political process and EU law.

The flow of political events has been deduced from official materials such as decisions by the EU institutions, press releases and other documents. Research literature on the events of the crisis and contemporary newspaper articles have

---

[39]   On these cases, see e.g. Beukers, de Witte and Kilpatrick (n 10).

[40]   See e.g. joined cases C-8/15 P–C-10/15 P *Ledra Advertising* EU:C:2016:701; joined cases C-105/15 – C-109/15 P *Mallis* EU:C:2016:702; C-258/14 *Florescu* EU:C: 2017:448.

[41]   See L. Ginsborg, 'The Impact of the Economic Crisis on Human Rights in Europe and the Accountability of International Institutions' (2017) *Global Campus Human Rights Journal* 1, 97–117.

[42]   See M. Canotilho, T. Violante and R. Lanceiro 'Austerity Measures Under Judicial Scrutiny: the Portuguese Constitutional Case-Law' (2015) *European Constitutional Law Review* 11(1), 155–83.

been used as secondary sources. The discussed national judgments have been sourced from several comparative studies that have included national reports from the Member States.[43] Research literature has been used as a secondary source in this aspect too.

Methodologically the reconstructions in the case studies draw inspiration from process tracing[44] and historical institutionalism, a theory of comparative politics often used in the study of European integration. Historical institutionalism emphasises 'how institutions emerge from and are embedded in concrete temporal processes'.[45] What this means is that importance is accorded to temporality: 'the timing and sequence of events shape political processes'. More specifically, historical institutionalism purports that factors such as unpredictability, inflexibility, nonergodicity and inefficiencies shape the outcome of political processes.[46] These might include, for example, how national constitutions set constraints for international action and how these constitutions are difficult to amend.[47] While a purely institutionalist analysis might be revealing in that it carves out why and how the crisis mechanisms came to be,[48] from the perspective of EU constitutional law, such analyses seem to stop halfway. This study utilises some of the insights of historical institutionalism in that the possible causal relations between the different political and legal instances are paid special attention. As will be shown in the case studies, the above-mentioned factors of unpredictability, inflexibility, nonergodicity and

---

[43] See U. Neergaard, C. Jacqueson and J. Hartig Danielsen (eds), *The Economic and Monetary Union: Constitutional and Institutional Aspects of the Economic Governance within the EU. The XXVI FIDE Congress in Copenhagen, 2014* (DJOF Publishing 2014); G. Bándi, P. Darák, A. Halustyik and P. L. Láncos (eds), *European Banking Union. Congress Proceedings Vol. 1. The XXVII FIDE Congress in Budapest, 2016* (Wolters Kluwer 2016); the European University Institute's project Constitutional Change Through Euro Crisis Law, http://eurocrisislaw.eui.eu/ (accessed 1 September 2020).

[44] See F. Schimmelfennig, 'Efficient Process Tracing: Analyzing the Causal Mechanisms of European Integration' in A. Bennett and J. T. Checkel (eds), *Process Tracing: From Metaphor to Analytical Tool* (Cambridge University Press 2015).

[45] See K. Thelen, 'Historical Institutionalism in Comparative Politics' (1999) *Annual Review of Political Science* 2(1), 369–404, p. 371.

[46] O. Fioretos, 'Historical Institutionalism in International Relations' (2011) *International Organization* 65(2), 367–99, p. 371.

[47] M. A. Pollack, 'The New Institutionalisms and European Integration' in A. Wiener and T. Diez (eds), *European Integration Theory* (Oxford University Press 2004), pp. 139–40.

[48] See e.g. L. Gocaj and S. Meunier, 'Time Will Tell: The EFSF, the ESM, and the Euro Crisis' (2013) *Journal of European Integration* 35(3), 239–53; A. Verdun, 'A Historical Institutionalist Explanation of the EU's Responses to the Euro Area Financial Crisis' (2015) *Journal of European Public Policy* 22(2), 219–37.

inefficiencies all seem to be present in the formulation and uptake of the crisis response mechanisms.

The tripartite contextuality of economic–politic–law that is looming behind the substantive topic of this study leads to one further methodological preconception: while political scientists and economists usually posit that material interests are primarily in charge of shaping the behaviour of actors, lawyers are quick to point out that legal norms and the ideas underlying them also affect the decisions that different actors take. Dehousse and Weiler most famously explained this by stating that law is 'both the object and agent of integration'.[49] Thus, the four case studies also try to highlight the dialectic relationship between economic interests, political forces and legal frameworks. This is important with regards to both research questions. On one hand, the EU's legal framework seems to have affected the reactions taken to the euro crisis and the national legal frameworks on how national courts interacted with the EU's political process. On the other hand, political differences concerning economic and fiscal policies, as well as idiosyncratic interests particular to each Member States' economic situation and banking sector, seem to have affected which types of legal reactions they favoured.

1.1.4   The Structure of the Book

The rest of this introduction first introduces the relevant aspects of the legal framework of the EMU and its asymmetrical structure (section 1.2.1). Next, the reasons for the euro crisis and the events surrounding the crisis, as well as the legal mechanisms of each case study are briefly introduced (section 1.2.2). The section then ends in a discussion on how the asymmetry of the EMU and constitutional pluralism are linked (1.2.3). Lastly, the theory of constitutional pluralism is introduced (section 1.3).

Overall, the book proceeds as follows: Chapters 2–5 contain the four case studies. Each case study begins with a chronological reconstruction of the events leading up to the adoption of the respective legal mechanism and its consequent review by national courts and the CJEU. Then, the interplay between economic, political and legal factors in the adoption of the respective mechanism is briefly discussed. Lastly, the constitutional significance of the respective mechanism, mainly with regards to how it relates to the asymmetry of the EMU, is analysed.

Chapters 6–8 are devoted to the main argument of the book, the inequality thesis, and the critique of constitutional pluralism.

---

[49]   R. Dehousse and J. Weiler, 'The Legal Dimension' in W. Wallace (ed.), *The Dynamics of European Integration* (Pinter Publishers 1990), p. 243.

Chapter 6 lays out the inequality thesis by explaining how differences in national legal frameworks allow for a varying degree of direct or indirect participation by national courts in the European-level political process. The chapter then addresses the problems that ensue from the fact that some national courts are in a privileged position vis-à-vis the others. It is argued that such inequality is problematic from both a political and a legal perspective. The national court's influence essentially usurps the Union's political process; in effect, they can even end up hijacking it. Legally speaking, the inequality of the national courts, or actually the dominant position of some, manifests itself in national courts questioning the interpretive *Kompetenz-Kompetenz* of the CJEU. Lastly, the chapter then turns to the normative basis of the inequality thesis: How according to Article 4(2) TEU, the 'Union shall respect the equality of Member States before the Treaties as well as their national identities, inherent in their fundamental structures, political and constitutional, inclusive of regional and local self-government'. The chapter presents a novel argument concerning the meaning of Article 4(2) TEU: The equality clause is there to guarantee horizontally the equality of the Member States vis-à-vis each other in relation to the EU, whereas the national identity clause is there to protect the Member States vertically from the EU.

Chapter 7 first focuses on the predicament that most of the national courts had when they reviewed the different legal mechanisms adopted pursuant to the crisis. It is argued that those national courts that were able to review the mechanisms at a later stage of the political and legal process, sometimes even after they had already entered into force, faced a strong predicament to find these measures in compliance with their national constitutions. Thus, review by these courts – as opposed to the privileged courts that were able to act early on and might have had an influence on the process – does not strengthen the legitimacy of the overhaul of the Union's economic governance regime either. Then, the chapter addresses the possibilities that the CJEU might have to address such inequality. Building on an analysis of *Gauweiler*, both a structural and a substantive alternative are presented. The first relates to whether the CJEU can affect the competences of national courts through its own doctrine, similar to what the outcome of the *Simmenthal* revolution was.[50] The second is about what types of preliminary references the CJEU admits and how it answers them. Lastly, the chapter discusses the shortcomings of the substan-

---

[50] Case 106/77 *Simmenthal* EU:C:1978:49. See D. Piqani, 'The *Simmenthal* Revolution Revisited: What Role for Constitutional Courts?' in B. de Witte, J. A. Mayoral, U. Jaremba, M. Wind and K. Podstawa (eds), *National Courts and EU Law: New Issues, Theories and Methods* (Edward Elgar Publishing 2016).

tive alternative, which reveal the inadequacy of the EU's current constitutional constellation.

Chapter 8 addresses the idea of constitutional pluralism at a more conceptual and theoretical level. It first explores the different modalities of constitutional pluralism that can be identified through the case studies. The chapter then discusses whether constitutional pluralism is a valid normative theory of European constitutionalism. This is done by mapping out four different critiques of constitutional pluralism: the historical critique, the criticism of uncertainty, the criticism of equality, and the criticism of legitimacy. Finally, the chapter discusses epistemic constitutional pluralism as a means to cope with the EU's incomplete constitutional system.

Chapter 9 concludes the argument and summarises the main findings of the book.

1.2   THE ECONOMIC AND MONETARY UNION AND ITS CRISIS

1.2.1   The Constitutional Framework of the Economic and Monetary Union

1.2.1.1   The Maastricht compromise and the asymmetry of the EMU

The Maastricht Treaty marked the formal beginning of the Economic and Monetary Union (EMU).[51] With the Treaty,[52] the European Community was conferred the powers to establish the EMU.[53] This meant the adoption of irrevocably fixed exchange rate policies and a single currency, which were paralleled with a single monetary and exchange rate policy. These measures aimed to secure price stability and to support the general economic policies in the Community.[54] These activities were to comply with the following guiding principles: stable prices; sound public finances and monetary conditions; and a sustainable balance of payments.[55]

The key issue with the establishment of the EMU was how the Community's competences regarding economic policy were limited to coordination, while monetary policy was supranationalised as an exclusive Community competence. Despite this, it is sometimes forgotten that "'EMU' does not stand for

---

[51]   This section builds on T. Tuominen, 'Mechanisms of Financial Stabilisation' in F. Fabbrini and M. Ventoruzzo (eds), *Research Handbook on EU Economic Law* (Edward Elgar Publishing 2019).
[52]   OJ C191/35, 29 July 1992.
[53]   Art. 2 EC Treaty.
[54]   Art. 3a(2) EC Treaty.
[55]   Art. 3a(3) EC Treaty.

"*European* Monetary Union" but for "*Economic* and Monetary Union"', as Harden pointed out early on.[56] The term 'economic union' is a bit of a misnomer, as there is an open contrast between the single monetary policy and the multiple national economic policies.[57] Thus, because of no common economic policy, the monetary union exists in a 'dangerous political vacuum'.[58]

In practice, the establishment of the EMU meant that the participating Member States transferred the conduct of monetary policy to the Community – to the European Central Bank (ECB).[59] Yet, in the domain of economic and fiscal policy,[60] the Member States retained competence for crafting their national policies as they please, while the Community gained only some oversight and coordination powers.[61] In strict legal terms, when it comes to monetary policy, the actions of the Community are legally binding, whereas the coordination and oversight of economic policies consists of non-binding legal measures. This disparity between the two policies is commonly referred to as the *asymmetry* of the EMU.[62] This has led to a conclusion that the euro is a currency without a state.[63]

The founding fathers of the EMU specifically wanted an asymmetrical structure. This is visible in the Delors Report:

> Even after attaining economic and monetary union, the Community would continue to consist of individual nations with differing economic, social, cultural and political characteristics. The existence and preservation of this *plurality* would require

---

[56] I. Harden 'The Fiscal Constitution of the EMU' in P. Beaumont and N. Walker (eds), *Legal Framework of the Single European Currency* (Hart Publishing 1999), p. 71.

[57] R. M. Lastra and J.-V. Louis, 'European Economic and Monetary Union: History, Trends, and Prospects' (2013) *Yearbook of European Law* 32(1), 57–206, p. 90.

[58] K. Dyson, 'Fifty Years of Economic and Monetary Union: A Hard and Thorny Journey' in D. Phinnemore and A. Warleigh-Lack (eds), *Reflections on European Integration: 50 Years of the Treaty of Rome* (Palgrave Macmillan 2009), p. 159.

[59] Art. 105 EC Treaty.

[60] Fiscal policy is generally used to refer to government revenues and expenditures, e.g. taxes and social security benefits. Economic policy is a higher order concept, which also includes, in addition to fiscal policy, issues such as labour market conditions and industrial policy. Monetary policy is also understood as part of economic policy. See Tuori and Tuori (n 5), pp. 30–31. In this study, reference is mostly made to just economic and monetary policy, since the distinction between economic and fiscal policy is not relevant for the main argument, while the focus is on the distinction between economic and monetary policies.

[61] Arts 102a–104c EC Treaty.

[62] On this asymmetry, see Harden (n 56), pp. 71–4.

[63] See T. Padoa-Schioppa, *The Euro and Its Central Bank: Getting United After the Union* (MIT Press 2004), pp. 35–6.

a degree of autonomy in economic decision-making to remain with individual member countries and a balance to be struck between national and Community competences.[64]

If the problems that the asymmetry of the EMU posed were known already during the inception of the EMU,[65] why was such an arrangement agreed upon? To simplify a bit, the underlying cause for the compromise that resulted in this asymmetry is found in the debate between the differing attitudes of the so-called 'French economists' and the 'German monetarists'. The monetarists favoured furthering monetary cooperation first and they believed that monetary cooperation together with the legal rules on the internal market would create the necessary economic convergence that would be required later, when economic integration would take place. The economists instead thought that economic policies should be integrated first so as to create the necessary economic convergence that living with a common currency requires.[66] This debate provided the reason to negotiate a compromise, but the factors that contributed to the actual end result are found elsewhere.

The Maastricht Treaty and the EMU were negotiated during an era of great political change in Europe: the collapse of the Soviet Union and the unification of Germany were major events that shaped current day Europe. Garrett has argued that the German government was willing to accept the 'suboptimal', asymmetric structure of the EMU because they were keen on deepening European integration, which had now gotten new impetus due to these two large-scale political incidents. The creation of the EMU and the euro would be a logical step forward on this path.[67]

The German D-Mark had had a somewhat hegemonic position in Europe in terms of creating stability. Many states had actually pegged their currencies to the D-Mark, and trading prices were also relative to it.[68] Economically speaking, by insisting on an institutional structure for the EMU that secured the euro's equivalent stability to that of the D-Mark, the Germans were able to avoid heavy domestic costs, although they did lose the hegemonic position of

---

[64] Committee for the Study of Economic and Monetary Union (The Delors Committee), *Report on Economic and Monetary Union in the Community* (Office for Official Publications of the EC, 1989), para. 17, emphasis in the original.

[65] See Lastra and Louis (n 57), p. 5.

[66] See Dyson (n 58), pp. 158–61.

[67] G. Garrett, 'The Politics of Maastricht' in B. Eichengreen and J. Frieden (eds), *The Political Economy of European Monetary Unification. Second Edition* (Westview Press 2001), p. 111.

[68] See H. James, *Making the European Monetary Union: The Role of the Committee of Central Bank Governors and the Origins of the European Central Bank* (Belknap Press of Harvard University Press 2012), Chapter 2.

the D-Mark and their relatively low real interest rates. However, by achieving a stable euro, German politicians were able to sell the idea to the German central bank (*Bundesbank*) and also to the German people who were somewhat anxious of the common currency.[69] The legal structure of the EMU, and specifically that of the ECB, then followed from these political and economic imperatives.[70]

Furthermore, establishing a common monetary policy was made possible after the benefits of an independent central bank were recognised: essentially, how an independent central bank would insulate monetary policy and thus the achievement of price stability from politics. However, no similar reasons were found in favour of supranationalising economic policy. This was because economic policy was seen to include value judgments and trade-offs between competing interests. Such decisions, so it was seen, needed an adequate legitimacy basis that only the national polity could offer. For the same reason, no collective supervision and regulation for private banks was established, since the bailing-out of banks is done with taxpayers' money, which is also connected to similar legitimacy requirements and political sentiments.[71]

1.2.1.2 The legal rules of the EMU in the EU Treaties

Title VIII of the Treaty on the Functioning of the European Union contains the constitutional norms of the Economic and Monetary Union. Their content has remained essentially the same since their creation with the Maastricht Treaty, notwithstanding one small amendment adopted during the euro crisis. The asymmetrical relationship between the rules on economic policy and monetary policy is key to understanding the specific articles of Title VIII.

The general purposes and objectives of economic and monetary policy are outlined in Article 119 TFEU. The importance of Article 119 TFEU is in the principles and objectives that it contains, as these are central for the interpretation of the consequent Articles of Title VIII. The principle of an open market economy with free competition, specified in the first paragraph of Article 119 TFEU, is central for internal market law and competition law. More relevant for the context of this study are the objectives listed in the second paragraph: to maintain price stability and to support the general economic policies in the Union. Lastly, paragraph three also lists the following principles: stable prices, sound public finances and monetary conditions and a sustainable balance of payments.

---

[69] Dyson (n 58), p. 149.
[70] See S. Fabbrini, *Which European Union? Europe After the Euro Crisis* (Cambridge University Press 2015), pp. 21–6.
[71] Dyson (n 58), pp. 162–3.

With regard to economic policy, the EU's competences are limited to coordination. This is expressly stated in Articles 2(3) TFEU and 5(1) TFEU but also visible in the articles outlining the Union's competences in practice. These rules are found in Articles 121–126 TFEU. The purpose of these rules is to manage the asymmetry of the EMU, namely to prevent government budget deficits and to subject the Member States' economic policies to the logic of the markets.

The Stability and Growth Pact (SGP) is central in this framework. It consists of a preventive and a corrective arm. The first is based on Article 121 TFEU and the latter on Article 126 TFEU. The functioning of these mechanisms has been further specified by EU secondary law instruments,[72] which have been accompanied by a host of other legal instruments as a consequence of the euro crisis.[73] The preventive arm aims to ensure sound budgetary policies over the medium-term by setting parameters for Member States' economic policies and planning. These policies are assessed annually by the Commission. If a Member State fails to fulfil the set objectives, the Commission can issue the Member State with a warning and the Council can give the Member State recommendations for correcting the situation. The purpose of the corrective arm is to ensure that Member States adopt appropriate policy responses to correct excessive government deficits. The Council may sanction a Member State that has breached the objectives specified in the procedure of the preventive arm. Possible sanctions include a fine and, since 2014, the possibility to suspend part or all of the commitments or payments linked to European Structural and Investment Funds.

Article 136 TFEU provides a legal basis for developing the procedures prescribed in Articles 121 and 126 TFEU. Article 136(1) TFEU can be used to adopt measures to strengthen the coordination and surveillance of Eurozone Member States' budgetary discipline and to set out economic policy guidelines for them.[74] During the euro crisis, Paragraph 3 was added to Article 136 TFEU.[75]

3. The Member States whose currency is the euro may establish a stability mechanism to be activated if indispensable to safeguard the stability of the euro area as a whole. The granting of any required financial assistance under the mechanism will be made subject to strict conditionality.

---

[72] Regulation (EC) No 1466/97; Regulation (EC) No 1467/97.
[73] Regulation (EC) No 479/2009; Regulation (EU) No 1173/2011; Regulation (EU) No 1174/2011; Regulation (EU) No 1176/2011; Directive 2011/85/EU; Regulation (EU) No 473/2013; Regulation (EU) No 472/2013. See Vade Mecum on the Stability & Growth Pact. 2019 Edition. European Commission, Institutional Paper 101, April 2019.
[74] See e.g. the EU secondary law measures cited supra n 73.
[75] 2011/199/EU: European Council Decision.

The purpose of the amendment was to make it possible for the Member States to adopt a permanent financial assistance mechanism since Article 122 TFEU, discussed below, only mandates the adoption of temporary mechanisms. This amendment was effectuated through the simplified revision procedure of Article 48(6) TFEU. In the simplified revision procedure, amendments can be made to Part III of the TFEU without organising an intergovernmental conference, which is a prerequisite for amending the Treaties according to the normal revision procedure of Article 48(3) TEU. Hence, in this procedure, the European Council has to accept the proposed amendment unanimously. Following this, all Member States must ratify the change according to their national constitutions. The use of the simplified revision procedure, among other issues pertaining to the adoption of the European Stability Mechanisms (ESM), was challenged before the CJEU in *Pringle*.[76]

While Articles 121 and 126 TFEU can be seen to act as constraints on the Member States' economic policies, the Treaties also contain two rules that aim to corroborate the previously discussed framework by way of subjecting the Member States' economic policies to the logic of the markets. Article 123 TFEU specifies that overdraft facilities or any other type of credit facility with the ECB or a national central bank in favour of a Union institution or a Member State is prohibited. Furthermore, Article 123 TFEU also states that the ECB and national central banks are prohibited from directly purchasing debt instruments from the Union's institutions or the Member States. This is known colloquially as the ban on central bank financing. A related rule is found in Article 125 TFEU, according to which the EU or a Member State shall not be liable for or assume the commitments of another Member State. This is known as the no bail-out clause, since it essentially prohibits Member States from offering each other financial assistance when default is near.

The purpose of Articles 123 and 125 TFEU is to subject the Member States' economic policies to the logic of the markets: if they are unable to receive financing from the Union or other Member States, and if the Union and the other Member States are forbidden to offer financial assistance when nearing default, Member States must conduct an economic policy that allows them to secure financing from the markets. In practice, the interest rate at which a Member State can acquire financing from the markets should be dependent on their chosen economic policies, which in turn should guide them towards sustainable economic policies.

The purpose of Article 125 TFEU specifically is to ward off moral hazard concerns: if Member States or their creditors can assume that the indebted States will not ultimately be held responsible for their debt – which would

---

[76]   C-370/12 *Pringle* EU:C:2012:756.

be the outcome in case of a bail-out – Member States will have an incentive to become overly indebted and banks will see the possibility of credit losses as low and therefore continue to supply cheap funding irrespective of the economic policy of the respective Member State. Due to the asymmetry of the EMU, the other Member States cannot prevent this from happening, as each Member State is in charge of their own economic policy, while the negative consequences of this ultimately affect all Member States due to the common currency.

Thus, together Articles 123 and 125 TFEU can be seen as an expression of the principle of Member States' fiscal liability.[77] In other words, without these two articles the SGP would be meaningless, since independently conducted economic policies would not be independent if they were, in the end, backed up by mutual liability, that is, a bail-out by the other Member States or the ECB.

Finally, Article 122 TFEU provides for the possibility of Union financial assistance in case of crises. The first paragraph of the Article makes it possible to adopt measures to assist a Member State if severe difficulties arise in the supply of certain products, notably in the area of energy. The second paragraph facilitates giving financial assistance where a Member State is in difficulties or is seriously threatened with severe difficulties caused by natural disasters or exceptional occurrences beyond its control. Article 122 is essentially a legal base for Union action. It was first used during the euro crisis to create the European Financial Stabilisation Mechanisms (EFSM)[78] and more recently in the midst of the COVID-19 crisis to create the European instrument for temporary Support to mitigate Unemployment Risks in an Emergency (SURE).[79] What is important to note concerning the scope of Article 122 is that it can only be used to create mechanisms of a temporary nature, since it is meant to be used only in exceptional circumstances.[80]

When it comes to monetary policy, the EU has exclusive competence over monetary policy for the Member States whose currency is the euro, as specified in Article 3(1) TFEU. The ECB is tasked with defining and implementing this monetary policy,[81] the primary objective of which is to maintain price stability.[82] The tasks of the ECB also include the prudential supervision of

---

[77] See Tuori and Tuori (n 5), pp. 32–3.
[78] Regulation (EU) No 407/2010.
[79] Regulation (EU) No 2020/672.
[80] See C-370/12 *Pringle* EU:C:2012:756, para. 65.
[81] Art. 127(2) TFEU.
[82] Art. 127(1) TFEU.

credit institutions,[83] for which purpose there is also a separate legal basis in Article 127(6) TFEU.

The principle of central bank independence, defined in Article 130 TFEU, is vital in both institutionally positioning the ECB but also in substantively guiding its actions. The independence prescribed in Article 130 TFEU can be characterised as 'dual independence': the ECB is independent in relation to both the other EU institutions as well as the national authorities.[84] This aspect is often referred to as institutional independence. From a substantive perspective, it can be said that the ECB enjoys functional independence. What this means is that the ECB has the autonomy to decide – as long as it keeps within the powers conferred on it in the Treaties – how to pursue the objective of price stability.[85]

The relevance of both aspects of independence become visible when considered together with the asymmetrical structure of the EMU. Institutionally speaking, since there is no common economic policy, it would be wrong for the EU or the Member States to try to affect the content of the ECB's monetary policy so that it would support the desired economic policy. Functionally speaking, since there is no common economic policy, it would be wrong for the ECB to pursue policies that would in fact have the same effects as a common economic policy. Although according to Article 127(1) TFEU the ECB 'shall support the general economic policies in the Union', as the Union does not have a proper economic policy competence, therefore the ECB's monetary policy should be kept separate from the Member States' economic policies.

It is by now common knowledge that this legal framework did not work as was envisaged. The political nature of the SGP had already become apparent before the euro crisis, when it was not enforced against Germany and France even though they had breached the deficit and debt criteria.[86] During the economic boom prior to the crisis, Member States' economic policies and financial situations were not reflected in government bond interest rates.[87] The logic of the markets was not functioning. Herein lies the background to the euro crisis: a common monetary policy that creates mutual interdependence, but no

---

[83]   Art. 127(5) TFEU.

[84]   R. M. Lastra, *Legal Foundations of International Monetary Stability* (Oxford University Press 2006), p. 224.

[85]   R. Smits, *The European Central Bank: Institutional Aspects* (Kluwer Law International 1997), p. 162–8.

[86]   See C-27/04 *Commission v Council* EU:C:2004:436. See M. Heipertz and A. Verdun, *Ruling Europe: The Politics of the Stability and Growth Pact* (Cambridge University Press 2010).

[87]   See S. Barrios et al, 'Determinants of Intra-euro Area Government Bond Spreads During the Financial Crisis' (2009) *European Commission, DG Economic and Social Affairs.*

common economic policy that would stabilise this interdependence. Thus, the asymmetry of the EMU, as established in Maastricht, 'has come back to haunt Europe in the context of the European financial and euro area debt crisis'.[88]

1.2.2 Reasons and Reactions to the Euro Crisis

1.2.2.1 An economic narrative to the crisis

Soon after the onset of the global financial crisis, which began from the 2007 USA subprime mortgage crisis, the economic situation of certain Eurozone Member States started to deteriorate. International rating agencies lowered the ratings for Member States' government bonds as well as those of several important national banks. This started to threaten the stability of the banking system in the Eurozone since due to the common currency and mutual borrowing the still stronger countries and banks were also affected. If in the USA the fall of Lehman Brothers in 2008 was the decisive moment, in Europe it was the announcement by the Greek Prime Minister George Papandreou in October 2009 that the debt and deficit levels previously reported by Greece had been tremendously wrong. After this announcement 'the euro decisively ceased being boring'.[89]

While all of this affected various parts of the Eurozone differently, some common denominators can be found. Ireland and Spain were hit by the initial global financial crisis. When consumption plummeted, the construction sector in particular faced problems. Greece, Portugal and Italy were hit by a fiscal crisis caused by their own government spending. The northern European creditor countries were hit by a balance of payments crisis, as suddenly capital started to flow out from them. National governments failed to react to these problems, since cheap debt was available due to the euro. Monetary stability did not mean financial stability, and due to its strict monetary policy mandate, the ECB had no way of tackling this. The link between governments and banks meant that it was difficult for sovereigns to react to the crisis.

After the initiation of the financial crisis in Europe, it soon became obvious that the most indebted and economically weak Eurozone Member States might actually face default. This, so it was perceived, could consequently threaten the existence of the whole euro. Due to a home bias in holding of sovereign debt by banks, sovereign default in the Eurozone also results in the private banks of that country running into trouble, as they are no longer able to receive liquidity

---

[88] F. Amtenbrink, 'The Metamorphosis of European Economic and Monetary Union' in A. Arnull and D. Chalmers (eds), *The Oxford Handbook of European Union Law* (Oxford University Press 2015).

[89] J. Pisani-Ferry, *The Euro Crisis and Its Aftermath* (Oxford University Press 2014), p. 8.

from the ECB because the sovereign debt they hold is worthless and thus not suitable as collateral. The only option left would be to exit the Eurozone, and thus regain sovereignty over monetary policy. Furthermore, default by one Eurozone Member State would have given the markets a signal that investments in other crisis states were not safe either, resulting in their debt refinancing costs soaring and therefore also bringing them closer to default. Such contagion was seen to threaten the existence of the euro. Whether or not this would have resulted in the break-up of the euro, we will never know, but the economic consequences of this would have been catastrophic no doubt. In this situation, giving financial assistance to both states and banks seemed the best and only option, since the link between the two had not yet been severed.

However, it was the political consequences that were most feared. This sentiment is depicted well in the words of the German Chancellor Angela Merkel: 'If the euro fails, Europe fails.' [90] This attitude – of being ready and willing to do 'whatever it takes' to preserve the euro[91] – is important for understanding the political events that resulted in the uptake of the various crisis response mechanisms, as well as their subsequent constitutionalisation by the CJEU in *Pringle* and *Gauweiler*.[92]

1.2.2.2   An overview of the crisis response measures

The magnitude of the euro crisis is reflected well in the myriad legal measures that the EU and the Member States, both together and on their own part, took to combat the crisis and to prevent future crises. Although only one small amendment to the EU Treaties was adopted as a consequence of the crisis, several scholars have described these reactions as amounting to no less than the transformation of the EU's economic governance regime, if not its constitutional structure more generally speaking.[93] A general criticism towards these measures has been that they were adopted in haste and under enormous economic pressure, yet without due consideration for what would have been the best possible option.[94]

---

[90]   '"If the Euro Fails, Europe Fails": Merkel Says EU Must Be Bound Closer Together': *Spiegel Online* (7 September 2011) http://www.spiegel.de/international/germany/if-the-euro-fails-europe-fails-merkel-says-eu-must-bebound-closer-together-a-784953.html (accessed 1 September 2020).

[91]   Speech by Mario Draghi, President of the European Central Bank at the Global Investment Conference. London, 26 July 2012. The whole sentence was: 'Within our mandate, the ECB is ready to do whatever it takes to preserve the euro. And believe me, it will be enough.'

[92]   See C-370/12 *Pringle* EU:C:2012:756; C-62/14 *Gauweiler* EU:C:2015:400.

[93]   See e.g. Tuori and Tuori (n 5); Amtenbrink (n 88); Borger (n 6).

[94]   See Fabbrini (n 9), p. 1.

How these measures were adopted is not explained here, as that will be addressed in detail in the four case studies. The purpose of this section is to give a brief overview of the mechanisms. This will reduce the need for repetition later on and also familiarise the reader with these measures at once. Even though each mechanism is analysed in a separate chapter, due to linkages between the measures, references are made between the case studies. In other words, understanding the rationale of one measure requires understanding all of them.

During the height of the euro crisis, several Member States were either at the brink of defaulting on their creditors or their debt refinancing costs were so high that they would soon find themselves in such a position. For this reason, financial assistance was given to Member States, as it was seen as a better alternative than letting some of the states default and perhaps exit the Eurozone. Thus, the purpose of these measures was also to safeguard financial stability, for which reason these measures have also been referred to as financial stabilisation mechanisms. In practice, such measures can be termed rescue packages or even bail-outs.

Assistance given by the Member States was first based on direct bilateral loans between the Member States but was eventually formalised under three different mechanisms. First, there was the EFSM, established with Regulation (EU) No 407/2010.[95] Second, the European Financial Stability Facility (EFSF) was established as a company incorporated in Luxembourg under Luxembourgish law and owned by the Eurozone Member States. Third, the European Stability Mechanism (ESM) was adopted as a treaty between the Member States based on international law, concurrently with the above-mentioned amendment to Article 136 TFEU. Such financial assistance mechanisms were completely novel, as similar ones did not exist before the crisis.

Financial assistance was also given to private banks. The events of the banking crisis have been closely described in the literature.[96] Initially, the lack of EU-level resolution and recovery rules resulted in State aid rules taking their place. Financial assistance to private banks was given explicitly in the form of State aid, as prescribed in Article 107 TFEU, first on the basis of Article 107(3)(c) TFEU and the 2004 Restructuring Guidelines,[97] and later on

---

[95] Regulation (EU) No 407/2010.

[96] See e.g. F.-C. Laprévote and F. de Cecco (eds), *Research Handbook on State Aid in the Banking Sector* (Edward Elgar Publishing 2017).

[97] Communication from the Commission — Community guidelines on State aid for rescuing and restructuring firms in difficulty. OJ C 244, 1.10.2004, pp. 2–17.

the basis of Article 107(3)(b) TFEU and the 2008 Banking Communication.[98] The bulk of bank bail-outs were then made according to the 2008 Banking Communication, with Article 107(3)(b) TFEU as their legal basis.[99]

In 2013 a new Banking Communication was adopted.[100] This Communication reflected the change in European leaders' attitudes towards solving the crisis. As a result of Angela Merkel and Nicolas Sarkozy's meeting in Deauville on 19 October 2010,[101] the emphasis shifted from bail-out towards bail-in. Such a shift is in line with the Maastricht macroeconomic principle of Member States' fiscal liability and the no bail-out clause of Article 125 TFEU, as it aims at inducing market discipline. When the same approach is applied to private banks, it is called 'private sector involvement'.[102] It needs to be reiterated that the bail-out approach utilising State aid was used before the adoption of the Banking Union.

As giving financial assistance to profligate states amounts to a Sisyphean task – or at least so the sentiment seemed to be at the time – the adoption of financial assistance mechanisms was quickly followed by tighter budgetary constraints. The Six-Pack was introduced to increase the effectiveness of the preventive and corrective arms of the SGP.[103] The Six-Pack also created the European Semester, a procedure whereby the Member States' budgets are subjected to review by the Commission, who assesses whether the budgets meet the new criteria created by the Six-Pack.[104] Later, the Two-Pack was adopted to further increase the Commission's surveillance powers over the Member States' budgets, although still leaving the final decision on the content of the budgets to the national parliaments, as the EU has no proper economic policy competence.[105] The Two-Pack enhanced the surveillance of draft budgetary

---

[98] Communication from the Commission — The application of State aid rules to measures taken in relation to financial institutions in the context of the current global financial crisis, OJ C 270, 25.10.2008, pp. 8–14.

[99] See supra n 96.

[100] Communication from the Commission on the application, from 1 August 2013, of State aid rules to support measures in favour of banks in the context of the financial crisis ('Banking Communication'), OJ C 216, 30.7.2013, pp. 1–15.

[101] See 'Franco-German Declaration' (18 October 2010) https://archiv .bundesregierung.de/archiv-en/articles/franco-german-declaration-756384 (accessed 1 September 2020).

[102] See M. K. Brunnermeier, H. James and J.-P. Landau, *The Euro and the Battle of Ideas* (Princeton University Press 2016), pp. 1 and 29–33.

[103] Regulation (EU) No 1175/2011; Regulation (EU) No 1177/2011; Regulation (EU) No 1173/2011; Directive 2011/85/EU; Regulation (EU) No 1176/2011; Regulation (EU) No 1174/2011.

[104] See K. A. Armstrong, 'The New Governance of EU Fiscal Discipline' (2013) *European Law Review* 38(5), 601–17.

[105] Regulation (EU) No 473/2013; Regulation (EU) No 472/2013.

plans by building on the preventive arm of the SGP and it also facilitated the common budgetary timeline of the European Semester.

In addition to these EU secondary law measures the Treaty on Stability, Coordination and Governance in the Economic and Monetary Union (TSCG or Fiscal Compact) was adopted as a measure between the Member States, based on international law. Its objectives are similar to those of the Six-Pack and Two-Pack, but its mode of operation is to effectuate changes through the Member States' national laws. Thus, it complements the other measures in an innovative way.[106] As opposed to the new mechanisms of financial assistance, rules on budgetary constraints existed already prior to the crisis but they were made considerably more stringent with these amendments.

As the fate of the Member States' economies is heavily connected to the fate of the private banks domiciled in them, which was already pointed out above by the bail-outs given to private banks in the beginning of the crisis, a legal mechanism directed towards the problems that the banks were facing was also deemed necessary.[107] The regulatory actions aimed at private banks ('credit institutions') comprise a vast variety of measures. On one hand, there are the general measures that are in force in the whole EU. These were enacted first. They are referred to as the 'Single Rulebook' and they aim to complete the single market for financial services.[108] The Single Rulebook regulates capital requirement for banks, prevention and management of bank failures, and protection of depositors. In practice, the most important elements of the Single Rulebook are the Capital Requirements Directive IV (CRD IV),[109] the Capital Requirements Regulation (CRR),[110] the Bank Recovery and Resolution Directive (BRRD),[111] and the Deposit Guarantee Scheme Directive (DGSD).[112]

On the other hand, there is the European Banking Union, which is substantively based on the application of the EU secondary law instruments comprising the Single Rulebook, but which applies only to the Eurozone Member States (non-Eurozone countries can also join). The purpose of the Banking Union is to create centralised forms of supervision and resolution that apply

---

[106] See P. Leino-Sandberg and J. Salminen, 'A Multi-Level Playing Field for Economic Policy-Making: Does EU Economic Governance Have Impact?' in T. Beukers, B. de Witte, and C. Kilpatrick (eds), *Constitutional Change through Euro-Crisis Law* (Cambridge University Press 2017).

[107] On the link between the banks and the states, see N. Véron, *Europe's Radical Banking Union* (Bruegel 2015), pp. 14–19.

[108] See Council of the European Union, Presidency Conclusions, 11225/2/09. Brussels, 10 July 2009.

[109] Directive 2013/36/EU.

[110] Regulation (EU) No 575/2013.

[111] Directive 2014/59/EU.

[112] Directive 2014/49/EU.

to banks situated in the Member States that are part of the Banking Union. The new mechanisms established for this purpose are the Single Supervisory Mechanism (SSM)[113] and the Single Resolution Mechanism (SRM).[114] In order to provide a back-stop to wind down failing banks, the Single Resolution Fund (SRF) was attached to the SRM. National contributions to the SRF have been transferred and mutualised with the Single Resolution Fund Treaty (SRF Treaty).[115] The third pillar of the Banking Union, the proposed European Deposit Insurance Scheme,[116] has still not been adopted. While there were some rules related to banks prior to the crisis,[117] this regulatory dimension is mostly novel too.

Separately from the substantive banking regulations, and actually already before it, the European System of Financial Supervision was established in 2010. This supervisory architecture consists of three supervisory authorities – the European Banking Authority, the European Securities and Markets Authority, and the European Insurance and Occupational Pensions Authority – accompanied by the European Systemic Risk Board.[118] These bodies supervise the whole EU and not just the Eurozone.

The last group of measures that needs to be mentioned here are the various operations undertaken by the ECB. Their objective has been to support financial stability and economic recovery within the EMU. These activities have taken two forms. First, there are the open market operations, which aim to inject liquidity into the real economy and to signal the monetary policy stance in the euro area. Second, there are the various asset purchase programmes, which, by definition, are a form of non-standard monetary policy measures. Through such programmes the ECB purchases government bonds, securities issued by European supranational institutions, corporate bonds, asset-backed securities and covered bonds with the aim of thus influencing financial conditions such as economic growth and inflation. The three most discussed programmes are perhaps the Securities Markets Programme (SMP),[119] the

---

[113]   Regulation (EU) No 1024/2013; Regulation (EU) No 1022/2013.

[114]   Regulation (EU) No 806/2014.

[115]   Agreement on the transfer and mutualization of contributions to the Single Resolution Fund. Council of the European Union, ECOFIN 342. Brussels, 14 May 2014.

[116]   COM/2015/0586 final.

[117]   See L. Dragomir, *European Prudential Banking Regulation and Supervision: The Legal Dimension* (Routledge 2010).

[118]   Regulation (EU) No 1092/2010; Regulation (EU) No 1096/2010; Regulation (EU) No 1093/2010; Regulation (EU) No 1094/2010; Regulation (EU) No 1095/2010; Directive 2010/78/EU.

[119]   Decision of the European Central Bank of 14 May 2010 establishing a securities markets programme (ECB/2010/5).

Outright Monetary Transaction Programme (OMT),[120] and the Public Sector Purchase Programme (PSPP).[121] The controversial aspect of such programmes is how the ECB acquires Eurozone Member States' government bonds – from the secondary markets, since Article 123 TFEU forbids the ECB from buying them directly from the Member States – with the aim of thus lowering their interest rates or making them attractive to private investors in the first place. Thus, such programmes seem to contravene the rules of Articles 123 and 125 TFEU. For this reason, the OMT programme resulted in the case *Gauweiler* and the PSPP in the case *Weiss*.[122]

1.2.3 The Link Between an Asymmetrical Economic and Monetary Union and a Dysfunctional Constitutional Order

Soon after the adoption of the EEC Treaty, Mundell presented his theory of optimal currency areas, which contained the so-called unholy trinity argument.[123] According to this thesis, the following three conditions are mutually incompatible within a common currency area and only two can co-exist at any one time: fixed exchange rates; independent monetary policies; and full capital mobility. Economists have since widely accepted the thesis, and it has become the standard for assessing the EMU from an economic perspective.[124] In another influential model, free trade between the countries is added as a fourth variable, in which case the thesis is referred to as the inconsistent quartet.[125]

Later, similar theses have been presented that pose further challenges to the EMU. Rodrik's trilemma of globalisation posits the following three variables, out of which only two can co-exist: hyperglobalisation; the nation state; and democratic politics.[126] This results in the following three possible combinations: (i) choosing hyperglobalisation and democracy results in discharging

---

[120] Technical features of Outright Monetary Transactions. ECB press release, 6 September 2012, https://www.ecb.europa.eu/press/pr/date/2012/html/pr120906_1.en.html (accessed 1 September 2020).

[121] Decision (EU) 2015/774 of the European Central Bank of 4 March 2015 on a secondary markets public sector asset purchase programme.

[122] See C-62/14 *Gauweiler* EU:C:2015:400; C-493/17 *Weiss* EU:C:2018:1000.

[123] See R. Mundell, 'Theory of Optimum Currency Areas' (1961) *American Economic Review* 51(4), 657–66.

[124] See K. McNamara, 'Economic Governance, Ideas and EMU: What Currency Does Policy Consensus Have Today?' (2006) *Journal of Common Market Studies* 44(4), 803–21, p. 805.

[125] See T. Padoa-Schioppa, *The Road to Monetary Union in Europe: The Emperor, the Kings, and the Genies* (Oxford University Press 2000), Chapter 2.

[126] See D. Rodrik, *The Globalization Paradox: Democracy and the Future of the World Economy* (W. W. Norton & Company 2011), pp. 200–206.

with the nation state; (ii) selecting democracy and the nation state means that globalisation is not possible, at least to the same extent; (iii) opting for the nation state and hyperglobalisation results in sacrificing democracy. In the first case, rules are made internationally so there are no transaction costs, but then national sovereignty is lost since the nation state does not decide anymore. In the second case, having two different sets of rules results in transaction costs, which hinders international economic integration. The third case has been referred to as the 'Golden Straitjacket', since in this case, although decisions are made in the nation state, the decisions are affected by the pressure of the international markets and thus end up producing rules that favour the markets at the expense of democracy.

Snell has schematised the development of the EMU through the three different choices offered by Rodrik's trilemma. First, we had an incomplete EMU, which allowed us to preserve mass politics and nation states. This, however, resulted in the EMU being vulnerable and not working. Second, as a response to the Eurozone crisis, we now have an EMU in which we try to strengthen economic integration while still maintaining national sovereignty. This, however, has led to mass politics being disregarded and to decisions imposed by the 'Golden Straitjacket'. Third, we have the blueprints for the future EMU, which emphasise economic integration and mass politics. This, however, would lead to national sovereignty being sacrificed, since it would be replaced by supranational democracy.[127]

What would this third stage mean? Snell's analysis of this is especially relevant for this study. First, there is a trade-off between national sovereignty and a single currency. The former has to be limited if the latter is to work. Those wishing to preserve national sovereignty have to realise the price they must pay for it. The German Federal Constitutional Court was endeavouring to argue for national democracy (sovereignty) in *Gauweiler*.[128] In its argumentation, the German court effectively chose national democracy (sovereignty) over a functioning single currency.

Second, the legitimacy of the EMU can also be analysed through this framework. The initial EMU lacked output legitimacy, while the crisis response measures lacked input legitimacy. Despite the crisis response mechanisms being able to save the euro, due to their undemocratic nature, such output legitimacy might not be enough to counter the inadequacies in input legitimacy. In order to redress this, mass politics (democracy) should be deployed at the

---

[127] J. Snell, 'The Trilemma of European Economic and Monetary Integration, and Its Consequences' (2016) *European Law Journal* 22(2), 157–79, pp. 160–71.

[128] See 2 BvR 2728/13, 14 January 2014 (*OMT reference*); 2 BvR 2728/13, 21 June 2016 (*OMT final judgment*).

supranational level. This, though, can be difficult. Therefore, the legitimacy problem would be worsened when trying to transfer mass politics from the national to the supranational level. On the other hand, since returning to national currencies does not seem a plausible solution, what are we to do? These points notwithstanding, Snell concludes in a Habermasian fashion that we must strive to build a transnational model of democracy.[129]

Snell's analysis of the euro crisis and its consequences seems to reproduce the more general problem underlying European constitutionalism: due to the pluralist nature of the current constellation, the sovereignty debate is ever-persistent. Snell's analysis offers a substantive reason explaining why there are competing claims to sovereignty by the Member States and especially by national courts. It also brings forth why normative pluralism, based on mutual deference and concession, does not work: what if the different courts are not able to find mutual ground in such trade-off situations as presented by these trilemmas? The answer that Snell presents in relation to Rodrik's trilemma and the EMU also hints towards the same direction as the answer to countering the problems stemming from constitutional pluralism: of introducing a political union; of furthering European integration; and of having structural rules on settling such debates instead of relying on conflict rules applied by courts.

1.3   CONSTITUTIONAL PLURALISM

1.3.1   Introducing Constitutional Pluralism

Let us start with two contrasting narratives on European constitutionalism, one from Luxembourg and the other from Karlsruhe. According to the first, authority, as far as it is transferred to the EU according to the doctrine of conferred powers, rests with the Union and thus the Union's new legal order is autonomous. This is the view expounded by the CJEU in its landmark rulings.[130] The opposing view, offered by the German Federal Constitutional Court, holds that the authority that the Union is able to exert is deduced from the authority of the Member States, their national constitutions, which consequently means that they have the final say. This also ultimately means that the Member States retain absolute sovereignty.[131] Tuori's explanation of this in Kelsenian terms is

---

[129]   Snell (n 127), pp. 171–8.

[130]   See e.g. case 26/62 *van Gend en Loos* EU:C:1963:1; 6/64 *Costa v E.N.E.L.* EU:C:1964:66; C-399/11 *Melloni* EU:C:2013:107.

[131]   See e.g. BVerfGE 37, 271 (*Solange I*); BVerfGE 73, 339 (*Solange II*); BVerfGE 89, 155 (*Maastricht*); BVerfGE 123, 267 (*Lisbon*); 2 BvR 2661/06 (*Honeywell*); 2 BvR 2728/13, 14 January 2014 (*OMT reference*).

enlightening: the claim made in Luxembourg implied a change in the national *Grundnorm*, since through the principle of primacy, the CJEU claimed the highest position for EU law within the national legal order, which also meant that the Member States had divided their sovereignty to the benefit of the EU. Karlsruhe's reply was that the national constitution is still the *Grundnorm*, according to which EU law is to be interpreted and applied in Germany.[132]

Constitutional pluralism as an academic project was sparked by the German Federal Constitutional Court's decision regarding the ratification of the Treaty of Maastricht.[133] Simply put, constitutional pluralism can be described as an attempt to analyse the interaction between national courts and the CJEU and how conflicts between them could be avoided via some form of mutual deference. Such deference is seen to unfold through a dialogue between courts.[134] In essence, pluralists – those ascribing to constitutional pluralism as an apt normative theory of European constitutionalism – reject both the view of the CJEU and that of the German court and propose a third, alternative view. Under this view, both systems can co-exist, overlap and interlock without a hierarchy. Instead, they try to find other ways of reconciliation between the two systems.[135] Some, however, hold the view that constitutional pluralism is merely a theory that tries to validate and legitimise national courts giving precedence to national rather than EU law.[136] This perception is perhaps based on the finding that national constitutions can 'gain much more from pluralism than the European position'.[137]

In an early article on the topic, Walker mapped out the three claims of constitutional pluralism.[138] This categorisation is still a relevant starting point for understanding constitutional pluralism in general, and it also serves as an inroad into the discussion on constitutional pluralism conducted in this book.

---

[132] K. Tuori, 'The Many Constitutions of Europe' in K. Tuori and S. Sankari (eds), *The Many Constitutions of Europe* (Ashgate 2010), p. 20.

[133] BVerfGE 89, 155 (*Maastricht*). See Baquero Cruz (n 23).

[134] See e.g. T. Tridimas, 'The ECJ and the National Courts: Dialogue, Cooperation, and Instability' in Arnull and Chalmers (n 88); B. de Witte, 'The Preliminary Ruling Dialogue: Three Types of Questions Posed by National Courts' in B. de Witte et al (eds), *National Courts and EU Law: New Issues, Theories and Methods* (Edward Elgar Publishing 2016).

[135] See N. Walker 'The Philosophy of European Union Law' in Arnull and Chalmers, ibid., pp. 23–6.

[136] M. Claes, 'The Primacy of EU Law in European and National Law' in Arnull and Chalmers, ibid., p. 202.

[137] Baquero Cruz (n 23), p. 414.

[138] See N. Walker, 'The Idea of Constitutional Pluralism' (2002) *Modern Law Review* 65(3), 317–59, pp. 337–9. Also see N. Walker, 'Late Sovereignty in the European Union' in N. Walker (ed.), *Sovereignty in Transition* (Hart Publishing 2003), p. 4.

First, there is the *descriptive claim*. Namely, that we can observe the existence of overlapping constitutional regimes, since within the Member States both their national constitutions and the EU's constitutional order are in force simultaneously. These overlapping constitutional regimes posit competing constitutional claims. These claims are most clearly articulated in cases in which there is disagreement as to whether the issue should be settled according to national law or EU law, or whether the final arbiter in the situation is a national court or the CJEU. In the above-mentioned PSPP case, the CJEU first declared the ECB's PSPP as being within the ECB's mandate. This decision was based on an interpretation of the EU Treaties. The CJEU thought that it – and only it – had the competence to rule on the interpretation of the EU Treaties and on the validity of acts by an institution of the Union, as stipulated in Article 267 TFEU.[139] However, the German Federal Constitutional Court then declared the PSPP and the CJEU's judgments as *ultra vires*. The German court based its ruling both on its interpretation of the EU Treaties and the German constitution.[140] In essence, both courts assumed the position of the final arbiter in the matter, whereas in reality only one court can decide what happens to the ECB's PSPP.

Second, there is the *normative claim*, which goes beyond the mere descriptive claim by first acknowledging the plurality of constitutional regimes and constitutional claims, and then by embracing the implications of this. Thus, whereas the descriptive claim signals the mere acknowledgement of *plurality*, the normative claim embraces it and turns it into *pluralism*. The normative claim thus deduces what ought to be from what is. That is to say, normative pluralism recognises the somewhat incomplete nature of the EU's constitutional system (that there are competing constitutional claims), but decides to turn it into a virtue by positing that this is how it ought to be. Furthermore, most often normative pluralism also argues that such competing claims are in fact a beneficial way of reconciling the different political views as expressed by the constitutions of the Member States and the EU. Again, to use the PSPP case as an example, normative pluralism could argue, for example, that it is in fact desirable that national courts question the ECB's actions and pressure the CJEU to conduct its review in a prudent manner, since otherwise the ECB could act outside its mandate. The fact that the Federal Constitutional Court sends a tersely formulated referral to the CJEU will not result in the eradication of the EU's constitutional system, since in the end, a solution to the situation will be found by the courts.

---

[139] C-493/17 *Weiss* EU:C:2018:1000.
[140] 2 BvR 859/15, 05 May 2020 (*PSPP judgment*).

Third, there is the *epistemic claim*, which is necessitated by the normative claim, if taken seriously. If the EU and its Member States are understood as distinct constitutional sites, then this also implies the incommensurability of their respective claims to constitutional authority. Therefore, in order for us to understand the competing sovereignty claims as true sovereignty claims, we have to adopt a new, pluralist epistemology. That is to say, we have to appreciate the competing sovereignty claims from their own starting points – and thus as not mutually exclusive. This requires acknowledgement that 'there is no neutral perspective from which their distinct representational claims can be reconciled'.[141] In other words, various epistemic starting points need to be adopted. As sovereignty is traditionally understood in ultimate terms, terms such as 'shared' or 'disaggregated' sovereignty would be oxymorons, because for us to truly appreciate the normative claim of constitutional pluralism requires us to adopt a new conceptualisation of sovereignty, and along with that a new constitutional vocabulary and grammar with which to speak this new constitutional language. The epistemic strand of constitutional pluralism is geared towards this purpose.[142] In practice, this is perhaps best described as an exercise in constitutional and political theory that aims to develop old categories and concepts so as to better match current reality – and more importantly, to aid in further developing the EU as a polity beyond the constraints that the old state-based constitutional concepts place on our constitutional imagination.[143]

Having become the dominant theory and accepted paradigm in European constitutionalism, the literature on constitutional pluralism, as well as the different views expressed therein, is vast.[144] For the sake of brevity, the pluralist accounts are here divided into two groups. First, we have the normative pluralists, who focus their attention on creating or explicating conflict rules according to which the clashes between the national courts and the CJEU could be reconciled. Second, we have the epistemic pluralists, who in turn are more interested in conceptualising this new state of affairs in terms of constitutional theory. Both strands of scholarship will be briefly introduced next.

1.3.2 Normative Constitutional Pluralism

Since normative pluralism appraises the plurality of constitutional sites and constitutional claims, in order for it to offer a viable constitutional framework,

---

[141] Walker, 'The Idea of Constitutional Pluralism' (n 138), pp. 338–9.

[142] See Walker, 'Late Sovereignty in the European Union' (n 138), pp. 10–18.

[143] See N. Walker, 'European Constitutionalism in the State Constitutional Tradition' (2006) *Current Legal Problems* 59(1), 51–89.

[144] See *supra* n 11.

it needs to address the apparent clashes between national courts and the CJEU. So, how should situations in which a national law and EU law – or interpretation by a national court and the CJEU – contradict each other be resolved? Several different alternatives have been put forward in the literature. I will call such propositions conflict rules, since their purpose is to settle constitutional conflicts between the Member States and the EU.

Various sources have been used to distinguish such conflict rules. To begin with, for Maduro these are his 'harmonic principles of contrapunctual law', which include pluralism, consistency and coherence, universalisability, and institutional choice.[145] In a somewhat similar manner, Kumm has posited his 'principle of best fit', that is, rules that would best realise the ideals underlying legal practice in the EU and the Member States. In practice, these include the formal principle of legality, jurisdictional principles of subsidiarity, the procedural principle of democracy, and the substantive principle of the protection of basic rights or reasonableness.[146] For Besselink, a conflict rule is already provided by the principle of primacy of EU law, and granting primacy to EU law over national law is justified on the basis of the principles of the consistent interpretation and useful effect of EU law, which do not imply a hierarchy as such between the European and the national legal orders.[147]

Then there are approaches that build on the national identity clause of Article 4(2) TEU. According to von Bogdandy and Schill, the principle of national constitutional identity, as balanced against the principle of uniform application of EU law, contains the proper conflict rule.[148] In a somewhat similar manner, Bobic argues for an 'auto-correct function', which on behalf of the European Union is based on the national identity clause of Article 4(2) TEU, and on behalf of the Member States on an EU-friendly interpretation of national constitutional law (*Europafeindlichkeit*).[149]

---

[145] See e.g. M. P. Maduro, 'Contrapunctual Law: Europe's Constitutional Pluralism in Action', in N. Walker (ed.), *Sovereignty in Transition* (Hart Publishing 2003), pp. 524–31.

[146] M. Kumm, 'The Jurisprudence of Constitutional Conflict: Constitutional Supremacy in Europe Before and After the Constitutional Treaty' (2005) *European Law Journal* 11(3), 262–307, p. 299.

[147] L. Besselink, *A Composite European Constitution* (Europa Law Publishing 2007), p. 9.

[148] A. von Bogdandy and S. Schill, 'Overcoming Absolute Primacy: Respect for National Identity under the Lisbon Treaty' (2011) *Common Market Law Review* 48(5), 1417–54.

[149] A. Bobić, 'Constitutional Pluralism Is Not Dead: An Analysis of Interactions Between Constitutional Courts of Member States and the European Court of Justice' (2017) *German Law Journal*, 18(6), 1395–428.

A common argument made by the authors propagating the use of such conflict rules as an answer to the competing constitutional claims is that such claims actually induce legitimacy into the EU's constitutional and political system. This is because, as Maduro has explained, the normative claim of constitutional pluralism necessarily entails that such competing claims 'are of equal legitimacy or, at least, cannot be balanced against each other in general terms'.[150]

Under Maduro's account, as the competences of the EU are not and cannot be explicitly defined (in which case the Union's actions would be legitimised by the EU Treaties as such), the only way to constantly legitimise the Union's actions is through a constitutional discourse between the CJEU and the national courts.[151] This is also what occurred during the early days of European integration, when the CJEU was constructing the 'new legal order': 'It was the support of a broad constituency of legal actors (mainly national courts and lit-igants) that "authorised" the European Court of Justice to "free" EU law from indirect legitimacy through the State and make a claim of independent and political authority.'[152] Conversely, Kumm has argued that 'concerns related to democratic legitimacy override considerations relating to the uniform and effective enforcement of EU law' and thus national courts can in some cases set aside EU law if it conflicts with national law.[153] This is because of the dem-ocratic deficit of the EU.[154] Adopting a more theoretical perspective, Walker has maintained that under a pluralist framework, 'the overlap of heterarchically related constitutional authorities of the common part and the local parts, rather than undermining or eroding the legitimacy of each such authority, becomes a condition of legitimacy of the combined whole'.[155]

Such claims bring forth the question of whether national courts can actually induce legitimacy into the EU's constitutional and political system, be it con-ceptualised in pluralist or monist terms. It is of course true that in some cases the concerns with which national courts have pressed the CJEU have been very legitimate and have resulted in overall desirable outcomes – think of the original *Solange* case law and the introduction of fundamental rights into EU

---

[150] M. P. Maduro, 'Three Claims of Constitutional Pluralism', in M. Avbelj and J. Komárek (eds.), *Constitutional Pluralism in the European Union and Beyond* (Hart Publishing 2012), p. 75.

[151] Maduro (n 145), p. 537.

[152] Ibid., pp. 517–18.

[153] Kumm (n 146), p. 298.

[154] Ibid., p. 300.

[155] N. Walker, 'Constitutional Pluralism Revisited' (2016) *European Law Journal* 22(3), 333–55, p. 352.

law.[156] This is the 'bottom-up effect' that Maduro alludes to.[157] However, this is not always the case. Sometimes national courts defy decisions taken at the European level, yet on the basis of a single national constitution. The direst example of this is the German Federal Constitutional Court's *PSPP judgment*.

How can a single national court, acting as the guardian of its national constitution, induce legitimacy into a political process that has taken place at the highest level of politics in Europe? How can a national court, as a legal institution, induce legitimacy into a decision taken by technocratic experts of a given field (e.g. monetary policy)? Furthermore, as there are differences in the way in which national courts can engage in such activity, what does this mean with regards to the legitimacy of such actions? That is to say, if some national courts are better placed to engage in a dialogue with the CJEU, and to thus try to alter the course of European politics or the content of EU law, where does this leave the rest of the national courts? Is there an inherent inequality between the national courts in this regard? It would seem, thus, that both substantively and structurally, the actions of national courts often do exactly the opposite than to induce legitimacy.

1.3.3 Epistemic Constitutional Pluralism

Let us still briefly address epistemic pluralism. In addition to the above-discussed legitimacy issues, taking normative pluralism seriously also leads to acknowledging the necessity of epistemic pluralism. If the existence of simultaneously existing and truly competing sovereignty claims is acknowledged, then to account for this state of affairs we are required to adjust our understanding of what sovereignty means. The purpose of epistemic pluralism is just this: to envisage what constitutionalism beyond the state would look like. In fact, one of constitutional pluralism's aims is to offer an explanation of the current constitutional arrangement that would facilitate constitutional discourse in a new way. This is necessary if we are to avoid 'middle-range theorizing' – that is, explaining the system with the system's own terms.[158]

---

[156] See Stone Sweet (n 31), pp. 170–74.

[157] M. P. Maduro, 'Europe and the Constitution: What if This is as Good as it Gets?' in J. H. H. Weiler and M. Wind (eds), *European Constitutionalism beyond the State* (Cambridge University Press 2003), p. 98, where Maduro explains how 'the legitimacy of European constitutionalism has developed in close cooperation with national courts and national legal communities which have an increasing bottom-up effect on the nature of the European legal order'. See also Maduro (n 145), pp. 517–18.

[158] Walker (n 22), p. 585.

Walker, having coined the term epistemic pluralism,[159] is perhaps the leading figure within this group of scholars. Walker has posited that the originally international law-based Community, which has since claimed its 'independence' based on the existence of its own 'new legal order', now makes relevant constitutional claims; claims that exist in harmony with those older claims originating from the Member States. The relationship of the old and the new – the state and the post-state – is thus best characterised as 'horizontal rather than vertical – heterarchical rather than hierarchical'.[160] Consequently, a key point in Walker's pluralism is the acknowledgement that although there are different sites of constitutional authority, this does not necessarily lead to one site subsuming authority over the other, and furthermore, that there would not exist any constitutional authority without the existence of such a hierarchy. In this way constitutional pluralism tries to retain the key element of constitutionalism (a single authorising political domain) while also embracing the diversity of that domain (the multiple sites of authority).[161] Being the leading theory of European constitutionalism, constitutional pluralism encompasses a wide range of theories and premises. This notwithstanding, there seems to be one key element that unites all pluralists: a very thin understanding of heterarchy, as opposed to some form of hierarchy between the European and national levels.[162]

1.4   CONCLUSIONS

Following the German Federal Constitutional Court's *PSPP judgment* in May 2020, we can say that constitutional pluralism has now come full circle: the discussion was first sparked by the German court's ruling on the ratification of the Maastricht Treaty in 1993,[163] with which the EMU was established. Since then there have been several rulings by national courts that assumed similarly critical stances towards European integration and EU law. These judgments have been considered as parts of a dialogue amongst European courts, which, supposedly, induces legitimacy into the EU's constitutional order. A crucial

---

[159] See Walker (n 138), p. 338.

[160] Ibid., p. 337. Similarly, see N. MacCormick, 'The Maastricht-Urteil: Sovereignty Now' (1995) *European Law Journal* 1(3), 259–66, p. 264: 'the most appropriate analysis of the relations of legal systems is pluralistic rather than monistic, and interactive rather than hierarchical'.

[161] N. Walker, 'Constitutionalism and Pluralism in Global Context' in M. Avbelj and J. Komárek (eds), *Constitutional Pluralism in the European Union and Beyond* (Hart Publishing 2012), pp. 17–18.

[162] See Jaklič (n 13), especially pp. 165–73.

[163] BVerfGE 89, 155 (*Maastricht*). See Baquero Cruz (n 23).

point in this story has been that such judgments, critical as they might have been, have not actually threatened the functioning of EU law nor the existence of the Union. However, exactly this has now happened with the ruling of the German court that outright declared the answer it had received from the CJEU to its preliminary reference *ultra vires*, and thereby also the actions of the ECB. The Federal Constitutional Court's *PSPP judgment* affirms the topicality and necessity of the approach adopted in this book: to study the theory of constitutional pluralism in light of the events of the euro crisis. Furthermore, the judgment also highlights the practical relevance of the argument made herein as well as the criticism presented towards constitutional pluralism as a normative theory of European constitutionalism.

2. The Fiscal Compact and budgetary discipline

2.1   INTRODUCTION

The Treaty on Stability, Coordination and Governance in the Economic and Monetary Union (TSCG) is an intergovernmental treaty amongst the European Union Member States.[1] It is often referred to as the Fiscal Compact after Title III of the Treaty, which contains its operational part. The Fiscal Compact aims to 'strengthen the economic pillar of the economic and monetary union by adopting a set of rules intended to foster budgetary discipline' (Art. 1(1) TSCG). In other words, to cut budgetary deficits and indebtedness. In doing this, the Fiscal Compact 'represents a major step forward towards closer and irrevocable fiscal and economic integration and stronger governance in the euro area'.[2] Similar mechanisms to those employed in the Fiscal Compact had already been in place within the European Union before, namely in the Stability and Growth Pact (SGP).[3] However, the way in which the Fiscal Compact changes these, and the way in which it was created, are somewhat of a novelty in the European Union's (EU) legal framework.

This chapter highlights how such use of international law stems from the inadequacy of the Economic and Monetary Union (EMU), namely its asymmetry. As will be explained in this chapter, the decision to take the international law route was central for the participation of national courts, which, in turn, is one of the key mechanisms on which the inequality thesis is based and through which the theory of constitutional pluralism is assessed in this study.

This chapter proceeds as follows. First, the creation of the Fiscal Compact is explained by providing a reconstruction of its negotiating, drafting and implementation phase (2.2). Then, the underlying economic, political and legal reasons that may help to explain this process are highlighted (2.3). Following this, the content of the Fiscal Compact as a legal measure is analysed doctri-

---

[1]   Treaty on Stability, Coordination and Governance in the Economic and Monetary Union. Brussels, 1–2 March 2012.
[2]   Communication by the Euro Area Member States, 30 January 2012, para. 1.
[3]   See Chapter 1.2.2.2.

nally and its constitutional consequences are discussed (2.4). Finally, conclusions in relation to the overall aim and chosen framework of this study are presented (2.5).

2.2   RECONSTRUCTING THE BIRTH OF THE FISCAL COMPACT

2.2.1   The Political Process Behind the Fiscal Compact

The first reaction of the Member States to solving the euro crisis was to amend the EU Treaties, specifically the SGP as it is included in the Treaty on the Functioning of the European Union (TFEU). On 18 October 2010, France and Germany issued a joint declaration (the 'Deauville declaration') stating that the Treaties should be amended to facilitate the solving of the crisis in a more efficient manner.[4] A year later, just prior to the conclusive European Council meeting, German and French leaders met again and once more issued statements according to which amending the Treaties is the preferred way forward.[5]

During the same month, on 23 November 2011, the Commission issued its proposal for the Two-Pack.[6] In the proposal, the Commission envisaged that Member States should implement the Medium-Term Budgetary Objectives (MTBO) of the preventive arm of the SGP into their national constitutions.[7] Tuori and Tuori have speculated that attaining this objective might have been a reason for why amending the EU Treaties was seen as a viable solution. This is, so they argue, because enforcing changes to national constitutions through EU secondary law might have seemed too ambitious a goal.[8]

Amending the EU Treaties would have been a good option when considering the previous problems on enforcing the SGP through the Council against reluctant Member States.[9] However, since amending the EU Treaties requires unanimity it soon became clear that not all Member States were willing to go through with this. This should have been clear since not all Member States were members of the Eurozone, which was most affected by the crisis. Thus,

---

[4]   See 'Franco-German Declaration' (18 October 2010) https://archiv.bun desregierung.de/archiv-en/articles/franco-german-declaration-756384 (accessed 1 September 2020).

[5]   See 'Strategy to overcome the national debt crisis' (5 December 2011) https:// archiv.bundesregierung.de/archiv-en/articles/strategy-to-overcome-the-national-debt -crisis-471418 (accessed 1 September 2020).

[6]   COM/2011/0821 final.

[7]   COM/2011/0821 final, para. 7 of the Preamble.

[8]   K. Tuori and K. Tuori, *The Eurozone Crisis: A Constitutional Analysis* (Cambridge University Press 2014), pp. 109–10.

[9]   See case C-27/04 *Commission v Council* EU:C:2004:436.

on 9 December 2011, the European Council meeting had to abandon the idea of amending the TFEU because the United Kingdom (UK) vetoed the proposal, and instead agreement was reached on a new 'fiscal compact'.[10]

Following this, the Member States then started an intense round of negotiations on the actual content of this new treaty. Altogether six different versions of the treaty were devised during this process.[11] The final compromise was reached on 30 January 2012.[12] The final version differed in many crucial aspects from the first proposal.[13] Closer analysis of the drafts and the whole process has revealed that most of the changes were based in part on the compromise of the different parties, since they preferred preserving the status quo to increasing or decreasing the effectiveness of the SGP and the annexed EU secondary law.[14]

The final version of the Fiscal Compact was signed by the 25 participating Member States on 1 March 2012. It entered into force on 1 January 2013 after the required amount of signatory states had ratified it. The path between signing the Fiscal Compact and its consequent entry into force was, however, hard and thorny. Ratification and implementation were contested before courts and other institutions with constitutional review functions in many Member States.

2.2.2   The Fiscal Compact Before Courts

The national case law concerning the Fiscal Compact can be categorised in the following manner, mainly based on when the cases were decided and what effect they had from the European perspective: (i) cases preceding the whole Fiscal Compact; (ii) cases that affected the final form the Fiscal Compact took; and (iii) cases that concerned the national ratification and implementation of the Fiscal Compact but which did not have any effect at European level.

Before the Fiscal Compact was even under negotiation by the Member States, two countries amended their constitutions in a manner anticipating

---

[10]   See Statement by the Heads of State or Government of the Euro Area, Brussels, 9 December 2011. On the UK's position, see V. Miller, 'The Treaty on Stability, Coordination and Governance in the Economic and Monetary Union: Political Issues' (2012) *House of Commons Research Paper* 12/14, 1–58.

[11]   On the different versions, see G. Tsebelis and H. Hahm, 'Suspending Vetoes: How the Euro Countries Achieved Unanimity in the Fiscal Compact' (2014) *Journal of European Public Policy* 21(10), 1388–411.

[12]   See Communication by the Euro Area Member States, Brussels, 30 January 2012.

[13]   On these changes adopted during the negotiations, see Tuori and Tuori (n 8), pp. 110–11.

[14]   See Tsebelis and Hahm (n 11), pp. 1404–6.

the Fiscal Compact. In Romania, the constitution was amended in order to incorporate the SGP's debt and deficit requirements. The proposal was challenged before the Constitutional Court of Romania (*Curtea Constituţională a României*), which found, on 17 June 2011, the amendment constitutional since it only restated the obligations stemming from the SGP and Article 126 TFEU.[15]

In Spain, a similar case arose in September 2011 after the Spanish constitution was amended to include a balanced budget rule and a rule on the absolute priority of debt and interest repayment. Although not based on the implementation of the Fiscal Compact, similarly to the Romanian case, this change directly reflected the spirit of the forthcoming Fiscal Compact. The purpose of such an amendment was to reassure the markets and thus lower the interest rates on Spanish government bonds. This amendment was challenged before the Spanish Constitutional Court (*Tribunal Constitucional de España*) on the grounds that it infringed fundamental rights by prioritising the repayment of public debt over all other budgetary choices. Furthermore, the challenge argued that the amendment should have been decided according to the normal procedure for revising the constitution, which would have required dissolving the parliament, and not through the simplified amendment procedure, which required a decision by a qualified majority in the parliament. The Spanish court handed down its various judgments in these proceedings between October and December 2011. In essence, the actions were declared inadmissible. The Spanish court argued that the priority of debt requirement cannot be read in such a way as to affect other sections of the Spanish constitution.[16]

During the negotiation phase the Fiscal Compact was reviewed by the Constitutional Law Committee (*Perustuslakivaliokunta*) of the Finnish parliament. The committee considered the first draft versions of the Fiscal Compact in its opinion of 20 January 2012.[17] Under the committee's opinion, the substantive provisions of the Fiscal Compact did not significantly alter the already existing legal framework of the SGP, and as such, the Fiscal Compact was not problematic in relation to the Finnish constitution. However, the committee had some reservations when it came to the requirement to include the content of the Fiscal Compact into the Finnish constitution and the role envisaged

---

[15]   Constitutional Court of Romania, Decision 799 of 17 June 2011 (*SGP Decision*), published in the Official Journal 828 of 23.11.2011. V. Viţă, country Report on Romania at http://eurocrisislaw.eui.eu (accessed 1 September 2020).

[16]   Sentencias del Tribunal Constitucional 157/2011, 185–189/2011, 195–196/2011, 199/2011, 203/2011. M. Estrada-Cañamares, G. Gomez Ventura and L. Díez Sánchez, country report on Spain at http://eurocrisislaw.eui.eu/ (accessed 1 September 2020).

[17]   PeVL 24/2011 of 20 January 2011.

for national courts to monitor abidance of the MTBO-criteria.[18] It has been speculated that these reservations expressed by the Finnish committee had an effect on the final version of the Fiscal Compact.[19] At least the requirement to incorporate the content of the Fiscal Compact into the national constitution and the role envisaged for national courts in enforcing it were excluded from the final version.

After the Fiscal Compact was signed and national ratification begun, it was challenged before a host of national courts. The most notable of these decisions is perhaps the one by the German Federal Constitutional Court (*Bundesverfassungsgericht*). On 12 September 2012, the German court issued a preliminary injunction regarding claims brought before it on the ratification of the European Stability Mechanism Treaty (ESM) and the amendment of Article 136(3) TFEU pursuant to this,[20] as well as the ratification of the Fiscal Compact.[21] Due to the nature of the legal proceedings, the judgment only contained a 'summary review' of these legal mechanisms, but the court was, however, still able to properly assess their meaning from the perspective of the German constitution and its prior doctrine.[22]

In its judgment, the German court found that the national law on assent to the Fiscal Compact did not breach the German constitution. According to the court, the content of the Fiscal Compact largely coincides with constitutional requirements already in existence and with requirements stemming from the EU Treaties. The Fiscal Compact grants the institutions of the EU no powers that affect the overall budgetary responsibility of the German parliament and does not force Germany to lay down its economic policy permanently in a way that can no longer be reversed.[23] The German court delivered the final ruling on the Fiscal Compact on 18 March 2014.[24] This judgment essentially amounted

---

[18] See P. Leino-Sandberg and J. Salminen, country report on Finland at http:// eurocrisislaw.eui.eu/ (accessed 1 September 2020); K. Tuori and J. Raitio, country report on Finland in U. Neergaard, C. Jacqueson and J. Hartig Danielsen (eds), *The Economic and Monetary Union: Constitutional and Institutional Aspects of the Economic Governance within the EU. The XXVI FIDE Congress in Copenhagen, 2014* (DJOF Publishing 2014).

[19] See Tuori and Tuori (n 8), p. 199.

[20] The ESM Treaty and the amendment of Art. 136(3) TFEU are discussed in Chapter 3.

[21] 2 BvR 1390/12, 12 September 2012 (*ESM interim ruling*).

[22] On the nature of such summary review and the procedural background of the case, see M. Wendel, 'Judicial Restraint and the Return to Openness: The Decision of the German Federal Constitutional Court on the ESM and the Fiscal Treaty of 12 September 2012' (2013) *German Law Journal* 14(1), 21–52.

[23] 2 BvR 1390/12, 12 September 2012 (*ESM interim ruling*), para. 300.

[24] 2 BvR 1390/12, 18 March 2014 (*ESM final judgment*).

to a repetition of the earlier summary review, although it further specified some substantive questions.

In France, the Constitutional Council (*Conseil constitutionnel*) addressed the national ratification of the Fiscal Compact in its judgment of 9 August 2012.[25] The case was sent before the council by the French President pursuant to Article 54 of the French constitution with the question as to whether ratifying the Fiscal Compact required amending the French constitution or not. According to Article 89 of the French constitution, constitutional amendments are approved either through a referendum or by the parliament with a three-fifths majority. Thus, President François Hollande apparently thought that organising a referendum or reaching the required qualified majority would be either too slow or too uncertain of a process and thus he wanted to ratify the Fiscal Compact without amending the constitution. The council deemed the content of the Fiscal Compact similar to the commitments already made by France through the SGP. Thus, no change to the French constitution was necessary for the ratification of the Fiscal Compact, and the incorporation of the so called 'golden rule' (discussed below) could take place by way of a *loi organique*. Later on, the law used to implement the Fiscal Compact into French law was also challenged before the council.[26] The decision of the council allowed the law to be promulgated, except for three parts that were ruled unconstitutional. The council also issued two reservations of interpretation concerning parts it found problematic in light of the national constitution.[27]

The Constitutional Court of Hungary (*Magyarország Alkotmánybírósága*) reviewed the Fiscal Compact in its judgment of 11 May 2012.[28] The court found, contrary to some other national courts, that the Fiscal Compact does broaden the competences of the EU, and thus its national ratification requires a two-thirds majority in the Hungarian parliament. Central for the court's finding was how the Fiscal Compact widens the scope of application of EU law and creates new competences for several EU institutions.[29]

The High Court of Ireland (*An Ard-Chúirt*) decided on 6 June 2012 a case dealing with the ratification of the ESM and the Fiscal Compact.[30] Due to the nature of the case and Irish law, the court did not in fact assess the substantive

---

[25]　Décision n° 2012-653 DC du 9 août 2012.

[26]　Décision n° 2012-658 DC du 13 décembre 2012.

[27]　See R. Gadbled and D. Fromage, country report on France at http://eurocrisislaw .eui.eu/ (accessed 1 September 2020).

[28]　Decision 22/2012 (V. 11.) AB on the interpretation of para. (2) and (4) of Art. E of the Fundamental Law.

[29]　Decision 22/2012 (V. 11.) AB, para. 56 (English translation of the decision provided by the court itself).

[30]　*Doherty v Referendum Commission* [2012] IEHC 211.

compatibility of the Fiscal Compact with the Irish constitution but rather decided the case on purely procedural grounds.[31] The case did not affect the ratification of the Fiscal Compact, which was given presidential assent later that month.[32]

In Luxembourg, the Council of State (*Conseil d'Etat*) assessed the constitutionality of the law implementing the Fiscal Compact in its judgment from 21 December 2012.[33] The council did not have any objections with the national law implementing the Fiscal Compact when it came to the golden rule (Art. 3(1) TSCG), since its content was already enshrined in the earlier obligations regarding the EMU. Furthermore, because of an essentially monist system in relation to international law, the national law implementing the Fiscal Compact would not set any further obligations that would not already stem from the Fiscal Compact as such. However, the council considered that the requirements stemming from Articles 3(2) and 8 TSCG were not contained within the existing body of EU law and thus were a transfer of competence to the EU. For this reason, the appropriate committee of the national parliament had to approve the national implementing law with a two-thirds majority.[34]

The Fiscal Compact entered into force on 1 January 2013, which means that the national courts that addressed it after this date could only affect their country's participation to the Fiscal Compact but they could not stop the Fiscal Compact from coming into force. This is defined as the point of no return for the Fiscal Compact.

The Constitutional Tribunal of Poland (*Trybunał Konstytucyjny*) addressed the national ratification of the Fiscal Compact in a case brought before it by a group of national parliamentarians. Unfortunately, the tribunal did not address the substantive claims presented before it, since it decided the case on purely procedural grounds. In its decision of 21 May 2013, the tribunal held the claims as inadmissible because they were filed before the President of Poland had ratified the Fiscal Compact. Such *ex ante* review of international

---

[31] See S. Coutts, country report on Ireland at http://eurocrisislaw.eui.eu/ (accessed 1 September 2020). However, such procedural aspects can be significant from the European viewpoint. See J.-H. Reestman, 'Legitimacy Through Adjudication: the ESM Treaty and the Fiscal Compact before the National Courts' in T. Beukers, B. de Witte and C. Kilpatrick (eds), *Constitutional Change through Euro-Crisis Law* (Cambridge University Press 2017).

[32] See Thirtieth Amendment of the Constitution (Treaty on Stability, Coordination and Governance in the Economic and Monetary Union) Act 2012, signed on 27 June 2012.

[33] No° 6449², Chambre des Deputes, Session ordinaire 2012-2013. Avis du Conseil d'Etat, 21.12.2012.

[34] See M. Kroeger, country report on Luxembourg at http://eurocrisislaw.eui.eu/ (accessed 1 September 2020).

agreements is only possible in Poland on the request of the President, which was not the case in this situation.[35]

The Constitutional Court of Austria (*Österreichischer Verfassungsgerichts-hof*) ruled on the constitutionality of the Fiscal Compact on 3 October 2013.[36] The applicants, a group of Members of Parliament, argued that the Fiscal Compact should have been adopted by a two-thirds qualified majority because of its constitutional significance. The court, however, found to the contrary. According to the court, the Fiscal Compact is a treaty under international law and outside the scope of EU law. Therefore, its conclusion does not require a qualified majority in the parliament as do amendments to EU Treaties. Furthermore, the transfer of competences to institutions of the EU is of such a nature that it does not exceed the scope of what is admissible under constitutional law, and thus, the constitutional law provisions which govern the federal budget are not violated.[37]

Most recently, on 26 April 2016, the Constitutional Court of Belgium (*Cour constitutionelle*) found all of the challenges brought before it against the Fiscal Compact as inadmissible. The reason was that the people and groups seeking annulment were not affected directly and unfavourably by the national law implementing the Fiscal Compact. An abstract interest in the matter is not sufficient in and of itself. As part of its substantive analysis of the Fiscal Compact the Belgian court found that although the Fiscal Compact contains specified deficit and debt limits, it leaves national parliaments the freedom to decide how to stay within these limits. Thus, the Fiscal Compact does not breach the constitution of Belgium.[38]

2.3   THE TRIPARTITE CONTEXTUALITY OF ECONOMIC–POLITIC–LAW

In addition to the above events, which can be traced as parts of the causal process affecting the formation of the Fiscal Compact, there were also other underlying causes that might have affected the process and the end result.

---

[35]   Decision of 21 May 2013, K 11/13, 3/1/A/2015. K. Granat, country report on Poland at http://eurocrisislaw.eui.eu/; D. Adamski, country report on Poland in Neergaard, Jacqueson and Hartig Danielsen (n 18).

[36]   SV 1/2013-15, 03.10.2013 (English translation of the decision provided by the court itself).

[37]   See D. Jaros, country report on Austria at http://eurocrisislaw.eui.eu/ (accessed 1 September 2020).

[38]   Arrêt n° 62/2016 du 28 avril 2016. See P. Gérard and W. Verrijdt, 'Belgian Constitutional Court Adopts National Identity Discourse: Belgian Constitutional Court No. 62/2016, 28 April 2016' (2017) *European Constitutional Law Review* 13(1), 182–205.

These are situated mostly in the realms of economics and politics but also partially in the realm of law. In contrast to the above-described events the weight of these reasons is more difficult to assess, and thus they are of a more speculative manner. They are, however, important for the overall analysis, since they point out the interplay between economic, political and legal factors.

Since the Member States had a keen interest for doing something that would give a clear signal to the markets as well as to their national constituencies, in terms of fixing the supposed underlying causes of the euro crisis, the UK's veto on amending the Treaties left the Member States in a difficult situation. Craig has argued that since German Chancellor Angel Merkel and French President Nicolas Sarkozy had both publicly committed to doing something to solve the crisis, and resorting to mere EU secondary law would have seemed as a failure on their part, the next best thing after amending the Treaties seemed to be an agreement under international law.[39] In addition to this political- and market-based need for something stronger than just EU secondary law, there is also another reason for why the international law route was maybe chosen. According to Tuori and Tuori, the requirement to introduce the golden rule into national law (Art. 3(2) TSCG) is such a measure that it could not be undertaken by EU secondary law, and since primary EU law was not possible the only option was the international law route.[40]

A contending reason has been presented by de Witte, according to whom the reasons for why the Fiscal Compact was adopted outside the EU's legal framework are far less apparent than is the case regarding the ESM.[41] According to his analysis, the Germans would have wanted to amend the EU Treaties in a similar manner as was the case with the ESM and the addition of Article 136(3) TFEU. Including the rules on fiscal surveillance and curtailment into the EU Treaties would have made altering them more difficult later on and thus would have avoided the problems associated with the enforcement of the SGP, which had become apparent in 2004 when it was not enforced against Germany and France.[42] Since this was not possible, an international law-based treaty and the enactment of national debt brakes through it had to suffice. Furthermore, an international treaty is easier and faster to negotiate and to put

---

[39]   P. Craig, 'The Stability, Coordination and Governance Treaty: Principle, Politics and Pragmatism' (2012) *European Law Review* 37(3), 231–48, pp. 232–33. See also S. Peers, 'The Stability Treaty: Permanent Austerity or Gesture Politics?' (2012) *European Constitutional Law Review* 8(3), 404–41, p. 406.

[40]   Tuori and Tuori (n 8), pp. 109–10.

[41]   For the ESM, see Chapter 3.

[42]   See C-27/04 *Commission v Council* EU:C:2004:436.

together than amending the EU Treaties since amending the Treaties takes place through the procedure prescribed in Article 48 TEU.[43]

Although ultimately being only the second choice, the use of the international law route and the subsequent national implementation of the golden rule of Article 3 TSCG also has its own objective and rationale. As Besselink and Reestman have pointed out, making the commitment to a balanced budget rule through national law is more visible to the people than making it just through EU law, be that EU secondary law or the EU Treaties. Making such a rule part of national law also seems to give it more legitimacy, since then the rule is 'self-imposed' instead of being superimposed by EU law. In addition, making the rule part of national law excludes, or at least reduces, the possibility to blame the EU for the harsh financial decisions that Member States might have to make regarding their own budget as a consequence of the new tighter budgetary constraints.[44]

Furthermore, Chiti and Teixeira have posited that a multiplicity of factors led to using an international law-based instrument. The main reason was that the Member States were not willing to confer new competences onto the EU (fiscal competence and own budget), and thus national budgets had to be used, which also meant the involvement of national parliaments. In addition, the options available in such a situation were somewhat constrained by the prior doctrines of national constitutional courts, especially that of the German Federal Constitutional Court.[45]

The above-listed reasons are mainly political and legal. Since the purpose of the Fiscal Compact is not to give financial assistance to the Member States – on the contrary, its purpose is to restrict fiscal profligacy – therefore its creation did not involve similar economic concerns as was the case with the ESM or the European Central Bank's operations, which will be discussed in the following chapters.

---

[43]   B. de Witte, 'Using International Law in the Euro Crisis: Causes and Consequences' (2013) *ARENA Working Paper* 4, 1–23, pp. 8–9.

[44]   L. Besselink and J.-H. Reestman, 'The Fiscal Compact and the European Constitutions: "Europe Speaking German"' (2012) *European Constitutional Law Review* 8(1), 1–7, p. 6.

[45]   E. Chiti and P. G. Teixeira, 'The Constitutional Implications of the European Responses to the Financial and Public Debt Crisis' (2013) *Common Market Law Review* 50(3), 683–708, p. 689.

2.4   WHAT DID THE FISCAL COMPACT CONSTITUTIONALISE?

Unlike most instruments of EU law, the Fiscal Compact is fairly concise, consisting of only 16 Articles, and being written in a manner that makes it accessible also for those not yet deeply entrenched in the law of economic governance. But then again, the Fiscal Compact is not a part of EU law as it is an international treaty, and its main impetus seems to be its political significance and not its legal force. Actually, most legal scholars seem to think that its content could have been enacted through EU secondary law, and that it does not add much to what was created by the Six-Pack and Two-Pack.[46] Hence, this section first presents the core provisions of the Fiscal Compact (2.4.1), after which their constitutional significance is discussed (2.4.2).

2.4.1   Content of the Fiscal Compact

Article 3(1) TSCG contains the balanced budget rule, or the so-called golden rule. According to it, government budgets should be balanced or in surplus, although a structural deficit of 0.5 per cent of the GDP at market prices is suitable, and in exceptional situations a deficit of 1.0 per cent is acceptable if government debt does not exceed 60 per cent of GDP. These limits do not deviate much from what had already been defined in the SGP.

What is interesting, and what caused most of the uproar at the national level, is the requirement to incorporate the golden rule into national law. According to Article 3(2) TSCG, this should be done 'through provisions of binding force and permanent character, preferably constitutional, or otherwise guaranteed to be fully respected and adhered to throughout the national budgetary processes'. In addition to implementing the golden rule, the contracting states are also supposed to implement a correction mechanism, a 'debt brake'. This mechanism includes the obligation to implement measures to automatically correct significant observed deviations from the MTBO (Art. 3(1)(e) TSCG). What this correction mechanism means in practice is a bit unclear, since all parties to the Fiscal Compact have implemented it in their own manner.[47]

---

[46]   See Craig (n 39), p. 235; Peers (n 39), p. 441; A. Hinarejos, *The Euro Area Crisis in Constitutional Perspective* (Oxford University Press 2015), p. 39. For a description of the Six-Pack and the Two-Pack, see J.-P. Keppenne, 'Fiscal Rules' in F. Fabbrini and M. Ventoruzzo (eds), *Research Handbook on EU Economic Law* (Edward Elgar Publishing 2019).

[47]   See Report from the Commission presented under Article 8 of the Treaty on Stability, Coordination and Governance in the Economic and Monetary Union. C(2017) 1201 final. Brussels, 22.2.2017.

What is ironic in light of previous actions on part of the Member States is that Article 3(1)(c) TSCG effectively contains a safety-valve that allows for the Member States to use consideration when enforcing the TSCG against a state that is deviating from their MTBO. According to the rule, temporary deviation is allowed in 'exceptional circumstances', which are defined as a 'case of an unusual event outside the control of the Contracting Party concerned which has a major impact on the financial position of the general government or to periods of severe economic downturn' (Art. 3(3)(b) TSCG). The last clause of Article 3(3)(b) TSCG is apparently supposed to limit a Member States possibility, against which the Treaty is being enforced before the Court of Justice of the European Union (CJEU), of appealing to the 'exceptional circumstances' so easily. According to the last clause of Article 3(3)(b) TSCG, the deviation of 'exceptional circumstances' only applies 'provided that the temporary deviation of the Contracting Party concerned does not endanger fiscal sustainability in the medium-term'. Overall, Article 3(1) TSCG is perhaps not as dramatic as it might seem based on a first reading since it encompasses many exceptions.

Arguably the most important change introduced by the Fiscal Compact is found in Article 7 TSCG. Whereas the normal way of decision making under the excessive deficit procedure of Article 126 TFEU is that the Council decides by qualified majority whether or not an excessive deficit exists,[48] Article 7 TSCG specifies that decisions within the framework of the excessive deficit procedure are to be taken through a reverse qualified majority procedure. In practice, an excessive deficit is presumed to exist on the basis of the Commission's proposal unless a qualified majority of states specifically votes against it. The aim of this norm is to make it more probable that an excessive deficit is found to exist if the Commission makes such a proposal. This is supposed to fix the political nature of enforcing the SGP, which had caused problems in the past.[49]

From the perspective of EU law, Article 8 TSCG has been assessed as the most dubious one.[50] It provides for the enforcement of the Fiscal Compact through recourse to the CJEU, based on Article 273 TFEU. First, Article 8(1) TSCG grants the CJEU jurisdiction to decide whether a state has implemented the golden rule according to the way specified in the correction mechanism. In this case, the CJEU is supposed to specify a time period within which the

---

[48]   In this case the required majority is defined as at least 55 per cent of the members of the Council representing the participating Member States, comprising at least 65 per cent of the population of these States. See Arts 126(6), 126(13) and 238(3)(a) TFEU.

[49]   See C-27/04 *Commission v Council* EU:C:2004:436.

[50]   See D. Adamski, 'Europe's (Misguided) Constitution of Economic Prosperity' (2013) *Common Market Law Review* 50(6), 47–86, p. 61; Besselink and Reestman (n 44), p. 4.

state is to comply with the decision. In addition, the CJEU is also given jurisdiction to impose financial sanctions on a state that has not complied with the original judgement of the CJEU (Art. 8(2) TSCG). This financial sanction is to follow the criteria set out in Article 260 TFEU and can total 0.1 per cent of the non-compliant state's GDP. Furthermore, Article 8(3) TSCG specifies that '[t]his Article constitutes a special agreement between the Contracting Parties within the meaning of Article 273 [TFEU]' so as to shed all doubts about the CJEU's jurisdiction to hear cases brought to it based on Article 8 TSCG.

Article 8 TSCG is susceptible to the same problem as the golden rule and its application by the Council: is there enough political will? According to Article 8(2) TSCG, if a breach of the golden rule is found, the 'matter will be brought to the Court of Justice of the European Union by one or more Contracting Parties'. This statement in itself is not binding on the Member States since it does not even specify which of them will initiate the action or any other of the specifics required for such action. Political reality in the future will show how powerful such an assertion is. Moreover, even if a case were to be brought before the CJEU, Craig has speculated that it would be highly unlikely that a breach of the golden rule would be found by the CJEU since the rule in itself is written so vaguely.[51] In this light, Adamski's conclusion that Article 8 TSCG is 'all words and no substance' seems reasonable.[52]

Article 12 TSCG introduces the new unofficial euro-summit meetings that aim at strengthening the surveillance and guidance of the Eurozone. It prescribes that the Heads of State or Government of the Eurozone shall meet 'informally' in meetings with the president of the Commission, to which the president of the European Central Bank is also invited. In these meetings 'questions relating to the specific responsibilities which the Contracting Parties whose currency is the euro share with regard to the single currency' are to be discussed (Art. 12(2) TSCG). This is one of the features of the Fiscal Compact that has not been seen as problematic in the literature,[53] namely because it simply codifies an already existing practice.

These meetings, dubbed Euro Summits in the Fiscal Compact, are of an unofficial nature. They do not have any relation to the institutional architecture of the EU Treaties, and the Fiscal Compact does not in itself create any specific role for them in this regard. One could of course raise the issue that creating such 'unofficial' political institutions just takes powers away from the institutions to which they should be vested according to the EU Treaties; but

---

[51]   Craig (n 39), p. 237.
[52]   Adamski (n 50), p. 61.
[53]   See Peers (n 39), p. 434; N. de Sadeleer, 'The New Architecture of the European Economic Governance: A Leviathan or a Flat-Footed Colossus?' (2012) *Maastricht Journal of European and Comparative Law* 19(2), 354–82, p. 376.

then again there have always been, and will always be, unofficial meetings of politicians, which are in essence used to negotiate and actually decide matters before they reach the specific institutions that have the normative power to take the decisions.[54]

Probably to quell these arguments, the Fiscal Compact specifies that after each Euro Summit the president of these meetings shall present a report to the European Parliament (Art. 12(5) TSCG). Along the same lines, Article 13 TSCG also tries to involve the representatives of the European Parliament and national parliaments in the work of the Euro Summits. This is in line with the general trend of strengthening the role of the European Parliament, which has been on the EU's agenda for several decades. All in all, it seems a positive thing to spell out the existence of a meeting of politicians that has already existed and that influences the exercise of politics within the EU.[55]

The functioning of the whole system is enhanced by the fact that the operation of the Fiscal Compact is linked to the ESM. In order for a state to receive financial assistance from the ESM, it has to have ratified the Fiscal Compact (Preamble 25 TSCG). The ESM is also utilised in the sanctioning mechanisms of the Fiscal Compact in that the fine which is payable due to not implementing the correction mechanism properly is to be paid to the ESM (Art. 8 TSCG).

2.4.2   Constitutional Implications of the Fiscal Compact

2.4.2.1   How effective is the Fiscal Compact?

When it comes to assessing the constitutional significance of a norm, the first criteria should of course be its effectiveness: is it able to produce the types of results it is aiming for? If so, what does it actually produce? Further still, what is the nature of this norm, or what type of a tendency does it represent? Next, these issues are explored in relation to the TSCG.

Adamski has doubted whether a Member State (namely, Germany, which pushed most for the adoption of the Fiscal Compact) would be willing to start a judicial battle against another Member State that is unwilling to self-impose austerity measures as prescribed by the golden rule. He argues that the possi-

---

[54]   See e.g. C. Reh, A. Héritier, E. Bressanelli, and C. Koop, 'The Informal Politics of Legislation: Explaining Secluded Decision- Making in the European Union' (2013) *Comparative Political Studies* 46(9), 1112–42; D. Heisenberg, 'The Institution of "Consensus" in the European Union: Formal Versus Informal Decision-making in the Council' (2005) *European Journal of Political Research* 44(1), 65–90.

[55]   On the nature of the Euro Group and Euro Summits, see Opinion of Advocate General Pitruzzella delivered on 28 May 2020, Joined Cases C-597/18 P, C-598/18 P, C-603/18 P and C-604/18 P *Council v Dr. K. Chrysostomides & Co. LLC* EU:C:2020: 390.

bility for such actions is very low since within the current framework of the EU Treaties national budgets are still decided by nationally elected democratic institutions. The EU does not currently have enough legitimacy to challenge such national decisions, especially when taking into consideration how economists seem to agree on the negative effects of such austerity politics.[56]

While surely persuasive, this line of argumentation can easily be countered with the factual situation concerning the ESM. As can be seen, Member States in want of financial assistance were keen and able to implement harsh austerity measures as specified in the Memorandum of Understanding (MoU) that are prerequisites for assistance from the ESM.[57] If the Member States have been able to enforce such measures upon each other, then why would they have any problem making use of the Fiscal Compact? De Sadeleer pointed out early on that the ratification of the Fiscal Compact will probably not turn out to be that problematic. This is because in the Member States at the receiving end its ratification will go hand in hand with financial aid given through the ESM as such aid is conditional upon the ratification of the Fiscal Compact.[58] The above reconstruction seems to validate this argument. All this speaks in favour of the Member States being able and willing to politically make use of all these new legal mechanisms.

Furthermore, with his already above-mentioned statement that Article 8 TSCG is 'all words and no substance' Adamski is implying that it is ineffective because when applying it a distinction can be made between actual laws (have they implemented the golden rule to a binding law, preferably of constitutional status) and governmental practices (regardless of whether the golden rule is incorporated into the laws of that state, what is the financial policy of that state). His main fear is that the application of Article 8 TSCG will only pay attention to the laws and not the actual budgetary practices.[59] Craig has also pointed out the same issue when stating that '[i]t suffices in this respect that they [the demands of Article 3(1) TSCG] take effect in ordinary budgetary processes, which may not be defined in statute at all'.[60]

As true as these statements may be, they do not as such tell us about the possible effectiveness or ineffectiveness of the procedure prescribed in Article

---

[56]   Adamski (n 50), p. 62. For a concise overview of the effects of austerity politics adopted pursuant to the euro crisis, see P. de Grauwe, *The Limits of the Market: The Pendulum Between Government and Market* (Oxford University Press 2017), p. 122.

[57]   See e.g. Compliance Report: The Third Economic Adjustment Programme for Greece. First Review, June 2016. European Commission, DG ECFIN. Brussels, 9 June 2016.

[58]   de Sadeleer (n 53), p. 369.

[59]   Adamski (n 50), p. 61.

[60]   Craig (n 39), p. 237.

8 TSCG. As has been the case already for a while, Member States are free to implement EU law in a variety of manners. EU law even accepts that the implementation of directives does not need to take place through laws, regulations or administrative provisions, but that reproducing parts of a directive in the preparatory works for the law implementing that directive is sufficient.[61] That is to say, that although the concerns raised by Adamski and Craig are no doubt correct, allowing for such practices (implementation through practice and not explicit legislation) is entirely in line with current EU law and practice, and thus, this is an inherent feature of EU law more generally and not just a problem of the Fiscal Compact specifically.

Rosas and Armati have had a different stance on the effectiveness of the Fiscal Compact. The primary problem with the SGP has been the reluctance of the Council to enforce it upon Member States deviating from their MTBOs.[62] For this reason, the Fiscal Compact aims to strengthen the role of the Commission and make enforcement more automated through the use of reverse qualified majority decision making. There is so far no practical evidence on the effectiveness of these changes, but Rosas and Armati have assessed that the sanctions suggested by the Commission would be almost impossible to prevent due to the reversed voting procedure.[63] It is also worth noticing that together France and Germany possess enough votes to establish a decision under the reversed voting procedure when the issue concerns a Eurozone Member State, since in that case only Eurozone Member States participate in the vote and the relative amount of votes that France and Germany possess is larger than in issues concerning a non-Eurozone Member State.[64]

Although the Fiscal Compact has in practice been deemed as rather insignificant, since the same rules are already found in Article 126(1) TFEU and Article 2(a) of Regulation (EU) No 1175/2011,[65] the drafters of the Fiscal Compact seem to have thought otherwise. Why would they state in Article 16 TSCG that the substance of the TSCG needs to be incorporated into the legal framework of the EU within the next five years if they did not deem its content as important?[66]

---

[61]　See C-478/99 *Commission v Sweden* EU:C:2002:281.

[62]　So far all of the Eurozone Member States have broken the reference values of the SGP. Currently ongoing and already closed excessive deficit procedures are listed at https://ec.europa.eu/info/node/4287/ (accessed 1 September 2020).

[63]　A. Rosas and L. Armati, *EU Constitutional Law: An Introduction* (3rd edn, Hart Publishing 2018), p. 234.

[64]　Peers (n 39), p. 424.

[65]　See e.g. Craig (n 39), p. 235.

[66]　The Commission has made a proposal in this regard, but the issue has not progressed. See COM/2017/0824 final.

According to Besselink and Reestman, Article 16 TSCG reveals that the Union's legal order is not yet at a place where it could on its own merit handle situations like the euro crisis.[67] In addition, this final article of the Fiscal Compact also hints that its drafters were worried that it would face similar difficulties during ratification as the ESM Treaty.[68] For this reason, it was beneficial to concede that the Fiscal Compact is only a temporary solution and that the objectives that are pursued through it shall be given a firmer legal footing in the future. After the adoption of the Fiscal Compact it was highly questionable as to whether such an amendment of the EU Treaties would ever be possible since the UK had already once vetoed it. However, with the benefit of hindsight, after Brexit this might become possible.

2.4.2.2 What does the Fiscal Compact actually do?

The Fiscal Compact aims at revising national law in pursuit of its objectives of curtailing national budgetary deficits and the reinforcement of supranational economic governance as spelled out in the golden rule of Article 3 TSCG and subsequently Article 8 TSCG on its enforcement. The EU Treaties, on the other hand, whilst pursuing the same objectives as the Fiscal Compact, rely on their own procedures and penalties, as found in Articles 121 and 126 TFEU. Although the substantive differences between the new requirements established by the Fiscal Compact and the existing ones based on the TFEU are small, they are relevant in that the ones established by the Fiscal Compact aim at a hierarchically superior status since their implementation takes place through national constitutions. By doing so, the Fiscal Compact impacts the very core of parliamentary democracy by 'dislocating as a matter of constitutional principle the budgetary autonomy of the member states'.[69]

However, this observation seems to be true only on the textual level and regarding Member States that have a dualist stance towards international law, whereas states that assume a monist stance would not make a distinction between rules of national and international origin. Despite this remark, the act of dislocation is significant. After the golden rule and the debt brake have been incorporated into national law, national constitutional courts no longer have the possibility to resist their effects by opposing the primacy of EU law as they stem from national law. The only argument left would be a substantive one: such austerity measures impair the fulfilment of fundamental rights.[70]

---

[67] Besselink and Reestman (n 44), p. 5.
[68] See C-370/12 *Pringle* EU:C:2012:756.
[69] Besselink and Reestman (n 44), p. 5.
[70] Generally, see C. Kilpatrick and B. de Witte (eds), *Social Rights in Crisis in the Eurozone: The Role of Fundamental Rights' Challenges* (EUI Depart of Law Research Paper No. 2014/05).

The Fiscal Compact mainly impacts national budgetary autonomy through Article 8 TSCG, which in effect subordinates national budgetary processes to review by the CJEU. In some cases, the national laws implementing the golden rule and the debt brake are of a constitutional status, whereas in some cases they have been implemented with ordinary laws. Furthermore, in some Member States the constitution already contained similar rules before the crisis.[71] Regardless of their legal status as such, budgetary process and the principle of fiscal sovereignty are nevertheless sensitive constitutional matters. Thus, enforcement actions under Article 8 TSCG could lead to tensions between the CJEU and national courts, despite the fact that the Member States themselves enacted the Fiscal Compact and wanted to create such a mechanism.[72]

An interesting by-product of the legal nature of the Fiscal Compact is that it emphasises the constitutionalisation of the EU at the national level since it is the Member States that make these rules part of their national law, and not the EU that forces these rules on them. As such, according to Besselink and Reestman, the Fiscal Compact highlights the constitutional relationship between the national and the European legal orders.[73]

Perhaps the gravest constitutional concern that the Fiscal Compact gives rise to is the fact that it increases executive dominance (as opposed to parliamentary dominance). This is because the Fiscal Compact sidesteps the procedural requirements for amending the EU Treaties or adopting new EU secondary law. Such sidestepping raises democratic concerns since by using an international law-based treaty only the governments of the Member States participate, whereas EU institutions and national parliaments are left without a voice.[74] Furthermore, such actions have also enhanced the role of judicial control by courts, which is another step away from parliamentary control.[75]

2.4.2.3 Intergovernmental or supranational?

If we take intergovernmentalism and supranationalism as descriptive labels to assess modes of governance and normative categories (and not as theories that would causally explain European integration), how should the Fiscal Compact be assessed in light of them? Being an agreement under international law and not EU law, the Fiscal Compact is foremost an expression of intergovernmentalism as opposed to supranationalism. The Community method of decision

---

[71]   See Report from the Commission presented under Article 8 of the Treaty on Stability, Coordination and Governance in the Economic and Monetary Union (n 47).

[72]   See Peers (n 39), p. 420.

[73]   Besselink and Reestman (n 44), p. 7.

[74]   Tuori and Tuori (n 8), pp. 172–3.

[75]   Hinarejos (n 46), pp. 100–101.

making has been the core element of supranationalism within the Union.[76] Although the Fiscal Compact fortifies the supranational elements of economic governance within the EU, these changes are more cosmetic than legally binding, as was noted above.

The Fiscal Compact is foremost a political pact expressing the will of the contracting parties to take seriously the issue of sound fiscal policy at the national level. Amending the EU Treaties to include a stricter framework of economic governance – which was blocked by the UK's veto – would have been a true expansion of supranationalism on this front. The fact that the Fiscal Compact requires Member States to incorporate the golden rule into their national law further reinforces this view: were the amendments made to EU law, they would have had primacy over national law and no such incorporations would have been required. This also speaks in favour of classifying the Fiscal Compact under the heading of intergovernmental tendencies in the development of European integration. Imprints of intergovernmentalism can also be seen in the other crisis response measures.[77]

However, the whole discussion on whether the crisis represents intergovernmental or supranational tendencies is somewhat futile, since, as Peers points out, intergovernmentalism can sometimes (as for example during the euro crisis, when unanimity could not be reached within the EU 28) be an effective way of achieving supranational goals.[78] Fabbrini's analysis seems to support this view, since, as he points out, while the Fiscal Compact is an instrument of international law and thus a product of intergovernmentalism, it actually enhances the powers of the CJEU and the Commission – both of which are supranational institutions – against the Member States within the broad framework of European economic governance.[79]

---

[76] See J. Scott and D. M. Trubek, 'Mind the Gap: Law and New Approaches to Governance in the European Union' (2002) *European Law Journal* 8(1), 1–18.

[77] See e.g. S. Fabbrini, 'Intergovernmentalism and Its Limits: Assessing the European Union's Answer to the Euro Crisis' (2013) *Comparative Political Studies* 46(9), 1003–29.

[78] S. Peers, 'Towards a New Form of EU Law?: The Use of EU Institutions outside the EU Legal Framework' (2013) *European Constitutional Law Review* 9(1), 37–72, p. 39–40.

[79] F. Fabbrini, *Economic Governance in Europe: Comparative Paradoxes and Constitutional Challenges* (Oxford University Press 2016), p. 61.

2.5   CONCLUSIONS

2.5.1   Observations from the Reconstruction

The reconstruction of the birth of the Fiscal Compact showed that its legal form was affected mostly by the UK's veto, which prevented the other Member States from pursuing this objective through an amendment to the EU Treaties. The actual substance of the Fiscal Compact was not constrained by existing EU law or the doctrine of the CJEU but rather by the reservations of the Member States in relation to their national parliaments, constitutions and constitutional courts. Overall, those Member States that wanted to pursue stricter supranational budgetary constraints got their way, although in the form of an international law-based treaty that does not differ much from the SGP as altered by the Six-Pack. After the UK's veto, the process of reaching this point was rather straightforward, and there were no apparent obstacles during the whole process from drafting to entry into force.

As the chronological reconstruction highlighted – and this is crucial for the main argument of this study – none of the national courts that reviewed the Fiscal Compact during national ratification deemed it unconstitutional and turned it down. Thus, we can conclude that national judicial review at this stage had no effect on the European-level political process. The only thing that these judgments could achieve, from a European perspective, is the *ex post* legitimation of the decision to adopt the Fiscal Compact. But what is the worth of such legitimation by a non-majoritarian institution? We will return to this issue in Chapter 7 when assessing constitutional pluralism's credentials as a normative theory of European constitutionalism.

The only clearly established effect of the national cases regarding the Fiscal Compact – either before, during or after the negotiations – is that the original requirement of making the golden rule part of national constitutional law was watered down. Article 3(2) TSCG on the national debt brake now states that implementation shall take place 'through provisions of binding force and permanent character, preferably constitutional, or otherwise guaranteed to be fully respected and adhered to throughout the national budgetary processes'. It seems that only the German Federal Constitutional Court and the Finnish Constitutional Law Committee were able to influence the content of the Fiscal Compact. In both cases, this stemmed from the national constitutional frameworks and how they facilitate the institutions' interaction with international policy processes, whether focused on international law or EU law. The Finnish Committee participated more directly whilst assessing the different draft versions of the Fiscal Compact, whereas the German Federal Constitutional Court participated more indirectly through its various cases on the different crisis response mechanisms that were pending simultaneously and touching upon related issues.

However, the concrete influence of the Finnish Committee seems difficult to establish. While references to this are made in the literature,[80] systematic analyses of the drafting phase do not mention this at all.[81] On the one hand, the reason for such omission can simply be that scholars tend to focus on the big Member States and on countries whose politics and constitutions they are most familiar with. On the other hand, it is a fact that the biggest Member States – in this case the ones with the biggest budget and who thus covered most of the costs of the euro crisis, namely Germany – also have the most political say. But political say only carries so far. If an institution tasked with constitutional review has specifically declared something as unconstitutional, then it will surely constrain politics despite originating from a small Member State and going against the wishes of larger Member States. Ultimately, though, whether or not the Finnish Committee's opinion had an effect in this case is irrelevant for the more general argument put forth in this study. The fact is that due to its institutional position and role, it was able to participate in the European-level political process before the point of no return, and thus it at least had the possibility to influence this process.

An interesting fact can also be observed through a closer look at the German Federal Constitutional Court's two decisions in this case. One would assume that due to its previous case law and general attitude towards European integration if some court would raise constitutional concerns against the Fiscal Compact it would surely be the German court. A plausible counter argument to this view would be the fact that it was actually Germany who wanted to adopt the Fiscal Compact. Furthermore, since Germany had already adopted a similar debt break as the golden rule into its own national constitution in 2009, the Fiscal Compact as such was nothing new. Thus, the German court naturally had no objections towards the Fiscal Compact. Actually, in its final decision the court was of the opinion that the Fiscal Compact only restates that which is already found in the German constitution due to the national debt brake implemented before the crisis and the requirements of Article

---

[80]   See Tuori and Tuori (n 8), p. 199; J.-H. Reestman, 'The Fiscal Compact: Europe's not always able to speak German: On the Dutch' (2013) *European Constitutional Law Review* 9(3), 480–500, p. 496; P. ó Broin, 'The Euro Crisis: The Fiscal Treaty – An Institutional Analysis' (2012) *Institute of International and European Affairs Working Paper Series* 5, pp. 8–9.

[81]   See A. Verdun, 'A Historical Institutionalist Explanation of the EU's Responses to the Euro Area Financial Crisis' (2015) *Journal of European Public Policy* 22(2), 219–37; Tsebelis and Hahm (n 11).

126 TFEU.[82] Article 109(3) of the German constitution imposes a strict limit on government deficits: as a structural component where at the federal level (*Bund*) revenue from credits should not exceed 0.35 per cent of GDP, whereas for the states (*Länder*) the cap is set at 0.0 per cent. These limits can vary according to the cyclical component in accordance with the economic situation at hand. There is also an exception clause, which permits the limits to be broken in exceptional circumstances.[83]

2.5.2 The Rationality of the Fiscal Compact

The rationality of adopting the Fiscal Compact as well as its substantive content – its aims and objectives and the means it uses in pursuing them – can be questioned on several levels. Since, as was already stated, the Fiscal Compact was primarily the result of political aspirations and not of economic or legal necessity, such underlying irrationality is somewhat expected. First, as the legal analysis pointed out, if the Fiscal Compact's possibilities of legally enforcing change are questionable, why make such a system at all? Second, the rather stringent nature of the system and its reliance on sanctions has been questioned: is there any point in sanctioning a state that already is on the verge of financial breakdown? Does a fine imposed after the deficit has been established hold any preventive force, and will a fine in this situation be only counter-productive?[84] Third, such micro-management of constitutional issues actually just contributes towards the legitimacy deficit that the EU is said to suffer from because 'constitutionalisation means de-politicization'.[85] That is to say, that issues that have been decided at the constitutional level are no longer open for political debate.

The asymmetry of the EMU seems to underlie much of this. The new framework provided by the Fiscal Compact, the Six-Pack and Two-Pack enhance the surveillance and coordination of national economic policy, but they do not create a common economic policy for the EU. Creating a common economic policy would include granting fiscal powers for the Union, considerable

---

[82] 2 BvR 1390/12, 18 March 2014 (*ESM final judgment*), para. 244: 'The Treaty grants the bodies of the European Union no powers which affect the overall budgetary responsibility of the German *Bundestag* and does not force the Federal Republic of Germany to make a permanent commitment regarding its economic policy that can no longer be reversed.'

[83] See A. Thiele, 'The "German Way" of Curbing Public Debt' (2015) *European Constitutional Law Review* 11(1), 30–54.

[84] Rosas and Armati (n 63), p. 234.

[85] See D. Grimm, 'The Democratic Costs of Constitutionalisation: The European Case' (2015) *European Law Journal* 21(4), 460–73.

enlargement of the Union's budget and greater joint liability of state debt.[86] Due to the still existing asymmetrical structure of the EMU, probably the most important question regarding the effectiveness of the Fiscal Compact is as follows: will it induce structural changes in the economies of the Member States, or are these to be forced on to them also in the future through the MoUs when they ask for financial assistance from others? As Adamski has pointed out, in its current form 'the EMU makes strong and competitive countries stronger and even more competitive, at the expense of poorer and uncompetitive Member States'.[87] This is due to non-governance of macroeconomics in the monetary union. In other words, the fact that the Member States still lack a common economic and fiscal policy. The Fiscal Compact is missing the supranational approach, since it tries to tackle the sovereign debt crisis through national politics, through the national budgets and national debt brakes. As long as the supranational element is missing, the only way to induce structural changes is through the strict conditionality of rescue packages.

---

[86]   See F. Fabbrini, 'Fiscal Capacity' in Fabbrini and Ventoruzzo (eds) (n 46).

[87]   D. Adamski, 'National Power Games and Structural Failures in the European Macroeconomic Governance' (2012) *Common Market Law Review* 49(4), 1319–64, p. 1361.

3. The European Stability Mechanism and financial assistance

3.1 INTRODUCTION

The European Stability Mechanism (ESM) is one of the European Union's (EU) key measures for crisis resolution and prevention following the euro crisis.[1] The ESM is intended to safeguard the financial stability of the euro area. The ESM offers loans and direct financial assistance to Eurozone Member States and it can also be used to recapitalise private banks. It finances its actions by issuing debt instruments on the public markets. Technically speaking, the ESM is not part of EU law since it was established as an inter-governmental organisation operating under public international law. It is a permanent agency functioning in Luxembourg, although not officially an EU institution. It is based on a treaty under international law signed by all 19 Eurozone Member States on 2 February 2012.[2]

The ESM is the successor of two earlier financial assistance mechanisms, the European Financial Stability Facility (EFSF) and the European Financial Stabalisation Mechanism (EFSM). This chapter will mainly focus on the ESM because it is meant to be a permanent mechanism, whereas the other two mechanisms were ad hoc instruments. However, the creation and content of the EFSF and the EFSM are explained to the extent necessary to understand the context of the ESM, and also because the adoption of the ESM is part of the process that began with the creation of the two earlier mechanisms. Similarly to the previous case study on the Fiscal Compact, here too the process of adopting the ESM and its contestation before national courts is central for the main argument of this study. Likewise, the constitutional analysis will focus on how the asymmetry of the Economic and Monetary Union (EMU) is reflected in the content of the ESM and the consequences this has.

---

[1] This chapter draws on T. Tuominen, 'Mechanisms of Financial Stabilisation' in F. Fabbrini and M. Ventoruzzo (eds), *Research Handbook on EU Economic Law* (Edward Elgar Publishing 2019).

[2] Treaty Establishing the European Stability Mechanism. 2 February 2012, https://www.esm.europa.eu/legal-documents/esm-treaty (accessed 1 September 2020).

This chapter proceeds as follows. First, the creation of the ESM is explained by providing a reconstruction of its negotiating, drafting and implementation phase (3.2). Then, the underlying economic, political and legal reasons that may help to explain this process are highlighted (3.3). Following this, the content of the ESM as a legal measure is analysed doctrinally and its constitutional consequences are discussed (3.4). Finally, conclusions in relation to the overall aim and chosen framework of this study are presented (3.5).

3.2   RECONSTRUCTING THE BIRTH OF THE EUROPEAN STABILITY MECHANISM

3.2.1   The Political Process Behind the European Stability Mechanism

The road towards the establishment of the European Stability Mechanism in 2012 actually began three years earlier. On 21 October 2009 the newly elected Greek government revealed actual deficit levels that were considerably higher than had been reported by the previous government: 12.5 per cent of GDP instead of 3.7 per cent.[3] To simplify a bit, this announcement by the Greek government is here taken as the triggering effect that started the whole process that eventually resulted in the establishment of the ESM, an amendment to the Treaty on the Functioning of the European Union (TFEU), and the constitutionalisation of bail-outs for Member States facing financial difficulties. This entire process consisted of several different incidents that as a whole approved of these developments, both at the European and national level.

During the spring of 2010 several meetings by the Eurozone Heads of State or Government were held in which the will to and the form of how to resolve the crisis were carved out. On 11 February 2010, an informal meeting of the Eurozone Member States was held in which the Member States declared that they 'will take determined and coordinated action, if needed, to safeguard financial stability in the euro area as a whole'.[4] At this stage, Greece had not yet asked for financial assistance, but its need for assistance was becoming evident. After this, the Council adopted an opinion, a decision and a recommendation in its meeting on 16 February 2010, all of which pertained to the deficit and debt levels in Greece and how to reduce them.[5]

---

[3]   COM/2010/0001 final, Report on Greek Government Deficit and Debt Statistics. Brussels, 8 January 2010.
[4]   Statement by the Heads of State or Government of the European Union. Brussels, 11 February 2010.
[5]   Press Release, 2994th Council meeting, Economic and Financial Affairs. Brussels, 16 February 2010.

The form of assistance that was going to be given to Greece was decided in the meeting of the Heads of State or Government of the Eurozone on 25 March 2010.[6] Prior to this, there had been proposals from Germany to amend the EU Treaties and to establish a European alternative to the International Monetary Fund (IMF). German Chancellor Angela Merkel had endorsed such ideas, but since amending the EU Treaties would have required the consent of all Member States, and it could also have been deemed *ultra vires* by the German Federal Constitutional Court, these German aspirations had to be abandoned.[7]

Thus, the rescue package was to take the form of coordinated bilateral loans between the Member States with the involvement of the IMF. This is usually referred to as the Greek Loan Facility (GLF). Then, on 11 April 2010, the Eurozone Member States issued a joint statement in which they specified some of the conditions for this bilateral assistance; for example, the interest rates and the maturity of these loans.[8] Due to these excessive preparatory arrangements (both at the political level and also at the practical level by the Commission and the IMF), when Greece finally requested assistance on 23 April 2010 the formal agreement on granting this was reached in under two weeks on 2 May 2010.[9]

However, this was not the end of the crisis; far from it. There was the fear of contagion from Greece to the considerably bigger economies of Spain and Italy, and there was the possibility that the now agreed measures would not be enough for Greece. For these reasons, other additional measures were seen as necessary. The following week, on 7 May 2010, the Eurozone Heads of State or Government issued a statement in which they spelled out some of their aspirations on how to solve the current crisis and prevent future crises.[10] One of these measures included 'a European stabilization mechanism to preserve financial stability in Europe'. This was basically the announcement of both the EFSM and the EFSF. Following this, the Council meeting on 9–10 May 2010 decided on the EFSM Regulation (EU) No 407/2010, with Article 122(2) TFEU as its legal basis. Then, the Eurozone Heads of State or Government

---

[6]   Statement by the Heads of State or Government of the euro area. Brussels, 25 March 2010.

[7]   L. Gocaj and S. Meunier, 'Time Will Tell: The EFSF, the ESM, and the Euro Crisis' (2013) *Journal of European Integration* 35(3), 239–53, p. 242.

[8]   Statement on the support to Greece by Euro area Members States. Brussels, 11 April 2010.

[9]   Statement by President Van Rompuy following the Eurogroup agreement on Greece. Brussels, 2 May 2010, PCE 80/10.

[10]   Statement by the Heads of State or Government of the euro area. Brussels, 7 May 2010.

agreed on the EFSF as a special purpose vehicle outside of the European Union's legal framework.[11]

Soon thereafter, on 14 May 2010, the European Central Bank (ECB) decided on its Securities Markets Programme (SMP). The SMP was a precursor to the ECB's Outright Monetary Transactions (OMT) programme. At this stage what is important to note is how there is a link between the Member States' incorporating the EFSF and the ECB launching the SMP. Ohler has argued that the ECB persuaded the Member States to do so, since it felt that its own measures were not enough and that it was unable to act because of the constraint set by the ban on central bank financing (Art. 123 TFEU).[12] This further shows the interdependence of these events and is revealing about the role of the ECB, which are analysed later in Chapter 5.

The reasons for adopting two separate bail-out mechanisms were rather simple. First, it was thought that because the EFSM was an EU law instrument and the EU had only a limited budget, the EFSM would not be enough to deal with the crisis. Therefore, a substantially larger fund was seen as necessary. Second, a mechanism based on EU secondary law and thus applicable to all Member States required those outside the Eurozone to participate in giving financial assistance in a crisis that was inherently seen as one belonging only to the Eurozone and not to the whole Union. Therefore, something in addition to the EU law based EFSM was seen as necessary.[13] The form and content of the EFSF was modelled on the GLF.[14]

Immediately after this, the *Euro rescue package* case was submitted before the German Federal Constitutional Court (*Bundesverfassungsgericht*) by a group of German scholars who argued, among other things, that Article 122(2) TFEU was not an adequate legal basis for the EFSM Regulation and that both the EFSM and the special purpose vehicle EFSF violated the no bail-out clause of Article 125 TFEU.[15] This had the effect that, in fear of the German court accepting such claims, Chancellor Merkel had to come up with a more reliable way of dealing with the crisis. Thus, the idea for a Treaty

---

[11]   ECOFIN Council 265, Annex. Brussels, 10 May 2010.

[12]   See C. Ohler, 'The European Stability Mechanism: The Long Road to Financial Stability in the Euro Area' (2011) *German Yearbook of International Law* 54, 47–74.

[13]   B. de Witte and T. Beukers, 'The Court of Justice Approves the Creation of the European Stability Mechanism outside the EU Legal Order: Pringle' (2013) *Common Market Law Review* 50(3), 805–48, p. 808–9.

[14]   A. Verdun, 'A Historical Institutionalist Explanation of the EU's Responses to the Euro Area Financial Crisis' (2015) *Journal of European Public Policy* 22(2), 219–37, p. 225.

[15]   See 2 BvR 987/10, 7 September 2011 (*Euro rescue package*).

amendment and the ESM was born.[16] Following this, on 18 October 2010, France and Germany issued a joint declaration (the 'Deauville declaration') that the Treaties should be amended to facilitate the solving of the euro crisis in a more efficient manner.[17]

Then, in the following European Council meeting of 28–29 October 2010, all Member States reached a consensus on the establishment of a permanent aid mechanism.[18] It was agreed that the permanent mechanism would be based on a limited change of the EU Treaties, thus leaving the no bail-out clause of Article 125 TFEU intact and that it would be the Member States themselves and not the EU that would establish this mechanism. The permanent mechanism was to replace the EFSM and the EFSF in 2013. This approach had the effect that, first, the mechanism would be based on international law and not EU law, and second, that the simplified revision procedure of Article 48(6) TEU could be used to facilitate the necessary Treaty amendment.[19] The European Council then adopted a draft decision for amending Article 136 TFEU in its meeting on 16–17 December 2010,[20] and the final decision was taken on 25 March 2011.[21]

The need for a permanent mechanism became evident during January 2011, when, despite the EFSF bond auction for Ireland going through well, there was much speculation of Portugal, Spain and Italy also needing support from the EFSF and that its capacity would not be enough to bail-out all three in addition to Greece. The underlying reason limiting the EFSF's capacity was Germany's determination to retain the AAA rating of bonds issued by the EFSF, which limited its actual capacity compared to that initially intended. This left the Member States underprepared to deal with possible future crises. These negative market reactions also forced the Member States to establish a permanent mechanism faster than Germany would have wanted to.[22]

At this point national constitutional avenues also started to react to these European events. On 8 March 2011, the European Union Committee of the House of Lords of the United Kingdom (UK) delivered its report on the

---

[16]   G. Barrett, 'First Amendment? The Treaty Change to Facilitate the European Stability Mechanism' (2011) *The Institute of International and European Affairs*, 1–27, p. 15.

[17]   See 'Franco-German Declaration' (18 October 2010) https://archiv.bun desregierung.de/archiv-en/articles/franco-german-declaration-756384 (accessed 1 September 2020).

[18]   European Council conclusions, EUCO 25/1/10. Brussels, 30 November 2010.

[19]   de Witte and Beukers (n 13), p. 811.

[20]   European Council conclusions, EUCO 30/1/10. Brussels, 25 January 2011.

[21]   2011/199/EU: European Council Decision.

[22]   Gocaj and Meunier (n 7), pp. 247–8.

amendment of Article 136 TFEU. In its concise assessment, the committee found that:

> [T]he amendment does not appear to us to fall within the classes of amendment which, under Clause 4 of the European Union Bill, would trigger a requirement for a referendum. Clause 4 applies (broadly speaking) where an amendment would add to EU competences or remove Treaty safeguards for Member States.[23]

Initially, the British had vetoed changing the EU Treaties for establishing the ESM within the framework of EU law. What made them accept creating the ESM outside the remit of EU law? One possible explanation is that they were willing to amend Article 136 TFEU to facilitate the creation of the ESM outside the framework of the EU law precisely because in this way the other Member States could enact it in a fashion that made it possible for them to stay out. The committee's opinion, on its part, made amending Article 136 TFEU possible in this regard since such amendments require ratification by all Member States, even though the reason for why this was done, the ESM, does not concern the UK.

The Finnish Parliament's Constitutional Law Committee (*Perustuslakivaliokunta*) assessed a draft version of the ESM Treaty on 14 June 2011.[24] The committee expressed that it is essential that decisions within the ESM are taken by unanimity, which essentially guarantees Finland – and every other participating Member State for that matter – a veto power on the future use of its funds. In addition, the committee thought it important that the Finnish parliament should have proper knowledge of the functioning and operation of the ESM so as to make informed decisions on its possible use.

The German Federal Constitutional Court's decision in *Euro rescue package* was delivered on 7 September 2011.[25] In this case, the national laws implementing the direct bilateral aid measures to Greece and the establishment of the EFSF were challenged by arguing that the financial commitments that these laws actually amounted to violated the right to vote (Art. 38.1 German constitution) and the right to property (Art. 14 German constitution). The Federal Constitutional Court admitted the case on the basis of the first but held the latter complaint as inadmissible.

The right to vote has been a central part of the German Federal Constitutional Court's jurisprudence on European integration. It was also invoked in its

---

[23]   European Union Committee – Tenth Report: Amending Article 136 of the Treaty on the Functioning of the European Union. London, 8 March 2011.

[24]   PeVL 1/2011 of 14 June 2011.

[25]   2 BvR 987/10, 7 September 2011 (*Euro rescue package*).

Maastricht and *Lisbon* judgments.[26] In the latter judgment, the court had already specified that the principle of democracy and the right to vote prohibit the transfer of budgetary powers to the supranational level 'to a considerable extent'.[27]

The ruling in *Euro rescue package* further defined the doctrine that the German Federal Constitutional Court had established in these previous judgments and, importantly, also set the tone for the court's following judgments on the crisis response mechanisms. According to the previously established doctrine, the constitutional right to vote (Art. 38.1 German constitution) guarantees not only the right to elect the *Bundestag* but also makes sure that the rights of the *Bundestag* are not transferred to supranational institutions. Basically, *Euro rescue package* seems to assert a certain openness towards international cooperation and suggests that supranationalisation of budgetary powers is possible if the adequate participation of the *Bundestag* in the decision-making process is guaranteed.[28] However, at the same time the judgment asserts that the limits to integration cannot be circumvented by shifting to special purpose vehicles of international law.[29] The crucial points of this judgment regarding the formation of the ESM were that: (i) the German *Bundestag* cannot consent to an unknown amount of financial liabilities; (ii) the *Bundestag* must approve all large aid measures individually; and (iii) this means that decisions within the ESM must be made unanimously so as to retain a veto power for Germany.

During the negotiation process the Finnish Constitutional Law Committee assessed the draft ESM Treaty a second time. The committee concluded in its opinion of 8 December 2011 that a formulation of the emergency voting procedure of Article 4(4) ESM – that allowed it to be used not only for already paid in capital but also for calling in authorised unpaid capital – would amount to a violation of budgetary sovereignty since Finland would not have a blocking minority on its own due to the size-dependent voting rules.[30] Accepting such a treaty would require amending the Finnish Constitution, namely accepting the treaty with a qualified majority in the Finnish Parliament.

The position that the German Federal Constitutional Court took in September 2011 in *Euro rescue package* is effectively the same position that the Finnish Constitutional Law Committee had already assumed in January of that year,

---

[26] BVerfGE 89, 155 (*Maastricht*); BVerfGE 123, 267 (*Lisbon*).

[27] BVerfGE 123, 267, (*Lisbon*) para. 256.

[28] A. von Ungern-Sternberg, 'German Federal Constitutional Court Parliaments — fig leaf or heartbeat of democracy? Judgment of 7 September 2011, Euro rescue package 1' (2012) *European Constitutional Law Review* 8(2), 304–322, p. 313–319.

[29] P. M. Huber, 'The Federal Constitutional Court and European Integration' (2015) *European Public Law* 21(1), 83–108, p. 99.

[30] PeVL 22/2011 of 8 December 2011.

although the German court's argument was much more elaborate and analytical. Huber has proposed that *Euro rescue package* affected the way the ESM was convened.[31] In a similar fashion, the second decision of the Finnish Committee from December 2011 has also been seen, by Tuori and Tuori, to have affected the final formation of the ESM Treaty.[32]

To what degree these instances affected the final content of the ESM, as signed on 2 February 2012, remains contested, but both the Finnish committee and the German court also assessed the legality of this final product. The Finnish committee delivered its final opinion on 7 June 2012 in which it relied on its earlier opinions on the EFSF. It stressed the fact that ratifying the ESM Treaty was possible by simple majority, since within the ESM decisions are taken by unanimity, and the Finnish Parliament (its Grand Committee) has the possibility to advise the Finnish representative on how to vote.[33] Therefore, it does not impinge upon sovereignty or the budgetary powers of the Finnish Parliament.[34]

In its interim ruling of 12 September 2012, the German Federal Constitutional Court reviewed the ratification statutes introducing the ESM into the German legal order.[35] The judgment followed largely the court's earlier argumentation in *Euro rescue package*. As part of its judgment the court set as a condition for national ratification that assurances under international law should be obtained for two things. First, that Article 8(5) of the ESM Treaty should limit the amount of all German payment obligations to the amount stipulated in Annex II in a way that higher obligations require the agreement of the German representative. Second, that the *Bundestag* should have adequate access to information on the ESM regardless of the ESM Treaty's Articles on inviolability of documents, professional secrecy and immunity. The result of this was that a joint interpretive statement was issued by the Contracting Parties on 27 September 2012 that satisfied the conditions set by the German court.[36] Due to the German court's ruling this statement was needed in order for Germany to be able to ratify the ESM.

---

[31]   Huber (n 29), p. 99.
[32]   K. Tuori and K. Tuori, *The Eurozone Crisis: A Constitutional Analysis* (Cambridge University Press 2014), p. 198.
[33]   PeVL 13/2012 of 7 June 2012.
[34]   See Tuori and Tuori (n 32), p. 197.
[35]   2 BvR 1390/12, 12 September 2012 (*ESM interim ruling*).
[36]   See Declaration on the European Stability Mechanism. Brussels, 27 September 2012.

3.2.2   The European Stability Mechanism Before Courts

The previous section addressed those national cases that took place before the signing of the ESM Treaty and which where thus able to affect its formation. Next, attention is given to cases concerning the national ratification of the ESM. These cases are addressed in chronological order. The landmark ruling of the Court of Justice of the European Union (CJEU) in *Pringle* will only be shortly mentioned here since the CJEU's ruling is addressed in more detail later.[37] If the CJEU's judgment in *Pringle* is taken as the point of no return, it can be observed that four cases were decided before this (the Netherlands, Estonia, Ireland and Belgium) and two afterwards (Austria and Poland). In the end, one outlier case (Slovenia) will also be assessed.

Geert Wilders, a Member of Parliament in the Dutch House of Representatives, challenged the participation of the Netherlands in the ESM before a local district court (*Rechtbank Den Haag*). There is no constitutional court in the Netherlands and Article 120 of the Dutch constitution explicitly prohibits judicial review by courts.[38] Thus, it was not surprising that the court rejected this challenge and did not engage in a substantive review of the ESM or the amendment of Article 136 TFEU.[39]

In Estonia, ratification of the ESM was challenged *ex officio* by the Chancellor of Justice before the Supreme Court (*Riigikohus*) in an abstract review proceeding. The emergency voting procedure of Article 4(4) ESM was claimed to infringe the financial competences of the Estonian parliament. The court found that Article 4(4) ESM interferes with the financial competence of the Estonian parliament and with the financial sovereignty of the state of Estonia. This infringement was weighed up against the objective of the ESM: to contribute towards 'the financial stability of the euro area as a whole'. Estonia is a member of the euro area. Based on a proportionality review, the court found that Article 4(4) ESM provides for an appropriate, necessary and reasonable measure for the achievement of the objective of financial stability and furthermore that the objective of the ESM is sufficiently significant to

---

[37]   C-370/12 *Pringle* EU:C:2012:756.

[38]   The Article reads: 'The constitutionality of Acts of Parliament and treaties shall not be reviewed by the courts.' See M. de Visser, *Constitutional Review in Europe: A Comparative Analysis* (Hart Publishing 2014), p. 79.

[39]   Rechtbank Den Haag 1 June 2012, case nr. 419556 / KG ZA 12-523. LJN: BW7242. See J. Mulder, country report on the Netherlands at http://eurocrisislaw .eui.eu (accessed 1 September 2020); S. Van den Bogaert, T. de Gans and J. van de Gronden, country report on the Netherlands in U. Neergaard, C. Jacqueson and J. Hartig Danielsen (eds), *The Economic and Monetary Union: Constitutional and Institutional Aspects of the Economic Governance within the EU. The XXVI FIDE Congress in Copenhagen, 2014* (DJOF Publishing 2014).

justify the interference with national financial competences and financial sovereignty. Hence, the court found that Article 4(4) ESM is not in conflict with the constitution of Estonia. The assessment of the court was rather thorough and included the dissenting opinion of nine of the 19 judges of the full court.[40]

Thomas Pringle, a Member of Parliament in Ireland, challenged both the ESM and the amendment of Article 136 TFEU before the High Court of Ireland (*An Ard-Chúirt*). He argued that participation in the ESM amounted to an unconstitutional delegation of sovereignty and that the ESM and the Council Decision amending Article 136 TFEU were both in violation of EU law. By its judgment of 17 July 2012, the High Court dismissed the sovereignty claim but decided to ask for a preliminary reference on the claims relating to the legality of these measures under EU law.[41] Mr. Pringle then appealed to the Supreme Court of Ireland (*Cúirt Uachtarach na hÉireann*), which in its decision of 31 July 2012 was basically of the same opinion as the High Court and decided to ask the CJEU for a preliminary ruling on the matter. The final judgment on the national aspects of the claims was delivered by the Supreme Court on 19 October 2012.[42] The court found that the decision of the Irish government to enter into the ESM was a policy decision within its executive powers and as such did not involve an impermissible transfer of sovereignty.[43]

On 20 December 2012 the Constitutional Court of Belgium (*Cour constitutionelle*) dismissed an action for annulling the national law on ratifying the ESM. Although the Belgian court is known for constantly broadening its own jurisdiction through its case law,[44] in this case it dismissed the action on procedural grounds since the action was lodged after the deadline.[45]

The CJEU delivered its judgment in *Pringle*, given by a full court of all 27 judges, on 27 November 2012. Even though the accelerated procedure was applied to the case by the decision of the President of the Court, the ESM Treaty had already entered into force on 27 September 2012; that is, before the CJEU had assessed the legality of the ESM under EU law. The CJEU's

---

[40]   Judgment of the Supreme Court En Banc of July 12, 2012 in Case No. 3-4-1-6-12. M.-L. Laatsit, country report on Estonia at http://eurocrisislaw.eui.eu (accessed 1 September 2020); A. Tupits, country report on Estonia in Neergaard, Jacqueson and Hartig Danielsen, ibid.

[41]   *Pringle v Government of Ireland and others* [2012] IEHC 296.

[42]   *Pringle v The Government of Ireland* [2012] IESC 47.

[43]   See S. Coutts, country report on Ireland at http://eurocrisislaw.eui.eu (accessed 1 September 2020).

[44]   See de Visser (n 43), p. 230.

[45]   Arrêt n° 156/2012 du 20 décembre 2012. See W. Vandenbruwaene, country report on Belgium at http://eurocrisislaw.eui.eu (accessed 1 September 2020).

judgment has been both criticised and applauded by academics.[46] Unlike the German Federal Constitutional Court, the CJEU accepted the amendment to Article 136 TFEU and the establishment of the ESM Treaty without any reservations or preconditions.[47] This is not the place for a substantive analysis of the CJEU's argumentation in *Pringle* since the primary concern here lies with the consequences of such a decision rather than with the merits of the decision.[48] In the effort to reconstruct the birth of the ESM, this ruling is taken as the point of no return since it was effectively the last instance that had an effect at the European level. Effectively, in *Pringle* the CJEU confirmed the legality of the approach chosen for crisis resolution already much earlier: the choice to venture outside the scope of EU law with such rescue mechanisms was taken already when direct bilateral loans to Greece were initiated and the EFSF was established as a limited liability company under Luxembourg law. The ESM follows this path as it is not formally part of EU law. However, some incidents did still occur that could possibly have had impacts at the national level.

The Constitutional Court of Austria (*Österreichischer Verfassungsgerichtshof*) assessed the legality of the ESM on the basis of a provision in the national constitution which governs the transfer of federal competences to intergovernmental organisations. The applicants argued, in addition to certain procedural grounds, that the ESM was contrary to Article 125 TFEU and that the ESM ran counter to the obligation of the national constitution to have a balanced budget. In its judgment of 16 March 2013, the Austrian court, citing the CJEU's ruling in *Pringle*, dismissed the claim that the ESM is contrary to Article 125 TFEU. Furthermore, the court saw participating in the ESM as a means to avoid unforeseeable economic damage and thus not to contradict the requirements of the constitution in regard to the efficiency of public administration and the objective of a balanced budget.[49]

In Poland the Constitutional Tribunal (*Trybunał Konstytucyjny*) also had to assess the ESM in addition to the Fiscal Compact. In specific, the case

---

[46] See e.g. B. de Witte and T. Beukers, 'The Court of Justice Approves the Creation of the European Stability Mechanism outside the EU Legal Order: Pringle'; P. Craig, 'Pringle and Use of EU Institutions outside the EU Legal Framework: Foundations, Procedure and Substance' (2013) *European Constitutional Law Review* 9(2), 263–284.

[47] C-370/12 *Pringle* EU:C:2012:756.

[48] See e.g. G. Beck, 'The Legal Reasoning of the Court of Justice and the Euro Crisis – The Flexibility of the Court's Cumulative Approach and the Pringle Case' (2013) *Maastricht Journal of European and Comparative Law* 20(4), 635–48; P. Craig, 'Pringle and the Nature of Legal Reasoning' (2014) *Maastricht Journal of European and Comparative Law* 21(1), 205–20.

[49] SV 2/12-18, 16.3.2013. D. Jaros, country report on Austria at http://eurocrisislaw .eui.eu (accessed 1 September 2020); A. Lengauer, country report on Austria in Neergaard, Jacqueson and Hartig Danielsen (n 39).

concerned the national ratification of the amendment to Article 136 TFEU, but in practice it was about the content of the ESM and the Fiscal Compact. The Polish tribunal found that out of the two possible means of national ratification, it was enough to use the lighter option; in the tribunal's conclusion the amendment of Article 136 TFEU neither subordinates the Member States to any international organisation nor transfers competences of the Polish state to the ESM. In its analysis, the Polish tribunal, too, followed the CJEU's ruling in *Pringle* but also its own previous ruling on the Treaty of Lisbon.[50]

In addition to these six national cases the final judgment of the German Federal Constitutional Court on the ESM, delivered on 18 March 2014,[51] deserves to be mentioned here. In this judgment the German court confirmed the findings of its 2012 interim ruling. The underlying tone of the ruling was that decisions on resolving the euro crisis should be taken by politicians and that they should enjoy a margin of appreciation while formulating this policy, which is to some extent exempt from control by the court. In practice, according to the German court, Germany's budgetary sovereignty is not compromised since decisions within the ESM are taken either by unanimity or by an 80 per cent qualified majority in the emergency procedure of Article 4(4) ESM. Since Germany's voting rights exceed the 20 per cent threshold (they hold 27,0716 per cent of the votes to be exact) they possess a blocking minority in both cases. The anticipated consequence of this ruling is that it will make amending the ESM Treaty's voting procedures (which might happen when new members are taken into the Treaty) difficult, since the German court stated that the German government has an obligation to make sure that the blocking minority in the emergency procedure is not lost in the future.

Lastly, to make the venture into the national case law on the ESM complete, the decision of the Constitutional Court of Slovenia (*Ustavno sodišče Republike Slovenije*) from 3 February 2011 has to be mentioned. The case concerned Slovenia's participation in the EFSF. As was pointed out by the examples on Finland and Germany, these older cases on the mechanisms preceding the ESM have had effect on the final form the ESM took. However, the Slovenian EFSF case is here presented as an outlier since it did not have effect at the European level.

Several Slovenian Members of Parliament challenged the national act on the EFSF. They argued, first, that the national act did not fulfil the constitution's requirements of regulating state guarantees by 'acts'. Second, they argued that

---

[50]   Decision of 26 June 2013, K 33/12, 63/5/A/2013. K. Granat, country report on Poland a http://eurocrisislaw.eui.eu (accessed 1 September 2020); D. Adamski, country report on Poland in Neergaard, Jacqueson and Hartig Danielsen (n 39).

[51]   2 BvR 1390/12, 18 March 2014 (*ESM final judgment*).

the act infringed on the national parliament's powers since according to the act the government was only required to inform the parliament of the guarantees but an approval by the parliament was not required. Adopting a deferential approach, the Slovenian court found no basis for these claims and saw the act as falling within the margin of appreciation of the legislator. Interestingly, the court did mention, in an *obiter dictum* manner, how the possible upper limit of state debt could be calculated in order to ensure adequate funding for social costs for the future generations.[52] However, it seems that this ruling did not affect the future formulation of the various crisis response measures at the European level.

3.3 THE TRIPARTITE CONTEXTUALITY OF ECONOMIC–POLITIC–LAW

In addition to the above events, which can be traced as being parts of the causal process affecting the formation of the ESM, there were also other underlying causes that might have affected the process and the end result. These are situated mostly in the realms of economics and politics but also partially in that of law. In contrast to the above-described events, the weight of these reasons is more difficult to assess, and thus they are of a more speculative manner. They are, however, important for the overall analysis, since they point to the interplay between economic, political and legal factors.

Several reasons can explain Germany's influence on and its preferences for the formation of the crisis response mechanisms. Being the largest Member State, it is also the largest contributor to the different funds, which gave it leverage in the negotiations. Conversely, Merkel's government was constrained by public opinion and the fear of the German Federal Constitutional Court not approving certain measures. This public fear maybe affected the interest rates on which the EFSF leant to Greece, since loans without any interest would have been seen as subsidies. However, the rather high interest did not help to alleviate the situation in Greece. Furthermore, the EFSF was not to resemble anything like a Eurobond.[53] A further reason was that German banks were heavily exposed to the risk of Greece defaulting on its creditors, since in addition to the Member States and the ECB, private German banks had also

---

[52]   Decision of the Constitutional Court, 3 February 2011, U-I-178/10. U. Petrovcic, country report on Slovenia at http://eurocrisislaw.eui.eu (accessed 1 September 2020); M. Ahtik, M. Brkan and Ž. Nendl, country report on Slovenia in Neergaard, Jacqueson and Hartig Danielsen (n 39).

[53]   See COM/2011/0818 final, Green Paper on the feasibility of introducing Stability Bonds.

acquired a vast amount of Greek government bonds.[54] Since this was known, it hindered the bargaining power of Germany but also affected the solution that Germany favoured.[55]

The other large Member States had different reasons for their preferences. French banks were also entrenched with bonds from Greece and other problem states, but their proposal was to have the Commission mobilise funds and to force the ECB to act. The United Kingdom, instead, had a different view. Gocaj and Meunier have argued that the UK vetoed the proposal to enlarge the EU's own budget because they did not want to participate in a Eurozone measure, despite the fact that British banks also held large amounts of Spanish and Irish debt.[56]

When the GLF was formulated it was not yet known that a permanent mechanism would be established later. This might have affected the form of that temporary mechanism, which then again affected the form the EFSF took and on which the permanent mechanism ESM was eventually based.[57] This might also explain why at first the EFSF was formulated as a special purpose vehicle outside the EU legal order, and following this, the ESM too. Furthermore, the reasons for establishing the EFSF as a private company under Luxembourg law are not entirely clear. It has been suggested that practicality and time constraints were probably the main reasons behind this choice: establishing such a mechanism could be decided by the Member States' governments without the consent of national parliaments and national ratification, which meant that the process was both politically easier to take through and also faster. Due to market pressure the Member States wanted to react quickly. A quick reaction would not have been possible had the EU Treaties been changed.

In the 9–10 May 2010 European Council meeting Germany opposed a more ambitious bail-out effort by the Commission, which essentially amounted to Eurobonds issued by the Commission. The EFSF was the solution that Germany wanted instead of control by the Commission. The Member States, and especially those outside the Eurozone, wanted to retain control of the mechanism for themselves and not let the Commission act as the instigator. Thus, the EFSF model was chosen. Furthermore, this was the fastest option.

---

[54]   On the development of banks' exposure to Greece, see Silvia Merler 'Who's (still) exposed to Greece?', 3 February 2015, http://bruegel.org/2015/02/whos-still -exposed-to-greece/ (accessed 1 September 2020). On the effects that such exposure creates, see H. Geeroms, S. Ide and F. Naert, *The European Union and the Euro: How to Deal with a Currency Built on Dreams* (Intersentia 2014), pp. 178–80.

[55]   Gocaj and Meunier (n 7), pp. 244–7.

[56]   Ibid., p. 244.

[57]   Verdun (n 14), p. 226.

The Commission was only given charge of the considerably smaller EFSM.[58] Ohler has presented a similar argument concerning the ESM. The decision to establish the ESM outside the EU legal order and to base it on the simplified revision of Article 136 TFEU was not only motivated by the fact that simplified revision is simpler and faster than ordinary revision (under Art. 48(2)–(5) TEU). More crucially, it was probably motivated also by the fact that the Member States 'were reluctant to lay the decision on the capitalisation of the ESM and accordingly the use of their budgetary resources in the hands of the EU legislator'.[59]

A further point regarding the ESM is that when the need for a sufficiently large enough permanent mechanism became evident it was thought that creating a new structure would take time and money and would have possibly not had the desired market reaction. In addition, it could also have faced legal or political opposition in the Member States. Therefore, it was easier to transform the EFSF into the ESM since the EFSF was already working and had been accepted in all Member States according to their national legal frameworks.[60]

3.4 WHAT DID THE EUROPEAN STABILITY MECHANISM CONSTITUTIONALISE?

As an intergovernmental organisation operating under public international law – that is, functioning outside the remit of EU law – the ESM might at first sight seem like a rather straightforward institution with uncomplicated legal mechanisms and thus easy to comprehend. This impression is strengthened by the fact that the ESM is not associated with a complicated set of EU secondary law measures.[61] However, a closer reading of the ESM Treaty reveals many pressing constitutional concerns. Out of the myriad of issues the ESM pertains to, this section will focus on those that are relevant for the overall argument of this study. To this end, the first sub-section presents the core provisions of the ESM (3.4.1), after which their deeper constitutional meaning is discussed (3.4.2).

3.4.1 Content of the European Stability Mechanism

While strict observance of the Stability and Growth Pact (SGP) and the accompanying legal framework on economic governance should remain the first line

---

[58] Gocaj and Meunier (n 7), p. 245.

[59] Ohler (n 12), p. 59.

[60] Gocaj and Meunier (n 7), p. 249.

[61] However, some of the tasks of the ESM have been codified into EU law. See Regulation (EU) No 472/2013.

of defence against confidence crises that affect the stability of the euro area (Recital 4 ESM), the Member States nevertheless saw it necessary to establish a permanent stability mechanism for the euro area (Recital 1 ESM). According to the Member States, the need for such a mechanism stems from the strong interrelation within the euro area. Due to this, severe risks to the financial stability of the Member States whose currency is the euro may put at risk the financial stability of the euro area as a whole. Therefore, the ESM is needed to provide stability support, although based on strict conditionality, and only if it is indispensable to safeguard the financial stability of the euro area as a whole and of its Member States (Recital 6 ESM). For this purpose the ESM is entitled to raise funds by issuing financial instruments or by entering into financial or other agreements or arrangements with ESM members, financial institutions or other third parties (Art. 3 ESM).

The ESM has a three-layer governance structure (Art. 4(1) ESM). At the top sits the Board of Governors, which is comprised of the national finance ministers of the Members of the ESM. They decide on the most important issues by mutual agreement. These include granting financial assistance, the terms and conditions of such assistance, the total lending capacity of the ESM and possible changes to the menu of instruments available to the ESM (Art. 5 ESM). The Board of Governors is essentially a political organ as it is comprised of national politicians and it decides upon issues that require political legitimacy – that is, use of the ESM, which in essence constitutes bail-out by taxpayers' money. Next there is the Board of Directors to which each Member shall appoint one director. These are experts in economic and financial matters. They are to carry out specific tasks that the Governors delegate to them or that are assigned to them in the ESM Treaty itself (Art. 6 ESM). Finally, there is the Managing Director, appointed by the Governors, who is responsible for the day-to-day management of the ESM (Art. 7 ESM).

The capital structure of the ESM consists of paid-in capital and callable capital. As of 2020, the total authorised capital stock is €704,8 billion, of which €80,5 billion is paid-in capital and €624,3 billion callable capital (Art. 8 ESM). Contributions by the Members are divided according to their contributions to the ECB's capital, pursuant to Article 29 of the ESCB Statute (Art. 11 ESM). The liability of each ESM Member is limited to its portion of the authorised capital stock, and the Members are not liable for the obligations of the ESM. This is where the ESM differs from its predecessor the EFSF, since the EFSF was guaranteed by its Members' commitments.[62]

---

[62] See A. de Gregorio Merino, 'Legal Developments in the Economic and Monetary Union During the Debt Crisis: the Mechanisms of Financial Assistance' (2012) *Common Market Law Review* 49(5), 1613–46, pp. 1622–3.

The Board of Governors may decide, by mutual agreement, to call in authorised unpaid capital at any time and set an appropriate time period for its payment to the ESM Members. In practice, it seems that this would be done in a situation where the credit rating of the ESM is under threat of being lowered. The Board of Directors may decide, by simple majority, to call in authorised unpaid capital to restore the level of paid-in capital if it has gone below the €80,5 billion threshold due to the absorption of losses (Art. 9 ESM). The level of authorised capital stock can be changed by the Board of Governors, by mutual agreement, but it also requires national ratification in accordance with national law (Art. 10 ESM).

The amendment to Article 136 TFEU does not mention which forms of assistance are available to the ESM, but the ESM has a host of different assistance instruments under its belt.[63] These include direct loans (either precautionary or actual loans, Arts 14 and 16 ESM), loans for the recapitalisation of banks (Art. 15 ESM) and primary or secondary market support by acquiring the Member's government bonds from the markets (Arts 17 and 18 ESM). It is important to note that the ESM is thus allowed to purchase government bonds directly from the primary markets – something which the ECB is explicitly prohibited from doing under Article 123 TFEU.

The possible activation of the financial assistance instruments begins with a request for assistance by an ESM Member. The request shall indicate which assistance instrument should be used. The Commission and the ECB are then asked to assess the overall situation from the perspective of the requesting Member as well as the whole euro area. Based on this assessment the Board of Governors may decide to grant financial assistance after which it shall entrust the Commission to negotiate a Memorandum of Understanding (MoU) with the requesting Member. This decision to grant assistance is made by the mutual agreement of the Governors. The technicalities of the financial assistance facility are drawn up by the Managing Director and accepted by the Board of Directors (Art. 13 ESM).

An essential element in granting assistance is whether the situation adheres to the four principles spelled out in Article 12 ESM:

If [i)] indispensable to safeguard the financial stability of the euro area as a whole and of its Member States, the ESM may provide stability support to an ESM Member [ii)] subject to strict conditionality, [iii)] appropriate to the financial assistance instrument chosen. Such [iv)] conditionality may range from a macro-economic

---

[63]   See V. Borger, 'The European Stability Mechanism: A Crisis Tool Operating at Two Junctures' in M. Haentjens and B. Wessels (eds), *Research Handbook on Crisis Management in the Banking Sector* (Edward Elgar Publishing 2015), p. 161–6.

adjustment programme to continuous respect of pre-established eligibility conditions. (Roman numbering added)

The Council of the EU is also involved through the Two-Pack legislation. An ESM Member requesting financial assistance has to prepare a macroeconomic adjustment programme in agreement with the Commission. This programme has to be fully consistent with the MoU that has been agreed by the Commission and the requesting Member. The Council, acting by a qualified majority on a proposal from the Commission, shall approve the macroeconomic adjustment programme prepared by the Member requesting financial assistance. Furthermore, the Commission and the ECB shall then monitor the implementation of the programme after financial assistance is granted.[64]

Although the ESM is in some sense a bail-out mechanism, the involvement of the private sector (bail-in) is also included to a certain extent (Recital 13 ESM). The Eurogroup has stated that the ESM loans will enjoy preferred creditor status: 'In all cases, in order to protect taxpayers' money, and to send a clear signal to private creditors that their claims are subordinated to those of the official sector, an ESM loan will enjoy preferred creditor status, junior only to the IMF loan.'[65]

Furthermore, as already stated in the previous chapter, assistance through the ESM is made conditional upon the ratification of the Fiscal Compact (Recital 5 ESM). This, and the Two-Pack legislation,[66] connects the ESM to the EU's economic governance regime.

3.4.2   Constitutional Implications of the European Stability Mechanism

3.4.2.1   Pringle: constitutionalising financial assistance
Mr. Pringle had two main arguments before the CJEU, a structural and a substantive one. First, that the European Council conclusion on amending Article 136 TFEU is contrary to Article 48(6) TEU on the simplified revision procedure since the amendment broadens the EU's competence, which would require the use of the ordinary revision procedure of Article 48 (2)–(5) TEU. Second, that the ESM violates the emergency financial assistance clause of Article 122 TFEU and the no bail-out clause of Article 125 TFEU.[67]

---

[64]   Art. 7 Regulation (EU) No 472/2013.
[65]   Statement by the Eurogroup. Brussels, 28 November 2010.
[66]   Regulation (EU) No 472/2013 and Regulation (EU) No 473/2013.
[67]   C-370/12 *Pringle* EU:C:2012:756, para. 28. The referring court actually presented the CJEU with three questions, but their relevant meaning can be simplified to these two points.

The main legal question in *Pringle* is connected to the asymmetrical structure of the EMU. According to Article 3(1)(c) TFEU the EU has exclusive competence over monetary policy (for the Member States within the Eurozone), whereas regarding economic policy, under Articles 2(3) and 5(1) TFEU, the Union has only coordinating competences. These articles on the Union's competences are found in Part One of the TFEU, but the amended Article 136 TFEU is located in Part Three of the TFEU. The ESM does not violate the Union's competences if it is interpreted as an economic policy measure since the Union only has a coordinating competence within this policy area, which does not preclude actions by the Member States. In contrast, if the ESM is interpreted as a monetary policy measure then it does violate the exclusive competence of the Union, and thus the amendment of Article 136 TFEU is contrary to the rules on the simplified revision procedure in Article 48(6) TEU since the competences of the Union are regulated in Part One of the TFEU.

The CJEU found that the ESM is not a monetary policy measure but instead an economic policy measure. It based this finding on the different aims of economic and monetary policies and the different tools used in attaining those aims. While monetary policy is primarily concerned with achieving and maintaining price stability (Arts 119(2) and 127(1) TFEU), economic policy is geared towards macroeconomic stability and the sustainability of public finances in general. The ESM complements the Union's existing economic governance regime (the SGP as amended and enforced by the Fiscal Compact and the Six-Pack) and is supposed to be used as a crisis management tool if the preventive measures are not successful. Furthermore, the CJEU emphasised that granting financial assistance to Member States is clearly not a part of monetary policy. Because the Union does not have an exclusive competence to establish a mechanism like the ESM, the Treaties do not prevent the Member States from enacting it outside the scope of EU law.[68]

In addition to this, the CJEU also considered the effects of Articles 122(2) and 352 TFEU on the issue of competences. According to the CJEU, the emergency financial assistance clause of Article 122(2) TFEU does not apply to this situation since the euro crisis is not an environmental disaster and the ESM is meant as a permanent financial assistance mechanism. Article 352 TFEU, which contains the residual competence clause of the Treaties, on the other hand, does not impose any obligation on the EU to act. Since Article 352 TFEU does not set the Union any obligation to act, it means that the Union does not have any competence that would preclude the Member States from enacting the ESM. Thus, the European Council decision of 25 March 2011

---

[68]   Ibid., paras 57–64.

does not alter the Union's competences and has therefore been taken in accordance with the simplified revision procedure of Article 48(6) TEU.[69]

When it came to the amendment of Article 136 TFEU itself, the CJEU stated bluntly that according to the added third paragraph the Member States 'may establish' a stability mechanism. On a literal reading, this amendment does not confer on the EU any new competences or a new legal basis, so it does not alter the existing competences of the Union.[70]

The CJEU's analysis of the substance of Articles 122(2) and 125 TFEU was more interesting. According to the CJEU, the ESM does not affect the Member States' capability of granting financial assistance under Article 122(2).[71] Conversely, the CJEU also thought that the Article does not confine the giving of financial aid to only the Union, and thus it does not preclude the Member States from doing so.[72]

The CJEU considered the joint meaning of Articles 122(2) and 125 TFEU and concluded that since Article 122(2) allows the granting of financial assistance in certain situations, Article 125 TFEU cannot be interpreted as banning financial assistance completely. In other words, Article 122(2) TFEU means that the no bail-out clause is not absolute.[73] In addition, granting financial assistance differs from taking responsibility for the commitments of others. After interpreting Article 125 TFEU through its aims, the CJEU concluded that it does not preclude financial assistance which is essential to safeguarding the financial stability of the euro area as a whole and which leads the recipient state conducting sound budgetary policy – that is, that the assistance is based on strict conditionality.[74] Therefore, the CJEU saw neither Article as obstructing the Member States from enacting the ESM.

3.4.2.2   Financial stability and strict conditionality

The constitutionalisation of financial assistance, and especially the way this was achieved by the CJEU in *Pringle*, gives rise to several concerns that relate to the asymmetrical structure of the EMU.

First, there are the evident moral hazard concerns related to such financial assistance and the dubious circumvention of the no bail-out clause of Article 125 TFEU. Moral hazard within the EMU occurs when Member States or their creditors assume that the indebted Member States will not ultimately be held responsible for their debts, but that the others will bail them out. Member States

---

[69]   Ibid., paras 65–70.
[70]   Ibid., paras 72–73.
[71]   Ibid., paras 104–106.
[72]   Ibid., para. 120.
[73]   Ibid., paras 130–131.
[74]   Ibid., paras 136–137.

will have an incentive to become overly indebted and banks will see the possibility of credit losses as low and therefore continue to supply cheap funding for these Member States. Due to the asymmetrical structure of the EMU the other Member States cannot prevent this from happening as each Member State is in charge of their own economic policy, but the negative consequences of this will ultimately affect all Member States due to the common currency.

The purpose of the no bail-out clause of Article 125 TFEU was to prevent this. In conjunction with the SGP, it was supposed to guide the Eurozone Member States towards a path of sound public finances and budgetary discipline. But as financial stability support has now been constitutionalised, how can such moral hazard concerns be alleviated nevertheless? The answer lies in the 'strict conditionality' (Arts 3 and 12 ESM) of such support. As explained by the CJEU, Article 125 TFEU 'prohibits the Union and the Member States from granting financial assistance as a result of which the incentive of the recipient Member State to conduct a sound budgetary policy is diminished'. Financial assistance is acceptable as long as the receiving Member State 'remains responsible for its commitments to its creditors provided that the conditions attached to such assistance are such as to prompt that Member State to implement a sound budgetary policy'.[75] In other words, the aid-receiving Member State has to agree to a new economic policy that is based on budgetary discipline and aims at the sustainability of public finances in the future.

However, the strict conditionality of stability support does not solve all aspects of the moral hazard problem. The current system just leads to a different, long-term and more profound moral hazard concern. According to the CJEU's reasoning in *Pringle*, the first-order objective of the no bail-out clause is to ward off moral hazard, but in some instances this is overridden by the second order-objective of financial stability, the protection of which justifies bail-outs. But as Tuori and Tuori have explained, although an individual bail-out might seem to serve the higher-order objective of safeguarding the financial stability of the euro area as a whole in the short term, in the long term it ends up creating a moral hazard as Member States and their creditors can assume that bail-outs will also be available in the future; and what is more, this eventually also leads to sacrificing the higher-order objective of financial stability. This is because, under the logic devised by the CJEU in *Pringle*, moral hazard is only taken into consideration with regard to the individual aid-receiving Member State, not the whole Eurozone.[76]

The rationale of the CJEU's interpretation of the no bail-out clause seems to rely on the following logic: a reading of Article 125 TFEU that would allow

---

[75]   Ibid., paras 136–137.
[76]   Tuori and Tuori (n 32), pp. 127–33.

no exceptions would transform it from a precautionary and moral hazard avoidance rule into an obstacle to combating a real crisis, which the Eurozone faced back then.[77] This is the logic behind elevating 'financial stability of the euro area as a whole' to the position of an overriding policy concern. However, adopting such a new meta-level objective has its own problems.

Second, and directly related to the previous point, is the fact that support through the ESM is premised upon 'strict conditionality' (Art. 12 ESM). This means that – in addition to the Fiscal Compact on its part – the ESM relativises budgetary sovereignty of the crisis states in regard to both the substance and overall volume of the budget. This is so because the MoUs that the recipient states have to sign not only go into detail on the type of policy choices to be made but also dictate the overall size of the budget.[78] Due to their nature, these measures not only impinge upon the recipient states' sovereignty in the fiscal sphere but also in the more general economic policy sphere. By explicitly referring to strict conditionality as a condition for the ESM not breaching Article 125 TFEU, *Pringle* constitutionalised this development too.[79] The fact that the EMU does not contain a proper economic policy competence has resulted in the strong public criticism towards the austerity policies that aid-receiving Member States have had to succumb to.[80]

Third, adopting financial stability as an overriding policy objective raises concerns due to the vagueness of the concept and a lack of normative justifications. The purpose of Articles 122 and 125 TFEU (the emergency assistance and no bail-out clauses) is to induce market discipline on the Member States, whereas the purpose of Articles 121 and 126 TFEU (the preventive and corrective arms of the SGP) is to induce self-restraint. Both of these aim at the Member States complying with the principle of sound public finances.[81] The need for the no bail-out rule stems from the finding that monetary policy cannot solely be in charge of anti-inflation measures, and because reliance on

---

[77]   See P. Athanassiou, 'Of Past Measures and Future Plans for Europe's Exit from the Sovereign Debt Crisis: What is Legally Possible (and What is Not)' (2011) *European Law Review* 36(4), 558–575, pp. 564–5.

[78]   For an example of how prescriptive the MoUs are, see Memorandum of Understanding between the European Commission acting on behalf of the European Stability Mechanism and the Hellenic Republic and the Bank of Greece. Brussels, 19 August 2015.

[79]   Tuori and Tuori (n 32), pp. 188–9.

[80]   See Y. Varoufakis, *Austerity* (Random House 2018).

[81]   V. Borger, 'The ESM and the European Court's Predicament in Pringle' (2013) *German Law Journal* 14(1), 113–140, pp. 118–19.

the markets in controlling the spending of States was thought to be insufficient by itself.[82]

Pace *Pringle*, the principle of price stability as the overriding objective of economic policies, including the monetary policy of the ECB, has been replaced by the 'financial stability of the euro area as a whole'. The monetary policy objective of price stability has become a second-order objective, the purpose of which is to serve the first-order objective of financial stability. This way *Pringle* confirmed the legality of the objective that the Eurozone Member States had assumed in their informal meeting in February 2010.[83]

Yet, to what exactly does the 'financial stability of the euro area as a whole' refer?[84] According to Article 127 TFEU price stability is the primary objective of the ECB's monetary policy, whereas stability in the SGP refers to sound public finances and how they help in pursuing price stability.[85] Neither of these two are the same as the 'financial stability of the euro area as a whole'. As no one seems to know what the concept actually means, it is problematic to give it a pinnacle position as the objective of the EMU.[86] Is Article 127(5) TFEU, according to which the ESCB shall contribute to the 'stability of the financial system' a clear enough norm to warrant such a change in the order of policy objectives?[87] Perhaps no, since the crisis mostly concerned the stability of national financial systems, which are composed of private banks.[88]

The end result of this paradigm shift is, that now the EMU contains not only prevention (the SGP), but also solution of sovereign insolvency crises (bail-out). Yet, this does not mean that the principle of states fiscal responsibility, as enshrined in the no bail-out clause, has been discarded. Rather, that the

---

[82]   See R. Smits, *The European Central Bank: Institutional Aspects* (Kluwer Law International 1997), pp. 74–5.

[83]   'Euro area Member states will take determined and coordinated action, if needed, to safeguard financial stability in the euro area as a whole', Statement by the Heads of State or government of the European Union. Brussels, 11 February 2010.

[84]   See T. Tuominen, 'The European Banking Union: A Shift in the Internal Market Paradigm?' (2017) *Common Market Law Review* 54(5), 1359–1380, pp. 1378–9.

[85]   See Resolution of the European Council on the Stability and Growth Pact, O. J. 1997, C 236/1, Preamble I: 'The European Council underlines the importance of safeguarding sound government finances as a means to strengthening the conditions for price stability and for strong sustainable growth conducive to employment creation. It is also necessary to ensure that national budgetary policies support stability oriented monetary policies.'

[86]   See Tuori and Tuori (n 32), pp. 120–36.

[87]   This change and the reasons for it are explained and analysed in V. Borger, *The Currency of Solidarity: Constitutional Transformation during the Euro Crisis* (Cambridge University Press 2020).

[88]   Tuori and Tuori (n 32), pp. 183–4.

scope of the no bail-out prohibition has been narrowed down; that '[i]t is only valid for good times but no longer for bad times'.[89]

3.5   CONCLUSIONS

3.5.1   Observations from the Reconstruction

The reconstruction of the birth of the ESM showed that its legal form was affected mostly by the events that preceded its formation: it became an intergovernmental instrument due to the fact that its temporary predecessors had been such, although it is supposed to be a permanent mechanism itself. Furthermore, the substance of the ESM was also directly affected by these earlier, rather ad hoc measures, which had been devised under economic, political and legal pressure. Despite being encumbered by these issues, or perhaps because of a predicament stemming from just the same pressures, the CJEU accepted the constitutionalisation of bail-outs through the ESM in *Pringle*. Thus, it seems that also in this case, similarly to the Fiscal Compact,[90] those Member States which wanted to pursue this path of crisis resolution and future management got their way in the end, although not through the primary option of amending the EU Treaties.

Even though the ESM was the subject of several legal proceedings, both national and European, in the end its establishment was not blocked by judicial review – as was the case with the Fiscal Compact too. But why was this the case? Were all the national courts constrained by the same predicament that according to Borger affected the CJEU in *Pringle*?[91] This might well be so, and depending on the chosen standpoint, it can also be seen as favourable that the courts did not block the political process. Although proper normative analysis is often revealing and thus convincing enough, since it is impossible to see behind a court's reasoning, a different path of assessing the first question is needed. The answer lies in differences in the national legal frameworks, which, as the reconstruction pointed out, allows for different courts to participate at different times through different vantage points. Being able to participate before the point of no return made it possible for certain courts to affect the ongoing process. Some courts had no other possibility but to dismiss the claims brought before them as their competences or rules of procedure allowed no other outcome.

---

[89]   Ibid. p. 187.
[90]   See Chapter 2.
[91]   See Borger (n 81).

This observation leads to an answer to the second question. Those courts that were only able to react after the point of no return had obvious constraints, since their possibilities for affecting the European-level political process were severely limited if non-existent. Thus, it seems more likely that these national courts had an even stronger predicament than the CJEU in *Pringle* when ruling on the legality of the ESM and national participation in it after the point of no return. As they were obviously aware of the restrictions their position put them in – that they no longer had the possibility of precluding the signing or coming into force of the ESM by themselves – they most likely realised that finding the ESM to breach their national constitution would only result in a national political and constitutional crisis. This predicament might explain why none of them found there to be sufficient enough of a breach of their national constitution so as to preclude national ratification. Granted, these latter courts' rulings might end up affecting political decisions in the future if they contain a doctrine that constrains that particular Member State's participation in a future EMU related mechanism. There are traces of such doctrines in the rulings, but their closer analysis is beyond the scope of this study.[92]

3.5.2   The Rationality of the European Stability Mechanism

As the reconstruction showed, one of the key reasons why some courts were able to affect the final formation of the ESM is based purely on the way the ESM was created. This argument is in line with Fabbrini's 'paradox of judicialization'[93] – that the heavy involvement of national courts was caused by the use of international law-based measures – but goes a step further by highlighting how also the crisis response mechanisms preceding the ESM affected its formation. The fact that the ESM was based on the preceding GLF and EFSF made it possible that the various constitutional speech acts concerning these preceding instruments could be taken into consideration when drafting the final form of the ESM. Had the process been different the involvement, or actually the effects, of courts would have been more restricted. Furthermore, the reconstruction displayed how the gradual formation of the EU's constitutional order – in the manner that the adoption of the ESM and its constitutionalisation in *Pringle* factually occurred – takes place through a process that is not centrally orchestrated but rather cacophonic. That is to say that there

---

[92]   See J.-H. Reestman, 'Legitimacy Through Adjudication: the ESM Treaty and the Fiscal Compact before the National Courts' in T. Beukers, B. de Witte and C. Kilpatrick (eds.), *Constitutional Change through Euro-Crisis Law* (Cambridge University Press 2017).

[93]   See F. Fabbrini, *Economic Governance in Europe. Comparative Paradoxes and Constitutional Challenges* (Oxford University Press 2016), Chapter 2.

is no internal logic (from the perspective of the EU as a polity) according to which the national courts participate into the European-level political process and what types of effects their rulings may or may not have. This leads to the following questions: is this way of taking political decisions and drafting legal frameworks – based on contestation and compromise – the best possible way? What does this mean regarding the form of the ESM as a mechanism?

The reconstruction pointed out that the ESM's final form was based on several compromises that stemmed from a particular line of political and legal decisions. Furthermore, it showed that the interlinkages of these decisions and the end results they produced were not coordinated in any fashion. It is thus not surprising that de Witte was amazed by the 'seemingly arbitrary nature of those actions by the governments' during one point of the process.[94] Although a deeper analysis, both legal and economic, would be needed to assess how close the final form of the ESM comes to what could be described as its optimal form, the reconstruction warrants at least an intermediate conclusion on the form of the said measure as well: a policy process that would facilitate informed decision making, based on evidence and not fear of contestation, would surely produce better results.

In the conclusions of the previous chapter it was stated that the Fiscal Compact does not introduce a common economic policy, and thus whether it can reach its stated objectives depends on whether it will induce structural changes into the Member States' economic policies that will result in deficit and debt ratios being lowered.[95] What about the ESM, what does it do for the asymmetry of the EMU? It does not create common economic or fiscal policy but only the possible mutualisation of debt if the loans granted through it are not repaid, either due to default or an agreed cut on the amount of the debt.[96] Creation of the ESM reflects the realisation that the accumulation of unsustainable government debts cannot always be prevented and that their resolution cannot be left solely to the markets. In addition, the establishment of the ESM reflects a recognition that it was undesirable for the ECB to constantly have to act as a policy-maker of last resort by purchasing crisis states' debt, since that was the only way of containing and resolving the crisis.[97] In this way, the ESM complements the Fiscal Compact. Although the ESM does not actually fix the

---

[94]   B. de Witte, 'Using International Law in the Euro Crisis: Causes and Consequences' (2013) *ARENA Working Paper*, 4, 1–23, p. 1, referring to the decision to adopt the EFSF on 9 May 2010, which subsequently led to the ESM.

[95]   See Chapter 2.5.2.

[96]   The repayment of some of the loans granted to Greece has already been postponed. See Eurogroup statement on Greece of 22 June 2018.

[97]   See B. Eichengreen, 'European Monetary Integration with Benefit of Hindsight' (2012) *Journal of Common Market Studies* 50 (Supplement 1), 123–136, p. 131.

asymmetry of the EMU, the way it functions and the results it aims for hint in that direction.

4. The European Banking Union and the vicious circle between banks and sovereigns

4.1 INTRODUCTION

The European Banking Union is a bank supervision and resolution system that operates on the basis of EU law rules and applies only to the Eurozone Member States, although it is open for the other Member States to join as well. The Banking Union aims to ensure that the banking sector of the euro area is functioning and stable, that non-viable banks are resolved without recourse to taxpayers' money and with minimal impact on the real economy. In other words, it aims to ensure that bank crises do not occur and if they do, that failing banks are resolved through controlled bail-ins as opposed to bail-outs utilising taxpayers' money. By doing this, the Banking Union aims to strengthen financial stability in the euro area. The three pillars of the Banking Union are supervision, resolution and deposit guarantee. These three regulatory areas comprise the measures through which the Banking Union sets out to achieve its objectives.

Whereas in the previous two case studies the participation of national courts in the European-level political process was central, here the opposite is the case. The same reason why the national courts were able to review the Fiscal Compact Treaty and the European Stability Mechanism Treaty (ESM) also meant that the Banking Union did not face judicial review to the same extent: it is more difficult for national courts to review EU secondary law measures than international law-based treaties. It can also be speculated that since there was only one case before a national court in which the Banking Union as such was challenged, the chances of a national court making a preliminary reference to the Court of Justice of the European Union (CJEU) were also smaller. This might partly explain why the CJEU has not had to assess the validity of the Banking Union.

The purpose of this chapter in relation to the overall argument of this study is the following: Just like the other crisis response mechanisms, the Banking Union aims to safeguard the 'financial stability of the euro area as a whole'.

Although a plausible goal as such, the way the Banking Union pursues this goal can be doubted. While with the Fiscal Compact and the ESM the substantive question was about the distinction between economic and monetary policy, here the question is, in addition, about the distinction between the internal market and economic policy more generally. The Banking Union is an internal market measure, but its aims fall under economic policy. Is such use of internal market measures for economic policy purposes acceptable? This is problematic in light of the asymmetry of the EMU: as the EMU does not contain a proper economic policy competence, economic policy related objectives should not be pursued through internal market measures. A practical issue through which these concerns arise is how the Banking Union is a step towards a transfer union. There is no denying this point, since that is what breaking the vicious circle between banks and sovereigns requires.

This chapter proceeds as follows: First, the creation of the Banking Union is explained by providing a reconstruction of its negotiating, drafting and implementation phase (4.2). Then, the underlying economic, political and legal reasons that may help to explain this process are highlighted (4.3). Next, the constitutional consequences, as relevant for the aims of this study, of adopting the Banking Union are discussed (4.4). Finally, conclusions in relation to the overall aim and chosen framework of this study are presented (4.5).

4.2   RECONSTRUCTING THE BIRTH OF THE BANKING UNION

4.2.1   The Political Process Behind the Banking Union

As with all four case studies, the reconstruction of the birth of the Banking Union has its shortcomings. First, due to the sheer number of events that took place during the summer of 2012, it is impossible to map out unambiguously the causality between them.[1] Second, a variety of competing economic interests have been distinguished behind the events,[2] for which reason only sophisticated guesses can be made on what were actually the main motivations behind the process. Third, although the Single Rulebook is the foundation on which the Banking Union sits,[3] and its adoption the starting point of the reconstruction, the analysis does not consider the developments leading up to

---

[1]   See N. Véron, *Europe's Radical Banking Union* (Bruegel 2015), p. 14.

[2]   See e.g. S. de Rynck, 'Banking on a Union: The Politics of Changing Eurozone Banking Supervision' (2016) *Journal of European Public Policy* 23(1), 119–35.

[3]   See Chapter 1.2.2.2.

and affecting the formation of the Single Rulebook,[4] since these are somewhat different as to the reasons that affected the adoption of the Banking Union.

Furthermore, it is difficult to pinpoint a single starting point or moment of rupture that set the development of the Banking Union on a roll. The European Council of June 2012 is perhaps the definitive point in the political spectrum, but there were a host of incidents leading up to it that created the required economic and political pressure as well as the legal foundations (or restrictions) for that decision. In fact, the term 'banking union' did not exist before 2011, when it was first coined by Véron.[5] The mapping process will begin from the first reactions following the initial banking crisis of 2007–2008, when the preliminary policy initiatives concerning the regulation of banks were issued; it was only later that the crisis escalated into a sovereign debt crisis and a crisis of the euro.

In February 2009, after the onset of the financial crisis, the de Larosière report recommended to the Commission that cooperation of national supervisors should be strengthened and formalised by creating a European Banking Authority (EBA). The report, though, rejected the notion of a single supervisor for the entire internal market.[6] The Commission was also in favour of such a diffused model of supervision at this point.[7] The European Council endorsed this version in its meeting on 18–19 June 2009.[8] Conjoining with the views of the de Larosière report, the Commission proposed the establishment of a European System of Financial Supervision (ESFS) on 23 February 2009.[9]

The June 2009 European Council also endorsed the uptake of the Single Rulebook, but the Commission's proposals on the contained three elements followed only later. The most controversial of these three was put forward first, when the proposal for the Deposit Guarantee Scheme Directive (DGSD) was issued on 12 July 2010.[10] The proposal for the Capital Requirements Directive

---

[4]   On these, see D. Howarth and L. Quaglia, 'Banking on Stability: The Political Economy of New Capital Requirements in the European Union' (2013) *Journal of European Integration* 35(3), 333–46.

[5]   See N. Véron, 'Europe must change course on banks', VoxEU, 22 December 2011, http://voxeu.org/article/europe-must-change-course-banks (accessed 1 September 2020).

[6]   Report by The High-Level Group of Financial Supervision in the EU: Chaired by Jacques De Larosiére. Brussels, 25 February 2009.

[7]   J.-M. Barroso, 'Europe: Working together to shape a new financial system', Speech by the President of the European Commission. Brussels, 16 June 2009.

[8]   Council of the European Union. Conclusions, 11225/09. Brussels, 19 June 2009.

[9]   COM/2009/0499 final.

[10]   COM/2010/0368 final.

package (CRD IV) was issued on 20 July 2011.[11] Finally, the proposal for the Bank Recovery and Resolution Directive (BRRD) was given on 6 June 2012.[12]

In the heat of the crisis, when the idea of a Banking Union had not yet been adopted by policy makers, the Heads of State or Government of the euro area decided in October 2011 that the tighter capital ratios of the Basel III Accord would be enacted in time.[13] Furthermore, if markets failed to recapitalise banks so as to meet these new criteria, 'national governments should provide support', which should originate from state budgets, or if not possible, via a loan from the European Financial Stability Facility (EFSF).[14] Simultaneously, negotiations on the Fiscal Compact – the objective of which was to limit the indebtedness of the Member States – were taking place. This view of national fiscal responsibility, as expressed by the Fiscal Compact, together with the approach of the EFSF (future European Stability Mechanism (ESM)) loans meant that there was not yet room for a policy choice for the establishment of the Banking Union.[15]

The actual decision or the political commitment to centralise supervisory authority was made at the 28–29 June 2012 European Council, or actually, the adjoining Eurozone summit,[16] although the other Member States later endorsed this decision as well.[17] As said in the statement, introducing the Banking Union 'is imperative to break the vicious circle between banks and sovereigns'. Note, however, that at this stage political leaders were talking only about supervisory functions and not of resolution. This shared destiny, the vicious circle between banks and sovereigns, can only be broken by establishing a fiscal union or a banking union. Since there was no political will for the first, the Member States thought that they had to act on the second option.[18]

In the 29 June 2012 statement, the establishment of centralised banking supervision was linked to the ESM's capability to recapitalise banks directly: when the first was in place, the second could be put in place also. ESM direct bank recapitalisation meant that no further direct liability would be incurred by the already distressed host Member States of those banks that might need recapitalisation. This gave these Member States incentives to accept the centralisation of bank supervision. Conversely, centralised supervision was also necessary for the ESM to assist national banks, since the ESM needed to

---

11   COM/2011/0452 final; COM/2011/0453 final.
12   COM/2012/0280 final.
13   On the Basel III Accord, see https://www.bis.org/ (accessed 1 September 2020).
14   Euro Summit Statement. Brussels, 26 October 2011.
15   See de Rynck (n 2), pp. 127–8.
16   Euro Area Summit Statement. Brussels, 29 June 2012.
17   European Council Conclusions, EUCO 205/12. Brussels, 13–14 December 2012.
18   See Véron (n 1), p. 16.

be able to supervise their actions in order to take the risk of financing them.[19] Finalising the conditions for the use of direct recapitalisation took quite some time, and the ESM Board of Governors finally adopted the direct recapitalisation instrument in December 2014.[20]

According to Véron's interpretation, the policy declaration in the 29 June 2012 statement contained the commitment to give such supervisory tasks to the European Central Bank (ECB).[21] This was certainly the outcome of that decision, but it makes more sense to say that supervision was centralised in this manner because of the existence of Article 127(6) TFEU. According to Article 127(6) TFEU, the Council may, by way of acting unanimously, confer specific tasks upon the ECB concerning policies relating to the prudential supervision of credit institutions and other financial institutions. Using Article 127(6) TFEU as a legal basis for centralising prudential supervision was the easiest option, since it specifically allowed for the establishment of such functions and was thus beyond any uncertainty on the correct use of Treaty-prescribed legal bases. In other words, the existence of Article 127(6) TFEU led to the supervisory task being conferred to the ECB because, at least legally, this was the easiest option. In this way, the existing Treaty framework dictated who should be in charge of this new competence bestowed upon the Union. Giving this task to some other institution would have required the usage of some other legal basis, which would not have had such a firm footing.

After the June 2012 commitment, the Commission started to advance quickly on this front. On 12 September 2012, the Commission published its plan for the Banking Union[22] in addition to its proposal for the Single Supervisory Mechanism (SSM) Regulation.[23] The Commission then further developed its plan in a communication published in November 2012,[24] which was followed by the so-called Four Presidents' Report that contained the European Union's leaders' views on the future Banking Union.[25] On 13–14 December 2012, at a meeting of the European Council, principled agreement

---

[19]   See de Rynck (n 2), pp. 123–5.

[20]   'ESM direct bank recapitalisation instrument adopted', ESM Press Release, 8 December 2014.

[21]   N. Véron (n 1), pp. 16–19. The part he is referring to reads: 'The Commission will present Proposals on the basis of Article 127(6) for a single supervisory mechanism shortly.'

[22]   COM/2012/0510 final, A Roadmap towards a Banking Union.

[23]   COM/2012/0511 final; COM/2012/0512 final.

[24]   COM/2012/0777, A blueprint for a deep and genuine economic and monetary union: Launching a European Debate.

[25]   'Towards a Genuine Economic and Monetary Union'. Brussels, 5 December 2012.

was reached on supervision and resolution within the Banking Union as well as the Single Rulebook.[26]

These initial proposals were based on the supranationalisation of supervisory functions and the inclusion of all banks under this centralised supervision. However, Germany opposed this, for reasons that will be addressed below. A compromise was presented by the Presidency of the Council on 3 December 2012,[27] which was accepted by the Council on 12 December.[28] The SSM Regulation (EU) No 1024/2013 and an amendment to the European Banking Authority Regulation (EU) No 1093/2010 were adopted in October 2013.[29] The result of this compromise was that only the supervision of most significant banks was centralised to the ECB, while the national competent authorities (NCAs) were entrusted with the supervision of other, less significant banks.[30] The ECB assumed the new tasks conferred onto it on 4 November 2014.[31]

In its June 2013 meeting, the European Council committed to finalising the Banking Union.[32] Europe's political leaders thought this was 'key to ensuring financial stability, reducing financial fragmentation and restoring normal lending to the economy' and necessary to 'break the vicious circle between banks and sovereigns'.[33] With this commitment, essentially, they approved the creation of the Single Resolution Mechanism (SRM) and called for a proposal for a Deposit Guarantee Scheme. The Commission's proposal for the SRM was given shortly thereafter,[34] but the path of the Deposit Guarantee Scheme was not that straightforward. The Commission's initial proposal from 2010 had not progressed due to political disagreements. After the June 2013 statement from the European Council, the Commission issued a recast proposal in March 2014.[35]

After the Commission had issued the proposal on the SRM and the renewed proposal on the DGSD, the European Parliament wanted to move

---

[26] European Council Conclusions (EUCO 205/12). Brussels, 13–14 December 2012.

[27] Presidency compromise, Council of the European Union (ECOFIN 1011). Brussels, 3 December 2012.

[28] 'Council agrees position on bank supervision', PRESSE 528, Council of the European Union. Brussels, 13 December 2012.

[29] Regulation (EU) No 1024/2013 ('SSM Regulation'); Regulation (EU) No 1022/2013 ('EBA Amending Regulation').

[30] Art. 6 SSM Regulation.

[31] Art. 33 SSM Regulation.

[32] European Council, Conclusions, Brussels, 27–28 June 2013 (EUCO 104/2/13, REV 2).

[33] Ibid., p. 9.

[34] COM/2013/0520 final, given on 10 July 2013.

[35] COM/2014/0140 final, given on 4 March 2014.

quickly with their adoption in order to accept them before the end of its term in May 2014. The Parliament and the Council reached an agreement on the SRM on 20 March 2014.[36] The compromise gave more independence to the SRM's decision-making body (the Single Resolution Board (SRB)), as per the European Parliament's wishes, whereas the Member States would have wanted the Council to have a strong participatory role in the resolution of failing banks. The SRM Regulation (EU) No 806/2014 became applicable on 1 January 2016.[37]

Since the orderly resolution of banks is not just about letting banks default and guiding them into liquidation, money is needed for alternative resolution instruments. Thus, the SRM needed a fund, which became known as the Single Resolution Fund (SRF). The legal basis of the SRM Regulation was Article 114 TFEU, which was, despite the constraints of the *Meroni* doctrine,[38] deemed adequate for establishing the SRB, the acting body of the SRM. However, Article 114 TFEU was not seen as an adequate legal basis for establishing a common bank resolution fund that would in essence mutualise the risks associated with bank resolution. This was what the Germans argued, in fear of the German Federal Constitutional Court's (*Bundesverfassungsgericht*) prior doctrine,[39] while such mutualisation was also seen to breach the no bail-out clause of Article 125 TFEU.[40] Therefore, the Council decided on 14 May 2014 to adopt an intergovernmental agreement on the SRF (the SRF Treaty), which would provide its own legal basis outside EU law for the transfer and mutualisation of national contributions to the SRF.[41] On 21 May 2014, on the side of a Council meeting, 26 Member States signed the SRF Treaty.[42]

While the SRM Regulation establishes the SRF under the authority of the SRB, financing of the SRF is based on the separate SRF Treaty. As an international law-based instrument, the SRF Treaty is not part of EU law. It defines

---

[36]   'European Parliament and Council back Commission's proposal for a Single Resolution Mechanism: a major step towards completing the banking union', European Commission Statement. Brussels, 20 March 2014.

[37]   Regulation (EU) No 806/2014 ('SRM Regulation'), Art. 99.

[38]   Case 9/56 *Meroni* EU:C:1958:7.

[39]   N. Moloney, 'European Banking Union: Assessing its Risks and Resilience' (2014) *Common Market Law Review* 51(6), 1609–70, p. 1658; A. Hinarejos, *The Euro Area Crisis in Constitutional Perspective* (Oxford University Press 2015), p. 92.

[40]   K. Alexander, 'European Banking Union: A Legal and Institutional Analysis of the Single Supervisory Mechanism and the Single Resolution Mechanism' (2015) *European Law Review* 40(2), 154–87, p. 156.

[41]   Agreement on the transfer and mutualisation of contributions to the Single Resolution Fund. Council of the European Union. Brussels, 14 May 2014.

[42]   'Member states sign agreement on bank resolution fund', Council of the European Union, Presse 302. Brussels, 21 May 2014.

how national contributions are levied and transferred to the SRF. The SRF Treaty was adopted to take the issue of the mutualisation of resolution funds outside the scope of the SRM Regulation and thus also of Article 114 TFEU.[43] The European Parliament initially opposed the use of such a legal measure outside the scope of EU law, since going beyond the community method of decision making excludes the European Parliament from the whole process.[44]

The DGSD, which is an element of the Single Rulebook, was adopted on 16 April 2014.[45] This was a somewhat substantially amended version compared to the original Commission proposal from 2010. The level of coverage was retained at €100,000, but the contributions from banks to a deposit guarantee fund were somewhat altered due to the compromise reached between the Commission and the European Parliament.[46] By retaining the national funds in charge of the repayment of deposits, the DGSD does not optimally contribute to breaking the vicious circle between banks and sovereigns. As Véron explains, '[w]ithout an EDIS, national budgets remain the backstop for national deposit insurance schemes that rely principally on the quality of European-level supervision'.[47] Thus, the Commission issued a proposal for a European Deposit Insurance Scheme (EDIS) in November 2015, this time in the form of a Regulation.[48] As of September 2020, negotiations on it are still pending.

The Summer of 2012 deserves extra focus, since the events that took place then are crucial in understanding the causality behind the birth of the Banking Union as well as the fourth case study on the ECB's Outright Monetary Transactions programme (OMT). On 26 July 2012, a month after the announcement of the SSM by the Euro Group summit, ECB President Mario Draghi delivered a speech that will be forever ingrained in the history of the EMU. Draghi promised that the ECB would do 'whatever it takes' to

---

[43]   Moloney (n 39), p. 1658.

[44]   See Presidency Report to the Council, consideration of the European Parliament's amendments in preparation for political agreement, Council Document 6187/14, 7 February 2014 (2014 SRM Coreper Report); European Parliament Press Release, 5 March 2014; European Parliament Committee on Economic and Monetary Affairs, Letter to the Greek Presidency of the EU, 15 January 2014.

[45]   Directive 2014/49/EU ('DGSD').

[46]   See COM/2014/0140 final.

[47]   N. Véron, 'European Deposit Insurance: a response to Ludger Schuknecht', 16 February 2016, http://bruegel.org/2016/02/european-deposit-insurance-a-response-to-ludger-schuknecht/ (accessed 1 September 2020). See also the stances of the IMF https://www.imf.org/external/pubs/ft/sdn/2013/sdn1301.pdf; and the ECB https://www.ecb.europa.eu/press/key/date/2015/html/sp151104.en.html (accessed 1 September 2020).

[48]   COM/2015/0586 final.

preserve the euro.[49] This was the starting point for the ECB's infamous OMT programme, which was initially announced the following week, on 2 August 2012, and the technical details of which were spelled out in a press release on 6 September 2012.[50]

The vicious circle between banks and sovereigns works in two directions. On one hand, the credibility of banks is based on the perception that their host states will support them in situations of difficulty, the possibility of which is of course predicated upon the financial resources available to that state. On the other hand, the weaknesses of sovereigns are transmitted to banks through the erosion of the public guarantees that they can offer banks: the more foreign debt a state holds from a crisis state, the more diminished its possibilities to guarantee the actions of banks domiciled in it become. In fact, a correlation has been observed between the credit ratings of banks and sovereigns.[51] As long as this circle is not broken, it would be futile for the ECB to support states through bond-buying programmes, since there would be no guarantee of this actually helping the target states. In other words, crisis states needed help, but the ECB was unwilling to help before the vicious circle was broken, and this is where the Banking Union stepped in. Introducing the SSM, and especially in the form that made the ECB itself the supervisory body, would break this circle, since it allowed for the ECB to supervise these banks as well as to give aid to their host states, for which purpose it subsequently introduced the OMT programme. Véron's interpretation of this causality is based on the nature of the vicious circle and on statements by participating officials in which they explicitly acknowledged this link.[52]

To conclude, the main argument of this section is as follows: the 29 June 2012 euro area summit decision meant the creation of the SSM, which made it possible for the ECB to establish the OMT, which in turn led to a decrease in sovereign bond spreads. Both of these decisions had legal imperatives that affected their content and plausibility. The supervisory tasks had to be given to the ECB because of Article 127(6) TFEU, while the ECB could not take other action except the OMT due to Article 123(1) TFEU, which was only made possible by the prior decision to establish the SSM. The SRM, conversely,

---

[49]   Speech by Mario Draghi, President of the European Central Bank at the Global Investment Conference. London, 26 July 2012. The whole sentence was: 'Within our mandate, the ECB is ready to do whatever it takes to preserve the euro. And believe me, it will be enough.'

[50]   'Technical features of Outright Monetary Transactions', ECB Press Release. Frankfurt am Main, 6 September 2012.

[51]   See A. Baglioni, *The European Banking Union: A Critical Assessment* (Palgrave Macmillan 2016), pp. 13–15.

[52]   Véron (n 1), pp. 14–19.

took its final form on the basis of a political compromise between the Member States and the European Parliament, although the SRF Treaty was invented due to legal constraints stemming both from EU law (is Article 114 TFEU an adequate legal base for this) and national law (will the German Federal Constitutional Court allow this).

4.2.2   The Banking Union Before Courts

In stark contrast to the Fiscal Compact and the ESM, the Banking Union has not been the object of fierce litigation. It has not been reviewed by the CJEU and apparently it has only been reviewed by one national court.[53] This is perhaps explained by what Fabbrini has called 'the paradox of judicialization'.[54] As was seen with the case studies on the Fiscal Compact and the ESM, using international law-based measures allowed national courts to participate in the crafting and assessment of the EU's new economic governance regime to an unprecedented degree. In many Member States, courts can review international treaties and the legislative measures implementing them, whereas it is more difficult and rarer for national courts to review EU secondary law. Thus, there have been fewer possibilities to challenge the Banking Union before courts, since it was established by EU secondary law.

To be precise, the functioning of the Banking Union has resulted in a wealth of case law before the CJEU,[55] as well as some cases before national courts, but these cases are not about the adoption and existence of the Banking Union as such but rather they focus on the application of the individual legal mechanisms constituting the Banking Union. These cases are mainly interesting from a technical banking regulation perspective, although some of them might of course also have relevance for general EU constitutional law. These cases are beyond the scope of this chapter and the overall argument of this study, however, as they do not address the interplay between courts and the European-level political process.

---

[53]   The UK lodged an action for annulment against one legislative measure of the Banking Union, but the action was later withdrawn. See Case C-507/13 Action brought on 20 September 2013 — United Kingdom of Great Britain and Northern Ireland v European Parliament, Council of the European Union, 2013/C 359/05.

[54]   See F. Fabbrini, *Economic Governance in Europe. Comparative Paradoxes and Constitutional Challenges* (Oxford University Press 2016), Chapter 2.

[55]   For a constantly updated list, see https://ebi-europa.eu/publications/eu-cases-or-jurisprudence/ (accessed 1 September 2020).

It seems that the establishment of the Banking Union was challenged only before a national court in Germany.[56] In this case, the members of the Europolis Gruppe[57] sought to challenge the establishment of the Banking Union before the German Federal Constitutional Court by arguing that the EU has no competence to enact the Banking Union; specifically, that the creation of the SSM on the basis of Article 127(6) TFEU and the SRM on the basis of Article 114 TFEU are *ultra vires* acts by the Union legislator. Furthermore, the applicants also questioned the possible mutualisation of bank refinancing costs that can occur through the use of the SRM and the SRF. As a consequence of being *ultra vires*, the SSM and the SRM would also violate the German constitution.

The case was brought before the German Federal Constitutional Court as early as 2014, but it was only on 30 July 2019 that the court was able to deliver its ruling on the matter.[58] Unlike in *Gauweiler* or *Weiss*,[59] here the German court did not make a preliminary reference to the CJEU. The German court was of the opinion that the scope of Articles 114 and 127(6) TFEU as legal bases were covered by the *acte éclairé* doctrine, so therefore it could rule on the issue on the basis of its own interpretation.[60] As the transfers of competence to the EU effectuated by the establishment of the Banking Union did not manifestly exceed the competences of the EU, the German court did not have to order the German government and the parliament to take action against the Banking Union.[61]

Although a similar point of no return was not defined for the process of adopting the Banking Union as was done with regards to the Fiscal Compact and the ESM, we can observe that the German Federal Constitutional Court's judgment was delivered at a very late stage in the European-level political process; the Banking Union had already been in operation for three years when the judgment was delivered. Furthermore, it needs to be remembered

---

[56]　No such national cases were reported in U. Neergaard, C. Jacqueson and J. Hartig Danielsen (eds.), *The Economic and Monetary Union: Constitutional and Institutional Aspects of the Economic Governance within the EU. The XXVI FIDE Congress in Copenhagen, 2014* (DJOF Publishing 2014); G. Bándi, P. Darák, A. Halustyik and P. L. Láncos (eds.), *European Banking Union. Congress Proceedings Vol. 1. The XXVII FIDE Congress in Budapest, 2016* (Wolters Kluwer 2016); the EUI project Constitutional Change through Euro Crisis Law, http://eurocrisislaw.eui.eu/ (accessed 1 September 2020).

[57]　See https://www.europolis-online.org/ (accessed 1 September 2020).

[58]　2 BvR 1685/14, 30 July 2019 (*Bankenunion*).

[59]　C-62/14 *Gauweiler* EU:C:2015:400; C-493/17 *Weiss* EU:C:2018:1000.

[60]　2 BvR 1685/14, 30 July 2019 (*Bankenunion*), paras. 314–319.

[61]　2 Ibid.; See P. Faraguna and D. Messineo, 'Light and Shadows in the Bundesverfassungsgericht's Decision Upholding the European Banking Union' (2020) *Common Market Law Review* 57(5), 1629–46.

that a national court cannot rule on the validity of EU law.[62] Thus, since the judgment was given after the political process had already ended, it could not have affected the European-level political process.

The existence of such a case highlights how differences in national constitutions affect how national courts can engage with the European-level political process or EU law. The case was brought before the German Federal Constitutional Court as an individual constitutional complaint (*Verfassungsbeschwerde*) under Article 93(1)(4a) of the German constitution. The existence of such a competence and the German court's tradition of reviewing EU law made this case possible. Could such a case have taken place in any other Member State? We will return to this issue in Chapter 6.

4.3   THE TRIPARTITE CONTEXTUALITY OF ECONOMIC–POLITIC–LAW

In addition to the above events, which can be traced as parts of the causal process affecting the formation of the Banking Union, there were also other underlying causes that might have affected the process and the end result. These are situated mostly in the realms of economics and politics but also partially in the realm of law. In contrast to the above-described events, the weight of these reasons is more difficult to assess, and thus they are of a more speculative manner. They are, however, important for the overall analysis, since they point out the interplay between economic, political and legal factors.

Although the above reconstruction partly explains the incidents contributing to the uptake of the Banking Union, a complete explanation of everything related to its establishment has not been determined, either on the political spectrum or in regard to its legal imperatives. For example, the order in which events occurred (first SSM, second SRM and no common deposit guarantee fund, at least as long as the EDIS has not been enacted) and their extent (strong SSM, weak SRM, no common deposit guarantee fund) cannot be completely explained.[63]

Moreover, the content of the individual Banking Union measures was also affected by inter-state bargaining. Every Member State wanted to both gain something and protect their national banks, although it had become obvious that these national sentiments were one of the reasons for the original banking crisis of 2007–2008.[64] For example, the original proposition for the SRM was

---

[62]   See case 314/85 *Foto-Frost* EU:C:1987:452, para. 15: '[national courts] do not have the power to declare acts of the Community institutions invalid'.

[63]   See Véron (n 1), p. 49.

[64]   See ibid., pp. 14–19.

based on strong supranational autonomy so that Member States' interests could not play a role in its operation. In the Commission's original proposal, the Council was not granted a role in the resolution procedure.[65] However, Germany was able to change this, and now the final decision on resolution is made by the Council.[66] On the other hand, Germany had to concede to German banks paying levies into the SRF.[67] Similarly, Member States' differing interests as to whether stricter supervision and capital standards or more public support in the case of default have resulted in the EDIS proposal not being actualised.[68]

The national preferences behind these negotiations are explained by the configurations of each Member State's banking systems. On one hand, the degree and form of internationalisation of the banks' activities, or the high amount of national bank holdings of EU sovereign debt from the crisis-ridden Member States, led to a high incentive to establish the Banking Union. On the other hand, the healthier the banking sector, namely the better it could withstand possible crises, or the more manageable the vicious circle between banks and sovereigns, the lower the incentive to establish the Banking Union.[69] The historical baggage from previously existing national deposit guarantee schemes, and the related legal frameworks, also likely affected the negotiations on the proposed EDIS and why it has been turned down.[70]

4.4   WHAT DID THE BANKING UNION CONSTITUTIONALISE?

In stark contrast to the two previous case studies, the Banking Union stands out because it regulates the actions of private undertakings and not the Member States themselves. Therefore, this case study does not deal with just the EMU and its underlying political rationale but also its interconnection with other policy areas, namely the internal market. This section first outlines the content of the EU secondary law measures constituting the Banking Union (4.4.1). Following this, the underlying rationale of the Banking Union is discussed and

---

[65]   See Art. 16 in COM/2013/0520 final.

[66]   See Art. 18 SRM Regulation.

[67]   See de Rynck (n 2), p. 125.

[68]   See S. Donnelly, 'Advocacy Coalitions and the Lack of Deposit Insurance in Banking Union' (2018) *Journal of Economic Policy Reform* 21(3), 210–23.

[69]   See D. Howarth and L. Quaglia, *The Political Economy of European Banking Union* (Oxford University Press 2016), p. 50–88.

[70]   See D. Howarth and L. Quaglia, 'The Difficult Construction of a European Deposit Insurance Scheme: A Step Too Far in Banking Union?' (2018) *Journal of Economic Policy Reform* 21(3), 190–209.

the constitutional significance of this, particularly in relation to the asymmetry of the EMU, is analysed (4.4.2).

4.4.1 The Content of the Banking Union

The Single Rulebook is the foundation on which the Banking Union is established. The Single Rulebook consists of a set of legislative texts with which all financial institutions within the European Union must comply. It has three elements:

- Capital requirement rules that consist of the Capital Requirements Directive (CRD IV)[71] and the Capital Requirements Regulation (CRR);[72]
- The harmonisation of national deposit guarantee schemes with the Deposit Guarantee Scheme Directive (DGSD);[73]
- The rules and procedures relating to the recovery and resolution of banks in the Bank Recovery and Resolution Directive (BRRD).[74]

Before the crisis, banking regulation was based on minimum harmonisation, which led to divergences between the national legal frameworks and thus contributed to the crisis. The novelty of the Single Rulebook lies in creating a level playing field, as it is to some extent based on maximum harmonisation. The role of the EBA is central for the functioning of the Single Rulebook, as the EBA's role is to promote supervisory convergence.[75]

The first pillar of the Banking Union is established with the SSM,[76] which entrusts the ECB with the surveillance of the most important banks within the Eurozone whilst leaving the supervision of other banks to the NCAs. Cooperation between the ECB and the NCAs is central for the functioning of the SSM. It is imperative to highlight that while the ECB has been tasked with supervisory duties, it is not in charge of resolution. The purpose of this was to shield the ECB from the fiscal consequences of bank failures.[77]

---

[71] Directive 2013/36/EU.
[72] Regulation (EU) No 575/2013 ('CRR').
[73] Directive 2014/49/EU ('DGSD').
[74] Directive 2014/59/EU ('BRRD').
[75] See V. Babis, 'The Single Rulebook and the European Banking Authority' in F. Fabbrini and M. Ventoruzzo (eds), *Research Handbook on EU Economic Law* (Edward Elgar Publishing 2019).
[76] SSM Regulation (EU) No 1024/2013; EBA Amending Regulation (EU) No 1022/2013; also see EBA Regulation (EU) No 1093/2010.
[77] See T. H. Tröger, 'The Single Supervisory Mechanism' in Fabbrini and Ventoruzzo (n 75).

The second pillar of the Banking Union is established with the SRM,[78] through which the rules of the BRRD are applied within the Banking Union.[79] The central decision-making body within the SRM is the SRB, with resolution being financed through the SRF. Contributions from national resolution schemes were transferred and mutualised into the SRF with the Single Resolution Fund Treaty (SRF Treaty).[80] As opposed to insolvency measures, the objective of resolution is not the maximisation of creditors' value but to prevent contagion and spillover effects from one bank to another, and furthermore, to prevent bail-out by recourse to taxpayers' money. Resolution under the SRM is to serve five objectives: continuation of critical functions; preservation of financial stability and avoidance of contagion; protection of public funds; protection of depositors covered by the DGSD; and protection of client funds and assets.[81]

The third pillar of the Banking Union is supposed to be established with the EDIS, but it is still just a Commission proposal.[82] The DGSD establishes the substantive rules that would be applied through the EDIS. A central innovation is the establishment of the Deposit Insurance Fund (DIF), through which homogeneous deposit insurance within the Banking Union is achieved. By pooling available financial means, the DIF can reinforce depositor confidence within the Banking Union, which is central for preventing future crises.[83]

4.4.2   Constitutional Implications of the Banking Union

4.4.2.1   The use of legal bases in the Banking Union
The SSM Regulation (EU) No 1024/2013 is based on Article 127(6) TFEU, which is specifically meant for conferring supervisory tasks to the ECB. Five of the EU secondary law instruments comprising the Banking Union are based on Article 114 TFEU: the CRR (EU) No 575/2013, the BRRD 2014/59/EU, the EBA Regulation (EU) No 1093/2010, the SRM Regulation (EU) No 806/2014 and the proposed EDIS Regulation. Article 114 TFEU is a general internal market harmonisation competence, which can be used to attain the objectives set out in Article 26 TFEU, namely, to ensure the functioning of the

---

78   Regulation (EU) No 806/2014.
79   Art. 5 SRM Regulation.
80   See 'Agreement on the transfer and mutualisation of contributions to the Single Resolution fund', Council of the European Union, 8457/14. Brussels, 14 May 2014.
81   See C. V. Gortsos, 'The Single Resolution Mechanism' in Fabbrini and Ventoruzzo (n 75).
82   See COM/2015/0586 final ('EDIS proposal').
83   See C. V. Gortsos, 'The European Deposit Insurance Scheme' in Fabbrini and Ventoruzzo (n 75).

internal market. Two instruments are based on Article 53(1) TFEU: the CRD IV 2013/36/EU and the DGSD 2014/49/EU. Article 53(1) TFEU is an internal market legal base for regulating the provision of services.

As noted above, the stated objective of the Banking Union is to contribute towards the 'financial stability of the euro area as a whole'.[84] This objective, and the fact that the Banking Union is based mainly on the two internal market legal bases of Article 114 TFEU and Article 53(1) TFEU, has given rise to the question of whether such use of legal bases is appropriate. Furthermore, what does such use of legal bases mean from a constitutional perspective?[85] The obvious reason for the use of Article 114 TFEU is that, unlike the centralisation of supervision, there is no legal basis in the EU Treaties for crisis resolution. Thus, the general internal market harmonisation competence of Article 114 TFEU was perhaps the only alternative to achieve the chosen objectives without amending the EU Treaties.[86]

The Commission has been able to spell out internal market-related concerns that, according to its view, justify the use of Article 114 TFEU as a legal base. These justifications are rooted in the nature and effects of the euro crisis, namely, that differences in the national regulatory environments partly resulted in the crisis, as the internal market for financial services was fragmented. Harmonising the rules on financial services creates a level playing field and thereby contributes to the functioning of the internal market.[87] If we study the Commission's proposals for the five measures based on Article 114 TFEU and the content of the actual measures, we can distinguish a host of ways in which they purport to support the functioning of the internal market. All of them, thus, contain an 'internal market rationale'.[88] Yet, in addition to this internal market rationale, all of the said measures also contribute, either

---

[84] European Council, Conclusions, Brussels, 27–28 June 2013 (EUCO 104/2/13, REV 2), p. 9.

[85] See T. Tridimas, 'The Constitutional Dimension of Banking Union' in S. Grundmann and H. W. Micklitz (eds), *The European Banking Union and Constitution: Beacon for Advanced Integration or Death-Knell for Democracy?* (Hart Publishing 2019); T. Tuominen, 'The European Banking Union: A Shift in the Internal Market Paradigm?' (2017) *Common Market Law Review* 54(5), 1359–180.

[86] See O. Capolino, 'The Single Resolution Mechanism: Authorities and Proceedings' in M. P. Chiti and V. Santoro (eds), *The Palgrave Handbook of European Banking Union Law* (Palgrave Macmillan 2019), pp. 250–51.

[87] See G. S. Zavvos and S. Kaltsouni, 'The Single Resolution Mechanism in the European Banking Union: Legal Foundation, Governance Structure and Financing' in M. Haentjens and B. Wessels (eds), *Research Handbook on Crisis Management in the Banking Sector* (Edward Elgar Publishing 2015), pp. 123–4.

[88] See Tuominen (n 85), pp. 1374–7.

directly or indirectly, towards the 'financial stability of the euro area as a whole'. Therefore, they also contain a 'financial stability rationale'.[89]

The financial stability rationale is present in the instruments in a variety of manners.[90] In the CRR, the smooth functioning of the internal market is linked to financial stability through the capital requirements.[91] In the framework established by the SRM Regulation, uniform resolution tools increase market confidence and thus stability.[92] Finally, the financial stability rationale is visible in the proposed EDIS Regulation in how it aims to spread risks associated with deposit guarantee.[93]

These factual circumstances and the constitutional concerns underlying them are perhaps best captured in a statement by Tridimas:

> Banking Union was conceived as a response to the Eurozone crisis. The outbreak of the sovereign debt crisis unveiled the unsustainable fragility of the single currency which was attributed not only to the asymmetric governance arrangements concerning monetary and fiscal policy within the EMU but also deficiencies in the EU legal framework governing financial supervision.[94]

Simply put, although the Banking Union is based mainly on internal market legal bases and regulates the actions of private banks, the real reasons for its existence are found in the more general objective of financial stability, which pertains to the economic policies of the Member States. Indeed, it has been argued in the literature that the Banking Union's relevance for the EMU actually explains its existence.[95] The internal market rationale and the more general financial stability rationale are connected, since the Banking Union seeks to sever the vicious circle between banks and sovereigns.[96] This reveals the problematic nature of establishing the Banking Union on the internal market legal bases.

While in the two previous case studies one of the main constitutional concerns was how the distinction between economic and monetary policy is being eroded with the adoption of the Fiscal Compact and the ESM, with the Banking Union the concern is, namely, that EMU-related policy goals are

---

[89]   See ibid., p. 1377–9.
[90]   See C. B. Morra, 'The Third Pillar of the Banking Union and Its Troubled Implementation' in Chiti and Santoro (n 86), pp. 403–5.
[91]   Recital 7 CRR. Also see COM/2011/0452, section 4.1.
[92]   Recital 12 SRM Regulation.
[93]   See COM/2015/0586 final, pp. 3–4 and Art. 41h(2) of the EDIS proposal.
[94]   T. Tridimas, 'General Report' in Bándi, Darák, Halustyik and Láncos (n 56), p. 68.
[95]   See A. de Gregorio Merino, 'Institutional Report' in Bándi, et al, ibid., pp. 153–8.
[96]   Véron (n 1), p. 12.

pursued through internal market measures. These types of developments have been seen to signal a shift in the way the internal market functions, perhaps towards an economic union paradigm.[97] Furthermore, just like in the previous case studies, here too the asymmetry of the EMU is in the background of why such creative use of legal bases was necessary and what types of constitutional concerns flow from this.

There is, of course, a natural link between the internal market and the EMU. Issues that can be categorised as falling under economic policy (but not fiscal policy, which is more strictly defined) are of the sort that they relate to the internal market, such as economic reforms relating to goods, capitals and labour markets. Yet, it is debatable how such intertwinement has been facilitated through the use of the internal market legal bases. This argument is based on the fact that it was an explicit political decision in Maastricht to have an asymmetrical EMU – that is, that there is no common economic policy.[98] Is it legitimate to pursue economic integration through an internal market legal base?

It has been debated at length in the literature whether such use of legal bases, especially Article 114 TFEU, is justifiable.[99] Views supportive of the use of Article 114 TFEU as a legal base for the Banking Union seem to resemble the 'two-order telos' argument, which Tuori and Tuori have identified from the CJEU's reasoning in *Pringle*.[100] Let us first recount the ethos of this argument.[101]

To justify the bail-out of Greece and the formation of the ESM, the Member States created the concept of 'the financial stability of the euro area as whole'.[102] This concept was used to legitimise bail-outs, both legally and politically. The CJEU accepted this 'two-level teleology' in *Pringle*: the no

---

[97] See J. Snell, 'The Internal Market and the Philosophies of Market Integration' in C. Barnard and S. Peers (eds), *European Union Law. Third Edition* (Oxford University Press 2020), pp. 347–354; Tuominen (n 85).

[98] See Chapter 1.2.1.1.

[99] See e.g. de Gregorio Merino (n 95), pp. 204–6; Tridimas (n 94), pp. 74–85; Moloney (n 39), pp. 1654–8; Tuominen (n 85); G. Lo Schiavo (ed.), *The European Banking Union and the Role of Law* (Edward Elgar Publishing 2019); E. Ferran, 'European Banking Union. Imperfect, But It Can Work' in D. Busch and G. Ferrarini (eds), *European Banking Union* (Oxford University Press 2015); Tridimas (n 85), pp. 35–42.

[100] See C-370/12 *Pringle* EU:C:2012:756, para. 136.

[101] See K. Tuori and K. Tuori, *The Eurozone Crisis: A Constitutional Analysis* (Cambridge University Press 2014), pp. 120–36.

[102] See L. Lionello, *The Pursuit of Stability of the Euro Area as a Whole: The Reform of the European Economic Union and Perspectives of Fiscal Integration* (Springer 2020), p. 1.

bail-out clause of Article 125 TFEU was given a different interpretation – in contrast to its literal meaning – with the help of the higher order objective of safeguarding the financial stability of the euro area as a whole. This development harmonised crisis prevention (prohibition of bail-outs) with crisis resolution (rescue-packages). The conclusion from *Pringle* is 'that the interpretation and application of the no-bailout clause should not prevent attaining the higher-level objective it shares with crisis management'. Such assimilation of the resolution and prevention objectives and instruments is detrimental, since it can lead to moral hazard problems in the future. This was noted by the policy makers whilst drafting the ESM and by the CJEU in *Pringle*. The solution was to make assistance conditional upon strict conditionality.[103]

According to Tuori and Tuori, a convincing justification for the ESM needs to resort to such two-level teleology and a discussion between the first- and second-order objectives of the no bail-out clause of Article 125 TFEU. However, they see using such two-level teleology as problematic, since the higher-order objective of 'financial stability of the euro area as a whole' does not originate from the EU Treaties.[104] The fact that all of the crisis response measures are related to this new paradigm,[105] in one way or the other, points to the conclusion that the objective defies definition. Nevertheless, it is understandable why policy makers and the CJEU would assume such a pattern of argumentation. Various economic, political and legal reasons led to this option becoming the most attractive one, whereas the CJEU probably had its own predicament for finding whatever line of reasoning it could to accept the taken path.[106]

How is this pattern of analysis applicable to our current case on the use of internal market legal bases for measures that are clearly aimed at something else than just the harmonisation of the internal market? In comparison to *Pringle* and the CJEU's two-order telos justification, the order of arguments is reversed here. Let us rephrase the two-order telos argument from *Pringle*: the first-order objective of the no bail-out clause of Article 125 TFEU would have prevented the adoption of the ESM, but reading into the Article the second-order objective of financial stability, and giving it a higher status, reversed this position.

Borrowing this taxonomy, we can map out that the first-order objective of, for example, the SRM Regulation is to establish uniform rules and procedures

---

[103] Tuori and Tuori (n 101), pp. 129–30.
[104] Ibid., pp. 131–2.
[105] See G. Lo Schiavo, *The Role of Financial Stability in EU Law and Policy* (Wolters Kluwer 2017); and Chapters 2–5 in this study.
[106] See Chapter 3.

for the resolution of failing banks.[107] This is an acceptable aim for a measure that is based on Article 114 TFEU. However, the second-order objective of the SRM Regulation clearly is to safeguard the financial stability of the euro area as a whole, and the Commission's proposal even seems to broaden this to encompass general 'economic stability'.[108] This is something else than what Article 114 TFEU is supposed to be used for, as how it is defined in Article 26(1) TFEU: 'establishing or ensuring the functioning of the internal market'. Furthermore, the risks that such use of Article 114 TFEU contain are a violation of both the principle of conferral and also the institutional structure and balance of the EU and the checks and balances that the system contains. Thus, the outcome of the two-order telos argument is reversed in this case, since the existence of the second-order objective actually effects breaching the first-order objective, and no valid reasons for accepting such a breach are found in the EU Treaties due to the vagueness of the objective of 'safeguarding the financial stability of the euro area as a whole'.

Accepting the use of the internal market legal bases for establishing the Banking Union is a pragmatic solution, of course. Who would not want a functioning banking sector and a stable EMU? But finding higher aims between the lines of the text of the EU Treaties and then using them to argue against explicit prohibitions in the Treaties (like the CJEU did in *Pringle*, according to Tuori and Tuori) or for something that is not found in the Treaties and thus forbidden (broadening the scope of Art. 114 TFEU as a legal base) is perhaps reaching a bit too far. In a system that posits democracy and the rule of law as central values (Art. 2 TEU), political and constitutional structures should be respected. Just as we can argue that the explicit decision taken in Maastricht to not have a common economic policy should not be circumvented by trying to drive one in through the back door with mechanisms like the Fiscal Compact and the ESM, so too can we argue that the conferral of powers to the Union and the division of competences between the Union and the Member States is defined in its current from in the EU Treaties for a reason, and thus we should

---

[107] Art. 1(1) SRM Regulation.

[108] See COM/2013/0520 final, emphasis added: 'Swift progress towards a Banking Union is indispensable to ensure *financial stability* and growth in the Euro Area and in the whole internal market', p. 2; 'It is therefore necessary to set out a framework that allows for the in-depth restructuring of banks by authorities whilst avoiding the very significant risks to *economic stability* and costs derived from their disorderly liquidation under national insolvency laws, and putting an end to the need to finance the process with public resources', p. 3; 'Compared to a network of resolution authorities, a Single Resolution Mechanism with a central decision-making body and a Single Bank Resolution Fund will provide key benefits for Member States, taxpayers, banks, and *financial and economic stability* in the entire EU', p. 3.

preferably try to alter EU Treaties explicitly instead of circumventing the conferred competences with the creative use of existing legal bases.

4.4.2.2 Establishing a transfer union

Three of the EU secondary law instruments based on Article 114 TFEU seem to contain elements that take the Eurozone towards a transfer union. The BRRD contains a 'European system of financing arrangements'.[109] The purpose of financing arrangements is to ensure the effective application of the resolution tools, for which purpose the Member States shall establish one or more financing arrangements.[110] These financing arrangements are in practice national resolution funds, contributions to which are collected from banks nationally.[111] Their purpose is to support the bail-in mechanism in order to avoid possible risks to financial stability.[112] The financing arrangements consist of national financing arrangements,[113] borrowing between national financing arrangements,[114] and the mutualisation of national financing arrangements in the case of a group resolution.[115] Group resolution refers to the resolution of a bank operating in multiple Member States.

Mutualisation, in this case, means that the national financing arrangements of each institution that is part of the group under resolution contribute to the financing of the said group resolution. Principally, the amount contributed by each participating national financing arrangement (namely fund) is calculated on the basis of how the group's risk-weighted assets, other assets, losses, and resources are distributed amongst the different Member States' jurisdictions. However, the BRRD does grant the group-level resolution authority the possibility to agree otherwise in its group-level resolution plan.[116]

The SRM Regulation provides the institutional framework for bank resolution for the Member States participating in the Banking Union, by way of applying the substantive rules of the BRRD. Therefore, it also uses the same 'financing arrangements'.[117] However, in practice the SRF provides the financing for resolution taking place under the SRM.[118] Due to the substantive link with the BRRD, the SRM Regulation also contains the equivalent provision

---

[109] Art. 99 BRRD.
[110] Arts 100 and 101 BRRD.
[111] Arts 102–104 BRRD.
[112] See COM/2012/0280 final, pp. 15–17.
[113] Art. 100 BRRD.
[114] Art. 106 BRRD.
[115] Art. 107 BRRD.
[116] Art. 107(5) BRRD.
[117] Art. 68 SRM Regulation.
[118] Art. 67 SRM Regulation.

on the mutualisation of national financing arrangements in the case of group resolution involving institutions from Member States outside the Banking Union.[119]

The main difference between the BRRD and the SRM regimes is that the SRF mutualises the contributions raised at the national level in accordance with the BRRD and the SRM Regulation after the transitional period of eight years has ended (2016–2023).[120] The SRF Treaty contains detailed rules on how the national contributions are to be used during the transitional period, determining when and how contributions from the other Member States' compartments can be used.[121] After the end of the transitional period, the national contributions that have been irrevocably transferred to the SRF can be used for resolution by the SRB in a manner that it sees fit, whilst of course following the rules set out in the SRM Regulation.

The Commission's EDIS proposal aims to establish a common deposit guarantee fund, although it is referred to as an insurance scheme.[122] The proposed EDIS differs from the DGSD in that the latter only harmonised the level of deposit guarantee and the way the national systems work, whereas the EDIS would establish a joint fund – the DIF – into which national contributions are collected, and which can subsequently be used to repay depositors during a crisis.

The naming of this proposal is somewhat misleading.[123] The proposal builds on three stages. During the first two transitional stages, the EDIS – in accordance with its name – insures the national deposit guarantee schemes. In the first stage, it covers those repayments that a national scheme does not have funds for.[124] In the second stage, it contributes to repayment along with the national schemes with a share ranging from 20 per cent to 80 per cent.[125] However, in the final, 'full insurance' stage, when a national scheme encounters a pay-out event, it may claim funding from the DIF for the full amount of deposits that it has guaranteed under the DGSD.[126] In the case of such a pay-out, the participating national scheme shall repay the amount of funding provided by the SRB, less the amount of any excess loss cover.[127] However, what if the national scheme cannot do this, as the crisis is so severe? The third and final stage is

---

[119] Art. 78 SRM Regulation.
[120] Art. 1(1)(b) SRF Treaty.
[121] Art. 5 SRF Treaty.
[122] See COM/2015/0586 final.
[123] See Gortsos (n 83), p. 369.
[124] Arts 41a–41c EDIS Proposal.
[125] Art. 41e EDIS Proposal.
[126] Art. 41h(2) EDIS Proposal.
[127] Art. 41o EDIS Proposal.

supposed to take effect in 2024. Furthermore, according to the DGSD,[128] the national deposit guarantee funds can also be used for bank resolution under the BRRD in certain situations.[129] Due to the link between the proposed EDIS (and the DIF contained therein) and the DGSD, the EDIS can also be used for such financing of bank resolution.[130] Compared to other EU instruments and policy areas, the Banking Union generally speaking and the proposed EDIS particularly represent a high redistributive impact between the Member States.[131]

This brief overview has outlined how these three mechanisms can be used to create common liability by way of using national funds for resolution in other Member States, or through mutualising national funds and then using them for resolution. The essence of this is captured well by Teixeira, according to whom:

> [the Banking Union] is the result of a *quid pro quo* between the transfer of competences and the mutualisation of risks at the European level through the direct recapitalization of banks by the ESM, the financing of resolution by the SRF, and the minimum coverage of bank deposits by EDSI.[132]

Does such joint liability or mutualisation of risks signal the creation of some form of a transfer union? The relevance of this questions, too, is closely linked to the asymmetric structure of the EMU. Is joint liability and the transfer of funds from one Member State to another a form of centralised economic policy?

Furthermore, it needs to be stressed that the whole purpose of the Banking Union, how it severs the vicious circle between banks and sovereigns, is to mutualise risks. The possibility of direct recapitalisation of banks by the ESM was linked to the centralisation of supervisory functions to the ECB, as discussed above.[133] Recapitalisation through the ESM means that 'the burden of rescuing an undercapitalised bank would not fall on national public accounts and increase the debt of a Member State'.[134] Granted, the conditions for resolution, especially those in Article 32(4)(d) BRRD, or the fact that under Article

---

[128] Art. 11(2) DGSD.

[129] See Art. 109 BRRD.

[130] Arts 41a–41h EDIS Proposal. See COM/2015/0586 final, p 8.

[131] See R. Epstein and M. Rhodes, 'From Governance to Government: Banking Union, Capital Markets Union and the New EU' (2018) *Competition & Change* 22(2), 205–24, p. 210.

[132] P. G. Teixeira, 'The Legal History of the Banking Union' (2017) *European Business Organization Law Review* 18(3), 535–565, p. 562.

[133] See Chapter 4.2.1.

[134] P. G. Teixeira, 'The Future of the European Banking Union: Risk-Sharing and Democratic Legitimacy' in Chiti and Santoro (n 86), p. 140.

6(6) SRM Regulation the use of the SRF 'shall neither require Member States to provide extraordinary public financial support nor impinge on the budgetary sovereignty and fiscal responsibilities of the Member States' means a shift from public bail-outs to private risk-sharing (bail-in).[135]

However, it has been strongly speculated whether the Banking Union, in its current form, is able to actually sever the vicious circle between banks and sovereigns, and whether therefore the choice to prioritise bail-in instead of bail-out will hold if a banking crisis occurs in the future. The fact that supervision has been centralised but deposit guarantee, resolution and the backstop function have been retained in the hands of the Member States does not help in severing the vicious circle.[136] Public risk-sharing mechanisms through backstops have been deemed as necessary additions to the Banking Union.[137] Under certain factual circumstances, bail-outs to private banks might be more effective and less costly than bail-ins, for which reason the adoption of the SRM as the second pillar of the Banking Union might not put an end to bail-outs.[138]

4.5   CONCLUSIONS

4.5.1   Observations from the Reconstruction

The reconstruction of the birth of the Banking Union showed how the compromises relating to the adoption of the SSM and the SRM, along with the pending process on the EDIS, were affected by both political disagreement and the framework of the EU Treaties. The disagreements stemmed from differences in the national banking sectors and the thus prevalent national attitudes on banking regulation. Although we can observe the economic, political and legal forces in play in the adoption of the Banking Union, the political, as pressured by the economic, seems to have been most decisive element in this case study.

These factors notwithstanding, legal concerns did play a minor role although not as significant as with the Fiscal Compact and the ESM. This is evident for three reasons. First, there was no legal baggage from preceding old regula-

---

[135]   See ibid., pp. 140–43.

[136]   See S. Donnelly, 'Expert Advice and Political Choice in Constructing European Banking Union' (2016) *Journal of Banking Regulation* 17, 104–18, p. 116.

[137]   See Teixeira (n 134), p. 149–151, citing A. Enria, 'Fragmentation In Banking Markets: Crisis Legacy and the Challenge of Brexit', Speech at the BCBS-FSI High-Level Meeting for Europe on Banking Supervision, 17 September 2018, available at https://eba.europa.eu/documents/10180/2353431/Andrea+Enria+speech+on+Fragmentation+in+banking+at+BCBS-FSI+High+Level+Meeting+170918.pdf (accessed 1 September 2020).

[138]   See M. Bodellini, 'To Bail-In, or to Bail-Out, that is the Question' (2018) *European Business Organization Law Review* 19(2), 365–92.

tory frameworks that would have acted as models for the three pillars of the Banking Union.[139] Second, the available legal bases did not affect, or had only minor effects, on the form or substance that the enacted measures eventually took. They mainly affected to whom the new supervisory duties were given. Third, although the Banking Union was no less politically contradictory from the perspective of the Member States, legally speaking its establishment was easier since this was possible through EU secondary law. However, the SRF Treaty was concluded as an international law-based agreement between the Member States, but its overall relevance is minor in comparison to the whole legal framework of the Banking Union.

Unlike with the Fiscal Compact or the ESM, there is no case law relating directly to the adoption of the Banking – aside from the German Federal Constitutional Court's ruling from July 2019, in which it deemed the Banking Union, already adopted five years prior to the ruling, as constitutional both in light of EU law and the German constitution. From the lack of relevant case law, two conclusions can be made. First, from the perspective of national constitutions, the establishment of the Banking Union was not legally as controversial as was the establishment of the Fiscal Compact or the ESM. Second, the fact that the Banking Union was established through EU secondary law measures meant that national courts did not have a possibility to participate in a similar manner as was the case with the Fiscal Compact and the ESM.

Nevertheless, even though courts did not directly affect the process of adopting the Banking Union, they seem to have exerted some level of influence by subjugating the legislator under their prior doctrine – in a way, turning the legislator into their agent through a process of 'autolimitation'.[140] As indicated above, the fears of the German Federal Constitutional Court possibly interfering might have influenced the choice to use Article 127(6) TFEU as the legal basis for the SSM, and in turn supervision being centralised to the ECB and the creation of the SRF Treaty outside the scope of EU law.

---

[139]   Yet, it needs to be acknowledged that the EU secondary law instruments comprising the Single Rulebook did not appear out of thin air but had their predecessors. See, Teixeira (n 132).

[140]   See A. Stone Sweet, *Governing with Judges. Constitutional Politics in Europe* (Oxford University Press 2000), p. 75. Specifically, in the context of the Banking Union, see S. Saurugger, A. Hofmann and T. Warren, 'National Constitutional Courts as Veto Players in the EMU Crisis' (January 7, 2020). Available at SSRN: https://ssrn.com/abstract=3599037 or http://dx.doi.org/10.2139/ssrn.3599037 (accessed 1 September 2020).

4.5.2   The Rationality of the Banking Union

As was the case with the Fiscal Compact and the ESM, the ultimate concern, or from where the two discussed constitutional concerns associated with the Banking Union stem, seems to be the asymmetry of the EMU. It is also the reason why the Banking Union has one foot in the internal market and the other in the EMU.[141] However, what differentiates the Banking Union from the two previous case studies is how here the main legal concern was the use of correct legal bases, whereas with the two others it was that of venturing outside the legal bases altogether. Both of these are tell-tale signs of the inadequacy of the EU Treaties and specifically of the asymmetrical structure of the EMU: with the Fiscal Compact and the ESM, the Member States had to venture outside the scope of the EU Treaties to achieve their desired objectives; with the Banking Union, the Member States had to resort to a questionable interpretation of Article 114 TFEU to achieve their desired objectives. What is more, an internal market legal base is thereby used to take steps towards a transfer union. In both cases, it was the need to protect to common currency that necessitated these actions, and, at least partly, the lack of common economic policy that resulted in the crisis and prevented other forms of crisis resolution.

All of this goes to show how the establishment of the Banking Union seems to have been an inevitable outcome of the compromise reached in Maastricht. As Underhill has stated, 'in a world of global market integration, the effectiveness of national policies and policy capacity are increasingly called into question, especially where cross-border capital mobility is concerned'.[142] In other words, having a common currency and the free movement of capital would eventually also require common regulation in the field of banking.

It is not as if this was not known or could not have been anticipated during the creation of the EMU. As Andenas and Hadjiemmanuil explained a decade before the eruption of the global banking crisis, banks and the effects of banking activities can be analysed through the relationship between banking services, the prudential supervision of banks, the internal market and the monetary union. There exists an intimate relationship between these elements: an internal market for banking requires the free movement of capital, which then again requires a certain economic policy from the Member States. The adoption of a single currency is the culmination of the development for an internal market in banking activities. However, the Member States did not want

---

[141]   See de Gregorio Merino (n 95), p. 153.

[142]   G. Underhill, 'The Political Economy of (eventual) Banking Union' in T. Beck (ed.), *Banking Union for Europe: Risks and Challenges* (Centre for Economic Policy Research (CEPR) 2012), p. 137.

common banking supervision when negotiating on the Treaty of Maastricht and the establishment of the ECB.[143] The chosen structure – a common currency and the free movement of capital, but no common rules on supervision or resolution – is similar to the asymmetry of the EMU with a common monetary policy but no common economic policy. This can be seen as one of the root causes of the initial banking crises, which then later escalated into the sovereign debt crisis due to the vicious circle between banks and sovereigns.

---

[143]   M. Andenas and C. Hadjiemmanuil, 'Banking Supervision, the Internal Market and European Monetary Union' in M. Andenas, L. Gormley and C. Hadjiemmanuil (eds.), *European Economic and Monetary Union: The Institutional Framework* (Kluwer Law International 1997), p. 375.

5. The Outright Monetary Transactions programme and preserving the euro

5.1 INTRODUCTION

The Outright Monetary Transactions (OMT) programme was intended as the European Central Bank's (ECB) tool for safeguarding the functioning of its monetary policy transmission mechanism and the singleness of its monetary policy. Under the OMT programme, the ECB could have purchased Member States' sovereign bonds from the secondary markets but not directly from the issuing state, that is from the primary markets. Since such purchases are not specifically regulated by the EU Treaties or the ESCB Statute,[1] the conditions for the use of the OMT programme were drawn up by the Governing Council of the ECB itself. According to the ECB, the necessity for the OMT programme stemmed from the magnitude that the sovereign debt crisis had reached in 2012: the normal monetary policy tools of the ECB were not functioning, hence in order to conduct its primary task of maintaining price stability it had to revert to such unconventional monetary policy measures.[2] The mere announcement of the OMT programme had the intended market reaction. The OMT programme was never actually used and it has since been replaced by other bond purchasing programmes.[3]

Similarly to the European Stability Mechanism (ESM), the OMT programme also had its predecessor, the Securities Markets Programme (SMP). This chapter will mainly focus on the OMT programme and thus highlight the

---

[1] Protocol (No 4) on the statute of the European System of Central Banks and of the European Central Bank, annexed to the Treaty of Lisbon.

[2] The ECB's standard monetary policy measure is the adjustment of its interest rates. When this is deemed not effective or not effective enough, the ECB can initiate a host of unconventional monetary policy measures. For an explanation and assessment of these measures during the crisis, see P. Cour-Thimann and B. Winkler, 'The ECB's Non-Standard Monetary Policy Measures: The Role of Institutional Factors and Financial Structure' (2013) *European Central Bank Working Paper Series*, (1528), 1–44.

[3] See ECB, 'Asset purchase programmes', https://www.ecb.europa.eu/mopo/implement/omt/html/index.en.html (accessed 1 September 2020).

SMP only to the extent that it affected the adoption or content of the OMT pro-gramme. Special attention will be given to the link between the establishment of the OMT programme and the Banking Union, which was also discussed in the previous chapter. The OMT programme was also linked to the ESM, as the latter was a threshold criterion for the use of the former. All this goes to show how the four studied crisis response mechanisms are interlinked and how they all relate to the asymmetry of the EMU.

The case studies on the Fiscal Compact and the ESM pointed out how there are differences in how national courts can interact with the European-level political process, the Court of Justice of the European Union (CJEU) and EU law. Those findings create the descriptive base for the inequality thesis put forth in this book. This case study focuses on one particular event of interac-tion: the *Gauweiler saga*.[4] The findings of this chapter enable a substantive assessment of the inequality thesis and its broader constitutional significance, which is at the root of the criticism presented towards constitutional pluralism in this book.[5] From a substantive perspective, the discussion in this chapter revolves around whether the intended OMT programme breached the pro-hibition on central bank financing found in Article 123 TFEU, and whether due to the link with the ESM it was also an economic policy measure. These questions relate directly to the asymmetry of the EMU in that the prohibition in Article 123 TFEU exists because of there being no common economic policy and how due to there being no common economic policy the mandate of the ECB is strictly limited to the domain of monetary policy.

This chapter proceeds as follows. First, the reasons that led to the announce-ment of the OMT programme by the ECB are explained by providing a recon-struction those events, followed by the challenges the programme faced before courts (5.2). Then, the underlying economic, political and legal reasons that may help to explain this process are highlighted (5.3). Following this, the content of the OMT programme as a legal measure is analysed doctrinally and its constitutional consequences discussed (5.4). Finally, conclusions in relation to the overall aim and chosen framework of this study are presented (5.5).

---

[4]   2 BvR 2728/13, 14 January 2014 (*OMT reference*); C-62/14 *Gauweiler* EU:C: 2015:400; 2 BvR 2728/13, 21 June 2016 (*OMT final judgment*). See T. Tuominen, 'Aspects of Constitutional Pluralism in Light of the *Gauweiler saga*' (2018) *European Law Review* 43(2), 186–204.

[5]   See Chapters 6 to 8.

5.2   RECONSTRUCTING THE BIRTH OF THE OMT PROGRAMME

5.2.1   The Political Process Behind the OMT Programme

This reconstruction will start from the adoption of the SMP, which was the ECB's first unconventional monetary policy measure. The Governing Council of the ECB established the SMP on 14 May 2010.[6] The decision was based on Article 18(1) ESCB Statute, according to which the ECB may, in order to conduct its monetary policy and to achieve its objective of maintaining price stability, operate in the financial markets by way of, inter alia, buying and selling outright marketable instruments. Due to the exceptional circumstances prevailing in the financial markets the Governing Council of the ECB thought that it needed to act in order to reinstate the functioning of its monetary policy transmission mechanism. It saw purchases of government bonds on the secondary markets as the correct solution. The SMP also covered certain debt instruments issued by private entities, both through the primary and secondary markets.[7]

Although Article 18(1) ESCB Statute specifically allows the ECB to purchase government bonds on the secondary markets, it was still questioned whether such actions breach the prohibition of monetary financing found in Article 123 TFEU. Early discussants were of the opinion that the SMP did not circumvent the prohibition on monetary financing, and that the SMP was actually conducive to attaining the primary objective of maintaining price stability.[8] The element of conditionality was also present already in the SMP. The governments of the Eurozone Member States had stated that they 'will take all measures needed to meet their fiscal targets this year and the years ahead in line with excessive deficit procedures', while some governments had already made additional commitments towards accelerating fiscal consolidation and ensuring 'the sustainability of their public finances'.[9] However, the SMP did not contain any precautionary conditions for the purchase of government bonds. Thus, purchases through the SMP could involve bonds from

---

[6]   Decision of the European Central Bank of May 14, 2010 establishing a securities markets programme [2010] ('SMP Decision').

[7]   Recitals 1–3 SMP Decision.

[8]   See P. Athanassiou, 'Of Past Measures and Future Plans for Europe's Exit from the Sovereign Debt Crisis: What is Legally Possible and What Not' (2011) *European Law Review* 36(4), 558–75, pp. 566–8.

[9]   Recital 4 SMP Decision.

any Eurozone Member States, also including those outside a formal financial assistance programme. Indeed, it was mainly used to support Italy and Spain.[10]

Before the European Financial Stability Facility (EFSF) was adopted, the ECB conducted two large purchases under the SMP in May and June 2010. The ECB resumed these actions in August 2011 mainly due to the spreads of Italy's bonds being so wide. On both occasions, in 2010 and 2011, the use of the SMP initially caused a decline in government bond spreads. However, this relief was only short lived since spreads still continued to show high volatility. Purchasers of these bonds required enormous risk surcharges, that is, higher interest rates.[11] This was due to a certain inherent flaw in the SMP. Purchasing government bonds with the aim of lowering their interest rates is one form of financial assistance since the total costs from government debt interests can be overwhelming. Giving financial assistance to a state without requiring it to change its economic policy choices does not create incentives to implement essential adjustments to strengthen competitiveness or to try to achieve the target levels of the Stability and Growth Pact. In other words, the SMP did not require structural changes from the target states.[12]

To counter the economic shortcomings of the SMP, the ECB decided to replace it with the OMT programme. According to Mr. Benoît Cœuré, ECB Executive Board Member, adoption of the OMT programme was necessary both for economic and political reasons: economically speaking, since the SMP had not restored the ECB's monetary policy transmission mechanisms; politically speaking, since all of the associated troubles threatened to break up the euro area.[13]

On 26 July 2012, ECB President Mario Draghi delivered a speech that contained the now infamous 'Draghi's bazooka': he promised that the ECB will do 'whatever it takes' to preserve the euro.[14] The OMT programme was officially

---

[10] See D. Adamski, 'Economic Constitution of the Euro Area After the Gauweiler Preliminary Ruling' (2015) *Common Market Law Review* 52(6), 1451–90, p. 1454.

[11] See P. Scherer, 'European Monetary Policy – What Works Legally and What Doesn't? The ECJ's Judgment Regarding the OMT Programme' (2015) *European Law Reporter* (4), 106–12, p. 106.

[12] See H. Geeroms, S. Ide and F. Naert, *The European Union and the Euro: How to Deal with a Currency Built on Dreams* (Intersentia 2014), pp. 229–35.

[13] 'Outright Monetary Transactions, one year on', Speech by Benoît Cœuré, Member of the Executive Board of the ECB, at the conference 'The ECB and its OMT programme', organised by Centre for Economic Policy Research, German Institute for Economic Research and KfW Bankengruppe. Berlin, 2 September 2013.

[14] Speech by Mario Draghi, President of the European Central Bank at the Global Investment Conference. London, 26 July 2012. The whole sentence was: 'Within our mandate, the ECB is ready to do whatever it takes to preserve the euro. And believe me, it will be enough.'

announced the following week, on 2 August 2012, and its technical details were spelled out in a press release on 6 September 2012.[15] The way in which the announcement of the OMT programme was linked with the concurrent announcement of the Banking Union was discussed in the previous chapter,[16] but we will return to it later in this chapter.

According to the 6 September 2012 press release, through the OMT programme the ECB could purchase bonds issued by Eurozone Member States from the secondary markets without limits, although subject to certain conditions. Thus, the OMT programme was also an unconventional monetary policy instrument. Unlike the earlier SMP, the OMT programme applied only to a select number of Member States: target states had to be under a macroeconomic adjustment programme and had to have received financial assistance from the ESM. Thus, intervention through the OMT programme had a residual character: 'the ECB would intervene only if that proved necessary, after the Eurozone governments had collectively decided to commit their own funds' through the ESM.[17]

The reconstruction of the birth of the OMT programme is rather brief for two reasons. First, because the ECB did not actually use the OMT programme as its mere announcement achieved the desired market reaction.[18] Thus, its use did not create additional political tension or legal hurdles. Second, and more importantly, because the political process leading up to the adoption of the OMT programme was rather straightforward.[19] This probably stems from the fact that it was not formally speaking a political decision but rather a technocratic decision by an institution that is by its very nature supposed to be insulated from political influence.[20] Although the ECB's decision to establish the OMT programme was linked to the political decision to establish

---

[15] 'Technical features of Outright Monetary Transactions', ECB Press Release. Frankfurt am Main, 6 September 2012.

[16] See Chapter 4.2.1.

[17] T. Tridimas and N. Xanthoulis, 'A Legal Analysis of the Gauweiler Case: Between Monetary Policy and Constitutional Conflict' (2016) *Maastricht Journal of European and Comparative Law* 23(1), 17–39, p. 19.

[18] See the analysis in European Central Bank Monthly Bulletin from September 2013 https://www.ecb.europa.eu/pub/pdf/mobu/mb201309en.pdf (accessed 1 September 2020).

[19] This is not to say that there would not have been economic or political imperatives affecting at the background. On these, see V. Borger, *The Currency of Solidarity: Constitutional Transformation during the Euro Crisis* (Cambridge University Press 2020), Chapter 6.

[20] It was of course political in the sense that it aimed to safeguard the euro 'whatever it takes', whether this meant stretching the limits of the ECB's legal mandate or not and whether the Member States protested against it or not.

the Banking Union, the ECB was free to make its decision without similar political hurdles as was the case regarding the Euro-Summit decision on the Banking Union.[21] This does not, however, mean that it would have been an easy decision. Indeed, contestation within the ECB against such a policy stance had taken place already during the uptake of the SMP. In September 2011 the German representative of the ECB's Executive Board resigned as a protest.[22]

5.2.2 The OMT Programme Before Courts

It seems that there were only two attempts to legally challenge the OMT programme. The first, which has received little attention in the literature, was an action for annulment lodged by a group of politically active German individuals. The General Court found the actions inadmissible and the CJEU upheld this decision upon appeal.[23]

Similarly as with the Banking Union, the legality of the OMT programme was also challenged before the German Federal Constitutional Court (*Bundesverfassungsgericht*), and subsequently before the CJEU due to a preliminary referral.[24] Out of the different cases relating to the crisis response mechanisms, the *Gauweiler saga*,[25] spurred by the OMT programme, is perhaps the most interesting and significant. However, it has not been any more influential in practice than the cases concerning the Fiscal Compact and the ESM as the ECB was not blocked from adopting the OMT programme nor was it declared *ultra vires* by either court. Furthermore, the outcome of the *Gauweiler* litigation has not prevented the ECB from adopting other bond purchasing programmes later.

---

[21]   See Euro Area Summit Statement. Brussels, 29 June 2012. See Chapter 4.2.1.
[22]   'Jürgen Stark resigns from his position', ECB Press Release, 9 September 2011, https://www.ecb.europa.eu/press/pr/date/2011/html/pr110909.en.htmlhttp://www.bbc.com/news/business-14858155 (accessed 1 September 2020).
[23]   See T-492/12 *von Storch and Others v ECB* EU:T:2013:702; C-64/14 P, *Sven A. von Storch v European Central Bank* EU:C:2015:300.
[24]   No such national cases were reported in U. Neergaard, C. Jacqueson and J. Hartig Danielsen (eds), *The Economic and Monetary Union: Constitutional and Institutional Aspects of the Economic Governance within the EU. The XXVI FIDE Congress in Copenhagen, 2014* (DJOF Publishing 2014); G. Bándi, P. Darák, A. Halustyik and P. L. Láncos (eds), *European Banking Union. Congress Proceedings Vol. 1. The XXVII FIDE Congress in Budapest, 2016* (Wolters Kluwer 2016); the EUI project 'Constitutional Change through Euro Crisis Law', http://eurocrisislaw.eui.eu/ (accessed 1 September 2020).
[25]   See 2 BvR 2728/13, 14 January 2014 (*OMT reference*); C-62/14 *Gauweiler* EU: C:2015:400; 2 BvR 2728/13, 21 June 2016 (*OMT final judgment*).

Before addressing the *Gauweiler saga*, a brief discussion on the actions lodged against the OMT programme's predecessor, the SMP, is in place. Analysing the German Federal Constitutional Court's decision on the SMP is essential due to the similarities between the two programmes.

5.2.2.1   Prelude: the *Euro rescue package* case

On 7 September 2011, the German Federal Constitutional Court delivered its ruling in the *Euro rescue package* case.[26] While the case primarily concerned the compatibility of the Greek rescue package with the German constitution and the adoption of the EFSF, it also addressed the validity of the SMP. The complaints made against these measures were based on the argument that the said measures violate the constitutional principle of democracy (the right to vote, Art. 38 German constitution) since they constrict the budgetary autonomy of the German parliament. Ruling against the complainants, the German court spelled out its stance on this question in the following manner. First, all large-scale financial assistance programmes have to be approved by the parliament, or the parliament needs to be involved even if the decision is taken by the government. Second, Germany's commitments to such rescue mechanisms cannot be open-ended; there needs to be an upper limit to what the government or parliament can oblige Germany to commit. The court did not, however, specify this limit.

The ECB adopted the SMP in order to avoid a similar market crisis as the one that took place in 2008–2009. It hoped that buying crisis states' bonds would reintroduce confidence on the financial markets. But since the ECB could only operate on the secondary markets, it persuaded the Member States to establish the EFSF for giving direct support to these states.[27] Thus, the SMP fits into the *Euro rescue package* case through its link with the EFSF. The legal concern centred on whether the SMP breaches the prohibition on monetary financing of Article 123 TFEU. While the German government argued that there is no such breach, the Federal Constitutional Court did not directly address this point in its ruling. The court found the claim related to the ECB's decision to buy government bonds (through the SMP) inadmissible, because it was not based on qualified subject matters of constitutional complaints. More specifically, the ECB's decision was not considered a sovereign act of German state authority and thus could not be challenged before the court on the basis of the German constitution.[28] Yet, although the German court dismissed a large

---

[26]   2 BvR 987/10, 7 September 2011 (*Euro rescue package*). See Chapter 3.2.1.

[27]   See C. Ohler, 'The European Stability Mechanism: The Long Road to Financial Stability in the Euro Area' (2011) *German Yearbook of International Law* 54, 47–74, pp. 48–9.

[28]   2 BvR 987/10, 7 September 2011 (*Euro rescue package*), para. 116.

part of the complaints in the proceedings, it still managed to articulate the above-mentioned criteria in its judgment.

After this judgment, it was not surprising that the legality of the OMT programme was also challenged before the German Federal Constitutional Court. However, what came as a surprise was that the German court decided to ask the CJEU for a preliminary ruling – something that the German court had never done previously.[29]

5.2.2.2 The decision to refer the case to the CJEU

The OMT programme ended up before the German Federal Constitutional Court for essentially the same reasons as all the other crisis response mechanisms. The tone behind the complaints was why should Germany pay for the reckless spending of other Eurozone Member States.[30] The claimants argued that the OMT breached both EU law and the German constitution. Due to the nature of the German constitution and the Federal Constitutional Court's doctrine, assessing the first necessarily entails an analysis of the second. While in its previous cases concerning European integration, the German court had refrained from making a preliminary reference to Luxembourg, surprisingly, this time it decided otherwise.

This immediately raised much speculation, since the Federal Constitutional Court could have dismissed the case as inadmissible,[31] as it did with the SMP, or it could have ruled on the case without requesting a preliminary ruling from the CJEU. If opting for the latter alternative, the German could have taken three actions. First, it could have pointed out some of the legal concerns that the OMT programme gives rise to from the perspective of both EU law and the German constitution. Following this it could have strongly criticised the programme but still find it to fall within the ECB's mandate. Finally, it could have tried to formulate the outer limits of the ECB's competences, with the intent of thus possibly affecting future actions by the ECB.

Interest in the Federal Constitutional Court's decision to admit the case in the first place stemmed from various reasons. This was even more so the case in regard to its decision to request a preliminary ruling. The first reason were

---

[29]   2 BvR 2728/13, 14 January 2014 (*OMT reference*). See I. Pernice, 'A Difficult Partnership Between Courts: The First Preliminary Reference by the German Federal Constitutional Court to the CJEU' (2014) *Maastricht Journal of European and Comparative Law* 21(1), 3–13.

[30]   See S. Dahan, O. Fuchs and M.-L. Layus, 'Whatever It Takes? Regarding the OMT Ruling of the German Federal Constitutional Court' (2015) *Journal of International Economic Law* 18(1), 137–51, p. 138.

[31]   See J. Snell, 'Gauweiler: Some Institutional Aspects' (2015) *European Law Review* 40(2), 133–4.

the possible immediate consequences the case could have for the survival of the euro if either the CJEU or the German court declared the OMT programme as *ultra vires*. The second reason was that the German court had already addressed the delineation of competences between monetary and economic policies within the EMU as well as the prohibition on monetary financing of Article 123 TFEU in its previous judgments.[32] The CJEU too had addressed these issues in its recent ruling in *Pringle*.[33] Nevertheless, the OMT provided a possibility for both courts to reconsider these issues. The third reason was the way in which the German court in practice executed its departure from its previous bark-but-no-bite approach: it spelled out the conditions that it wanted the CJEU to establish for the legality of the OMT, or otherwise it might still deem it *ultra vires* from the perspective of the German constitution. In other words, in its request the German court laid out the conditions for what type of an answer it would accept from the CJEU.[34]

From a practical viewpoint there seems to be one prominent reason for why the OMT programme ended up under review before the Federal Constitutional Court. The amount of purchases that the ECB could make through the OMT programme is unlimited. As the Member States are ultimately responsible for the liabilities of the ECB, if the target states of OMT purchases were to default on their government debt, the ECB would have to bear the losses. Since the Member States are liable for the ECB, they would ultimately end up footing the bill. The amount of these liabilities could be so vast that they would in essence curtail the budgetary sovereignty of the Member States responsible for them, since paying all of these would severely limit their budgetary choices elsewhere.

The German Federal Constitutional Court's doctrine regarding the principle of democracy and its different standards of judicial review to protect it will not be addressed here.[35] Suffice to say that the above-mentioned scenario was dressed in legal form in Germany with reference to the right to vote (the principle of democracy) and that use of state authority must stem from the people. If the state were to contract itself into an unknown and very large amount of possible liabilities, then these principles might be endangered since future parliaments would not have the option to conduct a budgetary policy of

---

[32]   See 2 BvR 987/10, 7 September 2011 (*Euro rescue package*); 2 BvE 8/11, 28 February 2012 (*Government guarantees*); 2 BvE 4/11, 19 June 2012 (*ESM and Euro Plus Pact*); 2 BvR 1390/12, 12 September 2012 (*ESM interim ruling*).

[33]   See C-370/12 *Pringle* EU:C:2012:756.

[34]   See Dahan, Fuchs and Layus (n 30), pp. 138–9.

[35]   The background of the preliminary reference has been assessed thoroughly in 'The OMT Decision of the German Federal Constitutional Court' (2014) *German Law Journal* [special issue] 15(2), 107–382.

their liking. In the words of the German court itself, in this case 'the German *Bundestag* would not remain the "master of its decisions" and could no longer exercise its budgetary autonomy under its own responsibility'.[36]

These issues translate into EU law in the following manner. First, is the OMT programme compatible with the strict monetary policy mandate of the ECB or is it instead an economic policy measure, and thus outside the scope of the ECB's competences? Second, is the OMT programme compatible with the prohibition of monetary financing found in Article 123 TFEU? Above has already been mentioned how the German court instructed the CJEU in its preliminary reference on how to interpret the ECB's decision on the OMT programme. The German court did this by attaching nine fears to the two questions.

The first question contained four such interpretive guidance points. Does the OMT programme breach the ECB's strict monetary policy mandate because: (i) its use is linked to the ESM, in that a Member State can only be subject to an OMT operation if it has received assistance from the ESM and is thus subject to the 'strict conditionality' of such aid (conditionality); (ii) the OMT programme can be used selectively towards a certain Member State, whereas the ECB's standard monetary policy measure (adjustment of interest rates) applies to all euro area Member States equally (selectivity); (iii) through the OMT programme the ECB will purchase government bonds of Member States in addition to assistance from the ESM, which is an economic policy measure (parallelism); and (iv) the OMT programme might undermine the terms and conditions of assistance from the ESM (bypassing)?[37]

The second question contained five such concerns. Does the OMT programme breach the prohibition on monetary financing of Article 123 TFEU because: (i) the OMT programme does not contain quantitative limits for the purchase of government bonds (volume); (ii) there is no specified time lag between the emission of government bonds on the primary markets and when they can be acquired by the ECB through the OMT programme (market pricing); (iii) the OMT programme allows that all purchased government bonds may be held to maturity (interference with market logic); (iv) the OMT programme contains no specific requirements for the credit rating of the government bonds that are to be purchased (default risk); and (v) the OMT programme contains equal treatment of the ECB and private bondholders (debt cut)?[38]

---

[36] 2 BvR 2728/13, 14 January 2014 (*OMT reference*), para. 102.
[37] See ibid., paras 70–83.
[38] See ibid., paras 84–100.

Due to these fears, the German Federal Constitutional Court was of the opinion that the OMT programme breached both the ECB's strict monetary policy mandate and the prohibition on monetary financing.[39] Notwithstanding, the German court submitted a referral to the CJEU. By doing this it seemed to acknowledge the CJEU's role as the interpreter of EU law. However, at the same time the German court seemed to think that only its own interpretation of the OMT programme is correct.[40] Lastly, the German court indicated that it might declare the OMT programme as *ultra vires* on the basis of the German constitution despite the answer provided by the CJEU.[41]

As Hinarejos has pointed out, the Federal Constitutional Court's attitude in *Gauweiler* signals a change both in relation to its previous case law on the other crisis response measures and also the doctrine it had created during the past decades on the relationships between EU law and the German legal order. While earlier it had always found that the EU act in question conforms to the German constitution 'so long as…', in this instance it turned the starting point around by effectively presuming that the OMT programme is *ultra vires*, unless proved otherwise.[42] In other words, prima facie the OMT programme is contrary to EU law and the German constitution, but it can be found to conform with them as long as the specified conditions are met.

5.2.2.3   The CJEU's judgment

Because the German Federal Constitutional Court's referral was worded in such a manner,[43] the CJEU had to first assess whether the referral was truly a referral in the meaning of Article 267 TFEU.[44] By reserving itself the right to possibly decline to accept the ruling given by the CJEU, the German court was not acting according to what is expected of national courts under Article 267 TFEU and the CJEU's doctrine on the nature of the preliminary ruling procedure. Notwithstanding, the CJEU decided to admit the case even though it was worded in an unorthodox manner.

Furthermore, whilst considering whether to admit the referral, the CJEU had to also consider the nature of the case pending before the German Federal Constitutional Court.[45] The Italian government argued in its intervention that the main proceedings are contrived and artificial because there is no legal right

---

[39]   See ibid., para. 55.
[40]   See ibid., para. 100.
[41]   See ibid., paras 102–103.
[42]   A. Hinarejos, *The Euro Area Crisis in Constitutional Perspective* (Oxford University Press 2015), pp. 149–50.
[43]   2 BvR 2728/13, 14 January 2014 (*OMT reference*), paras 99–100.
[44]   C-62/14 *Gauweiler* EU:C:2015:400, paras 11–17.
[45]   Ibid., paras 18–31.

of the applicants that would already at this point be violated, and furthermore, that the questions submitted to the CJEU are therefore abstract and hypothetical. The CJEU rebutted this by essentially saying that it is for the referring court to decide, on the basis of national law, whether a preliminary ruling is necessary in order to adjudicate on the case before it. The admissibility of a case before the national court is for the national court decided, also on the basis of national law. The crucial point of the CJEU's judgment regarding the main argument of this study comes at this part of the judgment: by stating that 'since under German law preventive legal protection may be granted in such a situation if certain conditions are met',[46] and thus accepting the referral, the CJEU acknowledged how differences in national legal orders affect the interaction between national courts and the CJEU. In practice, how the broad jurisdiction of the German Federal Constitutional Court made this case possible.[47]

An interim conclusion is at place here: the CJEU did not allow to challenge the OMT programme under the legal framework provided by EU law,[48] but it did allow to challenge it through the legal framework provided by German law. This was despite the fact that the dispute in the main proceedings was abstract and hypothetical, and only made possible by the peculiar conceptualisation of the principle of democracy enshrined in the German constitution and how the Federal Constitutional Court is to protect it. It needs to be restated at this point that the OMT programme was not challenged before any other national court, as the reconstruction pointed out. In terms of the inequality thesis, then, it seems that citizens from other Member States did not have an equal possibility to challenge the legality of the OMT programme before the CJEU.

Having settled the admissibility issue, the CJEU then turned to the substantive issue at stake. Here, the CJEU did not have to wander into the unknown, since it could rely heavily on its earlier argumentation in *Pringle*.[49] In practice, the current case concerned evaluating the nature of the OMT programme as announced in the ECB's press release of 6 September 2012. Although the CJEU did not address the two substantive issues as specifically and directly as the Federal Constitutional Court had formulated them in its preliminary reference (the nine fears), it did succeed in giving a straight answer on both issues.

The first substantive question was as follows: Does the OMT programme exceed the ECB's strict monetary policy mandate? In other words, is the OMT programme a monetary or economic policy measure. The CJEU started its answer by a teleological interpretation of the Treaties; a method of interpreta-

---

[46]   Ibid., para. 27.
[47]   See Tuominen (n 4), pp. 189–90.
[48]   See T-492/12 *von Storch and Others v ECB* EU:T:2013:702; C-64/14 P, *Sven A. von Storch v European Central Bank* EU:C:2015:300.
[49]   C-370/12 *Pringle* EU:C:2012:756.

tion very commonly used by the CJEU.[50] According to Article 127 TFEU, the ECB's primary objective is to 'maintain price stability' and to 'to define and implement the monetary policy of the Union'. While the content of monetary policy has not been explicitly defined in the Treaties, the aims of monetary policy and the means that the ECB has at its disposal in pursuing those aims are spelled out in Articles 127–133 TFEU. Therefore, in order to determine whether a measure falls under the ECB's monetary policy mandate, the aims of the said measure and the actions through which the measure is put into practice have to be analysed. According to the CJEU, the ECB's primary objective of maintaining price stability can be read to include the securing of the functioning of the monetary policy transmission mechanism, which the OMT programme is specifically aimed at. The 'functioning of the monetary policy transmission mechanism' simply means, that the ECB's monetary policy measures have an effect on the markets. If this transmission mechanism is defunct, the ECB cannot take care of its monetary policy duties and safeguard the singleness of this monetary policy. Singleness of the monetary policy is one of the aims or preconditions of a functioning monetary policy according to Article 119(2) TFEU.[51]

Having defined the content of monetary policy in this manner, the CJEU could then assess the delineation between monetary and economic policy. Here, the CJEU also resorted to teleology by stating that a monetary policy measure does not turn into an economic policy measure only because it would also affect the latter policy domain; in this case supporting the stability of the Eurozone. Instead, relevance must be given to the primary objective of the said measure, which in this case fell under monetary policy.[52] The CJEU did not find the requirement for a link between the OMT programme and the ESM – that the state towards which an OMT procedure is targeted must adhere to the strict conditionality of ESM assistance – to mean that the OMT programme would constitute an economic policy measure. Besides, the ECB's secondary task is to support the general economic policies in the Union as spelled out in Article 127(1) TFEU.[53]

Having established that the OMT programme falls within the ECB's monetary policy mandate, the CJEU then had to assess whether the OMT programme is proportionate. The principle of proportionality requires that acts of the EU institutions are appropriate for attaining the legitimate objectives

---

[50] See K. Lenaerts and J. A. Gutiérrez-Fons, 'To Say What the Law of the EU Is: Methods of Interpretation and the European Court of Justice' (2014) *The Columbia Journal of European Law* 20(2), 3–61, pp. 31–7.

[51] C-62/14 *Gauweiler* EU:C:2015:400, paras 34–50.

[52] Ibid., paras 51–52.

[53] Ibid., paras 57–59.

pursued by the legislation at issue and do not go beyond what is necessary in order to achieve those objectives (Art. 5(4) TEU). While the CJEU acknowledged that the ECB must be given broad discretion when making 'choices of a technical nature and to undertake forecasts and complex assessments',[54] it also noted that the ECB has to still comply with some procedural guarantees. These include the obligation 'to examine carefully and impartially all the relevant elements of the situation in question and to give an adequate statement of the reasons for its decisions'.[55]

In this case, these criteria are found in the ECB's press release on the OMT programme. In assessing these conditions the CJEU relied on the argumentation presented by the ECB itself. Although acknowledging that one could easily disagree with the reasoning of the ECB, the CJEU concluded the following:

> In that regard, the fact, mentioned by the referring court, that that reasoned analysis has been subject to challenge does not, in itself, suffice to call that conclusion into question, since, given that questions of monetary policy are usually of a controversial nature and in view of the ESCB's broad discretion, nothing more can be required of the ESCB apart from that it use its economic expertise and the necessary technical means at its disposal to carry out that analysis with all care and accuracy.[56]

The CJEU's conclusion on this first part of the proportionality analysis was that the ECB's decision on the OMT was not vitiated by a manifest error of assessment, and hence the OMT programme is appropriate for the purpose of contributing to the ECB's objectives and, therefore, to maintaining price stability.

The second leg of the proportionality analysis concerned whether the OMT programme goes manifestly beyond what is necessary to achieve the objective of maintaining price stability. Noting that there are several limitations to the use of the programme – although no quantitative limit per se – and that it has not even been used after its announcement, the CJEU found that it does not breach the limits of necessity when trying to achieve the objective of maintaining price stability. As a direct reply to the Federal Constitutional Court's concerns on the selectivity of the programme, the CJEU stated that selectivity is a key element of the programme as it aims to restore the functioning of the ECB's monetary policy transmission mechanism, which is not working as a result of the particular situation of government bonds issued by the crisis

---

[54]   Ibid., para. 68.
[55]   Ibid., para. 69.
[56]   Ibid., para. 75.

states.[57] The proportionality analysis conducted by the CJEU has been criticised in the literature for failing to tackle all of the three stages that usually are part of a proportionality analysis.[58]

Answering the second substantive issue was a bit trickier. The question was: Does the OMT programme violate the prohibition of central bank financing as laid out in Article 123 TFEU? According to Article 123 TFEU, the ECB is prohibited from directly purchasing 'debt instruments' from Member States as well as granting them 'overdraft facilities or any other type of credit facility'. One easily gets the impression that the OTM programme is being deliberately used to circumvent the prohibition of Article 123 TFEU, because the programme is supposed to be used to purchase government bonds from the secondary markets as opposed to purchasing them directly from the states. Such an interpretation is backed up by how the President of the ECB conceived the role of the OMT: 'This will ultimately lead to greater overall stability. The benefits of this do not accrue only to countries in difficulty. They accrue to the euro area as a whole.'[59] Pursuing such stability seems to go further than the ECB's strict monetary policy mandate. Yet, Article 18(1) ESCB Statute specifically grants the ECB the power to conduct secondary market operations to achieve its objectives. Therefore, the interpretive question is as follows: To what extent can the competences based on Article 18(1) ESCB Statute be used before they breach the prohibition of Article 123 TFEU?[60]

When conducting this analysis the CJEU again started with a teleological interpretation of Article 123 TFEU.[61] Citing the preparatory works of the Maastricht Treaty, the CJEU stated that 'the aim of Article 123 TFEU is to encourage the Member States to follow a sound budgetary policy, not allowing monetary financing of public deficits or privileged access by public authorities to the financial markets to lead to excessively high levels of debt or excessive

---

[57] Ibid., paras 81–92.

[58] See T. Tuominen, 'The "Financial Stability of the Euro Area as a Whole": Between Jurisdiction and Veridiction' (2019) *No Foundations: An Interdisciplinary Journal of Law and Justice* 17, 161–82, pp. 171–5.

[59] See 'Building the bridge to a stable European economy', Speech by Mario Draghi, President of the ECB, at the annual event 'Day of the German Industries' organised by the Federation of German Industries. Berlin, 25 September 2012.

[60] C-62/14 *Gauweiler* EU:C:2015:400, paras 93–97.

[61] Cf. F. Fabbrini, *Economic Governance in Europe: Comparative Paradoxes and Constitutional Challenges* (Oxford University Press 2016), p. 96, who calls this a 'historically-informed interpretation of the treaties'. On the use of such preparatory materials by the CJEU, see S. Miettinen and M. Kettunen, 'Travaux to the EU Treaties: Preparatory Work as Source of EU Law' (2015) *Cambridge Yearbook of European Legal Studies* 17(1), 145–67.

Member State deficits'.[62] Thus, the crucial point is whether the OMT programme lessens the Member States' impetus for following sound budgetary policy.[63] In assessing this, the CJEU accepted the ECB's arguments on how it will use the programme and to what effect. According to the ECB, the prohibition of central bank financing is not breached as long as the programme is used in a manner that guarantees the free formation of government bond prices at the markets. In practice, this means that the primary markets cannot form an assumption that the ECB will buy government bonds from private undertakings after they have first acquired these bonds from the states themselves.[64]

The CJEU's above-mentioned use of teleological interpretation is open to criticism: What are the CJEU's aims with this interpretation? It aims to provide a broad understanding of the monetary policy mandate of the ECB and the economic policy competences of the EU. But the OMT programme could have also been interpreted in light of another principle found in the EU Treaties: the principle of conferral (Art. 3(6) TEU).[65] According to this principle the Union shall pursue its objectives only on the basis of those competences that are conferred to it by the Member States. A teleological interpretation based on Article 3(6) TEU would have likely found the actions of the ECB to breach its monetary policy mandate as well as Articles 123 and 125 TFEU.

The edifice of the CJEU's ruling can be summarised with the following points. The decisions and acts taken by the ECB are subject to judicial review by the CJEU. The OMT programme is a monetary policy measure and thus within the competence of the ECB. Furthermore, the programme conforms with the principle of proportionality. The OMT programme does not infringe the prohibition on monetary financing. Thus – unlike what the Federal Constitutional Court was asking for and what Advocate General Cruz Villalón acceded to in his opinion[66] – the CJEU did not set any further limitations on the use of the OMT programme.

---

[62]   C-62/14 *Gauweiler* EU:C:2015:400, para. 100.
[63]   Ibid., paras 98–102.
[64]   Ibid., paras 103–122.
[65]   On the teleological interpretation of the principle of conferral, see R. Schütze, *European Constitutional Law* (Cambridge University Press 2012), pp. 152–7. Borger has argued that the CJEU should have based its interpretation on Article 18(1) ESCB Statute. See Borger (n 19), p. 336.
[66]   See Opinion of Advocate General Cruz Villalón delivered on 14 January 2015, C-62/14 *Gauweiler* EU:C:2015:7, paras 151, 165–168, and 199.

5.2.2.4   The final judgment in the main proceedings

The German Federal Constitutional Court delivered its final ruling in the main proceedings on 21 June 2016.[67] The German court found as inadmissible the constitutional complaints that challenged directly the action of the ECB but assessed the challenges brought against German state organs (the government and the parliament). The German court deemed these complaints as unfounded.

The Federal Constitutional Court began by first spelling out the framework within which it functions.[68] This framework includes the following: Given that the German constitution allows to transfer sovereign powers to the European Union (Art. 23 German constitution), it also allows the precedence of application of EU law. When the German legislature decides on matters pertaining to European integration, it can exempt EU and national bodies from the German constitution's guarantees (referring to the principle of democracy). However, the precedence of EU law only extends as far as the German constitutions permits the transfer of sovereign powers. Therefore, the principle of constitutional identity (Art. 79 German constitution) limits the extent to which sovereign powers can be transferred to the EU. The fundamental elements of the principles of democracy (Art. 20 German constitution) are part of the constitutional identity enshrined in the German constitution, which are protected by its eternity clause (Art. 79 German constitution). Therefore, state authority requires legitimation by the people through elections, which cannot be depleted by transferring powers and tasks to the EU. Thus, the principle of sovereignty of the people (Art. 20 German constitution) is violated if the EU exercises public authority that lacks adequate democratic legitimacy by the German constitution (the integration agenda laid down in the Act of Approval).

Furthermore, the German constitution contains the German citizens' right to vote (Art. 38 German constitution) and the principle that all state authority must be derived from the people (Art. 20 German constitution). If the citizens are not themselves able to ensure the integrity of these rights then the constitutional organs of the German state have a responsibility to ensure their protection. Therefore, the German state organs have to make sure that as European integration is deepened, the citizens' right to vote is not diminished due to a decrease in their influence, which would mean a restriction on the voters' right to democracy. In principle, this means that German state organs must actively work towards the EU respecting the German integration agenda (Art. 23 German constitution). Furthermore, this means that the EU is not to exceed its competences in a manifest and structurally relevant manner. These actions can contain both political and legal means to revoke an EU act that infringes

---

[67]   2 BvR 2728/13, 21 June 2016 (*OMT final judgment*).
[68]   Ibid., paras 80–84.

the German constitution or that in some other way restricts the measure's effects in Germany.

The German government or parliament (*Bundestag*) had not taken action against the OMT programme. In its judgment, the Federal Constitutional Court listed conditions that have to be met in order for the inaction of these state organs not to violate the citizens' (complainants') rights under Article 38.1 (the right to vote) as well as Article 20.1–2 (the principle of democracy and that authority stems from the people) read in conjunction with Article 79.3 (eternity clause) of the German constitution. The fulfilment of these conditions would also mean that the parliament's rights and obligations with regard to European integration, including its overall budgetary responsibility, are not impaired.[69]

The German Federal Constitutional Court based its review of the OMT programme on the CJEU's findings and acknowledged that the CJEU's findings are within its mandate as stipulated in Article 19(1) TEU.[70] However, the German court raised the following objections towards the CJEU's judgment. To begin with, the CJEU based its conclusion that the OMT programme is a monetary policy measure on a rather light review; the CJEU did not engage directly with all the nine fears that the German court had spelled out in its referral.[71] Although the CJEU acknowledged that economic and monetary policy overlap, it relied solely on the arguments given by the ECB itself.[72] Furthermore, the CJEU did not address the issue that granting considerable independence to the ECB, which leads to a reduction in its democratic legitimation, should be counterbalanced with a restrictive interpretation of its mandate and subjecting it to strict judicial review. On this basis, the principles of democracy and sovereignty of the people may be sacrificed and come into conflict with the constitutional identity of the Member States (at least in Germany), which the EU is supposed to respect under Article 4(2) TEU.[73]

Despite these concerns the Federal Constitutional Court concluded that the OMT programme, if interpreted in the way the CJEU did, does not 'manifestly' exceed the ECB's competences. Although the CJEU did not question the objectives of the OMT programme and did not perform an overall evaluation, this is acceptable because the CJEU's decision in essence amounts to a restrictive interpretation of the OMT programme, which the German court held possible in its referral. The restrictions that the CJEU posited for the implementation of the OMT programme, along with its procedural grounds

69   Ibid., paras 174–220.
70   Ibid., paras 175–180.
71   Ibid., para. 182.
72   Ibid., paras 183–186.
73   Ibid., paras 187–189.

that enable it to limit the ECB's competences through judicial review based on proportionality, are sufficient enough to limit the unlimited potential of the OMT programme. Although following this the OMT programme can still be seen as encroaching on the economic competences of the Member States, it appears acceptable to assume that 'the OMT Programme is at least predominantly of a monetary policy character'.[74]

If interpreted in accordance with the CJEU's judgment, the policy decision on the technical framework conditions of the OMT programme as well as its possible implementation do not manifestly violate the prohibition of monetary financing as found in Article 123 TFEU, although its possible implementation must fulfil the conditions referred to by the CJEU.[75] Thus, the OMT programme constitutes an *ultra vires* act if these conditions are not met, and in such a case the German central bank (*Bundesbank*) may not participate in the programme's implementation.[76]

Due to the above, the OMT programme did not represent a constitutionally relevant threat to the German parliament's right to decide on the budget and its overall budgetary responsibility. Thus, the German government or parliament were not required to act against the OMT programme.[77] Notwithstanding, the German government and parliament are under a duty to closely monitor the possible activation of the OMT programme.[78]

Overall, the outcome of the case seems to suggest, that the German Federal Constitutional Court accepted that the CJEU is the ultimate interpreter of EU law. The German court also showed a degree of deference towards the CJEU whilst exercising its *ultra vires* review, although simultaneously implying that the CJEU had exceeded its powers – although not 'manifestly' enough as per the German court's *Honeywell* doctrine.[79] The Federal Constitutional Court's ruling is perhaps more important when it comes to its own judicial review doctrine, whereas its direct relevance for the EU not as significant. This conclusion seems to be backed up by how the German court continued this debate in its *PSPP judgment*.[80]

---

[74]   Ibid., paras 190–196.
[75]   Ibid., paras 197–204, citing C-62/14 *Gauweiler* EU:C:2015:7 paras 106–118.
[76]   Ibid., paras 205–209.
[77]   Ibid., paras 210–219.
[78]   Ibid., para. 220.
[79]   See 2 BvR 2661/06 (*Honeywell*); C. Möllers, 'German Federal Constitutional Court: Constitutional Ultra Vires Review of European Acts Only Under Exceptional Circumstances; Decision of 6 July 2010, 2 BvR 2661/06, Honeywell' (2011) *European Constitutional Law Review* 7(1), 161–7.
[80]   See 2 BvR 859/15, 05 May 2020 (*PSPP judgment*).

5.3　THE TRIPARTITE CONTEXTUALITY OF ECONOMIC–POLITIC–LAW

In addition to the above events, which can be traced as being parts of the causal process affecting the formation of the OMT programme, there were also other underlying causes that might have affected the process and the end result. These are situated mostly in the realms of economics and politics but also partially in that of law. In contrast to the above-described events, the weight of these reasons is more difficult to assess, and thus they are of a more speculative manner. They are, however, important for the overall analysis, since they point to the interplay between economic, political and legal factors.

The link between the establishment of the OMT programme and the Banking Union is worth assessing. The vicious circle between banks and sovereigns necessitated the uptake of both mechanisms: private banks' weaknesses affect their host states, which necessitated adopting the Banking Union; Member States' weaknesses affect their banks, for which reason the OMT programme was needed.[81] These reasons and events are connected to the lender of last resort function, which Eurozone Member States have relinquished to the ECB.[82]

The vicious circle between banks and sovereigns in the Eurozone could be broken either through establishing a fiscal union or by establishing a banking union. Since political support was not found for the former, the latter option was chosen. In order to do this, the 29 June 2012 euro area summit statement contained two commitments: that bank supervision would be centralised to the ECB and the ESM would be allowed to recapitalise banks directly.[83] Although such a pledge was made in the euro area summit statement, major disagreements on direct ESM recapitalisation soon followed. This uncertainty did not, however, stop the ECB from acting, since in its view centralising bank supervision under its control was enough to break the vicious circle between banks and sovereigns. Therefore, it saw the risk of initiating the OMT programme as worth taking and announced it in the 6 September 2012 press release,[84] as was discussed above in the reconstruction. Later developments have shown that the ECB was correct in its assessment, since just the announcement of the OMT in itself had a massive positive market reaction.[85]

---

[81]　See N. Véron, *Europe's Radical Banking Union* (Bruegel 2015), pp. 14–18.

[82]　See D. Gros, 'On the Stability of Public Debt in a Monetary Union' (2012) *Journal of Common Market Studies* 50 (Supplement 2), 36–48, pp. 36–8.

[83]　See Euro Area Summit Statement. Brussels, 29 June 2012.

[84]　See 'Technical features of Outright Monetary Transactions', ECB Press Release. Frankfurt am Main, 6 September 2012.

[85]　See Véron (n 81), pp. 14–18.

5.4   WHAT DID THE OMT PROGRAMME CONSTITUTIONALISE?

While the first three case studies focused on initiatives taken by the Member States, either through international law or EU secondary law, the OMT programme as a crisis response mechanism is based on an act by an EU institution. Moreover, even the legal nature of that act – a press release – has been disputed. Furthermore, the whole mechanism was not used and has since then been replaced by other mechanisms.[86] Therefore, the legal significance of the OMT, or why it is interesting from a constitutional perspective, is not found in what it actually did but rather in the interpretations of the EU Treaties that were constitutionalised as a consequence of the *Gauweiler* litigation. These questions all pertain to the asymmetry of the EMU. To this end, the first sub-section will lay out the content of the OMT programme as well as the context within which it was initiated and on which its underlying logic is based (5.4.1). The second subsection will discuss the constitutional implications of OMT programme in light of the asymmetry of the EMU (5.4.2).

5.4.1   Content of the OMT Programme

5.4.1.1   ECB's press release
The objective of the OMT programme was to restore the functioning of the ECB's monetary policy transmission mechanism; that is, it intended to enable interest rates set by the ECB to affect how sovereign bond yields are formed on the markets. Previously, crisis states' interest rates had been high and remained unaffected by the ECB's standard monetary policy measures, while the fate of these states had become the target of market speculations: would some of these states default on their creditors or even end up exiting the Eurozone? In practice, this meant that the OMT programme was aimed at preventing possible negative scenarios that might have threatened price stability within the Eurozone. It was also argued by the applicants in the main proceedings in *Gauweiler* that the objective of the OMT programme 'was rather to "save the single currency" by making the ECB into a lender of last resort for the Member States, thereby redressing some of the design faults of monetary union'.[87]

The programme was established by a decision of the Governing Council of the ECB, and its core content was defined in the already mentioned press

---

[86]   See ECB, 'Asset purchase programmes', https://www.ecb.europa.eu/mopo/implement/omt/html/index.en.html (accessed 1 September 2020).

[87]   Opinion of Advocate General Cruz Villalón delivered on 14 January 2015, C-62/14 *Gauweiler* EU:C:2015:7, para. 137.

release.[88] Later on, during the proceedings in *Gauweiler*, the ECB provided further explanations and clarifications on some points relating to the possible use of the programme.[89]

Activation of the OMT programme would have required, in practice, that four criteria are met. The targeted state has to have first received financial assistance through the ESM and also followed the Memorandum of Understanding (MoU) that stipulates the conditions for ESM assistance. Following this, the state must have issued bonds on the primary markets since OMT purchases can only take place on the secondary markets. Finally, and most crucially, the ECB must have found that the market yields for the target state's bonds are higher than what could be assumed from various economic indicators concerning that state.

Thus, the crucial points with regards to how the OMT programme was to function are: (i) that the amount of purchases was not limited in advance to any specific quantity; and (ii) that while through the ESM bonds can be acquired directly from the target states, with the OMT programme they can only be acquired from the secondary markets.

5.4.1.2   Bundesbank's impression

What the OMT programme intended to do and why the ECB initiated it was explained above in the words of the ECB itself. There is, however, an alternative way of conceptualising the OMT programme's true nature – the one assumed by the German Federal Constitutional Court on the basis of 'the convincing expertise of the *Bundesbank*'.[90] Next, this version of the story will be explored.

The ECB adopted the OMT programme on the basis of false premises: market reactions, such as sovereign bond spreads, cannot be divided into rational and irrational. The fact that certain Member States needed to pay higher interest rates for refinancing their government debt was based on a genuine fear by the markets that these states would default on their creditors. This logic is fully in line with the rational of the no bail-out clause of Article 125 TFEU, which is meant to induce market discipline on to the Member States. Furthermore, the CJEU also assumed this view of Article 125 TFEU in *Pringle*.[91]

---

[88]   'Technical features of Outright Monetary Transactions', ECB Press Release. Frankfurt am Main, 6 September 2012.

[89]   In several passages, the CJEU mentions the explanations provided by the ECB without, however, clarifying their actual content. See C-62/14 *Gauweiler* EU:C:2015: 7, paras 72, 74, 105 and 106.

[90]   2 BvR 2728/13, 14 January 2014 (*OMT reference*), para. 71.

[91]   2 BvR 2728/13, 14 January 2014 (*OMT reference*), para. 71. See C-370/12 *Pringle* EU:C:2012:756, para. 135:

The ECB's standard monetary policy tools apply uniformly to the whole Eurozone, whereas the OMT programme is based on a targeted approach as it differentiates between individual Member States. Yet, the role of the markets is to take care of differentiation by producing different yield rates for different states. This is based on Article 127(1) TFEU, according to which the ECB shall act in accordance with the principle of an open market economy with free competition, favouring an efficient allocation of resources. On the one hand, OMT operations would skew the functioning of the markets by lowering the interest rates of the target states, and on the other hand, they would thus leave the government bonds of other Member States in a disadvantaged position.[92]

The ESM is an institution whose activities fall within the scope of economic policy, as has been established by the CJEU in *Pringle*.[93] In accordance with Article 136 TFEU, the granting of any financial assistance under the ESM is subject to strict conditionality. The terms of this conditionality are laid down in the MoU between the European Commission and the recipient state. OMT operations would only be directed towards Member States that have received financial assistance from the ESM and that are following the conditions specified in their respective MoU. If the target state of an OMT operation would not comply with the conditions in the MoU, the OMT operation would be terminated. This link between OMT purchases and the MoUs proves that OMT purchases are an economic policy measure. Furthermore, this also means that the OMT programme is essentially a similar financial assistance mechanism as the ESM, although its use is beyond any parliamentary legitimation and monitoring.[94]

The ESM has a host of different instruments under its belt which it can use to achieve its objective of 'safeguarding the financial stability of the euro area as a whole'. However, their use is subject to 'strict conditionality' (Art. 12(1) ESM Treaty). These include, inter alia, a secondary market support facility in which the ESM conducts secondary market operations in relation to the bonds of the object state (Art. 18(1) ESM Treaty). These operations are possible in case of 'exceptional financial market circumstances and risks to financial stability' (Art. 18(2) ESM Treaty). The use of the OMT programme, on the other hand, is not limited by similar conditions. Thus, the OMT programme would

---

The prohibition laid down in Article 125 TFEU ensures that the Member States remain subject to the logic of the market when they enter into debt, since that ought to prompt them to maintain budgetary discipline. Compliance with such discipline contributes at Union level to the attainment of a higher objective, namely maintaining the financial stability of the monetary union.

[92]   2 BvR 2728/13, 14 January 2014 (*OMT reference*), para. 73.
[93]   See C-370/12 *Pringle* EU:C:2012:756, para. 60
[94]   2 BvR 2728/13, 14 January 2014 (*OMT reference*), paras 74–78.

likely bypass the conditions and conditionality of the ESM. Consequently, it might also undermine the objectives of the ESM.[95]

Although the ECB 'shall support the general economic policies in the Union with a view to contributing to the achievement of the objectives of the Union' (Article 127(1) TFEU), the ways in which the OMT programme is intended to be used in conjunction with the ESM goes beyond a mere supporting role in economic policy. First, the volume of assistance granted through the ESM could be considerably broadened through parallel OMT purchases. Such actions by the ECB are not mere support. Second, according to Article 130 TFEU the ECB shall be independent in its actions, especially from the influence of other European Union institutions. Thus, when deciding on the use of the OMT programme, the ECB should not take into consideration the decisions of the Commission. If the first condition is accepted, then such independent decisions by the ECB are not merely supporting the Union's economic policy since the ECB would be conducting its own independent economic policy choices. Since there is no quantitative limitation for OMT purchases, they cannot be considered as merely supportive economic policy measures.[96]

While the above-mentioned issues concerned how the practical use of the OMT breaches the ECB's strict monetary policy mandate, the *Bundesbank* also presented several reasons for why the use of the OMT also breaches the prohibition on monetary financing of Article 123 TFEU.

Purchases through the OMT programme would have accepted the same treatment as private creditors that have purchased bonds issued by euro area Member States. Under Article 12(3) ESM Treaty, collective action clauses shall be included in all new euro area government securities. What this means is that debt cuts of such bonds are possible if the majority of creditors agree to them. Loans that do not have to be paid back can be seen to breach the prohibition on monetary financing as found in Article 123 TFEU.[97] Bonds purchased through the OMT programme would carry a high risk, because due to the nature of the programme it would specifically target states that have high bond yields. The possibility of a debt cut further enhances the risks associated with the use of the OMT programme. While the EU Treaties do not prohibit the ECB from taking risks neither do they contain an authorisation to take large and unnecessary risks.[98]

If a large amount of government bonds is permanently removed from the market, which would occur through OMT purchases, this would have

---

[95] Ibid., para. 79.
[96] Ibid., paras 80–83.
[97] Ibid., para. 88.
[98] Ibid., para. 89.

two effects: it would skew the functioning of the markets and the pricing of these bonds, and it would violate Article 123 TFEU as it would be a form of financing the target state's budget. Furthermore, holding government bonds until maturity delays the disclosure of losses by the ECB.[99] Purchasing a large amount of government bonds on the secondary markets immediately after their emission can also skew the proper formation of market pricing and this would thus be a circumvention of monetary financing. In other words, if the private banks that have bought bonds on the primary markets assume that they will be able to directly sell them to the ECB via the OMT programme on the secondary markets, they will be willing to pay more for them than they would otherwise.[100]

Even though the *Bundesbank* considered the monetary policy transmission mechanism of the ECB to be disrupted, this did not change its above analysis of the OMT programme breaching the ECB's strict monetary policy mandate or the prohibition on monetary financing. Although the OMT programme might support the functioning of the ECB's monetary policy transmission mechanism, it does not mean that the OMT programme itself is a monetary policy measure. Rather ironically, vice versa, as the CJEU concluded in *Pringle*,[101] the fact that the ESM also has effects on monetary policy does not mean that it is a monetary policy measure as such. Furthermore, in all debt crises the monetary policy mechanism of the central bank deteriorates due to the link between the sovereign and its banks. If the disruption of the ECB's monetary policy transmission mechanism would always allow for the ECB to purchase government bonds, the prohibition on monetary financing would be meaningless. Lastly, the ECB's premise that its monetary policy transmission mechanism is not functioning if government bond spreads are determined irrationally by the markets is false and leads to tampering with the free functioning of the markets. As such, the ECB's deciding on when price formation is irrational is a form of arbitrary market interference.[102]

5.4.1.3   ECB's view

It can be claimed that the CJEU averted addressing the majority of the issues raised by the German Federal Constitutional Court (on behalf of the *Bundesbank*). While this is true to some extent – the CJEU did not explicitly address all of the nine fears expressed by the German court – the CJEU did brush upon at least all of those aspects that are crucial from the viewpoint of

---

[99]   Ibid., paras 90–91.
[100] Ibid., paras 92–93.
[101] See C-370/12 *Pringle* EU:C:2012:756, para. 56.
[102] 2 BvR 2728/13, 14 January 2014 (*OMT reference*), paras 95–98.

a strictly literal reading of the EU Treaties. What follows is a short summary of the position of the CJEU, in the form influenced by the ECB's testimony.

When assessing the delimitation of monetary policy, the CJEU raised the following points. The nature of a programme is to be assessed on the basis of its aims, and the fact that it might also contribute to another policy area, namely economic policy, does not fundamentally alter its nature.[103] The CJEU did not see the OMT programme's selectivity as a problem since the EU Treaties do not specify that the ECB's financial market operations must be general and not directed towards specific states.[104] The link between the OMT programme and the ESM was deemed as indirect, and thus the CJEU did not see it as an issue even though the OMT programme might give a Member State a further incentive of following the conditionality prescribed to it as a condition for assistance from the ESM. Moreover, the argument was actually turned on its head when the CJEU stated that this link assures that the ECB's monetary policy measure will not work against the Member States' economic policy measures.[105] Again, based on its premise that the objective of the programme defines its policy categorisation, the CJEU held that although similar purchases by the ESM can be classified as economic policy, purchases through the OMT programme are nevertheless of a monetary policy nature due to their objective.[106]

When it came to the proportionality of the OMT programme, the CJEU first stated that since the ECB is to make choices of a technical nature and to undertake forecasts and complex assessments, it must be allowed in that context a broad discretion. Yet, to be in compliance with certain procedural guarantees the ECB must give an adequate statement of the reasons for its decisions, which can nevertheless be expressed in rather broad terms since it is to be assessed in light of the context of that decision.[107] Although the economic analysis conducted by the ECB of the market situation – that the bond yields of certain Member States were not rationally formed – can be disputed, the ECB's assessment was not vitiated by a manifest error and is thus proportionate.[108] In fact, according to the CJEU:

> given that questions of monetary policy are usually of a controversial nature and in view of the ESCB's broad discretion, nothing more can be required of the ESCB

---

[103] C-62/14 *Gauweiler* EU:C:2015:400, paras 51–52. Here the CJEU also cited C-370/12 *Pringle* EU:C:2012:756, para. 56.

[104] Ibid., para. 55.

[105] Ibid., paras 57–60.

[106] Ibid., paras 63–64, citing C-370/12 *Pringle* EU:C:2012:756, paras 56 and 60.

[107] Ibid., paras 68–70.

[108] Ibid., paras 72–74.

apart from that it use its economic expertise and the necessary technical means at its disposal to carry out that analysis with all care and accuracy.[109]

The second leg of the proportionality analysis, whether the OMT programme goes manifestly beyond what is necessary to achieve its objectives, was concluded by the CJEU with the finding that the criteria that the ECB has devised for its use seem to be restrictive enough since the OMT programme has never been used.[110] What came to the selectivity of the programme, the discretion given to the ECB in assessing the market situation also leads to the ECB having the possibility to use such a selective monetary policy instrument.[111]

Finally, as to the prohibition on monetary financing, the CJEU ruled that the explanations provided by the ECB have made it clear that the implementation of the OMT programme is subject to such conditions that its intervention on secondary markets does not have an effect equivalent to that of a direct purchase of government bonds on the primary market for the following reasons. First, the minimum period between the issuing of a security on the primary market and its purchase on the secondary markets and the total amount of OMT purchases will not be disclosed. Second, the fact that OMT purchases might, despite these safety measures, still have some effect on the primary and secondary markets is merely an inherent effect of the purchases and one that is not prohibited by the EU Treaties. Third, in any case, such effects are essential if the OMT programme is to be used effectively in the framework of monetary policy.[112]

The OMT programme does not implicitly transgress the prohibition on monetary financing by way of lessening the impetus for the target state to follow a sound budgetary policy. This is because OMT purchases will cease once their objective of reinstating the ECB's monetary policy transmission mechanism has been achieved, which means both that a Member State cannot rely on the ECB purchasing bonds on the secondary markets and the use of the OMT programme will not bring about the harmonisation of interest rates applied to government bonds. Consequently, Member States being targeted by an OMT operation would still need to conduct a budgetary policy that avoids deficits since they need to be able to seek financing from the public markets.[113] The OMT programme's impact is limited in that it can only buy bonds that a Member State has first successfully issued on the primary markets, and the ECB has the option of selling the bonds it has purchased at any time; these

---

[109] Ibid., para. 75.
[110] Ibid., para. 84.
[111] Ibid., para. 89.
[112] Ibid., paras 106–108.
[113] Ibid., paras 112–114.

bonds are not permanently withdrawn from the markets. Whether or not the ECB will hold the bonds until maturity depends on the market reactions, and such a possibility is not precluded by Article 18(1) ESCB Statute.[114] Finally, the link between OMT purchases and ESM conditionality means that Member States cannot rely on the OMT programme as a source of financing but have to continue with fiscal consolidation.[115]

By way of conclusion, the CJEU stated that the other features of the OMT programme, to which the Federal Constitutional Court drew attention to, but which the CJEU did not specifically assess, do not alter the conclusions drawn by the CJEU.[116] Here the CJEU effectively dismissed some of the German court's nine fears.

5.4.1.4 The middle ground

Reading the insights of political scientists leads to understanding that no political choice is 'necessary' as such; there are always other alternatives, although these may come with certain consequences. The policy trade-offs related to the EMU, as conceptualised through the different economic trilemmas, highlight this well.[117] Notwithstanding, it is submitted that announcing the OMT programme was if not necessary for the survival of the euro then at least conducive to it.[118] However, this does not invalidate or negate the relevant concerns raised by the German Federal Constitutional Court and the *Bundesbank*.

It seems that in this case the argumentation of both sides is correct, at least when seen from their own premises. The ECB was perhaps correct in establishing the programme and thus reducing the possibility of the break-up of the Eurozone. The views of the *Bundesbank*, and the sentiments expressed towards them by the German Court, are also true in that they convey how the ECB had to tread a difficult path in trying to come up with a mechanism to save the euro whilst being handicapped by the underlying asymmetry of the EMU. Since there is no common economic policy, and as such the ECB was only granted a strict monetary policy mandate, the prohibition on monetary financing and the no bail-out clause were intended to induce market discipline onto the Member States that share the euro as their common currency. Sentiments for saving the euro and thus accepting the reasoning put forth by the ECB are understandable, but at the same time the shortcomings of the current system

---

[114] Ibid., paras 116–118.
[115] Ibid., paras 120–121.
[116] Ibid., para. 122.
[117] See Chapter 1.2.3.
[118] For how an ECB insider argued why the OMT was necessary, see 'Outright Monetary Transactions, one year on', Speech by Benoît Cœuré, Member of the Executive Board of the ECB, at the conference (n 13).

and how its rescue has arguably circumvented the original intentions on which the EMU was established in Maastricht need to be acknowledged.

5.4.2   Constitutional Implications of the OMT Programme

5.4.2.1   Delineation between economic and monetary policy and the CJEU's predicament

The CJEU found, that although the OMT programme affects also the Member States' economic policies, it is still a monetary policy measure due to its primary aim. Although the CJEU's argumentation is logical in this regard, it contains some inherent flaws.

Without the linkage between the OMT programme and the ESM, OMT purchases would only help those banks that are big creditors to the crisis states. Were the ECB to buy government bonds from secondary markets without any conditions directed towards those governments (in addition to conditionality they also receive financial assistance through the ESM), it would only relive the position of large creditors since they would thus wash their hands of the possibly worthless bonds. By contrast, when usage of the OMT programme is linked to the structural changes preconditioned by the ESM and the possible primary market operations, the ECB is able to affect directly the budgets of the crisis states – that is, their economic policies. This shows that although the primary objectives of the OMT programme might lie in monetary policy, its principal effects fall under economic policy.[119] The CJEU's claim that such effects on economic policy are just incidental, or that they can be mitigated by the supportive role the ECB is to play on economic policy, cannot be shrugged off lightly.

This problem between objectives and effects also concerns the CJEU's argumentation regarding the prohibition on central bank financing. Article 123 TFEU contains a primary rule and an exception to that rule. According to Article 123 TFEU, the ECB is not allowed to purchase government bonds from the primary markets, that is, directly from the states. The exception to this primary rule is that such purchases are however possible on the secondary markets. The prohibition concerning primary markets and the exception for secondary markets have very different aims: where the first is supposed to prevent the ECB from supporting governments' budgets by bond purchases, the latter is there to make it possible for the ECB to conduct normal monetary policy operations and to ensure liquidity in the marketplace. Therefore, the OMT programme is problematic because even though it functions on the

---

[119]   Elsewhere I have called this the CJEU's 'indirect effects doctrine'. See Tuominen (n 58), pp. 169–71.

secondary markets its principal effects are seen at the primary markets. In this sense, it pursues the same objective as buying government bonds from the primary markets.

A further problem is that although purchases from secondary markets are on the face of it allowed under Article 123 TFEU, they should not be used to circumvent the no bail-out clause of Article 125 TFEU. The no bail-out clause shares the same objective as the primary rule of Article 123 TFEU, and as such they should both be interpreted in conjunction with each other. As Tuori and Tuori have explained: 'The telos of the exception made in Article 123(1) [TFEU] in favour of secondary-market purchases is to facilitate "normal" liquidity operations and not emergency measures amounting to the bailout of a Member State threatened by insolvency.'[120]

Direct financing by the ECB would violate the no bail-out clause since it is the Member States that are ultimately responsible for the commitments of the ECB. The CJEU's remark,[121] that as a central bank the ECB is obliged to take decisions which, like open market operations, inevitably expose it to a risk of losses totally ignores the real problem: decisions on the use of the ESM are taken by democratically accountable politicians, whereas decisions to activate the OMT programme are taken by the Governing Council of the ECB, which is comprised of the six ECB Executive Board members and the Governors of the 19 national central banks. In both cases the Member States are ultimately responsible in case of default by the aid receiving or bond releasing state, while only in the former case is the decision taken by a democratically accountable body.

Conversely, the CJEU's position on the legality of the OMT programme, notwithstanding the above interpretations of Articles 123 and 125 TFEU, could be justified by the 'two-order telos' argument that the CJEU applied in *Pringle.* This is essentially a re-reading of the CJEU's argumentation by Tuori and Tuori.[122] In *Pringle,* the CJEU thought that 'the financial stability of the euro area as a whole' was such a higher-order objective that it validated the ESM despite the no bail-out clause.[123] In *Gauweiler,* the CJEU did not refer to this higher-order objective, although the same pattern could have been used here. Still, the CJEU's logic was similar in both cases: in *Pringle* it was possible to breach the no bail-out clause as long as the financial assistance given to Member States was 'subject to strict conditionality';[124] whereas in *Gauweiler*

---

[120] See K. Tuori and K. Tuori, *The Eurozone Crisis: A Constitutional Analysis* (Cambridge University Press 2014), pp. 165–6.

[121] C-62/14 *Gauweiler* EU:C:2015:400, paras 123–126.

[122] See Tuori and Tuori (n 120), pp. 120–36.

[123] C-370/12 *Pringle* EU:C:2012:756, para. 136.

[124] Ibid., para. 111.

breaching the prohibition on central bank financing was possible as long as the use of the OMT programme does not interfere with the normal functioning of the bond markets and 'does not lessen the impetus of the Member States concerned to follow a sound budgetary policy'.[125] In other words, in both cases there seemed to be at play a higher-order objective working for the common good of the Eurozone, which allowed for, if not a *contra legem* interpretation of the no bail-out clause and the ECB's strict monetary policy mandate, at the very least a stretching of the limits of those provisions to accommodate for the crisis response measures aiming to purport this common good.

After this, it is still worth returning to the demarcation between economic and monetary policy and to take notice of the fact that while in *Pringle* it was the CJEU's 'predicament' to find that the ESM constituted economic policy,[126] in *Gauweiler* the CJEU had to establish whether the OMT programme was truly a monetary policy measure. In other words, if such a predicament existed in either or both of the cases, it is ironic how the CJEU had to argue towards opposite ends in these two cases. What is interesting is that in both cases the CJEU used a methodologically similar pattern of argumentation but reached opposite conclusions. The outcome and how it was reached by the CJEU in *Gauweiler* seems to support Borger's reading of the CJEU's predicament in *Pringle*: as with the ESM in *Pringle*, the stakes for invalidating the OMT programme in *Gauweiler* were politically just too high, and thus the CJEU had to assume the above criticised line of reasoning.

If the actions of the ECB are, at least arguably, violating its strict monetary policy mandate, and if, when conducting these actions, the ECB has had to take heed of the political process, as was expressed by the link between the OMT programme and the Banking Union, then the following questions seem to be worth asking. First, taking into consideration how the ECB's actions have effects on economic policy, be they intended or just coincidental, is the ECB's independence and counter-majoritarian position justifiable and legitimate? Second, taking into consideration how the ECB has had to conform its actions to the political reality surrounding it, what is left of its independence? These questions are worth addressing as the independence of the ECB is linked strongly to the asymmetry of the EMU, which is being eroded with the announcement of the OMT programme and the CJEU's ruling in *Gauweiler*.

---

[125] C-62/14 *Gauweiler* EU:C:2015:400, paras 99–108 and 121.
[126] See V. Borger, 'The ESM and the European Court's Predicament in Pringle' (2013) *German Law Journal* 14(1), 113–40.

5.4.2.2   The independence of the ECB

Many things can be meant by the independence of the ECB,[127] but perhaps the key definition is the one found in the EU Treaties. The independence of the ECB as a constitutional principle is based on the role the ECB has regarding monetary policy within the Eurozone: the EU has exclusive competence in monetary policy for the Member States whose currency is the euro (Art. 3(1) (c) TFEU), and it is the ECB's basic task to define and implement this monetary policy (Art. 127(2) TFEU). The significance of the principle of ECB independence is heightened by the fact that no common economic policy exists to complement the common monetary policy.

Article 130 TFEU and Article 7 ESCB Statute deem the ECB as politically independent. These articles have a dual nature in that they prohibit the ECB from taking instructions but also the EU and the Member States from seeking to influence the ECB.[128] In addition, the ECB's independence can also be conceptualised through a negative aspect, such as setting constraints: the ECB should not interfere with the Member States' economic policies since it is an issue not conferred on to the EU.[129] This constraining aspect of independence does not, however, mean that the ECB would function in isolation from politics; it only means that politicians are not to directly influence the decision making of the ECB in individual instances. However, the ECB of course can – or has to, depending on the perspective – take the surrounding political and economic context into consideration when making decisions.

The interdependence between the ECB's monetary policy and the wider economic policy conducted by the Member States is of course a truism. As has been pointed out by Smits, the framework set up by the EU Treaties for the regulation of the economy is such that the ECB is in charge of the stability of the currency, while several other actors influence other parts of the economy. While such a framework supports the independence of the ECB, it does not facilitate coordination between economic and monetary policy.[130] Thus, it is not surprising that informal links exist between the monetary policy functions conducted by the ECB and the economic policy functions conducted by the

---

[127]   See e.g. T. Beukers, 'The New ECB and its Relationship with the Eurozone Member States: Between Central Bank Independence and Central Bank Intervention' (2013) *Common Market Law Review* 50(6), 1579–620.

[128]   See R. Smits, *The European Central Bank: Institutional Aspects* (Kluwer Law International 1997), p. 161.

[129]   Although according to Art. 127(1) TFEU 'the ESCB shall support the general economic policies in the Union' the European Union does not have similar competence within economic policy as it has for monetary policy or the internal market.

[130]   R. Smits, 'The European Central Banks Independence and its Relations with Economic Policy Makers' (2007) *Fordham International Law Journal* 31(6), 1614–36, pp. 1617–18.

Member States. Actually, it might even seem rather normal when taking into consideration that a clear delineation between economic and monetary policy is not perhaps even possible. One such informal link is found beneath the concurrent establishment of the OMT programme and the Banking Union, discussed above and in the previous chapter. Another link can be seen in how the use of the OMT programme and the ESM are conjoined together through conditionality, as also discussed above.

Although the issue of independence did not directly surface in *Gauweiler*,[131] the reasons for the link between the OMT programme and the Banking Union, which also affect the independence of the ECB, were addressed by the CJEU. While the German Federal Constitutional Court was weary of the possible default risk associated with such a programme, and specifically formulated this as one of the nine fears it expressed in its request, the CJEU rather lightly dismissed such fears. Essentially, since the amount of OMT purchases is not limited, this can expose the Member States, as they are the ultimate guarantors of the ECB, to an unprecedented amount of liabilities if the target state defaults later. According to the CJEU, the interlinkage based on conditionality between the OMT programme and the ESM is likely to reduce the possible default risk.[132]

This risk is also associated with the shared destiny of banks and their host states, the so-called vicious circle.[133] As long as this link between the two exists, the risks associated with financing crisis states is amplified by the possible risks found on the balance sheets of that country's banks. The ECB was well aware of these risks, and national politicians had also protested against such aid mechanisms on the basis that they would essentially amount to risk sharing. The Single Supervisory Mechanisms (SSM), which is the first pillar of the Banking Union,[134] alleviated some of these risks on part of the ECB, since, to some extent, adoption of the SSM meant breaking the vicious circle; especially in a manner favoured by the ECB since supervision of banks was centralised under its control by this new mechanism. This causality between

---

[131] The independence of the ECB was only used as an argument to support the monetary policy nature of the OMT programme: because of the ECB's independence, the apparent links to economic policy do not turn the OMT programme into an economic policy measure. See C-62/14 *Gauweiler* EU:C:2015:400, para. 40.

[132] Ibid., paras 123–124.

[133] See R. M. Lastra, *International Financial and Monetary Law* (2nd edn, Oxford University Press 2015), p. 359; R. Smits, 'The Crisis Response in Europe's Economic and Monetary Union: Overview of Legal Developments' (2015) *Fordham International Law Journal* 38(4), 1135–91, p. 1172.

[134] See Chapter 4.4.1.

the establishment of the Banking Union and the OMT programme was discussed above and in the previous chapter.

The second link exposing the relative independence of the ECB is the one between the use of the OMT programme and the ESM. The German Federal Constitutional Court had highlighted in its referral how the use of the OMT programme is dependent on the object state being in observance with the strict conditionality required by an ESM assistance operation and how OMT purchases are a parallel support mechanism to the ESM.[135] Advocate General Cruz Villalón drew attention to this issue in his highly learned opinion. As the Advocate General pointed out, the ECB has a decisive role in the design, adoption and regular monitoring of the assistance programmes under the ESM. In other words, the ECB first takes part in the elaboration of conditionality and then also in monitoring compliance with conditionality, which is, finally, a condition for both the continuance of ESM support as well as an OMT operation. Due to this link the Advocate General considered that if the ECB were to activate the OMT programme, it should at that point resign from monitoring the object state's compliance with the conditionality of the ESM support. Otherwise the OMT programme will not retain its monetary policy nature since the ECB's role will exceed merely supporting the EU's economic policy.[136]

Do these links between the OMT and the two other crisis response mechanisms reveal the ECB's independence being sacrificed? Or do they perhaps reveal something else? It seems reasonable to conclude that such links do not indicate the ECB's independence per se being sacrificed by such actions but perhaps more about the ECB's delicacy in taking into consideration the economic, political and legal context within which it tries to fulfil its Treaty prescribed tasks. No institution is an island, not even one with rigid normative foundations that strive for its independence. Thus, institutions such as the ECB cannot function without taking into consideration the surrounding world and the underlying context of the decisions at hand. If the ECB is to take its primary objective of maintaining price stability seriously, this seems to be what it has to do.[137] That is, it seems that the asymmetry of the EMU both forces the ECB to act like this and also creates the basis of the criticism presented towards the ECB and the OMT programme in this chapter.

---

[135]   2 BvR 2728/13, 14 January 2014 (*OMT reference*), paras 74–78.

[136]   Opinion of Advocate General Cruz Villalón delivered on 14 January 2015, C-62/14 *Gauweiler* EU:C:2015:7, paras 140–151.

[137]   As ECB Executive Board Member Benoît Cœuré has stated (n 13): 'in the ECB's case, passivity is not an option if it means failing to reach our objective of price stability. It is our unequivocal duty, enshrined in the Treaty, to do whatever it takes within our mandate to fulfil our objective.'

5.5   CONCLUSIONS

5.5.1   Observations from the Reconstruction

The reconstruction of the process leading up to the announcement of the OMT programme highlighted the deep interconnectedness between economic and monetary policies within the EMU. Furthermore, it also emphasised the interlinkages between the political and technocratic institutions crafting and implementing these policies. Perhaps just for these reasons, the process also instigated the first direct judicial dialogue between the German Federal Constitutional Court and the CJEU.[138] But, similarly to what was observed with regard to the other crisis response mechanisms studied in the previous chapters, neither the national court nor the CJEU was ready to disrupt the process of safeguarding the financial stability of the euro area as a whole and the subsequent overhaul of the EU's economic governance regime. Both the CJEU and the German court accepted the OMT programme. It appears, then, that the CJEU was affected by the same predicament in *Gauweiler* as it was in *Pringle*. And maybe the Federal Constitutional Court, too, was affected by such a predicament, since its final judgment expressed a considerable degree of constraint, although one could have expected differently based on the defiance it expressed in its referral. Perhaps the political stakes were just too high for either court to declare the OMT programme *ultra vires*, either on the basis of the EU Treaties or the German constitution.

The reconstruction of the announcement of the OMT programme and its subsequent review by the Federal Constitutional Court and the CJEU add a further layer to the inequality thesis. Based on the analysis in this chapter, it truly seems that differences in the national constitutions and how the competence and jurisdiction of national courts are defined affect the way in which national courts can interact with the CJEU and the European-level political process; what is more, the CJEU seemed to acknowledge and accept this in its ruling in *Gauweiler* by admitting the case despite its abstract and hypothetical nature.

5.5.2   The Rationality of the OMT

There is perhaps less dispute amongst experts about the effectiveness or rationality of the OMT programme when compared to the other crisis response mechanisms; its mere announcement did the job and it was never used in practice. However, both its substantive rationality and its practical effective-

---

[138] On *Gauweiler* as a 'judicial dialogue', see Tuominen (n 4), pp. 200–203.

ness stem from the underlying issue of the EU still lacking a clear economic policy mandate in the EU Treaties. Since the EU lacks fiscal capacity, the ECB needed to resort to such bond purchases. The OMT programme did not alter the fundamental mismatch between economic and monetary policy related competence in the EMU. While both the German court and the CJEU deemed the OMT programme as constitutional, the cases nevertheless highlight how politicians and technocrats felt the need to do something, while being constrained by the mandate given by the EU Treaties.

While it can be argued that the distinction between economic and monetary policy is futile – since monetary policy should be understood as a part of broader economic policy in that monetary policy always effects economic policy in some way – this distinction cannot be reduced to insignificance. This is so, because it was an explicit political decision to create such an asymmetric EMU in Maastricht.[139] Although the problems associated with such asymmetry were acknowledged back then, and the Germans might have anticipated some sort of a functional spill-over from the common monetary policy to a common economic policy in the future, this does not mean that the distinction between these two policies is unnecessary and should not be upheld. The OMT programme further underscores how this original setup established in Maastricht does not function and continues to produce difficulties for the political, executive and judicial organs of the EU.

---

[139]   See Chapter 1.2.1.1.

6. The equality of the Member States and Article 4(2) TEU

6.1 INTRODUCTION

This chapter first introduces the inequality thesis by explaining how differences in national legal frameworks allow for a varying degree of direct or indirect participation by national courts in the European-level political process: when, how and to what degree national courts can engage with the European Union's political processes (6.2). Next, the chapter addresses the problems that ensue from the fact that some national courts are in a privileged position vis-à-vis other national courts. It is argued that such inequality is problematic from a political perspective: some national courts end up being able to affect the European-level political process in a way that they effectively hijack it from the political institutions (6.3). Following these descriptive accounts, the chapter then turns to the normative basis of the inequality thesis. According to Article 4(2) TEU, the 'Union shall respect the equality of Member States before the Treaties as well as their national identities, inherent in their fundamental structures, political and constitutional, inclusive of regional and local self-government'. Most of the literature on Article 4(2) TEU discusses the meaning of national identity for the primacy of EU law. Departing from this, this chapter presents a novel argument concerning the meaning of Article 4(2) TEU: the equality clause is there to guarantee horizontally the equality of the Member States vis-à-vis each other in relation to the EU, whereas the national identity clause is there to protect the Member States vertically from the EU (6.4). The final section concludes the discussion (6.5).

6.2 UNEQUAL IN DIVERSITY?

Under the system established by the EU Treaties, national courts are EU courts: they apply EU law in their rulings and also act as agents to the CJEU in that they can, and in some cases are obliged to, send preliminary references to the

CJEU.[1] Article 267(3) TFEU stipulates the circumstances in which a national court must refer a question to the CJEU. To which courts and to which types of decisions this rule applies was formulated in *Lyckeskog*.[2] However, the EU Treaties do not grant national courts constitutional review functions vis-à-vis EU law; on the contrary, the CJEU has the sole power to declare a Union act invalid, as was established in *Foto-Frost*.[3] The only instance in which national courts can review EU 'law'[4] is when the EU Treaties are amended and when the amendments are ratified nationally. In practice, this is an issue falling under the rubric of public international law, as the EU Treaties are like any other international treaty between sovereign states. Depending on the national constitutional framework, certain courts might have the competence to subject the ratification or implementation of such international agreements under their review.

This was the reason why the Treaty on Stability, Coordination and Governance in the Economic and Monetary Union (Fiscal Compact)[5] and the European Stability Mechanism Treaty (ESM)[6] were subjected to constitutional review in several Member States. They are treaties under international law, not legal instruments issued by the EU. If the measures had been enacted through the Community method, such constitutional review by national courts would not have been possible. Fabbrini has called this the 'paradox of judicialization'.[7] In which Member States and in which manner such judicial review was possible stemmed from the Member States' respective constitutional frameworks.

---

[1]   After the primacy and direct effect of EU law was established by the CJEU, private litigants started using national courts to enforce EU law against Member States. See K. J. Alter, *Establishing the Supremacy of European Law: The Making of an International Law Rule of Law in Europe* (Oxford University Press 2001), p. 210.

[2]   C-99/00 *Lyckeskog* EU:C:2002:329.

[3]   Case 314/85 *Foto-Frost* EU:C:1987:452, para. 15: '[national courts] do not have the power to declare acts of the Community institutions invalid'.

[4]   The EU Treaties are multilateral treaties between the Member States and thus they constitute the primary 'law' of the Union. However, they should not be called the primary 'legislation' of the Union, since they are not legal instruments issued by the Union. See R. Schütze, *European Union Law* (Cambridge University Press 2015), p. 923.

[5]   Treaty on Stability, Coordination and Governance in the Economic and Monetary Union. Brussels, 1–2 March 2012.

[6]   Treaty Establishing the European Stability Mechanism. 2 February 2012, https://www.esm.europa.eu/legal-documents/esm-treaty (accessed 1 September 2020).

[7]   See F. Fabbrini, 'The Euro-Crisis and the Courts: Judicial Review and the Political Process in Comparative Perspective' (2014) *Berkeley Journal of International Law* 31(1), 64–123, p. 65; F. Fabbrini, *Economic Governance in Europe: Comparative Paradoxes and Constitutional Challenges* (Oxford University Press 2016), Chapter 2.

In continental European states, there exist roughly three models of judicial review: abstract, concrete and review based on constitutional complaints.[8] The German Federal Constitutional Court (*Bundesverfassungsgericht*) is able to use all three of these due to the position the German constitution grants it.[9] Other newer forms of accessing a constitutional court with the intent of reviewing state actions include, for example, that state officials such as parliamentary ombudsmen or public prosecutors refer a case to the constitutional court. The Hungarian *actio popularis*, under which anyone could directly petition the constitutional court, was very powerful,[10] but it was recently abolished.[11] The development in Europe of rights-based constitutional review – that constitutional courts try to secure the protection of fundamental and human rights, and not just the observance of state-centred constitutional principles such as allocation of powers between government institutions or federal levels – has resulted in a situation in which no legal norm is beyond constitutional review.[12]

Such differences explain why the Fiscal Compact and the ESM Treaties were subjected to review in some Member States but not in all, and why the European Central Bank's (ECB) Outright Monetary Transactions (OMT) programme was challenged in Germany and subsequently before the CJEU in *Gauweiler*.[13] Thus, such differences explain why certain courts are better positioned to participate in the European-level political process and, perhaps, to affect it; in other words, why some courts are more influential than others. Yet, the impact of political significance cannot be dismissed completely. As was explained in the case studies, although the Finnish Constitutional

---

[8]   In addition to these basic models, there are also 'intermediary forms' of constitutional review. See K. Tuori, *Ratio and Voluntas: The Tension Between Reason and Will in Law* (Ashgate 2010), pp. 248–54.

[9]   See A. Stone Sweet, *Governing with Judges: Constitutional Politics in Europe* (Oxford University Press 2000), pp. 44–9; D. P. Kommers and R. A. Miller, *The Constitutional Jurisprudence of the Federal Republic of Germany.* (3rd edn, revised and expanded, Duke University Press 2012), pp. 10–16.

[10]   See G. Halmai, 'The Hungarian Approach of Constitutional Review' in W. Sadurski (ed.), *Constitutional Justice, East and West, Democratic Legitimacy and Constitutional Courts in Post-Communist Europe in a Comparative Perspective* (Kluwer International 2002).

[11]   See G. Spuller, 'Transformation of the Hungarian Constitutional Court: Tradition, Revolution, and (European) Prospects' (2014) *German Law Journal* 15(4), 637–92.

[12]   A. Stone Sweet, 'Constitutional Courts' in M. Rosenfeld and A. Sajó (eds.), *The Oxford Handbook of Comparative Constitutional Law* (Oxford University Press 2012), pp. 822–24.

[13]   C-62/14 *Gauweiler* EU:C:2015:400. See T. Tuominen, 'Aspects of Constitutional Pluralism in Light of the *Gauweiler saga*' (2018) *European Law Review* 43(2), 186–204.

Law Committee (*Perustuslakivaliokunta*)[14] is also in a privileged position in comparison to some constitutional courts with only concrete *ex post* review powers, it has nevertheless not been as influential as the German Federal Constitutional Court.

Since the German Federal Constitutional Court's scope of review is among the broadest in Europe, the majority of relevant case law stems from Germany. The way the German constitution facilitates accessing the Federal Constitutional Court has been criticised for judicialising politics. The way individual complaints work in the German system makes it possible that 'every anti-government paranoid fantasy that any citizen can dream up' can be challenged before the Federal Constitutional Court. This is not in line with how Kelsen initially intended that review by a constitutional court should function. The combination of abstract review and individual complaints is the primary reason for such judicialisation. The outcome of this has been that 'many of the most politically important complaints are, in fact if not in theory, completely abstract'.[15]

The German Federal Constitutional Court can conduct both abstract and concrete review.[16] All of the German court's cases that were assessed in the case studies were brought before it either as individual consti-tutional complaints under Article 93(1)(4a) of the German constitution (*Verfassungsbeschwerden*) or as disputes between high state organs under Article 93(I)(I) (*Organstreitverfahren festzustellen*). None of the cases was brought before the Federal Constitutional Court as actual abstract *ex ante* pro-

---

[14]   On the role of the Committee and the development of its doctrine, see J. Husa, *The Constitution of Finland: A Contextual Analysis* (Hart Publishing 2011), pp. 78–85. In the literature, its position and functions are usually compared to those of constitutional courts. See J. Lavapuro, T. Ojanen and M. Scheinin, 'Rights-Based Constitutionalism in Finland and the Development of Pluralist Constitutional Review' (2011) *International Journal of Constitutional Law* 9(2), 503–31. The Committee seems to fulfil all of the four constituent components of European, Kelsenian consti-tutional courts: that (i) it only has the power of constitutional review, whereas normal courts do not (they can only choose to disapply a law in an individual case, but not to declare it null or void); (ii) it does not decide on actual cases; (iii) it has links to politics and courts, but it is strictly speaking part of neither of the two; (iv) it conducts abstract *ex ante* review. On these criteria, see M. Shapiro and A. Stone Sweet (eds), *On Law, Politics, and Judicialization* (Oxford University Press 2002), pp. 343–4. Although they do not extrapolate on this point, Tuori and Tuori seem to equate the Committee with other institutions that perform constitutional review since they accord so much rele-vance to what the Committee did during the euro crisis. See K. Tuori and K. Tuori, *The Eurozone Crisis: A Constitutional Analysis* (Cambridge University Press 2014).

[15]   See Shapiro and Stone Sweet, ibid., p. 368.

[16]   See Kommers and Miller (n 9), pp. 10–16.

cedures under Article 93(2)(I) (*abstraktes Normenkontrollverfahren*).[17] Thus, what is here referred to as the 'abstract' nature of the Federal Constitutional Court's review, or how it could participate '*ex ante*' does not refer to its review under Article 93(2)(I), but rather how it was able to participate in this European-level process in a different manner from the majority of national courts and how from their perspective, and in relation to the point of no return, its review is characterised as abstract and *ex ante*.

The intervening Member States pointed out the abstract nature of the German Federal Constitutional Court's review in *Gauweiler*. For this reason, the CJEU stated that national divergences in the way that judicial review is facilitated in the different Member States neither constitutes an obstacle to the functioning of the preliminary reference procedure as it is spelled out in Article 267 TFEU, nor for the admissibility of this specific case.[18] The CJEU was of course correct with this conclusion, since the primary function of the preliminary reference procedure is to assure the uniformity of EU law,[19] which differences in national judicial frameworks should not obstruct. By comparison, it is interesting to note how the Constitutional Court of Belgium (*Cour constitutionelle*) found all of the challenges against the Fiscal Compact inadmissible because the people seeking annulment were not affected directly and unfavourably by the national law implementing the Fiscal Compact; an abstract interest in the matter was not sufficient in and of itself.[20] However, this is not what this section focuses on, and instead it looks at the consequences that follow from this.

Courts that are able to participate only after the point of no return – whether it be because they can only conduct concrete *ex post* review or the way their jurisdiction and rules of procedure otherwise facilitates the interaction between national constitutional law and EU law – have no way of affecting the content of European-level political processes and the created legal measures. When these courts are permitted to assess these measures, their content is already set in stone. The political pressure directed towards courts facing such 'take it or

---

[17] See 2 BvR 987/10, 7 September 2011 (*Euro rescue package*); 2 BvE 8/11, 28 February 2012 (*Government guarantees*); 2 BvE 4/11, 19 June 2012 (*ESM and Euro Plus Pact*); 2 BvR 1390/12, 12 September 2012 (*ESM interim ruling*); 2 BvR 1390/12, 18 March 2014 (*ESM final judgment*); 2 BvR 2728/13, 14 January 2014 (*OMT reference*); 2 BvR 2728/13, 21 June 2016 (*OMT final judgment*).

[18] C-62/14 *Gauweiler* EU:C:2015:400, paras 27–29.

[19] Case 66/80 *SpA International Chemical Corporation* EU:C:1981:102, para. 11: 'The main purpose of the powers accorded to the Court by Article 177 [Art. 267 TFEU] is to ensure that community law is applied uniformly by national courts.'

[20] See Arrêt n° 62/2016 du 28 avril 2016; P. Gérard and W. Verrijdt, 'Belgian Constitutional Court Adopts National Identity Discourse: Belgian Constitutional Court No. 62/2016, 28 April 2016' (2017) *European Constitutional Law Review* 13(1), 182–205.

leave it' decisions is surely strong, which can also create some sort of predicament for these courts to accept the measures under review.[21] It is in this sense that courts participating before the point of no return – whether it be through conducting abstract *ex ante* review or otherwise – are in a privileged position, whereas the aforementioned courts are in a far more disadvantaged position. Thus, the latter appear to be unequal in relation to the former.

As events during the euro crisis highlight, the only way that courts participating after the point of no return are able to influence the European-level political process is by being able to create an atmosphere of 'autolimitation' on part of the legislator; either the EU legislator concerning the Community method or the Member States concerning the supranational method based on international law. This means that the legislator starts self-restraining its actions in anticipation of an annulment by the court in question or the development of the court's review doctrine in the future.[22] The classical example of this is the German Federal Constitutional Court's *Solange* doctrine,[23] but the fear of courts, especially of the Federal Constitutional Court, has also affected the formation of many of the crisis response mechanisms, as pointed out in the case studies.

Courts that are able to participate before the point of no return can directly influence the outcome of the European-level political process. Take, for example, the Finnish Constitutional Law Committee. As explained in the case studies, and as discussed in the literature,[24] the Committee's opinions on both the drafts of the Fiscal Compact and the ESM Treaties might have affected the final versions of these instruments, or at least the aspects that the Committee deemed problematic on part of the Finnish constitution did not make it to the final versions. There also might have been, of course, other reasons for why this happened, so not all credit necessarily goes to the Committee.

---

[21] The same argumentation of course applies also to the CJEU when it is reviewing legal acts that have already been put to use. See V. Borger, 'The ESM and the European Court's Predicament in Pringle' (2013) *German Law Journal* 14(1), 113–40.

[22] See Stone Sweet (n 9), p. 75; S. Saurugger, A. Hofmann and T. Warren, 'National Constitutional Courts As Veto Players in the EMU Crisis' (January 7, 2020). Available at SSRN: https://ssrn.com/abstract=3599037 or http://dx.doi.org/10.2139/ssrn.3599037 (accessed 1 September 2020).

[23] On this doctrine and its effects on European integration, see P. M. Huber, 'The Federal Constitutional Court and European Integration' (2015) *European Public Law* 21(1), 83–108.

[24] Tuori and Tuori (n 14), pp. 198–9.

6.3 WHY IS INEQUALITY A PROBLEM?

The described inequality, that there are differences in national systems for judicial review, leads to the following problem: some national courts end up being able to affect the European-level political process in a way that they effectively hijack it from the political institutions. The causes for this were explained above, whereas this section focuses on the broader implications of such inequality.[25]

By posing its ultimatum in *Gauweiler*,[26] the German Federal Constitutional Court effectively tried to hold the CJEU and the whole Union to hostage by subjecting the legality of a Union act under its review – that is, review by a national court on the basis of a national constitution. It is important to note that while the Fiscal Compact and ESM are international law-based treaties adopted by the Member States, the ECB's OMT programme, the issue under review in *Gauweiler*, was based on a decision of the ECB and is thus classified as a legal act by the Union. While there are good reasons for why national constitutions facilitate the judicial review of the ratification of international treaties, the same does not hold for acts of the EU. The CJEU exists for the purpose of reviewing the legality of Union acts. The whole point of the principle of the primacy of EU law – as well as the fact that only the CJEU is to rule on the legality of Union acts – is to guarantee the functioning of the Union as a composite polity. Another goal is to make sure that all of the Member States are treated equally and that none of them has a prerogative over Union actions.

If the CJEU had accepted the ultimatum posed by the German Federal Constitutional Court, it would have effectively subsumed itself under the authority of a national court. The CJEU's adaptation to the Federal Constitutional Court's *Solange I* decision meant, to a certain extent, just this: as a result of the German court's ruling, the CJEU introduced the protection of fundamental rights into the EU's legal order through the development of what it called 'general principles' of EU law and by drawing inspiration from the European Convention on Human Rights.[27] This development was perhaps legitimate, as it concerned fundamental rights, whereas *Gauweiler* concerned the Union's economic governance regime. The CJEU's adaptation to *Solange I* is thus in line with the general trend of adopting rights-based constitutional review, whereas the regulation of economic governance is more an issue

---

[25] See also Tuominen (n 13), pp. 190–94.

[26] 2 BvR 2728/13, 14 January 2014 (*OMT reference*), paras 99–100. See Chapter 5.2.2.

[27] See case 4/73 *J. Nold* EU:C:1974:51, para. 13; case 36/75 *Roland Rutili* EU:C: 1975:137, para. 32; case 249/86 *Commission v Germany* EU:C:1989:204, para. 10.

of upholding federal principles and competences. Although there are good arguments for why the CJEU could have and perhaps should have found *Gauweiler* inadmissible,[28] it seems that the CJEU's choice was correct because it is the *de facto* supreme constitutional court of the Union: by admitting the case and assessing the OMT programme in substance, the CJEU asserted its interpretative supremacy over the German Federal Constitutional Court and did not allow the German court to affect the European-level political process in a manner that would go beyond what the EU Treaties recognise as the task of national courts. Although the CJEU took something of a risk in asserting its interpretative supremacy over the Federal Constitutional Court, the outcome of the *Gauweiler saga* proved that this risk was worth taking, since in the end, the German court conceded.

On a practical level, what would it lead to if all national courts started to pose similar ultimatums to the CJEU as the German Federal Constitutional Court did in *Gauweiler*? If even one national court is able to disrupt the system adopted by the EU Treaties by being able to affect the workings of the CJEU with its threats, it would be devastating if the courts of all of the Member States assumed a similar stance. As Kelemen notes, the EU is not a dyad but a multilateral organisation.[29] If such actions by national courts were allowed, the EU's political process, or the actions of EU institutions, as they are enshrined in the EU Treaties, would be taken hostage by national courts. As the Advocate General Cruz Villalón noted in *Gauweiler*, it would be 'an all but impossible task to preserve *this* Union, as we know it today, if it is to be made subject to an absolute reservation, ill-defined and virtually at the discretion of each of the Member States'.[30]

Moreover, what would the German Federal Constitutional Court's own stance be towards other national courts that acted like it does? Would it allow, say, the French *Conseil constitutionnel* to pose ultimatums that would affect the EU and the rights of German citizens ensuing from EU law? Most likely not. In this sense, the Federal Constitutional Court is trying to impinge on the EU and all EU citizens something that it would not accept itself. This, actually,

---

[28]   See T. Tridimas and N. Xanthoulis, 'A Legal Analysis of the *Gauweiler* Case: Between Monetary Policy and Constitutional Conflict' (2016) *Maastricht Journal of European and Comparative Law* 23(1), 17–39, pp. 21–3; I. Pernice, 'A Difficult Partnership Between Courts: The First Preliminary Reference by the German Federal Constitutional Court to the CJEU' (2014) *Maastricht Journal of European and Comparative Law* 21(1), 3–13, pp. 7–8.

[29]   R. D. Kelemen, 'On the Unsustainability of Constitutional Pluralism: European Supremacy and the Survival of the Eurozone' (2016) *Maastricht Journal of European and Comparative Law* 23(1), 136–50, p. 144.

[30]   Opinion of Advocate General Cruz Villalón delivered on 14 January 2015, C-62/14 *Gauweiler* EU:C:2015:7, para. 59, emphasis in the original.

is not that surprising, taking into consideration the Federal Constitutional Court's case law regarding the various crisis response measures. As Besselink has pointed out, Germany was at the forefront of the group of Member States that imposed strict austerity measures on Greece, whereas the Federal Constitutional Court's own case law seems to suggest that imposing similar measures on Germany would violate the German constitution.[31] It seems that the foundation for this line of reasoning was already laid with the Federal Constitutional Court's judgment on the Treaty of Maastricht. The German court ruled then that the Maastricht Treaty is compatible with the German constitution precisely because it adopts the German-inspired stability concept. The Federal Constitutional Court is still treading this path. As Joerges has nicely stated, it 'is precisely this kind of external effect of national decision-making that has to be avoided in a Union of equals'.[32] While the outcome of the *Gauweiler saga* was that the ECB could continue its bond purchasing programmes, it remains to be seen how disruptive the effects of the Federal Constitutional Court's recent *PSPP judgment* will be.[33]

An interesting conclusion surfaces when taking into consideration how the rulings of the German Federal Constitutional Court on the crisis response measures suggest that such austerity induced through conditionality is actually a prerequisite for the measures being acceptable under the German constitution: the Federal Constitutional Court seems to be impinging upon the Eurozone something which it would not accept being impinged upon Germany. In addition to placing national courts in an unequal position in relation to one another and enabling some to hijack the European-level political process, these national frameworks can also feed into formalising the direct clash between national courts and the CJEU by facilitating it. The next chapter will discuss this issue in more detail but before that, let us turn to the national identity clause of Article 4(2) TEU and an alternative way of conceptualising it and the relationship between the Member States and the EU.

---

[31] L. Besselink, 'Parameters of Constitutional Development: The Fiscal Compact In Between EU and Member State Constitutions' in L. Serena Rossi and F. Casolari (eds), *The EU After Lisbon: Amending or Coping with the Existing Treaties?* (Springer 2014), p. 29.

[32] C. Joerges, 'Constitutionalism and the Law of the European Economy' in M. Dawson, H. Enderlein and C. Joerges (eds), *Beyond the Crisis: The Governance of Europe's Economic, Political and Legal Transformation* (Oxford University Press 2015), p. 221.

[33] See 2 BvR 859/15, 05 May 2020 (*PSPP judgment*).

6.4   NATIONAL CONSTITUTIONAL IDENTITY AND THE EQUALITY OF THE MEMBER STATES

6.4.1   The Role of National Constitutional Identity in EU Law

The topic of national constitutional identity, as enshrined in Article 4(2) TEU, has become increasingly popular lately.[34] The issue has been discussed at length in the literature, and both the CJEU and national courts have started to apply the concept of national constitutional identity and Article 4(2) TEU in their judgments.[35]

The requirement that the EU respects the Member States' national constitutional identities was first introduced into the EU Treaties with the Maastricht Treaty. Article F (1) TEU proclaimed that: 'The Union shall respect the national identities of its Member States, whose systems of government are founded on the principles of democracy.' The current formulation of the national identity clause was adopted with the Lisbon Treaty. Now, under Article 4(2) TEU, the EU is to respect the national identities of the Member States, as they are 'inherent in their fundamental structures, political and constitutional'. While some have argued that the purpose of such a national identity clause is to appease the national constitutional courts' concerns resulting from the unconditional nature of the primacy of EU law, the drafting history of Article 4(2) TEU does not support such a view.[36]

Although not explicitly invoking the term national constitutional identity or the relevant Treaty Article, *Omega* is usually taken as the first influential judgment where the CJEU allowed for national restrictions to free movement rights on the basis of something echoing national constitutional identity.[37] The first case to draw major attention to Article 4(2) TEU was undoubtedly *Sayn-Wittgenstein*. There, the CJEU correlated pleading constitutional

---

[34]   See e.g. A. S. Arnaiz and C. A. Llivina (eds), *National Constitutional Identity and European Integration* (Intersentia 2013); E. Cloots, *National Identity in EU Law* (Oxford University Press 2015); J. Bast and L. Orgad (eds), 'Constitutional Identity in the Age of Global Migration' (2017) *German Law Journal* [special issue] 18(7); C. Calliess, and G. van der Schyff (eds), *Constitutional Identity in a Europe of Multilevel Constitutionalism* (Cambridge University Press 2019).

[35]   Although the semantics of this has been discussed in the literature, a distinction between 'national identity' and 'national constitutional identity' is not made here. See E. Cloots, 'National Identity, Constitutional Identity, and Sovereignty in the EU' (2016) *Netherlands Journal of Legal Philosophy* 45(2), 82–98.

[36]   See B. Gustaferro, 'Beyond the *Exceptionalism* of Constitutional Conflicts: The *Ordinary* Functions of the Identity Clause' (2012) *Yearbook of European Law* 31, 263–318.

[37]   C-36/02 *Omega* EU:C:2004:614, paras 37–41.

identity to relying on public policy as grounds for restricting free movement rights, while also citing Article 4(2) TEU in its reasoning.[38] Since then the CJEU has referred to the concept or the Article itself in a number of cases.[39] *Coman* serves as an example of a recent case. The legal question was whether Romania was allowed to violate Article 2(2) of the Citizens' Rights Directive 20004/38/EC by pleading that its national constitutional identity did not allow same-sex marriage.[40]

The academic discussion on the national identity clause of Article 4(2) TEU seems to focus on what exactly is mandated or allowed by it. What does the clause mean for both the CJEU and national courts when they try to solve a conflict between EU law and national law? Some have argued that the national identity clause enables national courts to decide when to disapply EU law if their national constitutional identity so requires,[41] whereas others maintain that the national courts' role is just to raise the issue through preliminary referrals, but that it is ultimately for the CJEU to decide whether it accepts the provided argument as a reason to breach EU law.[42]

From a structural perspective, these two contrasting views can be summarised as follows. According to the perspective of the national courts, the CJEU lacks the competence to assess whether EU law conflicts with a Member State's national constitutional identity since doing this requires interpreting the content of national constitutional law. As stated in Article 19(3) TEU, the CJEU has the competence to rule on the interpretation and validity of EU law, not national law. Logically speaking then, Article 4(2) TEU must be interpreted in the way that any EU law that does not respect national constitu-

---

[38]   C-208/09 *Sayn-Wittgenstein* EU:C:2010:806, paras 83–84 and 92. See L. Besselink, 'Respecting Constitutional Identity in the EU. A Case Note on C-208/09 Ilonka Sayn-Wittgenstein' (2012) *Common Market Law Review* 49(2), 671–94.

[39]   See e.g. C-438/14 *Nabiel Peter Bogendorff von Wolffersdorff* EU:C:2016:401; C-317/18 *Cátia Correia Moreira* EU:C:2019:499.

[40]   C-673/16 *Coman* EU:C:2018:385, paras 42–51. See J. J. Rijpma, 'You Gotta Let Love Move: ECJ 5 June 2018, C-673/16, Coman, Hamilton, Accept v Inspectoratul General pentru Imigrări' (2019) *European Constitutional Law Review* 15(2), 324–39.

[41]   See e.g. A. von Bogdandy and S. Schill, 'Overcoming Absolute Primacy: Respect for National Identity under the Lisbon Treaty' (2011) *Common Market Law Review* 48(5), 1417–54, pp. 1447–52; M. Kumm, 'The Jurisprudence of Constitutional Conflict: Constitutional Supremacy in Europe before and After the Constitutional Treaty' (2005) *European Law Journal* 11(3), 262–307, pp. 302–4.

[42]   See e.g. M. Claes, 'The Primacy of EU Law in European and National Law' in A. Arnull and D. Chalmers (eds), *The Oxford Handbook of European Union Law* (Oxford University Press 2015), pp. 204–6; A. Pliakos and G. Anagnostaras, 'Fundamental Rights and the New Battle over Legal and Judicial Supremacy: Lessons from Melloni' (2015) *Yearbook of European Law* 34, 97–126.

tional identity does not have primacy over national law.[43] The view from the CJEU holds that while the national identity clause mandates the CJEU to take such national pleas seriously, it has not fundamentally altered the principle of primacy of EU law, and therefore it is for the CJEU to decide which national circumstances classify as derogations from EU law.[44]

Regardless of which position one takes, the debate centres on what exactly are the criteria under which a national court can plead national constitutional identity as a justification for disapplying EU law, or, conversely, what criteria the CJEU should accept as justifiable causes for disapplying EU law. As the case law and literature on this topic is still developing,[45] definitive answers on what falls under the rubric of 'national constitutional identity' cannot be given.

As one can appreciate from the short literature review above, the issue of national constitutional identity is closely linked to constitutional pluralism. The position according to which Article 4(2) TEU empowers the national courts to decide when to disapply EU law basically amounts to the acknowledgement of normative constitutional pluralism.[46] Accepting this view thus means that Article 4(2) TEU is a legal norm through which constitutional pluralism has become constitutionalised within the EU Treaties.

While those advocating for normative constitutional pluralism or an interpretation of Article 4(2) TEU according to which the final decision on its extent is taken by the national courts have surely had good intentions whilst presenting their arguments, there is an evident caveat to this line of reasoning; namely, that by accepting such arguments, the national identity clause of Article 4(2) TEU might quickly become the margin of appreciation doctrine of EU law.[47] While the system created with the European Convention on Human Rights differs fundamentally from the 'new legal order' created by EU law, the criticism presented towards the margin of appreciation doctrine of the European Court of Human Rights can be applicable in the context of the EU too.[48]

---

[43] L. Besselink, 'National and Constitutional Identity Before and After Lisbon' (2010) *Utrecht Law Review* 6(3), 36–49, pp. 44–7.

[44] Claes (n 42), p. 205.

[45] See n 34.

[46] On the relationship between the discussion on national identity and constitutional pluralism, see C. Calliess and A. Schnettger, 'The Protection of Constitutional Identity in a Europe of Multilevel Constitutionalism' in C. Calliess and G. van der Schyff (eds), *Constitutional Identity in a Europe of Multilevel Constitutionalism* (Cambridge University Press 2019).

[47] See generally J. Gerards, 'Pluralism, Deference and the Margin of Appreciation Doctrine' (2011) *European Law Journal* 17(1), 80–120.

[48] See generally G. Letsas, 'Two Concepts of the Margin of Appreciation' (2006) *Oxford Journal of Legal Studies* 26(4), 705–32; J. Gerards, 'Margin of Appreciation

In fact, during recent years the concept of national constitutional identity and Article 4(2) TEU have been used rather maliciously by certain Member State governments. The authoritarian regimes in Hungary and Poland have both relied on national constitutional identity when arguing for their democratically questionable policies and affronts on the rule of law.[49] Furthermore, the majority of people in Europe would perhaps deem the Romanian government's argumentation in the above-mentioned *Coman* case questionable. However, such use of the national identity clause that questions the very values on which the EU is based is dubious.[50] Arguably, what has made such use of the national identity clause possible is its lack of a normative core.[51] As one can also observe in the diversity of the arguments presented in the literature, defining the content of national constitutional identity is so difficult that it can be utilised to argue for a variety of objectives, for which we can easily find resonance somewhere in the EU Treaties, as they foster so many values and objectives.

Take, for example, the recent case of *Commission v Poland*. Poland and Hungary refused to participate in the relocation of asylum seekers from Italy and Greece following Council Decisions 2015/1523 and 2015/1601. They argued that Article 72 TFEU, according to which the maintenance of law and order and the safeguarding of internal security is an exclusive competence of the Member States, read in conjunction with the national identity clause of Article 4(2) TEU, vindicates them from having disapplied the two Council Decisions. Following the opinion of Advocate General Sharpston, the CJEU noted that the Member States' legitimate interest in preserving social and cultural cohesion may be safeguarded effectively by other, less restrictive means than a unilateral and complete refusal to fulfil their obligations under EU law.[52]

---

and Incrementalism in the Case Law of the European Court of Human Rights' (2018) *Human Rights Law Review* 18(3), 495–515.

[49]   See R. D. Kelemen and L. Pech, 'Why Autocrats Love Constitutional Identity and Constitutional Pluralism: Lessons from Hungary and Poland' (2018) *Reconnect-Europe Working Paper* No. 2; G. Halmai, 'The Fundamental Law of Hungary and the European Constitutional Values' (2019) *DPCE Online* 39(2), 1503–24.

[50]   See O. Mader, 'Enforcement of EU Values as a Political Endeavour: Constitutional Pluralism and Value Homogeneity in Times of Persistent Challenges to the Rule of Law' (2019) *Hague Journal on the Rule of Law* 11, 133–70.

[51]   See F. Fabbrini and A. Sajó, 'The Dangers of Constitutional Identity' (2019) *European Law Journal* 25(4), 457–73.

[52]   Joined cases C-715/17, C-718/17 and C-719/17 *Commission v Poland* EU:C: 2020:257; Opinion of Advocate General Sharpston delivered on 31 October 2019, para. 227.

6.4.2   The Horizontal and Vertical Aspects of Article 4(2) TEU

Where does all of this leave us? If the national identity clause effectively insti-tutionalises constitutional pluralism and can be used maliciously, is there any other way of interpreting Article 4(2) TEU? Indeed, what exactly is the content of Article 4(2) TEU and how should it be construed as a whole? The content of Article 4(1)–(2) TEU is reproduced below in full.

> Article 4 TEU
> 1. In accordance with Article 5, competences not conferred upon the Union in the Treaties remain with the Member States.
> 2. The Union shall respect the equality of Member States before the Treaties as well as their national identities, inherent in their fundamental structures, polit-ical and constitutional, inclusive of regional and local self-government. It shall respect their essential State functions, including ensuring the territorial integrity of the State, maintaining law and order and safeguarding national security. In particular, national security remains the sole responsibility of each Member State.

The above-discussed growing body of literature seems to focus almost exclu-sively on the protection of national constitutional identity while disregarding the fact that according to Article 4(2) TEU, the EU is also to respect the equal-ity of the Member States. This reading of Article 4(2) TEU has slowly started gathering attention in the literature. The gist of this argument is that without strict adherence to the primacy of EU law – which is lost if national courts can decide, by relying on Article 4(2) TEU or some other norm, to disapply EU law on their own motion – equality of the Member States is lost. This results in a pick-and-choose model whereby Member States are bound by only those aspects of EU law that they see fit. This argument is based on recognising how a clash between a national court and the CJEU is actually not just about the relationship between that Member State and the EU, but in fact affects all of the Member States. This is because by acting this way, a national court can effectively prevent the Member States as a whole from pursuing policy choices that they see fit.[53]

The counterargument to this reading of Article 4(2) TEU is that if primacy is taken as unconditional, then the meaning of the national identity clause

---

[53]   See F. Fabbrini, 'After the OMT Case: The Supremacy of EU Law as the Guarantee of the Equality of the Member States' (2015) *German Law Journal* 16(4), 1003–24, pp. 1014–16; Tuominen (n 13), pp. 190–94. Also see M. Wilkinson, 'Economic Messianism and Constitutional Power in a "German Europe": All Courts are Equal, but Some Courts are More Equal than Others', *LSE Law, Society and Economy Working Papers* 26/2014 (2014).

becomes redundant.[54] This counterargument, however, does not hold when we take into consideration how the national identity clause has been applied by the CJEU and by the majority of national courts. In fact, in most cases the principle is applied in the manner of a proportionality test.[55]

The inequality thesis presented in this book stems from the above-conceptualised aspects of Article 4(2) TEU. A novel argument on the horizontal and vertical aspects of Article 4(2) TEU is presented: the national identity clause is there to protect the Member States vertically from the EU, whereas the equality clause is there to guarantee horizontally the equality of the Member States vis-à-vis each other in relation to the EU. This leads to the realisation that from the Member States' perspective it is not just about how the actions of the Union affect their own constitutions – that is to say, whether the EU breaches the competences conferred to it – but also about how the actions of other Member States affect the Union, with which all of the Member States have a common constitutional bond.

The 'equality' aspect of Article 4(2) TEU has been argued at least once before the CJEU, although in a different manner as is conceptualised here.[56] Poland had initiated an action for annulment against the National Emissions Ceilings (NEC) Directive (EU) 2016/2284. The Directive was based on Article 192(1) TFEU, which can be used to better the quality of environment and for protecting human health. The NEC Directive establishes, inter alia, national commitments for the reduction of certain emissions for 2030 onwards. One of the arguments presented by Poland was that the emission reductions envisioned by the NEC Directive breach of the principle of equality of Member States before the Treaties since the national emission reduction commitments provided for in the Directive did not take into account 'the social and economic situation, technological progress and the costs of implementing those commitments in the different Member States and regions of the European Union'.[57] In practice, this argument was based on the idea that the costs of implementing the NEC Directive in Poland are, relatively speaking, considerably higher than in other Member States. The CJEU did not, however, engage with Article 4(2)

---

[54]   A. Bobić, 'Constitutional Pluralism Is Not Dead: An Analysis of Interactions Between Constitutional Courts of Member States and the European Court of Justice' (2017) *German Law Journal* 18(6), 1395–428, p. 1407.

[55]   See e.g. D. Piqani, 'In Search of Limits for the Protection of National Identities as a Member State Interest' in M. Varju (ed.), *Between Compliance and Particularism* (Springer 2019).

[56]   See C-128/17 *Poland v European Parliament and Council* EU:C:2019:194. Also see C-364/10 *Hungary v Slovak Republic* EU:C:2012:630.

[57]   C-128/17, *Poland v European Parliament and Council* EU:C:2019:194, para 119.

TEU in its assessment of this argument. Instead, the CJEU discussed, mainly, the meaning of Article 191(3) TFEU, according to which Union's environmental policy shall take account of the economic and social development of the Union as a whole and the balanced development of its regions.[58]

The argument present by Poland in this case was essentially substantive. Poland argued that the effects of the NEC Directive are disproportionate in Poland and therefore the NEC Directive does not respect the equality of the Member States before the Treaties. This can also be seen in the fact that as part of its assessment, the CJEU concluded a proportionality analysis. The only novelty in Poland's argumentation, then, was in how it connected the equality clause of Article 4(2) TEU to a traditional proportionality argument. On the face of it, Poland's argument seems similar as to the 'horizontal aspect' of the equality clause that is presented here. However, it is actually quite different due to the very reason that it is substantive, whereas the argument presented here is structural in nature.

It is rather self-evident that the effects of EU law differ from one Member State to another when it comes to harmonisation. Some Member States might already have in place similar policies and legal rules as are mandated by a new directive. Thus, substantively speaking, all harmonisation treats Member States in an unequal manner. Yet, if we take into consideration what harmonisation is actually about, we realise that this is what it is actually supposed to do. Therefore, the way that Poland tried to utilise the equality clause of Article 4(2) TEU in its argumentation was somewhat redundant and it was not surprising that the CJEU did not engage with this argument. Another reason that might explain why the CJEU did not engage with Article 4(2) TEU in its argumentation is that perhaps the CJEU's understanding of the Article is conditioned by the prevailing view in the literature. As explained above, the literature seems to have disregarded the equality aspect of Article 4(2) almost completely.

In what types of situations, then, could the equality clause of Article 4(2) TEU be utilised in practice? The next chapter will address inequality and its consequent problems from a legal perspective. There, the possibility of the CJEU to affect the workings of national courts in a similar manner as was the result of *Simmenthal* will be discussed.[59] Could the equality clause of Article 4(2) TEU be used to argue to this end? Furthermore, the next chapter will also discuss the effects of the CJEU's *Foglia* doctrine and whether the CJEU could use it to decline to admit cases that stem from such inequality.[60] Perhaps the

---

[58] Ibid., paras 127–148.
[59] Case 106/77 *Simmenthal* EU:C:1978:49.
[60] Case 104/79 *Foglia* EU:C:1980:73; Case 244/80 *Foglia (No 2)* EU:C:1981:302.

equality clause of Article 4(2) TEU could be used to aid in the formulation of this doctrine too?

And what about Article 4(2) TEU as a whole? How should the equality clause (horizontal aspect) and national identity clause (vertical aspect) of Article 4(2) TEU affect each other? That is to say, if we accept that the national identity clause might in some circumstances allow for the Member States to breach EU law – but only if the CJEU has granted this in a preliminary reference procedure so as not to endanger the primacy of EU law unilaterally[61] – how should the horizontal aspect of the Article be taken into consideration in this process? These are open questions to which we do not yet have proper answers. Let us still consider the above-discussed case *Poland v European Parliament and Council* from another perspective. Although the annulment procedure functions *ex ante* whereas an action due to a failure to fulfil obligations is initiated *ex post*, from the perspective of what is argued, these two issues can overlap. If Poland had declined to transpose the NEC Directive and then, following an action for a failure to fulfil obligations by the Commission, had pleaded national constitutional identity as a reason for why it did not fulfil its obligations under the NEC Directive, how would the CJEU have reacted? This way, Poland could have utilised the national identity clause of Article 4(2) TEU to argue, effectively, for the same objective as it did by way of relying on the equality clause in an action for annulment. Yet, as the CJEU did not even recognise the use of the equality clause in the manner as attempted by Poland, we cannot conclude that it would be possible to use them in a similar manner. However, this case should not be interpreted to mean that that the equality clause cannot have its own independent and practically meaningful content.

Lastly, can the equality clause of Article 4(2) TEU affect the workings of national courts? That is, could national courts try to use it in some manner? Perhaps not, since the actions of national courts are guided by their national constitutions. It is difficult to conceive of a situation in which a national court would directly apply Article 4(2) TEU, as national courts do not apply rules of the Treaties, not at least in this manner. Furthermore, unlike the Charter of Fundamental Rights, which national courts can take into consideration, or the indirect (interpretive) effect of directives, which can guide the application of national law, Article 4(2) TEU does not seem to possess similar qualities so as to affect the interpretation of national law by national courts. It could, of course, be used by national politicians to argue for a variety of issues; in a similar manner as has been the case with the national identity clause, as was observed above in relation to the rule of law crisis in Hungary and Poland.

---

[61]   See T. Tuominen, 'Reconceptualizing the Primacy–Supremacy Debate in EU Law' (2020) *Legal Issues of Economic Integration* 47(3), 245–65.

6.5   CONCLUSIONS

This chapter has sought to describe how national courts are in an unequal position when it comes to their ability to interact with the European-level political process, the CJEU, and more generally speaking, EU law. The political ramifications of such inequality were discussed, especially how this affects the legitimacy of interventions by national courts. Furthermore, the related discussion on the national identity clause of Article 4(2) TEU was introduced, which is somewhat corollary to the discussion on constitutional pluralism. As part of this discussion, a novel reading on the two different aspects of Article 4(2) TEU was presented: the equality clause, which concerns the horizontal relationship between the Member States, and the national identity clause, which concerns the vertical relationship between the Member States and the European Union. After these mainly descriptive and rather tentative conclusions, the next chapter will discuss what should or could be done about inequality.

7.   The role of courts and the question of ultimate interpretive authority

7.1   INTRODUCTION

This chapter first focuses on the predicament that most of the national courts had when they reviewed the different legal mechanisms adopted pursuant to the euro crisis. It is argued that those national courts that were able to review the mechanisms at a later stage of the political and legal process, sometimes even after they had already entered into force, faced a strong predicament to find these measures in compliance with their national constitutions. Thus, review by these courts – as opposed to the privileged courts that were able to act early on and might have had an influence on the process – does not strengthen the legitimacy of the overhaul of the European Union's economic governance regime. Furthermore, the substantive and procedural guarantees in the EU Treaties through which the same issues that the national courts pursued by relying on their national constitutions are discussed. Here, the purpose is to question the constitutional nature of these national judicial review procedures and instead ask whether they served only political purposes (7.2).

Then, the chapter addresses the possibilities that the Court of Justice of the European Union (CJEU) might have to address such inequality. Building on an analysis of *Gauweiler*,[1] a structural and substantive alternative are presented. The first concerns the possibilities that the CJEU has to reshape the national courts' mandates through its own doctrines, with the view to thus alleviating the problem of inequality. It is concluded that this alternative does not seem like a plausible solution. The second relates to what types of preliminary references the CJEU admits and how it answers them. Here, the question revolves around the reasons for why the CJEU admitted the case and what consequences its dismissal might have had (7.3).

Lastly, the chapter discusses the shortcomings of the substantive alternative, which reveals the inadequacy of the EU's current constitutional constellation. The notion of constitutional pluralism was born out of the inter-court dialogue, which centres around the sovereignty debate: what is the meaning of the

---

[1]   C-62/14 *Gauweiler* EU:C:2015:400.

primacy of EU law with regards to the sovereignty of the Member States? Depending on one's viewpoint, constitutional pluralism can be seen either as an answer to the existing constitutional plurality or just as a means of trying to explain away the problem; of sweeping the sovereignty debate under the carpet. Although in *Gauweiler* the CJEU was able to assert its interpretive authority over the German Federal Constitutional Court (*Bundesverfassungsgericht*), but as we saw recently in *Weiss*, the Federal Constitutional Court is willing to disregard the judgments of the CJEU.[2] Furthermore, there are also other instances where highest national courts have not followed the ruling given by the CJEU in a preliminary reference procedure. This raises the fact that the CJEU is unable to unilaterally resolve the latent conflict between it and the national courts. On this basis it is argued that constitutional pluralism is not a valid normative theory of European constitutionalism (7.4).

The final section concludes the discussion (7.5).

7.2   THE NATIONAL COURTS' PREDICAMENT

The Member States established the EU for the specific purpose of governing common issues by way of creating a common legal framework. This common legal framework must produce legal effects within the Member States' legal orders if it is to fulfil these objectives. Advocate General Cruz Villalón alluded to this in his opinion in *Gauweiler*.[3] This is the harmonising nature of EU law. However, a central and often overlooked aspect of European constitutionalism is how the national affects the European. The effects of the national constitutional frameworks on the European level can stem from either written norms or court created doctrines. It needs to be remembered that constitutional pluralism, both as a phenomenon and subsequently as an intellectual project, was born out of the German Federal Constitutional Court's contestation against the Treaty of Maastricht.[4]

This section argues that the national courts had no reason to try to enforce certain national constitutional principles against the EU's political process as such, since they are already contained in EU law *sensu lato*. Furthermore, whilst doing so, the national courts that were able to act after the point of no return were all the same not able to strengthen the legitimacy of these

---

[2]   2 BvR 859/15, 05 May 2020 (*PSPP judgment*). See 'The German Federal Constitutional Court's PSPP Judgment' (2020) *German Law Journal* [special section] 21(5), 944–1127.

[3]   See Opinion of Advocate General Cruz Villalón delivered on 14 January 2015, C-62/14 *Gauweiler* EU:C:2015:7, para. 59.

[4]   See J. Baquero Cruz, 'The Legacy of the Maastricht-Urteil and the Pluralist Movement' (2008) *European Law Journal* 14(4), 389–422.

European-level measures; they faced a strong predicament to find these measures in compliance with their national constitutions. The point of no return means the stage of the European-level political process after which an individual national court was not able to prevent the European measure from being adopted or coming into force. In light of the case studies this point was as follows: for the Fiscal Compact Treaty, this was its entry into force in January 2013;[5] for the European Stability Mechanism Treaty (ESM), this was the CJEU's ruling in *Pringle*;[6] for the European Central Bank's (ECB) Outright Monetary Transactions (OMT) programme, this was the CJEU's ruling in *Gauweiler*;[7] finally, for the Banking Union no such point was distinguished mainly because it was only reviewed by the German Federal Constitutional Court and in that case the judgment was delivered several years after the entry into force of the EU secondary law measures constituting the banking union.[8]

7.2.1   The National Courts Assert – With a Predicament

A host of different national constitutional norms or doctrines can be distinguished from the national cases reviewing the different crisis response mechanisms. These took the form of either arguments presented to the courts by the various applicants or arguments the courts themselves employed as a basis for their findings. Since there is considerable overlap between these various national principles and the fact that each court presented them in relation to their national constitutional doctrine, it is difficult to compile a definitive list of them. Therefore, the following list aims to outline by way of compilation the most important principles that can be derived from the national cases:[9]

* The principle of democracy: containing the right to vote and a requirement that state actions are appropriately legitimised (Estonia, Germany).
* The principle of national sovereignty: in a variety of different meanings and aspects, some of which were clearly post-national (Estonia, Finland, France, Germany, Ireland and Poland).

---

[5]   See Chapter 2.2.
[6]   C-370/12 *Pringle* EU:C:2012:756. See Chapter 3.2.
[7]   C-62/14 *Gauweiler* EU:C:2015:400. See Chapter 5.2.
[8]   See Chapter 4.2.
[9]   For discussion on these national cases, see Chapters 2–5. A broader analysis, covering more than just the euro crisis, has distinguished the following principles or issues as being central to the debate on national constitutional identity: family law; protection of the welfare state; the form of state and the associated issue of local government; national preferences for foreign and military policy; national language; fiscal autonomy; and criminal law. See P. Faraguna, 'Taking Constitutional Identities Away from the Courts' (2016) *Brooklyn Journal of International Law* 41(2), 491–578.

- The principle of the budgetary powers of the parliament: also referred to as the budgetary autonomy or sovereignty of the parliament (Estonia, Finland, France, Germany and the Netherlands).
- The principle of the state's fiscal ability to meet its constitutional obligations: the state needs fiscal resources to fulfil the obligations that it has towards its citizens (Estonia, Finland and Germany).

Were these principles transposed to the European level through the national courts' judgments? In other words, did they have any effect on the formation of the crisis response measures, on their future operation or on the EU's constitutional framework in general? As was discussed in the case studies, some changes were made to the content of the Fiscal Compact and the ESM Treaties due to national constitutional constraints.[10] But were these changes introduced to safeguard the above-listed constitutional principles or purely for political convenience? One of the central reasons for adopting changes to these two treaties was that they could then be ratified by a simple majority instead of a qualified majority in the national parliaments.[11] This was central since securing a qualified majority behind these treaties would have been politically impossible in most Member States, and thus the measures would not have been ratified and implemented at all in the respective Member States.

According to the above-described view, the listed four principles did not as such lead to the contents of the crisis response measures being adapted to suit them, but rather national political situations forced these changes to be adopted. This line of argumentation can of course be disputed, or even claimed to be circular, since the reasons behind the pragmatic political consideration are the constitutional norms that prescribe qualified majority requirements for amending national constitutions or for adopting international treaties of constitutional relevance. Furthermore, the judicial review powers existing in national constitutions for enforcing these principles made it mandatory to take such political imperatives into consideration. However, this only means that the Member States' constitutional systems as such are functioning and not that the aforementioned principles expounded in the national case law would have per se affected the final formulation of the Fiscal Compact or the ESM Treaties.

---

[10] See Chapters 2.2 and 3.2.

[11] According to the constitutions of most Member States, the ratification and implement of an international treaty that has constitutional significance (that is contrary to some parts of the existing constitution) is possible but requires recourse to a process similar to constitutional amendment, necessitating a qualified majority in the parliament. See L. Besselink, M. Claes, Š. Imamović and J.-H. Reestman: *National Constitutional Avenues for Further EU Integration* (European Parliament, Directorate General for Internal Policies, Policy Department C, 2014), pp. 31–3.

But can a conclusion be drawn from the above, that national judicial review would have legitimised the Fiscal Compact and the ESM Treaties? Or, even more generally, can it be said that the national cases have helped to legitimise the overhaul of the EU's economic governance regime? Reestman has argued that the judicial review of these mechanisms by national courts had a legitimising force on the said measures. This is for three reasons. First, the way in which the national rulings have ended the discussion on the constitutionality of these measures; all the judgments are final and all approved the mechanisms. Second, the way in which the rulings have increased the national political acceptance of the measures by setting certain substantive limits for the mechanisms. Third, the way in which the judgments have indicated the limits to how far integration within the economic sphere can progress without recourse to amending national constitutions.[12]

Although all three points are facts as such, the argument that these national judgments had a legitimising force is difficult to accept. As Reestman himself points out,[13] the national courts reviewing the crisis response measures after the point of no return faced an enormous predicament to deem them as legal according to their respective national constitutions. Therefore, a more plausible argument would be that the national courts went to great lengths in coming up with the fitting procedural or substantive arguments for why this is so.[14] He seems to, however, dismiss this predicament rather lightly in a somewhat Tu Quoque fashion by pointing out how the courts acting before the point of no return were also faced with a predicament, although one of a slightly different nature.[15] But this does not negate the fact that there existed a real predicament towards the courts participating after the point of no return, and in no way does it increase the legitimacy of their judgments. It just shows how the courts participating before the point of no return too were faced with a predicament, and thus, how courts are perhaps not the best institutions for assessing such issues in the first place.

Regulating macroeconomic policies through legal means is difficult enough in itself, and furthermore, courts will inevitably have difficulties in review-

---

[12] See J.-H. Reestman, 'Legitimacy Through Adjudication: the ESM Treaty and the Fiscal Compact before the National Courts' in T. Beukers, B. de Witte and C. Kilpatrick (eds), *Constitutional Change through Euro-Crisis Law* (Cambridge University Press 2017).

[13] Ibid., pp. 268–9.

[14] Reestman has conducted a thorough analysis of the cases in this respect. See ibid., pp. 245–67. Also, see F. Amtenbrink, 'New Economic Governance in the European Union: Another Constitutional Battleground?' in K. Purnhagen and P. Rott (eds), *Varieties of European Economic Law and Regulation: Liber Amicorum for Hans Micklitz* (Springer 2014).

[15] Reestman, ibid., p. 269.

ing such measures and policies since they follow an economic logic instead of legal rationality.[16] Courts represent rights, but not expertise or voice.[17] Furthermore, such court-led constitutionalisation is open to criticism since, according to Curtin, 'it represents a rather haphazard and ad hoc approach to constitution-making', and as such it is an elitist and closed constitution-making process.[18] Thus, it would seem that the best source for realising legitimacy still resides with the national parliaments, as they are vested with democratic accountability.[19]

However, it can of course be argued that this conclusion applies only to Finland precisely for the reason that the Constitutional Law Committee of the Parliament has been able to act proactively. It could also be argued that the German Federal Constitutional Court would not have been able to assume such a central role if its interventions were not seen as legitimate from a substantive perspective. Notwithstanding, parliaments are still surely a better source of legitimacy than courts; courts can only fill the legitimacy gap if parliaments have been unable to do so in the first place. As a Habermasian transnational democracy has not yet surfaced in Europe,[20] national parliaments are the appropriate loci of such legitimacy.

7.2.2   The EU's Legal Order Protects – Independently

The above-listed four principles seem rational derivations of the core elements that modern rights-based constitutions contain and to which the Member States surely subscribe. Although there are variations in the national constitutional identities of the Member States, these principles seem to be dear to most of them, as is exemplified by the fact that they were expounded by many national courts. However, without disputing the relevance of these principles, it is worth asking whether there was a real need for national courts to assert these principles towards the EU? In other words, are these not already contained in the Union's own constitutional framework *sensu stricto*? This question is

---

[16]   See K. Tuori, *European Constitutionalism* (Cambridge University Press 2015), p. 323.

[17]   See F. Fabbrini, *Economic Governance in Europe. Comparative Paradoxes and Constitutional Challenges* (Oxford University Press 2016), pp. 108–12.

[18]   D. Curtin, *Executive Power of the European Union: Law, Practices, and the Living Constitution* (Oxford University Press 2009), pp. 13–14.

[19]   See P. Leino and J. Salminen, 'The Euro Crisis and Its Constitutional Consequences for Finland: Is There Room for National Politics in EU Decision-Making?' (2013) *European Constitutional Law Review* 9(3), 451–79, p. 477.

[20]   See J. Habermas, *The Lure of Technocracy* (Polity Press 2015), Chapter 2; and compare to J. Habermas, 'Remarks on Dieter Grimm's "Does Europe Need a Constitution?"' (1995) *European Law Journal* 1(3), 303–7.

made relevant when taking into consideration the following facts: none of the national legal proceedings in which these principles were evoked resulted in the Member States and the EU from being obstructed from setting up the crisis response mechanisms or an individual Member State from being obstructed to ratify and implement such a measure.

First, the values of the EU are listed in Article 2 TEU. These contain, inter alia, democracy and the rule of law. According to Article 10 TEU the functioning of the Union is built on representative democracy and according to Article 20 TFEU the citizens of the EU have the right to vote.

Second, although the principle of sovereignty is not directly mentioned in the EU Treaties, its core meaning is found in Articles 4 and 5 TEU on the principle of conferral and the allocation of competences between the EU and the Member States. Since the starting point of these Articles is that the Member States retain the competences that are not conferred onto the Union, the Member States are essentially sovereign. This view is corroborated by Article 50 TEU according to which the Member States may withdraw from the Union, which is a way of redeeming back the transferred sovereignty. Brexit makes such an interpretation also practically valid.[21]

Third, Article 5 TFEU on the Union's economic policy competence, as well as Articles 119 and 120 TFEU, all build on the idea of the Member States' independent economic policies, which are only coordinated by the Union. In fact, Article 5 TEU was formulated as it is because of the Member States' will to retain economic policy competences (i.e. fiscal sovereignty).[22] Moreover, this has also affected the fact that the Union's competences within the sphere of economic policy do not follow the logic of exclusive, shared or supplementary.[23] The underlying logic of the EMU – the Maastricht compromise – as enshrined in the prohibition on monetary financing (Art. 123 TFEU) and the no bail-out clause (Art. 125 TFEU) also corroborates this view.[24] Thus, in a certain sense, the EU Treaties also contain the principle of the budgetary powers of national parliaments.

Fourth, while the principle of the states' fiscal ability to meet their constitutional obligations is not found directly in the EU Treaties, it can be deduced

---

[21] For a further discussion, see T. Tuominen, 'Reconceptualizing the Primacy–Supremacy Debate in EU Law' (2020) *Legal Issues of Economic Integration* 47(3), 245–65.

[22] See P. Craig, *The Lisbon Treaty: Law, Politics, and Treaty Reform* (Oxford University Press 2013), p. 179.

[23] See R. Bieber, 'The Allocation of Economic Policy Competences in the European Union' in L. Azoulai (ed.), *The Question of Competence in the European Union* (Oxford University Press 2014), p. 90.

[24] See Chapter 1.2.1.

from the norms listed above that contain the first three principles. Furthermore, both the general obligation of the Member States to respect human rights (Art. 2 TEU) and the more specific obligations stemming from the Charter of Fundamental Rights – for example the right to social security and social assistance (Art. 34 EU Charter) or the right to healthcare (Art. 35 EU Charter) – require that Member States have at their disposal adequate fiscal means and that they duly allocate them for the fulfilment of these rights.

After having established that the EU's own legal order contains the principles that the national courts sought to safeguard on the basis of their national constitutions, the following residual and rather hypothetical position is still worth assessing: If the EU Treaties did not contain these principles, could the EU's legal order still have protected their realisation? In other words, could EU law, if understood in a composite manner,[25] protect their fulfilment through other means?

Two Treaty articles and requirements stand out in this respect. First, Article 7 TEU on national compliance with the values of Article 2 TEU. Second, Article 4(2) on the respect of the Member States' national constitutional identities. In fact, the functioning of these three articles needs to be understood as a whole. Article 2 TEU on the values of the Union is known as the homogeneity clause in that it constitutes 'the constitutional identity of the Union in as far as it coincides with the identity common to the Member States'.[26] Article 4(2) TEU states that the Union shall respect the national identities of the Member States, which are inherent in their constitutional structures. Thus, the EU should embrace the principles found in the Member States' constitutions and accord protection for their fulfilment. Understood in this way, EU law would contain the above-listed principles even if they were not found in the EU Treaties *sensu stricto*, since the homogeneity clause includes them anyway in EU law *sensu lato*.

7.3   HOW TO CREATE EQUALITY?

7.3.1   The Structural Alternative

Next, two different possibilities for how the CJEU could have tackled the inequality issue in *Gauweiler* are discussed: a structural and a substantive alternative.

---

[25]   See L. Besselink, *A Composite European Constitution* (Europa Law Publishing 2007).

[26]   L. Besselink, 'The Bite, the Bark and the Howl: Article 7 TEU and the Rule of Law Initiatives' in A. Jakab and D. Kochenov (eds), *The Enforcement of EU Law and Values: Ensuring Member States' Compliance* (Oxford University Press 2017), p. 129.

According to Article 4(2) TEU, the EU is to respect the national identities of the Member States' as they are inherent in their fundamental political and constitutional structures. This means that Member States are free to decide how their national constitutional frameworks are designed. One element of this is how constitutional review is conducted in a Member State – or whether they have such a legal institution or procedure at all. The freedom that Member States have in this regard is only circumscribed by their obligation to respect Union law, as specified in Article 4(3) TEU. However, as de Visser has pointed out, the case law of the CJEU does seem to affect this freedom of the Member States to some degree. The main point of concern of this case law has been the relationship between national constitutional courts and other national courts and how to ensure the procedural primacy of EU law.[27]

The most important ruling of the CJEU in this regard is *Simmenthal*.[28] The case concerned a situation in which an Italian magistrate had, based on a pre-liminary ruling it had received from the CJEU, ordered the Italian ministry of finance to refund fees that had been unlawfully placed on importers of goods. The ministry protested because under its interpretation the magistrate lacked the competence, under Italian law, to refuse to apply Italian law that was found to be inconsistent with EU law. Only the Italian constitutional court (*Corte constituzionale*) could, according to the Italian constitution, declare national laws as unconstitutional. Thus, under the Italian system, ordinary judges did not possess the competence to set aside national law that they found to breach EU law, and rather they should refer such issues to the constitutional court.

Such a view contradicts the EU law principles of primacy and direct effect.[29] Therefore, the Italian magistrate decided to send a second request to the CJEU. In its answer the CJEU found that all national courts must be able to refuse to apply national law that is incompatible with EU law. National courts cannot be required to direct such issues to a constitutional court. Effectively, then, the CJEU ruled on the national judicial enforcement of the doctrines of primacy and direct effect.[30] The judgment meant a model of decentralised review on the conformity of national law with EU law.[31]

Later on, in *Melki and Abdeli*, the CJEU ruled as follows: national laws which establish an obligation for national courts to refer an issue to the national constitutional court for a decision on constitutionality before they can

---

[27]   See M. de Visser, *Constitutional Review in Europe: A Comparative Analysis* (Hart Publishing 2014), pp. 417–27.

[28]   Case 106/77 *Simmenthal* EU:C:1978:49.

[29]   See Case 26/62 *Van Gend en Loos* EU:C:1963:1; Case 6/64 *Costa v ENEL* EU:C:1964:66.

[30]   See Case 106/77 *Simmenthal* EU:C:1981:102, paras 21–24.

[31]   de Visser (n 27), p. 419.

make a reference to the CJEU are contrary to EU law.[32] Such a rule effectively precludes national courts from referring cases to the CJEU as a preliminary reference under Article 267 TFEU before they have referred them to the national constitutional court. The case arose following changes made to the national system of judicial review in France.[33]

The usual conclusion on *Simmenthal* and consequent cases is that they resulted in the decentralisation of judicial review in the Member States.[34] If the CJEU has been able to harmonise certain aspects of national judicial review in this manner, could it then perhaps also tackle the inequality between the way in which national courts can participate to the European-level political process? Should, or could, the CJEU do something about such differences in national frameworks for judicial review?

At first glance the answer seems to be negative since both *Simmenthal* and *Melki and Abdeli* were about the preliminary reference procedure and making it possible for all national courts to participate in the European dialogue between courts by utilising this procedure; whereas the issue addressed here is somewhat of an indirect nature, and the solution would seem to be to limit the judicial review possibilities of certain national courts instead of granting all courts similar powers. Increasing the judicial review powers of all national courts would just deepen the said problem. However, as the case studies point out, some courts have been able to make preliminary references to the CJEU, while others have not purely due to differences in national legal frameworks. And as was argued before,[35] the CJEU seems to acknowledge and accept this since it first refused to admit an action for annulment against the OMT programme yet accepted the preliminary referral from the Federal Constitutional Court in *Gauweiler*.[36]

---

[32]   C-188/10 and C-189/10 *Aziz Melki and Sélim Abdeli* EU:C:2010:363, paras 52–53.

[33]   See de Visser (n 27), pp. 420–22; T. Tridimas, 'The ECJ and the National Courts: Dialogue, Cooperation, and Instability' in A. Arnull and D. Chalmers (eds), *The Oxford Handbook of European Union Law* (Oxford University Press 2015), pp. 415–16.

[34]   See L. Besselink, 'The Proliferation of Constitutional Law and Constitutional Adjudication, or How American Judicial Review Came to Europe After All' (2013) *Utrecht Law Review* 9(2), 19–35; D. Piqani, 'The *Simmenthal* revolution revisited: what role for constitutional courts?' in B. de Witte, J. A. Mayoral, U. Jaremba, M. Wind and K. Podstawa (eds.), *National Courts and EU Law: New Issues, Theories and Methods* (Edward Elgar Publishing 2016).

[35]   See Chapter 5.2.2.3.

[36]   See T-492/12 *von Storch and Others v ECB* EU:T:2013:702; C-64/14 P, *Sven A. von Storch v European Central Bank* EU:C:2015:300; C-62/14 *Gauweiler* EU:C:2015: 400.

However, it would perhaps be too bold of a conclusion to suggest that the CJEU could through its interpretation limit the national courts' competences as to when and how they can refer cases to it. Empowerment and disempowerment are quite different things, and while the effectiveness of EU law can logically be used to argue in favour of the *Simmenthal* revolution, it is difficult to find normative basis for an argument that would lead to the disempowerment of national courts. Such an interpretation of the equality clause of Article 4(2) TEU would perhaps breach the national identity clause of the same Article.

7.3.2   The Substantive Alternative

If the above-described structural solution, which pertains to the constitutional frameworks of the Member States, does not seem like a feasible solution for how the CJEU could tackled the issue of inequality, a substantive approach can also be explored. Let us take *Gauweiler* as an example: the CJEU could have declared the preliminary reference by the German Federal Constitutional Court as inadmissible and thus accepted the claims made by the intervening Member States.[37] Next, this alternative will be assessed in more detail.

The starting point of the preliminary reference procedure is that when a question submitted by a national court concerns the interpretation of a provision of EU law, the CJEU is obliged to give a ruling.[38] However, in order to police its own jurisdiction, the CJEU has to assess the nature of the preliminary reference and the content of the question referred to make sure that it does not exceed the limits of its competence. If the CJEU were to answer a preliminary reference that would not contribute towards resolving the dispute in the main proceedings because the question had no relevance to EU law, the CJEU would be overstepping its jurisdiction.[39] Therefore, the CJEU has started to assert authority over the cases referred. To this end, the CJEU has created the *Foglia* doctrine.[40] Under this doctrine, the CJEU ultimately decides on its own jurisdiction – not the referring court or the parties to the main proceedings. In other words, the CJEU has the competence to decide over the suitability of the reference. Although *Foglia* concerned a somewhat hypothetical situation, the created doctrine is more general and actually about control over the preliminary reference procedure and a judicial hierarchy between national courts and the CJEU.

---

[37]   See C-62/14 *Gauweiler* EU:C:2015:400, paras 18–31.

[38]   C-231/89 *Krystyna Gmurzynska-Bscher* EU:C:1990:386, para. 20.

[39]   K. Lenaerts, I. Maselis and K. Gutman, *EU Procedural Law* (Oxford University Press 2014), pp. 84–5.

[40]   See Case 104/79 *Foglia* EU:C:1980:73, paras 10–11; Case 244/80 *Foglia (No 2)* EU:C:1981:302, paras 12–25.

The *Foglia* doctrine has then been further elaborated to include various reasons for declining jurisdiction: hypothetical cases, irrelevant cases, unclearly articulated cases, and cases in which the facts are insufficiently clear.[41] The category on hypothetical cases has been addressed in several cases. The main point is that the justification for a reference for a preliminary ruling is not that it enables advisory opinions on general or hypothetical questions to be delivered, but rather that it is necessary for the effective resolution of a dispute.[42] There are both practical and conceptual reasons for why the hypothetical nature of the case has been used as an argument to decline jurisdiction. Regarding the former category, it would be a waste of resources to give a ruling in a case that is of no practical relevance due to its hypothetical nature.[43] However, deciding when an issue is of no practical relevance can be difficult.[44] The latter category concerns issues such as who are the correct parties to the case, and as such are the relevant arguments presented. Likewise, here too it is difficult to define when the question is hypothetical.[45]

Were the CJEU's arguments for dismissing the intervening Member States' claims of hypotheticality persuasive in *Gauweiler*, or should the CJEU have dismissed the preliminary reference instead? Craig and Markakis have presented the pragmatic answer to this question: the CJEU did not want to dismiss the case on the basis of its allegedly hypothetical nature since it would have given the German Federal Constitutional Court the impression that the CJEU did not want to engage with the substantive questions of the case and was not taking the German court's concerns seriously.[46]

While on the face of it this argument seems very valid, it nevertheless stems from a wrong premise. During the foundational period of Community law, it was essential for the CJEU to recruit the national courts into its endeavour of

---

[41] See P. Craig and G. de Búrca, *EU Law: Text, Cases, and Materials. Fifth Edition* (Oxford University Press 2011), pp. 467–71; Lenaerts, Maselis and Gutman (n 39), pp. 87–94.

[42] C-409/06 *Winner Wetten* EU:C:2010:503, para. 38.

[43] See C-492/11 *Ciro Di Donna* EU:C:2013:428, paras 30–31: the national legislation in question had been annulled during the proceedings, therefore questions regarding them had become devoid of purpose.

[44] Compare C-422/93, C-423/93 and C-424/93 *Teresa Zabala Erasun* EU:C:1995: 183, para. 29 with C-194/94 *CIA Security International* EU:C:1996:172, paras 19–20.

[45] See C-412/93 *Société d'Importation Edouard Leclerc-Siplec* EU:C:1995:26, paras 8–16, where the CJEU decided to give a preliminary ruling although there actually was no dispute between the parties in the main proceedings; C-458/06 *Skatteverket* EU:C:2008:338, paras 25–33, where the CJEU decided to give a preliminary ruling to a reference sent not from a court deciding an actual case but a tax authority giving a preliminary opinion on how certain products would be taxed if they were sold in Sweden.

[46] P. Craig and M. Markakis, 'Gauweiler and the Legality of Outright Monetary Transactions' (2016) *European Law Review* 41(1), 4–24, p. 15.

establishing the primacy of EU law and of acquiring direct effect in practice.[47] EU law was only able to achieve primacy and direct effect in practice due to such 'cooperative supranationalism' between national courts and the CJEU.[48] However, now that these doctrines have been established and accepted as part of the day-to-day practice of the majority of courts throughout the Member States,[49] the CJEU should focus on securing the coherence and efficacy of the established system; even if it means enforcing it against recalcitrant national courts. Since the CJEU came to the conclusion that its role is to interpret the content of EU law and that the referring court is obliged to follow this interpretation,[50] it would not have been difficult for the CJEU to continue on this strictly assertive path and to declare the referral as inadmissible due to its hypothetical nature.

A closer reading of the CJEU's argumentation reveals how, or actually why, it reached the conclusion it did. The CJEU first addressed the issue of what the roles are of the two courts within this procedure and how the national court is obliged to follow the interpretation reached by the CJEU.[51] The CJEU needed to state this due to the threat that the German Federal Constitutional Court had voiced in its referral: if the CJEU produced the wrong answer, it might not follow it. While it was necessary for the CJEU to state this in order to assert its interpretative authority over the German court, this statement then led the CJEU to conclude that the hypothetical nature of the referral is not an issue since it is within the margin of consideration left to the national court in deciding what questions to refer.[52] Furthermore, the CJEU concluded that it is not for it to determine whether the case has been admitted to the Federal Constitutional Court in accordance with the applicable German rules of proce-

---

[47]   See K. J. Alter, *Establishing the Supremacy of European Law: The Making of an International Law Rule of Law in Europe* (Oxford University Press 2001), Chapter 2.

[48]   Tridimas (n 33), p. 408.

[49]   However, some highest national courts have had difficulties in coming to terms with the primacy of EU law. For an overview of the positions, see B. de Witte, 'Direct Effect, Primacy, and the Nature of the Legal Order' in P. Craig and G. de Búrca (eds), *The Evolution of EU Law* (2nd edn, Oxford University Press 2011), pp. 346–57; C. Grabenwarter, 'National Constitutional Law Relating to the European Union' in A. von Bogdandy and J. Bast (eds), *Principles of European Constitutional Law* (2nd edn revised, Hart Publishing 2009).

[50]   C-62/14 *Gauweiler* EU:C:2015:400, paras 11–17. Similarly, see Opinion of Advocate General Cruz Villalón (n 4), paras 30–69.

[51]   C-62/14 *Gauweiler* EU:C:2015:400, paras 15–16.

[52]   Ibid., para. 24, citing para. 15.

dure.[53] In other words, the CJEU's will to employ the *Foto-Frost* doctrine led to the situation in which it was obstructed from applying the *Foglia* doctrine.[54]

Pernice has explained in more detail what options the CJEU had to dismiss the request due to its hypothetical nature. First, the reference concerned the legality of a decision that the ECB may take in the future; that is, that the press release on the OMT programme itself is not a legal act with the proper effects needed for it being amenable to judicial review. Second, the *ultra vires* review that the Federal Constitutional Court was conducting, and from which the preliminary reference stemmed, has resulted in the CJEU effectively having to decide whether or not the German Parliament (*Bundestag*) and the German Central Bank (*Bundesbank*) neglected their duty to try to annul the decision of the ECB in the first place. This too is a national issue that the CJEU should not be forced to get involved in.[55]

On the other hand, there is of course a rational reason for admitting the case. As Advocate General Cruz Villalón noted, finding the OMT press release as non-actionable would entail the risk of excluding a significant number of decisions of the ECB from all judicial review merely on the grounds that they have not been formally adopted and published in the Official Journal.[56] However, while this is surely a plausible recommendation when it comes to protecting the integrity of the EU's legal order, the separation of powers within the EU and the rights of EU citizens, in this case it was none of these reasons that initiated the proceedings. Rather, it was the will of the German Federal Constitutional Court to contest the ultimate interpretive authority of the CJEU.

All in all, convincing arguments can be presented, on the one hand, for appraising the CJEU's decision to admit the case, despite both the Federal Constitutional Court's threat and the hypothetical nature of the referral and, on the other hand, also for how the CJEU could have and why it should have dismissed the case. Be that as it may, although the CJEU could have dismissed *Gauweiler*, and maybe also could have formulated some sort of a doctrine to restrict national courts' possibilities to impact on the European-level political and legal processes, this would only have partially solved the problem. As is

---

[53]   Ibid., para. 26.
[54]   See Case 314/85 *Foto-Frost* EU:C:1987:452, para. 17:
    Since Article 173 [now Art. 263 TFEU] gives the Court exclusive jurisdiction to declare void an act of a Community institution, the coherence of the system requires that where the validity of a Community act is challenged before a national court the power to declare the act invalid must also be reserved to the Court of Justice.
[55]   I. Pernice, 'A Difficult Partnership Between Courts: The First Preliminary Reference by the German Federal Constitutional Court to the CJEU' (2014) *Maastricht Journal of European and Comparative Law* 21(1), 3–13, pp. 7–8.
[56]   Opinion of Advocate General Cruz Villalón (n 4), para. 89.

well known, courts are restricted by their dockets. That is to say, that they only have the possibility to rule on issues that are brought before them, and whilst doing so they have to follow their mandate as prescribed by the legal norms that create them and their jurisdiction. This results in two problems.

First, a pertinent example of this feature of courts' power are the various national cases on the different crisis response measures themselves. Because national cases are brought about under the conditions of the national constitutional framework, and usually based on national political debates, they end up assessing the legality of one specific measure at a time and from a very specific standpoint. Thus, they end up missing the EU's economic governance regime as a whole.[57] However, this also applies to the CJEU, as can be seen from what took place in *Pringle* and *Gauweiler*.[58] Although aiming for a comprehensive interpretation on the rules governing the EMU, the CJEU too is restricted by its docket and maybe also by certain political predicaments. This is exemplified by how in the two cases the CJEU argued towards different ends although employing similar methods of argumentation.[59] Second, in practice, the CJEU could only limit the national courts' possibilities of trying to directly challenge the validity of EU law, but national courts would still have the possibility of reviewing the national measures necessary for the implementation of European decisions. In this way, national courts would still be able to hijack the European-level political process.

This section assessed what the CJEU's possibilities might have been for trying to address the apparent inequality issue. This was done through discussing the structural and substantive alternatives that the CJEU might have taken. It is a plausible assertion that the CJEU could have dismissed the referral due to substantive reasons. The structural alternative, on the other hand, might be reaching a bit too far. And since the CJEU could have effectively come to the same result through the substantive alternative, it seems that there is no need to propagate for the structural alternative. Nevertheless, the fact that the CJEU took neither of the two distinguished paths leaves a further concern unaddressed.

---

[57]   Amtenbrink (n 14), p. 233.
[58]   C-370/12 *Pringle* EU:C:2012:756; C-62/14 *Gauweiler* EU:C:2015:400.
[59]   In the former case the CJEU's predicament was to classify the ESM as an economic policy measure, whereas in the latter the OMT programme was to be classified as a monetary policy measure. See Chapters 3.2 and 5.2.

7.4   THE PROBLEM OF ULTIMATE INTERPRETIVE AUTHORITY

7.4.1   Introducing the Problem

The attention now shifts to the most apparent feature of constitutional plurality: claims to ultimate interpretive authority by national courts vis-à-vis the CJEU and how the ongoing sovereignty debate between the national and the European manifests itself through this confrontation. The main instigator within this debate has undoubtedly been the German Federal Constitutional Court,[60] but recently also other national courts have started to act similarly.[61] This interaction could also be deemed as the most radical aspect of constitutional plurality, since the participating courts have formulated their constitutional speech acts in a clearly conflict-seeking manner.

Up until before the German Federal Constitutional Courts *PSPP judgment*,[62] direct confrontations between national courts and the CJEU had not resulted in any major negative outcomes at the European level. This is because cases like *Sayn-Wittgenstein*,[63] where the CJEU accepted a national derogation from EU law on the basis of Article 4(2) TEU on national identity, or instances where national courts have defied EU law and the rulings of the CJEU,[64] have concerned rather minor issues that affect mainly the Member State in question. However, while this is factually true, it does not take away the underlying issue and its continued relevance. Since these defiant constitutional speech acts have taken place, what stops national courts from revolting in a more serious manner? Mere political prudence? As the Federal Constitutional Court's *PSPP judgment* shows, national courts are ready and willing to openly defy the CJEU also in issues that concern the whole Union (or the Eurozone). Thus, while in individual cases it is possible to assess from a substantive perspective

---

[60]   See Baquero Cruz (n 4).

[61]   E.g. the Constitutional Court of the Czech Republic (*Ústavní Soud*) declared the CJEU judgment C-399/09 *Landtová* EU:C:2011:415 as *ultra vires* in its judgment of 31 January 2012, Pl. ÚS 5/12 (*Slovak Pensions*). See R. Zbíral, 'A Legal Revolution or Negligible Episode? Court of Justice Decision Proclaimed Ultra Vires' (2012) *Common Market Law Review* 49(4), 1475–91. The Supreme Court of Denmark (*Højesteret*) chose not to follow the CJEU's judgment C-441/14 *Ajos* EU:C:2016:278 in its judgment of 6 December 2016, Case 15/2014 (*Ajos A/S v Estate of A*). See M. Rask Madsen, H. Palmer Olsen and U. Šadl, 'Competing Supremacies and Clashing Institutional Rationalities: the Danish Supreme Court's Decision in the *Ajos* Case and the National Limits of Judicial Cooperation' (2017) *European Law Journal* 23(1–2), 140–50.

[62]   2 BvR 859/15, 05 May 2020 (*PSPP judgment*).

[63]   C-208/09 *Sayn-Wittgenstein* EU:C:2010:806.

[64]   See n 61 above.

whether an event of constitutional defiance and confrontation was acceptable or not, overall such a system is problematic. Therefore, although the critique of constitutional pluralism presented in this book stems from particular cases it is meant as a general critique.

That EU law takes precedence over national law is based on the primacy of EU law. Whether or not the primacy of EU law also entails the sovereignty of the EU over the Member States remains debated.[65] The question of whether the primacy of EU law also entails sovereignty of the Union over Member States is here called the sovereignty debate.[66] While political institutions, both of the Member States and the EU, seem to have grasped the relative nature of their power in the current post-state constellation and thus seldom make claims to ultimate sovereignty,[67] courts seem to have had more difficulty in conforming to this new situation.[68] This is perhaps because it is essentially a political question, although one that is 'tamed by constitutional rules and principles and thus also becomes a legal issue' and therefore ends up being decided by courts.[69]

It is from this inter-court debate that the whole notion of constitutional pluralism was born.[70] Depending on one's viewpoint, constitutional pluralism can be seen either as an answer to the existing constitutional plurality or just as a means of trying to explain away the problem; of sweeping the sovereignty debate under the carpet. It is in this respect that the *Gauweiler* saga[71] and the *Weiss* saga[72] are important. After a short excursus on *Weiss*

---

[65]   Elsewhere I have argued that as long as the Member States remain 'masters of the Treaties' the unconditional primacy of EU law, as enforced by the CJEU, does not mean that the Member States have somehow relinquished their sovereignty. See Tuominen (n 21).

[66]   See N. Walker (ed.), *Sovereignty in Transition* (Hart Publishing 2003); Alter (n 47); N. MacCormick, *Questioning Sovereignty: Law, State, and Nation in the European Commonwealth* (Oxford University Press 1999).

[67]   However, Brexit can be seen as an explicit claim to national sovereignty since by leaving the EU the UK has reclaimed back all of the competences it had transferred to the EU upon accession.

[68]   On how the stance of the national courts of the original six Member States towards the primacy of EU has developed, see A.-M. Slaughter, A. Stone Sweet and J. Weiler (eds), *The European Court and National Courts: Doctrine and Jurisprudence: Legal Change in its Social Context* (Hart Publishing 1998).

[69]   M. Claes, 'Negotiating Constitutional Identity or Whose Identity is it Anyway?' in M. Claes, M. de Visser, P. Popelier and C. Van de Heyning (eds), *Constitutional Conversations in Europe: Actors, Topics and Procedures* (Intersentia Publishing 2012), p. 206.

[70]   See Baquero Cruz (n 4).

[71]   2 BvR 2728/13, 14 January 2014 (*OMT reference*); C-62/14 *Gauweiler* EU:C: 2015:400; 2 BvR 2728/13, 21 June 2016 (*OMT final judgment*).

[72]   2 BvR 859/15, 18 July 2017 (*PSPP reference*); C-493/17 *Weiss* EU:C:2018: 1000; 2 BvR 859/15, 05 May 2020 (*PSPP judgment*).

(7.4.2), both viewpoints on constitutional pluralism will be assessed in light of these sagas. First, it will be asked why constitutional pluralism failed in both cases: in *Gauweiler* the CJEU was able to assert its interpretive authority over the Federal Constitutional Court and the German court did not get the answer to its preliminary reference that it hoped; in *Weiss* the German court attempted to corner the CJEU by building on the criteria that the CJEU had established in *Gauweiler*, but as the CJEU again deemed the ECB's actions valid, the German court then resorted to the utmost and declared the CJEU's judgment and the ECB's decision as *ultra vires*. In other words, it seems that neither court was able to get across to the other what they were hoping for and thus there does not seem to be any conciliatory potential in pluralism (7.4.3). Next, it will be asked why the CJEU is still unable to unilaterally resolve the sovereignty-debate (7.4.4).

7.4.2   Excursus: *Weiss*

The public sector purchase programme (PSPP) is one of the several bond-buying programmes that the ECB has initiated after the onset of the euro crisis. Similar to the OMT programme, through the PSPP the ECB can purchase government bonds from the secondary markets and thereby effectively circumvent the prohibition on central bank financing in Article 123 TFEU. According to the ECB, the PSPP is 'aimed at further enhancing the transmission of monetary policy, facilitating credit provision to the euro area economy, easing borrowing conditions of households and firms and contributing to returning inflation rates to levels closer to 2%, consistent with the primary objective of the ECB to maintain price stability'.[73] Before the adoption of the PSPP annual inflation was between -0.2 per cent and 0.6 per cent.[74] Through the PSPP the ECB in practice injects money into the Eurozone and thus boosts private spending, the assumption being that this should bring inflation back to the target level. This is called 'quantitative easing', a form of unconventional monetary policy.[75] What is important to note is that the objectives of the OMT programme and the PSPP are different. While the OMT programme was aimed at defusing speculation on the sovereign bond markets, the PSPP aims to bring inflation within the Eurozone closer to the target level of 2 per cent. A further difference is that

---

[73]   Decision (EU) 2015/774 of the European Central Bank of 4 March 2015 on a secondary markets public sector asset purchase programme (ECB/2015/10) ('PSPP Decision'), Recital 2.

[74]   C-493/17 *Weiss* EU:C:2018:1000, para. 39.

[75]   See M. Joyce, D. Miles, A. Scott and D. Vayanos, 'Quantitative Easing and Unconventional Monetary Policy – An Introduction' (2012) *The Economic Journal* 122(564), 271–88.

the OMT programme was never actually used, while in November 2020 the cumulative net purchases through the PSPP amounted to 2,400 billion euros.[76]

The procedure before the German Federal Constitutional Court was based on individual constitutional complaints (*Verfassungsbeschwerden*) under Article 93(1)(4a) of the German constitution. The applicants presented the following arguments: first, that the PSPP breaches the ECB's strict monetary policy mandate (Art. 119 TFEU); second, that the PSPP breaches the ban on central bank financing (Art. 123 TFEU); and third, that the possible sharing of losses stemming from the PSPP would affect the budgetary powers of the German Federal Parliament (*Bundestag*), which would infringe on the principle of democracy, as laid down in the German constitution, and therefore also undermine German constitutional identity. On the basis of these arguments, the German court subjected the PSPP to an *ultra vires* review.[77]

As the CJEU and the Federal Constitutional Court had both already previously accepted the OMT programme, and thus purchases on the secondary markets, the gist of the case did not revolve around the legality of the PSPP as such but rather on the details of that programme, specifically its volume, duration and effects. The Federal Constitutional Court's decision to refer the case to the CJEU focused especially on the prohibition on central bank financing (Art. 123 TFEU) and the proportionality of the PSPP.[78]

As was expected in light the CJEU's permissive stance in the previous euro crisis related judgments, the CJEU deemed the PSPP as being within the ECB's mandate.[79] The judgment addressed five issues. First, similarly as to what took place in *Gauweiler*,[80] the CJEU had to again address the admissibility of the case due to the way in which the referral was phrased. The three substantive issues of the case concerned the ECB's obligation to state reasons for the PSPP (Art. 296 TFEU), the delineation of the ECB's strict monetary policy mandate (Arts 119 and 127 TFEU), and the prohibition on central bank financing (Art. 123 TFEU). Whilst discussing the delimitation of competences the CJEU conducted a seemingly more thorough proportionality analysis as to that in *Gauweiler*. The CJEU's analysis concerning Article 123 TFEU again centred on whether the PSPP lessens the Member States' impetus to follow sound budgetary policy. The fifth issue concerned the claim as to whether

---

[76]   See https://www.ecb.europa.eu/mopo/implement/app/html/index.en.html (accessed 25 November 2020).

[77]   2 BvR 859/15, 18 July 2017 (*PSPP reference*).

[78]   See A. Lang, 'Ultra Vires Review of the ECB's Policy of Quantitative Easing: An Analysis of the German Constitutional Court's Preliminary Reference Order in the PSPP Case' (2018) *Common Market Law Review* 55(3), 923–52, pp. 928–33.

[79]   C-493/17 *Weiss* EU:C:2018:1000.

[80]   See Chapter 5.2.2.3.

the PSPP could result in loss sharing between the Member States. The CJEU found this question inadmissible.[81]

In its final judgment in the national proceedings the German Federal Constitutional Court disagreed with the findings of the CJEU.[82] The German court opined that the CJEU's assessment of the legality of the PSPP was wrong. Specifically, that the CJEU's proportionality analysis was lacking and that therefore the judgment as such is *ultra vires*. As a consequence of this the Federal Constitutional Court itself then assessed the legality of the PSPP. According to the court's analysis, the ECB failed to consider the PSPP's effects on economic policy and therefore the PSPP failed the court's proportionality test. The PSPP, too, was deemed *ultra vires*. Ultimately, the Federal Constitutional Court ordered the German government and parliament to take action against the PSPP in its current form.[83]

Early commentators noted that the Federal Constitutional Court's tone in this referral was not as terse as in its first referral in *Gauweiler*; it was 'much more conciliatory' and 'rather modest and neutral', and thus the chance of an *ultra vires* ruling by the German court seemed 'rather remote'.[84] After the German courts final ruling, some have been of the opinion that this outcome was not as unexpected when taking into consideration the court's prior doctrine.[85]

7.4.3   Why Pluralism Failed?

If we look at the *Gauweiler* and *Weiss* sagas, we can observe that pluralism is not what either court was after. To the contrary, both courts just sought to reinforce their own position and interpretive authority within the European constitutional constellation; instead of engaging in a dialogue, both courts were

---

[81]   See M. van der Sluis, 'Similar, Therefore Different: Judicial Review of Another Unconventional Monetary Policy in Weiss (C-493/17)' (2019) *Legal Issues of Economic Integration* 46(3), 263–84; A. Mooij, 'The Weiss judgment: The Court's further clarification of the ECB's legal framework' (2019) *Maastricht Journal of European and Comparative Law* 26(3), 449–65.

[82]   2 BvR 859/15, 05 May 2020 (*PSPP judgment*).

[83]   See P. Dermine, 'The Ruling of the Bundesverfassungsgericht in PSPP – An Inquiry into its Repercussions on the Economic and Monetary Union' (2020) *European Constitutional Law Review*, FirstView article published online 19 November 2020.

[84]   A. Pliakos and G. Anagnostaras, 'Adjudicating Economics II: The Quantitative Easing Programme Declared Valid' (2020) *European Law Review* 45(1), 128–46, pp. 138 and 145.

[85]   See D. Grimm, 'A Long Time Coming' (2020) *German Law Journal* 21(5), 944–9.

perhaps talking past each other.[86] In *Gauweiler* the CJEU prevailed as a clear winner. Regarding *Weiss*, it is not as easy to give a definite answer. Although the German Federal Constitutional Court found both the CJEU's ruling and the ECB's PSPP *ultra vires*, this judgment has no immediate consequences for the ECB as the ECB does not take orders from national courts.

Both courts had their own reasons for pursuing ultimate interpretive authority. For the German Federal Constitutional Court this was the German constitution and for the CJEU the EU Treaties. Instead of pluralism, the first was essentially pursuing 'nation-state constitutional monism' while the latter 'European constitutional monism'.[87] To some extent this is understandable, since both courts are just acting as guardians of different constitutions; constitutions, into which respect towards the other might be written into – the respect for national constitutional identity in Article 4(2) TEU and German constitution's 'openness to European integration' (*Europarechtsfreundlichkeit*) – but which nevertheless are based on monist rather than pluralism premises. In other words, both courts see their respective constitution as the *Grundnorm* that guides their actions.

In the current post-state polity, these two starting points seem to be worlds apart, or at least the results that their application produces are very different. In this sense, it can be observed how the German court, and every other national court for that matter, is captive of its own constitution: their role is to safeguard that constitution at whatever cost – even at the expense of the other Member States. Moreover, due to the content of the German constitution – its specific view of democracy (Art. 20) and how the eternity clause (Art. 79) is supposed to safeguard it – this insight seems to apply even more to it than some other national courts. Indeed, the German constitution's understanding of democracy is somewhat unique and perhaps not shared by other Member States and their constitutions.[88] The CJEU, on the other hand, while essentially doing the

---

[86]   See M. Dawson and A. Bobić, 'Quantitative Easing at the Court of Justice – Doing whatever it takes to save the euro: Weiss and Others' (2019) *Common Market Law Review* 56(4), 1005–40, pp. 1038–9; T. Tuominen, 'Aspects of Constitutional Pluralism in Light of the *Gauweiler* Saga' (2018) *European Law Review* 43(2), 186–204, pp. 200–203.

[87]   'European constitutional monism' refers to the situation where the EU subsumes final authority, whereas the opposite alternative to pluralism is offered by 'nation-state constitutional monism', which refers to the situation where the Member States retain sovereign authority with the Union's legal powers being just somehow derived from these. See K. Jaklič, *Constitutional Pluralism in the EU* (Oxford University Press 2014), p. 21.

[88]   See A. von Bogdandy, 'Common Principles for a Plurality of Orders: A Study on Public Authority in the European Legal Area' (2014) *International Journal of Constitutional Law* 12(4), 980–1007, pp. 995–6.

exact same thing, seems to have a firmer footing for its assertive actions since it has a specific role in the post-state polity – unlike the Federal Constitutional Court, since it is a national institution.

Having been the first ever preliminary reference from the German Federal Constitutional Court to the CJEU, the *Gauweiler* saga had the possibility of institutionalising constitutional pluralism; of expressing how the relationship between the national and European legal orders is now truly 'horizontal rather than vertical – heterarchical rather than hierarchical'.[89] However, following the *Weiss* saga, it seems that the CJEU's will to reinforce its position as the '*über*sovereign'[90] of the EU's legal order backlashed and led to the Federal Constitutional Court proclaiming its *ultra vires* judgment in the latter case.

What might explain this outcome is that the Federal Constitutional Court ruined the possibility of accomplishing mutual deference and finding common ground by assuming a clearly conflict seeking attitude in its referral in *Gauweiler,* and thus setting the whole process of dialogue and rapprochement off on the wrong foot.[91] By doing this, the German court did not offer the CJEU a respectable way of accommodating its views in a manner that would have made it possible to retain the core elements of the CJEU's doctrine concerning the role of the preliminary reference procedure and the CJEU's role as the ultimate interpreter of EU law.[92] As was discussed in the previous section, the CJEU seemed to have a strong preference for asserting its interpretive authority as based on the *Foto-Frost* doctrine. As the CJEU was unwilling to change its stance in *Weiss*, despite the German court enticing the CJEU to utilise the same criteria as formulated by itself in *Gauweiler*, the Federal Constitutional Court perhaps felt that it had no other option than to declare both the CJEU's ruling and the ECB's decision *ultra vires*. In other words, perhaps the German court felt that this was the only way to get its point across to the CJEU.

---

[89]   N. Walker, 'The Idea of Constitutional Pluralism' (2002) *Modern Law Review* 65(3), 317–59, p. 337.

[90]   The term is taken from N. Walker, 'Legal Theory and the European Union: A 25th Anniversary Essay' (2005) *Oxford Journal of Legal Studies* 25(4), 581–601, p. 592.

[91]   2 BvR 2728/13, 14 January 2014 (*OMT reference*). For an analysis of the of the BVerfG's reference as a 'chicken run', see F. Mayer, 'Rebels Without a Cause? A Critical Analysis of the German Constitutional Court's OMT Reference' (2014) *German Law Journal* 15(2), 111–46; M. Kumm, 'Rebel Without a Good Cause: Karlsruhe's Misguided Attempt to Draw the CJEU into a Game of "Chicken" and What the CJEU Might do About It' (2014) *German Law Journal* 15(2), 203–16.

[92]   On this doctrine, see Case 29/68 *Milch-, Fett- und Eierkontor GmbH v Hauptzollamt Saarbrücken* EU:C:1969:27, para. 3; Case 52/76 *Luigi Benedetti* EU:C: 1977:16, para. 26; Case 69/85 *Wünsche Handelsgesellschaft* EU:C:1986:104, para. 13.

At a more theoretical level, this outcome might also be explained by the fact that the lack of an '*über*sovereign', and instead building on 'mutually assured discretion'[93] or any other form of deference between courts, simply does not lead to practically viable results, but merely to relativising the whole sovereignty debate. The nature of law and the way courts function and apply law naturally leads to courts wanting to produce, retain and apply hierarchies.[94] While it is true that polities have moved from being purely national to post-national, and that this shift should also affect the scholars epistemic starting points,[95] the existence of plurality or the scholars' adoption of epistemic pluralism does not lead to courts changing their mode of operation. In other words, courts are bound by the constitutions that create them and define their jurisdiction. As long as expressing mutual deference and respecting plurality is not written into these constitutions as a task for courts, courts are bound to enforce these constitutions and the ensuing hierarchy that comes with them.[96] Furthermore, due to the self-referential nature of both the European and the national legal orders, even if they were to share common conflict rules to be used for settling individual debates, they would both end up applying them differently from their own perspectives.[97] Constitutional pluralism seems to concede this point, since if in a pluralist order 'the integrity of the whole necessarily remains a contingent achievement rather than a normative premise or guarantee'.[98]

7.4.4   Life after Pluralism?

Many academic commentators have criticised the German Federal Constitutional Court's referral in *Gauweiler*. The criticism expressed, among

---

[93]   See M. Goldmann, 'Constitutional Pluralism as Mutually Assured Discretion: The Court of Justice, the German Federal Constitutional Court, and the ECB' (2016) *Maastricht Journal of European and Comparative Law* 23(1), 119–35.

[94]   For a similar argument relying on the nature of legal systems and courts against constitutional pluralism, see J. Baquero Cruz, 'Another Look at Constitutional Pluralism in the European Union' (2016) *European Law Journal* 22(3), 356–374, p. 370.

[95]   See Walker (n 89), pp. 338–9. This issue is further discussed in Chapter 8.4.

[96]   Although in *Gauweiler* the German Federal Constitutional Court also stressed the German constitution's 'openness to European integration' (*Europarechtsfreundlichkeit*), the way the principle of democracy of Art. 20 German constitution is construed means that the European polity always comes second after the national polity. See 2 BvR 2728/13, 21 June 2016 (*OMT final judgment*) paras 155–157.

[97]   M. Claes, 'The Primacy of EU Law in European and National Law' in A. Arnull and D. Chalmers (eds), *The Oxford Handbook of European Union Law* (Oxford University Press 2015), pp. 202–3.

[98]   See Walker (n 90), p. 592.

other things, both how the German court's way of carrying out *ultra vires* review of EU law undermines the CJEU's interpretive authority under Article 19(1) TEU and Article 344 TFEU, and, what is more fundamental, also the primacy of EU law.[99] While in its final judgment in the main proceedings the Federal Constitutional Court accepted the CJEU's interpretation of the OMT programme, the judgment still contained the seeds of the *Solange* approach: it was only due to the (somewhat) strict criteria that the CJEU set for the implementation of the OMT programme that the German court decided to follow the CJEU's ruling. However, the German court still retained for itself the right to review the actions of EU institutions and EU law in the future if need be.

The outcome of the German Federal Constitutional Court's final judgment in *Gauweiler* was somewhat expected.[100] What was perhaps most interesting in that judgment was how the German court saw its own doctrine for *ultra vires* review and how it links it with identity review. This exemplifies how, on the one hand, the CJEU was able to assert its dominance in this individual case and how, on the other hand, the question of who is the ultimate interpreter of EU law is still up for debate as the German court keeps constructing its doctrines for reviewing EU law. Furthermore, it exemplifies how due to the latter the sovereignty debate is ever persistent. Now these fears seem to have materialised with the German court's *ultra vires* ruling in *Weiss*.[101]

All this seems to suggest that in the current pluralist constellation the various national courts have the possibility of continuously contesting the primacy of EU law, the interpretative authority of the CJEU, and consequently hijacking the whole European-level political process. Further still, it suggests also how through these actions national courts are able to assert nation-state constitutional monism over European constitutional monism. Concurrently, all the CJEU can do is keep restating its doctrine on the primacy of EU law; although only being able to do so when a national court feels like sending it a preliminary reference.

Thus, even if conflict rules or some principles of constitutional pluralism were able to produce viable results in individual cases,[102] which is highly questionable, conflict rules can never settle the debate between the national courts and the CJEU since their application by one part, and their acceptance by the other part, is always contingent upon the degree of mutual deference the courts are willing to express for each other. As the German Federal Constitutional

---

[99]   See M. Wendel, 'Exceeding Judicial Competence in the Name of Democracy: The German Federal Constitutional Court's OMT Reference' (2014) *European Constitutional Law Review* 10(2), 263–307, p. 265; Pernice (n 55), p. 4.

[100]   See e.g. Mayer (n 91), p. 123; Wendel, ibid., p. 305.

[101]   See 2 BvR 859/15, 05 May 2020 (*PSPP judgment*).

[102]   For a discussion on these, see Chapter 1.3.

Court's ruling in *Weiss* highlights,[103] the threat of an open and severe conflict is ever persistent. Therefore, the only way of settling this issue seems to be the structural solution: to amend the EU Treaties in a way that would more clearly delineate the roles of national courts and the CJEU. Since amending the EU Treaties requires national ratification, usually by way of or in a way comparable to constitutional amendment,[104] such national ratification procedures would settle and more crucially also legitimise the interpretive authority of the CJEU vis-à-vis national courts. The declaration annexed to the Lisbon Treaty does not establish this.[105] Although deepening integration seems to be constantly on the EU's agenda,[106] its likelihood in the current Eurosceptic environment seems rather scant.

7.5   CONCLUSIONS

Being led into to a difficult situation the CJEU chose to respect Member States' national identities at the expense of their equality by admitting *Gauweiler*. The case studies, and especially the *Gauweiler* saga, have exemplified how national constitutional frameworks make it possible for national courts to influence the European-level political process in two different ways. First, directly, either through the preliminary reference procedure or by being able to review EU law (or EU law-related international law) before the point of no return. Second, indirectly by those courts which are only able to participate after the point of no return, through so-called 'autolimitation'.[107] The courts in the first category are in a privileged position in relation to the courts in the

---

[103]   See 2 BvR 859/15, 05 May 2020 (*PSPP judgment*).

[104]   On these procedures and the 'procedural constitutional hurdles' that need to be overtaken in order to deepen EU integration, see Besselink, Claes, Imamović and Reestman (n 11).

[105]   Declaration 17 annexed to the Treaty of Lisbon states:
   The Conference recalls that, in accordance with well settled case law of the Court of Justice of the European Union, the Treaties and the law adopted by the Union on the basis of the Treaties have primacy over the law of Member States, under the conditions laid down by the said case law.

This was initially supposed to be an article in the Constitutional Treaty but the idea was abandoned because it was so controversial. See A. Rosas and L. Armati, *EU Constitutional Law: An Introduction* (Hart Publishing 2012), p. 69.

[106]   See e.g. COM/2017/2025 final, White Paper on the Future of Europe: Reflections and scenarios for the EU27 by 2025.

[107]   See A. Stone Sweet, *Governing with Judges. Constitutional Politics in Europe* (Oxford University Press 2000), p. 75; S. Saurugger, A. Hofmann and T. Warren, 'National Constitutional Courts as Veto Players in the EMU Crisis' (January 7, 2020). Available at SSRN: https://ssrn.com/abstract=3599037 or http://dx.doi.org/100.2139/ssrn.3599037 (accessed 1 September 2020).

latter category, and especially in relation to courts that have not been able to participate at all. What is interesting to notice is that the German Federal Constitutional Court's influence seems to take place through both categories, directly and indirectly. Furthermore, although a structural and a substantive way for the CJEU to address this issue was distinguished, this chapter made the case that there is very little that the CJEU as such can do to prevent the privileged national courts from hijacking the European-level political process.

EU law already contains the principles that national courts relied on when trying to participate in the European-level political process. Furthermore, EU law contains adequate safeguards for the protection of these principles. Thus, there was no actual need for the national courts to do so. Does this mean that these national cases were in vain? What further conclusions can be drawn from them or this outcome? The EU's constitutional order seems to be 'composite' in two ways.[108] First, how both the national constitutions and the EU Treaties contain the same constitutional principles. Second, how the EU Treaties contain the inbuilt mechanism for protecting these principles but also how the national courts to a certain extent were able to assert them against the EU.

In its current form, the EU's constitutional constellation seems to allow for constitutional pluralism in the form of claims to interpretive authority by national courts. Although the CJEU has been able to resist these claims, for the most part, the possibility of a national judicial revolution is ever lurking in the background.[109] One just needs to recall the German Federal Constitutional Court's recent ruling in *Weiss* to highlight this issue.[110] Thus, constitutional plurality has not manifested itself into constitutional pluralism, and instead one-sided constitutional monism seems to still prevail within the current European constellation.

Although in the *Gauweiler* saga European constitutional monism prevailed over national constitutional monism, as the *Weiss* saga has pointed out the ensuing sovereignty debate can resurface at any time. In addition to European constitutional monism being on a fragile footing, the underlying threat of a national judicial revolution also produces several problems for the policy process of the EU, as was exemplified by the case studies. Thus, MacCormick's old remark still seems valid: 'If despite this [concession and deference on part of the CJEU and national courts] conflicts come into being through judicial decision-making and interpretation, there will necessarily have to be some political action to produce a solution'.[111] The possibility of

---

[108]   Besselink (n 25).
[109]   See the text accompanying n 61 above.
[110]   See 2 BvR 859/15, 05 May 2020 (*PSPP judgment*).
[111]   N. MacCormick, 'The Maastricht-Urteil: Sovereignty Now' (1995) *European Law Journal* 1(3), 259–66, p. 265.

reaching one though, both due to the large number of Member States and the current political climate, seems scarce.

The previous chapter outlined the inequality thesis in descriptive form and then gave it normative character by discussing the results it has for the European-level political process. In this chapter, the argument was further developed by discussing how it could be addressed by the CJEU. In addition to the actions of national courts being questionable due to them creating such inequality, they are also questionable as national courts represent the individual national polities and not the European polity; the CJEU represents the European polity and as such is best suited for resolving such European disputes. National courts do not have the legitimacy to impose idiosyncratic national constitutional identities on the European Union or the other Member States, whereas the CJEU has the legitimacy to impose commonly agreed EU law on all of them.

While this chapter has argued for the absolute interpretive authority of the CJEU, this is not, however, equal to an argument for the 'sovereignty' of the EU over the Member States, nor does it preclude the possibility for the CJEU, on the basis of criteria established by itself, to limit the absolute primacy of EU law in certain situations.[112] Contestation by national courts in an area like fundamental rights can be acceptable,[113] or at least perhaps more acceptable than contestation in an area like economic governance. This is because, as discussed above, courts are experts in such rights-issues but perhaps not in economic governance related issues. Tuori's conceptualisation of the micro- and macroeconomic constitutions provides a further justification.[114] National constitutions do not usually regulate the economy at all, at least not to the same extent as do the EU Treaties. Therefore, since national constitutions do not usually regulate economic matters, national constitutional courts should not have a need to review EU related legal measures that are of an economic nature; whereas fundamental rights form the very core of national constitutions, and it is the courts' duty to protect them. It seems that in Germany, due to how judicial review by the Federal Constitutional Court functions, fundamental rights have been conflated to contain also issues that in other Member States fall under economic policy, and as such they do not occupy a central position in the constitutional order.

---

[112] See Tuominen (n 21).

[113] So as to avoid the 'downwards' interpretation of individuals rights as seems to have been the case in C-399/11 *Melloni* EU:C:2013:107. See L. Besselink, 'The Parameters of Constitutional Conflict after Melloni' (2014) *European Law Review* 39(4), 531–52, p. 533.

[114] See K. Tuori and K. Tuori, *The Eurozone Crisis: A Constitutional Analysis* (Cambridge University Press 2014), Chapter 2; K. Tuori (n 16), Chapters 5 and 6.

8.   The failure of European constitutional pluralism

8.1   INTRODUCTION

While Chapters 6 and 7 looked at issues stemming from the eminent constitutional plurality in Europe and explained in practical terms the problems that
such plurality creates, this chapter addresses the idea of constitutional pluralism at a more conceptual and theoretical level. The chapter begins by explor-
ing the different modalities of constitutional pluralism that can be identified
through the case studies. Constitutional pluralism affects how the European
Union's constitutional structure develops, but this development also creates
more plurality. This brings together the two themes of the book, as it is true
for both the EU's constitutional constellation in general and the Economic and
Monetary Union (EMU) in specific (8.2). Then, this chapter asks, is constitutional pluralism a valid normative theory of European constitutionalism. This
is done by mapping out four different critiques of constitutional pluralism: the
historical critique; the criticism of uncertainty; the criticism of equality; and
the criticism of legitimacy (8.3). After concluding that the answer to the above
question is no, the chapter then asks, what are the possible merits of epistemic
constitutional pluralism. To assess this, the analysis draws on the comparative
nature of European constitutionalism in general and the theory of comparative
law in particular (8.4). The chapter concludes by finding, that while constitutional pluralism as an academic effort has been useful, and especially its
epistemic strand, it has ultimately been unable to address the problems from
which it initially arose (8.5).

8.2   MODALITIES OF CONSTITUTIONAL
PLURALISM

In its practical perspective, constitutional pluralism can be seen to function
both as an input and output mechanism of European constitutionalism. That
is to say, that on the one hand the pluralist nature of the EU's constitutional
constellation on its part affects how the EU's constitutional structure develops,
but on the other hand this constellation also creates more pluralism. This is

true for both the Union's constitutional constellation in general and the EMU in specific.

All of the four case studies in this book expressed different modalities of constitutional pluralism. These refer to how legal mechanisms and frame-works bring about the interaction between the national and the European and the problems that this brings forth. Because of the event-driven and reactive characteristics of EU legal theorising,[1] and the very roots of constitutional pluralism as a theory being born out of practice,[2] these modalities should then re-contribute to the reflexive theory building on constitutional pluralism. In this way, constitutional pluralism should form its own hermeneutic circle in which each constitutional instance is to be interpreted as part of the whole constellation, but the whole is to be read through the individual parts and how the reflective interaction between theory and practice – the scholar and the judge – keeps affecting the development of European constitutionalism.[3] Thus, one way to understand the relation between the two conceptual starting points – the practical and the theoretical aspects of constitutional pluralism – is to see constitutional pluralism as an element of the form and formation of European constitutionalism. In other words, European constitutionalism as a process – the interaction between the European and the national – and its content are both affected by constitutional pluralism.

With this in mind, attention is next shifted to the different modalities of constitutional pluralism – that is, how constitutional pluralism functions as an input and output mechanism of European constitutionalism.

The following issues can be listed under the input category:

(1)   Instrumental variation. How different types of norms have been used in the adoption of the crisis response mechanisms: the Fiscal Compact and the European Stability Mechanism (ESM) being based on treaties under international law, whereas the Banking Union is based on EU secondary law and the Outright Monetary Transactions (OMT) pro-gramme on a mere press release of the European Central Bank (ECB). This is a constitutional issue since it ultimately stems from the division of competences between the Member States and the European Union as specified in the EU Treaties.

---

[1]   See N. Walker, 'Legal Theory and the European Union: A 25th Anniversary Essay' (2005) *Oxford Journal of Legal Studies* 25(4), 581–601.

[2]   See J. Baquero Cruz, 'The Legacy of the Maastricht-Urteil and the Pluralist Movement' (2008) *European Law Journal* 14(4), 389–422.

[3]   See K. Tuori, *European Constitutionalism* (Cambridge University Press 2015), pp. 1–9; K. Tuori, 'The Many Constitutions of Europe' in K. Tuori and S. Sankari (eds), *The Many Constitutions of Europe* (Ashgate 2010), p. 8.

(2) Institutional variation. How different institutions at different levels – political and legal institutions, national and European institutions – were able to participate to the process of adopting the crisis response mechanisms.

(3) Contextual variation. How different contexts – economic, political and legal – were able to influence, first, the actions of the different institutions, and second, the form of the adopted mechanisms.

Conversely, the following issues can be listed under the output category:

(4) Tendency of perpetuation. How, because of its incomplete nature, by allowing the participation, or at least indirect influence of, various institutions and contexts the current constitutional constellation on its part is responsible for re-creating the reality that perpetuates constitutional pluralism.

(5) Tendency of problematisation. How, by allowing such pluralist input tendencies, the current constitutional constellation in its current form creates problems within many of the foundational democratic issues. For example, those related to the dispersion and use of power within the composite polity.

(6) Missed tendency of re-theorisation. How, despite the event-driven and reactive characteristics of EU legal theorising, the crisis has not resulted in the upsurge of new perspectives on constitutional pluralism; at least not to the extent that could be assumed when taking into consideration all of the above-listed five modalities.

8.2.1 Instrumental Variation

Instrumental variation is rather visible at least when it comes to the use of international law to govern issues that relate exclusively to the EU or the Member States' relationship with the Union. This is also the aspect that has, perhaps, garnered most attention in the literature.[4] The use of different legal instruments was also focused upon by the CJEU in both of its seminal euro crisis related judgments. In *Pringle,* the CJEU came to the conclusion that Article 3(2) TFEU did not preclude the Member States from concluding the ESM Treaty or from ratifying it, although according to Article 3(2) TFEU the Union is to have exclusive competence for the conclusion of an international

---

[4] See e.g. B. de Witte, 'Using International Law in the Euro Crisis: Causes and Consequences' (2013) *ARENA Working Paper,* 4; K. Lenaerts, 'EMU and the EU's Constitutional Framework' (2014) *European Law Review* 39(6), 753–69.

agreement when its conclusion may affect common rules or alter their scope.[5] In *Gauweiler*, on the other hand, the CJEU stated that the fact that the OMT programme was announced in a press release and has not been implemented, and that its implementation will be possible only after further legal acts have been adopted, does not render the actions in the main proceedings devoid of purpose since under German law preventive legal protection may be granted in such a situation if certain conditions are met.[6] Therefore, the CJEU allowed to challenge a mere press release, although according to Article 267 TFEU the CJEU has jurisdiction to give preliminary rulings concerning the validity and interpretation of 'acts' of Union institutions.[7] When it comes to the Banking Union, the way that Article 114 TFEU was used as the legal basis of some of the EU secondary law measures was seen as problematic since by doing this aspects of a common economic policy are being introduced through internal market harmonisation measures.[8]

The reasons for such varied use of legal instruments and other acts were already discussed in each of the four case studies respectively. Suffice it to say, all of the three contexts – economic, political and legal – affected this outcome. Economic reasons, for example, affected the outcome in the way that it was wanted that the substantive content of the measures was large enough and that they should be set up quickly enough, but doing this within the confines of EU law would not have been possible. Political reasons stemmed mostly from the inability to attain unanimity or from specific safeguards that individual Member States required, which led to using international law-based measures. Legal reasons refer to how the existence of a legal base for the creation of, and an institution suitable for the allocation of, new tasks affected the formation of certain measures, for example the centralisation of supervisory tasks to the ECB.

Several different types of conclusions have been drawn from all of this in the literature. On the one hand, the use of such a broad array of legal instruments has been criticised as it leads to, first, creating a complex legal framework,[9] and second, accentuating the multi-speed development of the EU

---

[5]   C-370/12 *Pringle* EU:C:2012:756, paras 99–107.

[6]   C-62/14 *Gauweiler* EU:C:2015:400, para. 27.

[7]   Although the CJEU did not cite any, there is previous case law concerning which types of 'acts' are reviewable. See Case 9/73 *Schlüter* EU:C:1973:110 regarding a Council resolution; C-80/06 *Carp Snc di L. Moleri e V. Corsi v Ecorad Srl* EU:C:2007:327 regarding a Commission decision. Most of such cases concern actions of the Commission and are related to state aid issues. See K. Lenaerts and P. van Nuffel, *European Union Law* (3rd edn, Sweet & Maxwell 2011), pp. 919–25.

[8]   See Chapter 4.4.2.

[9]   P. Craig, 'Economic Governance and the Euro Crisis: Constitutional Architecture and Constitutional Implications' in M. Adams, F. Fabbrini and P. Larouche (eds), *The*

as these measures are not applied uniformly to all Member States.[10] On the other hand, the flexibility and inventiveness of the Member States and the EU in devising all of this has been appraised, and it has been claimed that the constitutional significance of the crisis response measures has been overstressed.[11] The urgency with which the EU needed to react to the crisis, too, has been seen to somewhat explain this state of affairs.[12] Regardless of which position one assumes, it is safe to say that this development discloses the inadequacies associated with the asymmetry of the EMU and the delicate balance on which the whole constitutional constellation is based upon. Thus, it still seems to be the case that '[t]the picture that emerges is one of fragmentation rather than unity, of bits and pieces rather than singleness'.[13]

8.2.2   Institutional Variation

Institutional variation manifests itself in two dimensions. First, the way in which both national and European institutions were able to participate in the European-level political process. An interesting observation is that although one of the novelties of the Lisbon Treaty was the new role accorded to the national parliaments on the basis of Article 12 TEU and Protocol No 1 On the Role of National Parliaments in the European Union,[14] the subsidiarity control mechanisms was not triggered for any of the studied crisis response mechanisms.[15] This is of course mostly due to the above-described instrumental variation – that only the Banking Union was based on EU secondary law – but on a larger scale it tells also of the more profound underlying problems: democratically accountable institutions are not given the chance to participate in the political process.[16]

Constitutionalization of European Budgetary Constraints (Hart Publishing 2014), p. 30.

[10]   A. Hinarejos, *The Euro Area Crisis in Constitutional Perspective* (Oxford University Press 2015), pp. 103–19.

[11]   B. de Witte, 'Euro-Crisis Responses and the EU Legal Order: Increased Institutional Variation or Constitutional Mutation?' (2015) *European Constitutional Law Review* 11(3), 434–57.

[12]   M. Markakis, *Accountability in the Economic and Monetary Union: Foundations, Policy, and Governance* (Oxford University Press 2020), pp. 50–51.

[13]   D. Curtin, 'The Constitutional Structure of the Union: A Europe of Bits and Pieces' (1993) *Common Market Law Review* 30(1), 17–69, p. 22.

[14]   See P. Craig, *The Lisbon Treaty: Law, Politics, and Treaty Reform* (Oxford University Press 2013), pp. 45–8.

[15]   So far the subsidiarity control mechanism has only been triggered three times. See https://ec.europa.eu/info/law/law-making-process/adopting-eu-law/relations-national-parliaments/subsidiarity-control-mechanism_en (accessed 1 September 2020).

[16]   Cf. Markakis (n 12), pp. 130–31.

The second dimension is how institutions with different roles have been able to participate and exert influence, perhaps in places where they should not. The most striking example of this is, as has already been discussed, the participation of national courts in the European-level political process. The separation of powers doctrine and its application to the EU,[17] or the legitimacy of judicial review as such,[18] are discussions in their own right, into which there is no need to venture here. However, there are very valid arguments for why courts, and especially national courts, should not be able to exert such judicial review powers over EU law. As Halberstam explains, the separation of powers between institutions should be based on their respective capabilities when it comes to expertise, voice and rights: national courts have expertise in national law, whereas the Commission and the ECB perhaps have more expertise when it comes to economic and monetary policy formation at the European level.[19] The latter institutions also represent better the shared concern of all of the Member States, whereas national courts are only able to exert the voice of their national constituencies, and even then, the legitimacy of that voice is questionable in comparison to the national governments and parliaments. In fact, governments achieve legitimacy through elections, whereas the legitimacy of judges is based on their claim of being 'non-political, independent, neutral servants of "the law"'. Thus, 'courts achieve legitimacy by claiming they are something they are not'.[20] Although the lack of economic resources can lead to issues in the implementation of social rights, as the broad case law on the national implementation of the Memorandums of Understanding testifies,[21] economic and monetary policy as such are not similar rights issues

---

[17]   The direct application of the principle of separation of powers to this situation is difficult since the national courts are not typically seen as EU institutions, whereas assessments of the principle in relation to the EU only take account of the EU's own institutions. Cf. R. Schütze, 'Constitutionalism and the European Union' in C. Barnard and S. Peers (eds), *European Union Law* (Oxford University Press 2014), pp. 88–91; S. Douglas-Scott, *Constitutional Law of the European Union* (Longman 2002), p. 49.

[18]   Generally, see J. Waldron, 'The Core of the Case Against Judicial Review' (2006) *The Yale Law Journal* 115(6), 1346–406; in the context of the European Union, see N. de Boer, 'The False Promise of Constitutional Pluralism' in G. Davies and M. Avbelj (eds), *Research Handbook on Legal Pluralism and EU Law* (Edward Elgar Publishing 2018).

[19]   D. Halberstam, 'Constitutional Heterarchy: The Centrality of Conflict in the European Union and the United States' in J. L. Dunoff and J. P. Trachtman (eds), *Ruling the World? Constitutionalism, International Law, and Global Governance* (Cambridge University Press 2009), pp. 336–53.

[20]   M. Shapiro and A. Stone Sweet (eds), *On Law, Politics, and Judicialization* (Oxford University Press 2002), p. 3.

[21]   On these cases, see Hinarejos (n 10), pp. 145–7; F. Fabbrini, *Economic Governance in Europe. Comparative Paradoxes and Constitutional Challenges* (Oxford University Press 2016), pp. 86–9.

as fundamental and human rights, and therefore the role of courts in reviewing economic and monetary policy decisions should be limited.

When a new constitution is drafted, it can be beneficial that the issues on which the associated parties cannot reach a compromise are left unsettled and thus to the future purview of the constitutional court. In this way the drafters of the constitution can progress in their work and eventually come up with a constitution.[22] Although this model has its advantages, it only works in relation to individual states and national constitutions; even if the EU Treaties were seen as an incomplete constitution,[23] such a view cannot be used to argue for a right for the national courts to disapply EU law. This concerns, on the one hand, the delineation of competences between the CJEU and national courts and, on the other hand, also those between political and judicial institutions.

The existence of both dimensions of institutional variation can be explained by the same contextual reasons as was the case with instrumental variation. Central, however, seem to be the legal reasons, especially the national constitutional frameworks, since it is according to them that the different national institutions function. Here, the difficulty of balancing between the equality of the Member States and the respect for national identity appears yet again.

8.2.3 Contextual Variation

Contextual variation stems from the innate contextuality of law and, as Tuori has described it, how constitution is a relational concept.[24] Namely, that just as all law is to be understood in its societal context, so too the constitution needs to be understood through the relation it has with its object of regulation. Since the substantive context of the case studies revolved around the euro crisis (i.e. essentially the economic) and the resultant political crisis (i.e. essentially the political), both of which are issues that are regulated by constitutional norms, it is only natural that the tripartite contextuality of economic–politic–law can be distinguished to have affected the formation of all of the legal mechanisms studied in the case studies. Thus, this tripartite contextuality must also be taken into consideration in the current analysis.

---

[22] See A. Stone Sweet, 'Constitutional Courts' in M. Rosenfeld and A. Sajó (eds), *The Oxford Handbook of Comparative Constitutional Law* (Oxford University Press 2012), p. 821.

[23] In relation to the role of the CJEU, see T. Tridimas, 'Constitutional Review of Member State Action: The Virtues and Vices of an Incomplete Jurisdiction' (2011) *International Journal of Constitutional Law* 9(3–4), 737–56.

[24] See Tuori (n 3), 'The Many Constitutions of Europe', pp. 7–10; Tuori (n 3), *European Constitutionalism*, pp. 9–10.

Such contextual variation is key to the existence of the whole phenomenon that this study focuses on. On the one hand, the fluidity of the problems results in various legal responses being called upon and, on the other hand, it also creates possibilities for ever new readings and interpretations of this phenomenon. In this way, contextual variation has been the driving force behind the first two modalities, but it also affects the fourth one.

8.2.4 The Tendency of Perpetuation

The tendency of perpetuation – the first of the three modalities falling under the output category – explains how the above-described plurality affects the overall results that the political and legal processes produce. It is because of the deficiencies in the EU's constitutional constellation – how it allows for the above-described input mechanisms to persist – that this constellation keeps reproducing even more plurality. In other words, plurality is both the cause and consequence of more plurality.

While perhaps during the early years of the Community it was legitimate for the CJEU to step in when the political process was not functioning and to further the aims of the EU Treaties with its own judgments,[25] this no longer seems to be the case. Now that the stated aims of the Treaties have been to a large extent realised,[26] the main problems of the Union seem to be its proper functioning amidst the variety of interests that the 27 Member States represent. Thus, nowadays the CJEU's main task is to guarantee the functioning of the Union's legal and political system, as established by the EU Treaties. But as the tendency of perpetuation explicates, these are problems largely outside the scope of the CJEU's jurisdiction; rather, it would require political decisions, both national and European, to fix this issue.[27] The tendency of perpetuation is also linked to constitutional pluralism being a meta-theoretical academic project, the epistemic claim, to which the penultimate section of this chapter will shortly return to.

---

[25] See J. Weiler, 'The Community System: the Dual Character of Supranationalism' (1981) *Yearbook of European Law* 1(1), 267–306; J. Weiler, 'The Transformation of Europe' (1991) *Yale Law Journal* 100(8), 2403–83.

[26] Notice, how the asymmetrical structure of the EMU is specifically written into the EU Treaties (Arts 2–6 TFEU) and thus the CJEU should not even try to broaden or deepen supranational economic governance.

[27] This issue was discussed in Chapter 7.

8.2.5 The Tendency of Problematisation

The tendency of problematisation gains impetus from all of the above-mentioned as the input mechanisms and the tendency of perpetuation create more problems than they are able to resolve. While the judicial aspect of constitutional pluralism seeks to alleviate the problem of clashes between courts – yet, without actually solving it – constitutional pluralism as a normative theory of European constitutionalism seems to have very little to offer for the other issues that follow from the existing plurality.

If constitutional pluralism aspires to be the normative theory of European constitutionalism, it should offer answers to the foundational problems that a constellation beset with plurality faces. But how does European constitutional pluralism propose to solve some of the fundamental issues of polity formation related to, for example, democracy and participation? Again, the position assumed in this study needs to be stressed: meta-theoretical propositions are not enough without practical solutions, while practical solutions based on conflict rules relativise the issue. Although the EU has been able to function in practice despite these shortcomings, the pluralists premise concedes that 'the integrity of the whole necessarily remains a contingent achievement rather than a normative premise or guarantee'.[28] The more national courts contest EU law and the role of the CJEU,[29] the more relevant such a conclusion becomes and the more there is need for solutions to the problems that have been described in the case studies and the previous two chapters. Although the purpose of epistemic pluralism is to find answers to these shortcomings, it has not yet proven to have any significance in the practical domain. The CJEU's case law, on the other hand, does seem to develop the concept of democracy in a more inclusive direction that would accommodate both European and

---

[28]   See Walker (n 1), p. 592.
[29]   The Constitutional Court of the Czech Republic (*Ústavní Soud*) declared the CJEU judgment C-399/09 *Landtová* EU:C:2011:415 as *ultra vires* in its judgment of 31 January 2012, Pl. ÚS 5/12 (*Slovak Pensions*). See R. Zbíral, 'A Legal Revolution or Negligible Episode? Court of Justice Decision Proclaimed Ultra Vires' (2012) *Common Market Law Review* 49(4), 1475–91. The Supreme Court of Denmark (*Højesteret*) chose not to follow the CJEU's judgment C-441/14 *Ajos* EU:C:2016:278 in its judgment of 6 December 2016, Case 15/2014 (*Ajos A/S v Estate of A*). See M. Rask Madsen, H. Palmer Olsen and U. Šadl, 'Competing Supremacies and Clashing Institutional Rationalities: the Danish Supreme Court's Decision in the *Ajos* Case and the National Limits of Judicial Cooperation' (2017) *European Law Journal* 23(1–2), 140–50. The German Federal Constitutional Court (*Bundesverfassungsgericht*) declared in 2 BvR 859/15, 05 May 2020 (*PSPP judgment*) the CJEU's judgment in C-493/17 *Weiss* EU:C:2018:1000 as *ultra vires*.

national views on democracy.[30] However, such development is based on European constitutional monism – not on European constitutional pluralism.[31]

8.2.6   The Missed Tendency of Re-theorisation

The missed tendency of re-theorisation asserts that it is somewhat strange how, despite the event-driven and reactive characteristics of EU legal theorising, the Eurozone crisis has not resulted in the refinement of the theory of constitutional pluralism, at least to any considerable degree.[32] Even though the euro crisis has been the epicentre of European constitutionalism during the previous decade, the literature on constitutional pluralism has, with few exceptions,[33] ignored the euro crisis as a constitutional relation and thus as a topic. The very few articles that have focused on the euro crisis have only paid due respect to the conflictual aspect of the issue. They have mainly analysed the meaning of the judicial decisions that make up the *Gauweiler saga*.[34] This is strange, since political science, the closest academic bedfellow of EU legal studies, has constantly been re-adapting its various integration theories on the basis of the experiences gathered during the crisis.[35]

---

[30]   See K. Lenaerts, 'The Principle of Democracy in the Case Law of the European Court of Justice' (2014) *International and Comparative Law Quarterly* 62(2), 271–315.

[31]   'European constitutional monism' refers to the situation where the EU subsumes final authority, whereas the opposite alternative to pluralism is offered by 'nation-state constitutional monism', which refers to the situation where the Member States retain sovereign authority with the Union's legal powers being just somehow derived from these. See K. Jaklič, *Constitutional Pluralism in the EU* (Oxford University Press 2014), p. 21.

[32]   However, the German Federal Constitutional Court's recent judgment 2 BvR 859/15, 05 May 2020 (*PSPP judgment*) might change this. See 'The German Federal Constitutional Court's PSPP Judgment' (2020) *German Law Journal* [special section] 21(5), 944–1127.

[33]   See e.g. M. Goldmann, 'Constitutional Pluralism as Mutually Assured Discretion: The Court of Justice, the German Federal Constitutional Court, and the ECB' (2016) *Maastricht Journal of European and Comparative Law* 23(1), 119–35; R. D. Kelemen, 'On the Unsustainability of Constitutional Pluralism: European Supremacy and the Survival of the Eurozone' (2016) *Maastricht Journal of European and Comparative Law* 23(1), 136–50.

[34]   2 BvR 2728/13, 14 January 2014 (*OMT reference*); C-62/14 *Gauweiler* EU:C: 2015:400; 2 BvR 2728/13, 21 June 2016 (*OMT final judgment*).

[35]   See e.g. D. Ioannou, P. Leblond and A. Niemann (eds), '*European Integration in Times of Crisis: Theoretical Perspectives*' (2015) *Journal of European Integration* [special issue] 22(2); R. Vilpišauskas, 'Eurozone Crisis and European Integration: Functional Spillover, Political Spillback?' (2013) *Journal of European Integration* 35(3), 361–73; S. Fabbrini, 'Intergovernmentalism and Its Limits: Assessing the

If the euro crisis has been, above all, a political and an existential crisis for the EU,[36] then it should offer both the perfect environment and opportunity for constitutional pluralism to reconfigure itself as the normative theory of European constitutionalism. Yet this reshaping of the theory is still missing. This is perhaps so, because the crisis just points out – as this study has tried to do throughout – that constitutional plurality in itself is problematic, and thus constitutional pluralism cannot be argued for coherently.

8.3   CRITIQUES OF CONSTITUTIONAL PLURALISM

Let us first shortly recapture the core tenets of constitutional pluralism. While various accounts have been presented in the name of constitutional pluralism,[37] the early and influential conceptualisation presented by Walker serves as a good starting point for defining constitutional pluralism. In the context of the EU, constitutional pluralism maintains three claims. First, that the national and the European sites, both of which are legally relevant for the EU, have their own claims to constitutional authority. Second, that there is no standard according to which their claims could be settled hierarchically, and rather each claim is plausible and stands independently of the other claims. Third, that to sustain this complex each site has to acknowledge and accommodate for the claims of the other. In this way, the absence of a single dominant authoritative framework is ensured.[38]

What this means is that constitutional *pluralism* maintains something more than just a description of constitutional *plurality*. That is to say, that the acknowledgement of the existence of multiple overlapping constitutional sites within the EU as a polity just expresses the *descriptive* claim of constitutional pluralism: there is plurality. However, what constitutional pluralism argues for is the *normative* acceptance of this state of affairs: no pre-ordered hierarchy should be established between these constitutional sites. Further still, constitutional pluralism has also an *epistemic* aspect to it. Accepting that there are distinct constitutional sites with incommensurable authority claims also requires assuming different epistemic starting points with regard to each of these sites and that there is no neutral perspective from which these claims could be

---

European Union's Answer to the Euro Crisis' (2013) *Comparative Political Studies* 46(9), 1003–29.

[36]   See J. Habermas, *The Crisis of the European Union: a Response* (Polity 2012).

[37]   See e.g. M. Avbelj and J. Komárek (eds), *Constitutional Pluralism in the European Union and Beyond* (Hart Publishing 2012); G. Davies and M. Avbelj (eds), *Research Handbook on Legal Pluralism and EU Law* (Edward Elgar Publishing 2018).

[38]   N. Walker, 'Constitutional Pluralism Revisited' (2016) *European Law Journal* 22(3), 333–55, pp. 333–4.

settled. The alternative, epistemic singularity, would invariably reduce constitutional pluralism to constitutional monism, either national or European,[39]
since it would not accommodate a true understanding of what it means to have
valid claims to sovereignty that are competing and overlapping but that still
manage to co-exist as true sovereignty claims. In essence, then, the epistemic
aspect of constitutional pluralism is about defining constitutional language in
this post-state era – of defining what is post-state constitutionalism.[40]

As was mentioned above, constitutional pluralism is a theory, and not just
a descriptive, normative and epistemic claim. But what does it mean that it is
a theory? Legal scholars have expounded several general theories of law.[41]
However, legal pluralism, as Patrignani has argued, is not a general theory
of law but a theory of law that focuses on the variability of legal phenomena.
Thus, if one is a pluralist, one's theory of knowledge changes – that is, one
adopts a different epistemic understanding.[42] This observation carries over
to constitutional pluralism in the way that constitutional pluralism is not just
a legal theory, since due to its relational object, the constitution, it must also
take heed of the political. Therefore, and especially if the normative claim
is to have force, constitutional pluralism must also be a normative theory of
European constitutionalism. That is to say, that it has to be able to account for
how different legal orders and their respective authority claims can mutually
co-exist within one polity.[43]

To summarise, the normative claim of constitutional pluralism maintains
that both national and European claims to ultimate constitutional authority
are equally plausible. To handle such disputes in practice, normative constitutional pluralism puts forth various conflict rules, according to which the
disputes can be settled on a case-by-case basis by courts. The epistemic claim
of constitutional pluralism, then, attempts to reconfigure the concept of sovereignty and our conceptualisation of it to fit the current post-state constellation.
Thus, constitutional pluralism is turned into a normative theory of European
constitutionalism. A normative theory of European constitutionalism ought to

---

[39] See supra n 31.
[40] See N. Walker, 'The Idea of Constitutional Pluralism' (2002) *Modern Law
Review* 65(3), 317–59; N. Walker, 'Constitutionalism and Pluralism in Global Context'
in Avbelj and Komárek (eds), (n 37).
[41] By a 'general' theory of law I am referring to legal theoretical accounts that try to
explain the ontology of law and the functioning of legal orders. Such theories claim to
be general in the sense that they are not presented in relation to any specific legal order
but are meant a universal. Well-known examples include Hans Kelsen's *Pure Theory of
Law* (1934), H.L.A. Hart's *The Concept of Law* (1961) and Ronald Dworkin's *Taking
Rights Seriously* (1977).
[42] See E. Patrignani, 'Complex Legal Pluralism' (2015) *Retfaerd* 38(4), 19–33.
[43] See Walker (n 38), p. 335.

tell us how conflicts between national law and EU law should be settled and what should the constitutional relationship between the two respective constitutional orders be like.

Both the normative and the epistemic aspects of constitutional pluralism have received widespread criticism in the literature. In other words, both the capacity of conflict rules as such, but also the credentials of constitutional pluralism as the normative theory of European constitutionalism have been contested. Next, the essential elements of this critique at the conceptual level are mapped out. Four such criticism can be distinguished.

8.3.1   The Four Critiques Outlined

The first critique can be called the historical critique. It is historical in that it bases its assessment and critique of constitutional pluralism on the past European but also more general constitutional experience. Two very different approaches employ such an historical account. The first recalls the horrors of the two world wars and how the European project was originally about committing France and Germany to a joint economic project, which was to be done in a manner that would make war between them impossible.[44] Based on such a historical reading and the original aim of European integration, a dualistic understanding of EU law has been presented. What this means is that EU law only states that it has the authority to determine its own effects, and that EU law has primacy over national law and direct effect in the national legal orders. In this way, the integrity of the common EU legal order can be assured. However, this does not mean that the authority of national law would somehow be derived from Union law or that national law would be hierarchically inferior to it.[45] Moreover, argumentation building on 'national identity' and Article 4(2) TEU actually empowers national courts even though it would be the CJEU who in the final instance decides whether the specific circumstance allows to breach EU law.[46]

---

[44]   See J. Baquero Cruz, 'Another Look at Constitutional Pluralism in the European Union' (2016) *European Law Journal* 22(3), 356–74; J. Baquero Cruz, *What's Left of the Law of Integration? Decay and Resistance in European Union Law* (Oxford University Press 2018).

[45]   J. Baquero Cruz, 'Another Look at Constitutional Pluralism in the European Union', p. 371.

[46]   See M. Claes, 'Negotiating Constitutional Identity or Whose Identity is it Anyway?' in M. Claes, M. de Visser, P. Popelier and C. van de Heyning (eds), *Constitutional Conversations in Europe: Actors, Topics and Procedures* (Intersentia Publishing 2012), pp. 229–30.

The other historical argument is actually comparative. According to this reading, both the *sui generis* theory on the nature of the EU's legal order and constitutional pluralism as it builds on this are mistaken in their precepts. This stems from them not having the correct understanding of the American federal experience. The American federal experience is essentially pluralist, since in federal orders constitutional conflicts are the norm; they are evidence of a living constitution. The pluralist description of the EU is essentially a description of the federal system of the United States of America (USA). However, what this pluralist description fails to notice is how in the federal system of the USA, while both the States and the Union present constitutional claims, only the States are conceived in statist terms. Constitutional conflicts between the EU and the Member States should be conceptualised in light of federal theory and not through constitutional pluralism, which is ahistorical and mistaken.[47] This line of criticism can also be seen as challenging constitutional pluralism's credentials as a normative theory of European constitutionalism, since the roots of American federalism are entrenched firmly in political theory. European integration has also been assessed in light of federal theory and the underlying political theories,[48] but pluralists fail to take notice of such analyses.[49]

The second line of criticism addresses the debate on interpretive *Kompetenz-Kompetenz*. Since pluralism argues that national courts should have the right, in certain situations, to set aside EU law, the outcome-based criticism concerning this debate can be called the *criticism of uncertainty*. Although concepts such as heterarchical and horizontal seem more intriguing than hierarchical and vertical, a legal order needs some structure in order to be functional and predictable. The preliminary reference procedure provides a mechanism through which a dialogue between the national courts and the CJEU can and must take place. Although this relationship is one of 'cooperative supranationalism' since both courts have distinct but complementary

---

[47]   See R. Schütze, *European Constitutional Law* (Cambridge University Press 2012), p. 68, fn. 114 and p. 378, fn. 128; R. Schütze, *From Dual to Cooperative Federalism: The Changing Structure of European Law* (Oxford University Press 2013), pp. vii–viii; R. Schütze, 'Federalism as Constitutional Pluralism: "Letter from America"' in Avbelj and Komárek (37).

[48]   See e.g. M. Burgess, *Federalism and European Union: The Building of Europe, 1950–2000* (Routledge 2000); K. Nicolaidis and R. Howse (eds), *The Federal Vision: Legitimacy and Levels of Governance in the United States and the European Union* (Oxford University Press 2001).

[49]   However, multi-level governance, a kindred spirit of constitutional pluralism, has been assessed in light of the federal experience. See T. Vandamme, 'EU Directives and Multi-Level Governance: Can Lessons Be Drawn from Cooperative Federalism?' (2014) *Maastricht Journal of European and Comparative Law* 21(2), 341–58.

functions,[50] this cooperation must take place on the terms of that procedure as is outlined in Article 267 TFEU.

National interpretations of EU law are not acceptable since they would sacrifice the whole point of EU law: that there is one set of legal rules that applies unilaterally to all of the 27 Member States and that it is the CJEU that interprets them. If national courts start to interpret the content or validity of EU law, they would start imposing limits set by themselves on to the rest of the Member States. The political process of enacting EU law already contains many safeguards for taking national interests into consideration.[51] Therefore, there is no need to add another level of review – review by the national courts, that is. Pluralism tries to absolve hierarchies, but there needs to be a hierarchy between EU law and national law at the level of application in the case of conflict. In whichever way a conflict is resolved, and whether it is solved by disapplication or annulment, the end result is that there is a hierarchy between the two orders: either EU law is applied or national law is applied.[52]

The criticism of uncertainty is given more force when the illogical and immoral aspects of constitutional pluralism, and especially the claims made by the German Federal Constitutional Court in its reference on the ECB's OMT programme, are taken notice of.[53] First, accepting the normative claims of constitutional pluralism would mean that there would be no uniform application of EU law and no coherent EU legal order. The unilateral power of national courts to disapply EU law would be counter to the whole purpose of establishing a common legal order. Second, such national practices would also be problematic in that no Member State would want other Member States to do so. In other words, they would be immoral as they would breach the Kantian categorical imperative.[54]

---

[50]   T. Tridimas, 'The ECJ and the National Courts: Dialogue, Cooperation, and Instability' in A. Arnull and D. Chalmers (eds), *The Oxford Handbook of European Union Law* (Oxford University Press 2015), p. 408.

[51]   It has been argued, that if such safeguards are not functioning, it would then be legitimate for national courts to step in. See M. Kumm, 'Rethinking Constitutional Authority: On the Structure and Limits of Constitutional Pluralism' in Avbelj and Komárek (n 37), p. 43.

[52]   Baquero Cruz (n 2), pp. 414–16.

[53]   2 BvR 2728/13, 14 January 2014 (*OMT reference*).

[54]   Kelemen (n 33), p. 143; M. Wilkinson, 'Economic Messianism and Constitutional Power in a "German Europe": All Courts are Equal, but Some Courts are More Equal than Others' (2014) *Law Society and Economy Working Paper Series WPS* 26, pp. 19–20.

The critique of uncertainty finds another expression through the following question: 'How could pluralism become constitutional?'[55] The problem with constitutional pluralism is that by definition the term constitutional implies a system of law; such a system must be coherent and must contain some sort of a hierarchy.[56] Yet, the whole purpose of constitutional pluralism is to create a constitutionalism without order and instead base it on heterarchy. This is because a move has occurred from the state to the post-state polity, and thus the used constitutional language and concepts should also be changed.[57] Such heterarchical concepts and conceptions of constitution and constitutionalism are presented at the metal-level, but, however, not operationalised at the practical level.

Third, there is the criticism of equality. This line of criticism was already addressed at length in the two preceding chapters, where the differences in how national courts are able to participate and affect the European-level political and judicial processes were discussed. However, a brief restatement and conceptualisation of this critique is useful here. From the perspective of the CJEU, if EU law is not applied uniformly throughout the EU, then the Union does not seem to have a legal order of its own. Thus, pluralism's claim for national courts to have the possibility to assess the validity of EU law – in essence to breach EU law, or to choose to disapply it – questions the equality of the Member States before the EU Treaties. Such unilateral disapplication of EU law by a national court would be against the reciprocal commitments that Member States have made when signing the EU Treaties and would not be in the best interest of any Member State – even that of Germany.[58]

The same can also be argued for by starting from a different premise. Such criticism is formal or structural, in that it states how the essence of a legal order is to produce security, predictability and certainty. The rule of law principle stems from the EU having a legal order. If the equal and universal application of EU law were sacrificed at the altar of national democracy – as has now taken place by the German Federal Constitutional Court declaring the CJEU's

---

[55] C. Timmermans, 'The Magic World of Constitutional Pluralism' (2014) *European Constitutional Law Review* 10(2), 349–58, p. 353.

[56] Ibid., p. 350.

[57] See N. Walker, 'Postnational Constitutionalism and the Problem of Translation' in J. Weiler and M. Wind (eds), *European Constitutionalism Beyond the State* (Cambridge University Press 2003); J. Weiler, *The Constitution of Europe: 'Do the new clothes have an emperor?' and other essays on European integration* (Cambridge University Press 1999), pp. 264–70.

[58] F. Fabbrini, 'After the OMT Case: The Supremacy of EU Law as the Guarantee of the Equality of the Member States' (2015) *German Law Journal* 16(4), 1003–24, pp. 1012–22.

judgment in *Weiss ultra vires*[59] – then the Union's democratic credentials would be damaged.[60] In other words, since the EU Treaties establish a common legal framework and rules on how to manage it, if one Member State assumes the privilege of not respecting it, then they are effectively denouncing the EU's legal order and the rule of law principle stemming from it – and also the underlying democratic decision taken together by the Member States to enact such a system. They are, thus, breaching the equality of the Member States vis-à-vis each other. With regard to the German court, a substantive approach would also lead to the same conclusion, as the German court's understanding of national identity seems to be detached from the holistic perspective offered by Article 4(2) TEU. While the point of Article 4(2) TEU is that the CJEU should take all national identities into consideration when interpreting the EU Treaties and EU secondary law, the German court persistently only accords weight to its own viewpoint.[61]

A fourth line of criticism, which goes to the very fundamentals of constitutional pluralism, is here called the criticism of legitimacy. This line of criticism stems from constitutional pluralism's main focus being on courts and how to avoid conflicts between them. However, courts are but one of the relevant constitutional institutions. If constitutional pluralism aspires to be the normative theory of European constitutionalism, it should also offer something in the form of how to develop the EU as a polity. Since issues of democratic legitimacy and accountability, both stemming from the perceived or argued democratic deficit of the Union, are central for the development of this polity, then constitutional pluralism should take a stance on them as well.

It may well be that the point of constitutional pluralism is not to offer any such guidelines for developing the polity but to just manage the explicit confrontations between courts. But this is a sort of normativity light as it does not address the deeper foundational issues. Doing this, though, in a manner that avoids federalising the EU, is perhaps only possible in some Habermasian fashion, but those pleas have not materialised even though they have been around for quite a while.[62] When it comes to the substantive topic of this study,

[59]   See 2 BvR 859/15, 05 May 2020 (*PSPP judgment*); C-493/17 *Weiss* EU:C:2018: 1000.

[60]   J. Baquero Cruz, 'Another Look at Constitutional Pluralism in the European Union' (n 44), pp. 368–73.

[61]   See Wilkinson (n 54), p. 19.

[62]   Compare J. Habermas, 'Remarks on Dieter Grimm's "Does Europe Need a Constitution?"' (1995) *European Law Journal* 1(3), 303–7; J. Habermas, *The Lure of Technocracy* (Polity Press 2015), Chapter 2.

many of the shortcomings of the EMU seem to be best addressed by taking example from the system of the USA.[63]

This legitimacy issue also surfaces when the interaction between national and European constitutional frameworks is analysed. In this pluralist constellation, there are certain instances of 'institutional interlocking' – that is, how national political institutions participate in the functioning of the EU, and thus their legitimacy is at least partly transposed onto the EU. Furthermore, there exists a degree of 'interlegality' between the national and the European legal orders, which is based on the various legal actors' legal cultural pre-understanding and how this, subsequently, is important for sustaining a dialogical relation between the different orders.[64] A similar critique can be presented based on a conceptual analysis of sovereignty, since the highest authority in a polity is not a court, but a legislature, the constitution or the constituent power.[65]

Furthermore, constitutional pluralism usually fails to address how it could be the normative theory of European constitutionalism. More specifically, that for pluralism, the existence of a European *demos* – which would be one precursor for a European polity and which constitutional pluralism should address if it were to be the normative theory of European constitutionalism – seems to be an all–or–nothing issue in that there is no half-way house between the national and the European *demos*, and thus we are stuck with the national *demois*. In addition, there is the question of how a pluralist order would have difficulties in creating the required solidarity between the peoples of Europe that the establishment of strong welfare mechanisms would require – a further issue which constitutional pluralism also fails to address.[66] This solidarity aspect also finds expression in another, rather unexpected form. Somewhat related to the third critique, but concerning equality in a deeper, systematic manner, it is worth first recalling how 'the national constitutional position … stands to gain much more from pluralism than the European position'.[67] However, there seems to be a structural bias within this discourse that favours certain Member States at

---

[63]   See Fabbrini (n 21). Although Fabbrini too shares the Habermasian tone by stressing that the EU is 'a Union of states and citizens' (e.g. on p. 241), his reform proposals are very practical.

[64]   See K. Tuori, *European Constitutionalism* (n 3), pp. 37–44 and 78–81, and Chapter 3 passim.

[65]   M. Loughlin, 'Constitutional Pluralism: An Oxymoron?' (2014) *Global Constitutionalism* 3(1), 9–33, pp. 16–17.

[66]   N. Krisch, 'Europe's Constitutional Monstrosity' (2005) *Oxford Journal of Legal Studies* 25(2), 321–34, pp. 322–4 and 332.

[67]   Baquero Cruz (n 2), p. 414.

the expense of the others; that 'the "universal" of the Union most often coincides with the "particular" of the centre'.[68]

The four case studies and the argument put forward in the two preceding chapters seem to confirm this. One simply needs to recall how dominant of a position the German Federal Constitutional Court assumed during the euro crisis, whereas the highest courts of other Member States have often found themselves in a situation in which they face an immense predicament to find that the European-level measures conform with their national constitutions.

8.3.2   The Fourth Critique in Focus

While the first three critiques are very practical in how they are centred on the outcomes of contestation or the institutional and constitutional praxis from which contestation stems from, the fourth critique is of a more fundamental character. That is to say, that the criticism of legitimacy also addresses constitutional pluralism as a normative theory of European constitutionalism, whereas the first three critiques just address the normative claim from a formal legal perspective.

The fourth critique focuses on the epistemic strand of constitutional pluralism.[69] This strand of constitutional pluralism can be seen to focus on meta-theoretical and epistemological issues.[70] The assessment conducted here takes as its starting point the conclusions drawn from the case studies, which are rather practical and therefore perhaps more closely associated with the first three critiques. Thus, the critique presented here might seem to be misplaced or even unfair.[71] This starting point could be criticised by asking, would it not be more fruitful to present such practical criticism towards those pluralists that have presented what could be called conflict rules.[72] That is, rules or principles that could be used to settle individual conflicts between constitutional actors

---

[68]   D. Kukovec, 'Law and the Periphery' (2015) *European Law Journal* 21(3), 406–28, pp. 422–4. Further, see D. Kukovec, 'Hierarchies as Law' (2014) *Columbia Journal of European Law* 21(1), 131–94, pp. 160–62.

[69]   On epistemic constitutional pluralism, see Chapter 1.3.2.

[70]   See e.g. N. Walker, 'Flexibility within a Metaconstitutional Frame: Reflections on the Future of Legal Authority in Europe' in G. de Búrca and J. Scott (eds), *Constitutional Change in the EU: From Uniformity to Flexibility?* (Hart Publishing 2000).

[71]   For an outline of such critiques and replies to them, see N. Walker, 'Taking Constitutionalism Beyond the State' (2008) *Political Studies* 56(3), 519–43, pp. 520–25; Walker, 'Constitutionalism and Pluralism in Global Context' (n 40) pp. 17–21; Walker (n 38), pp. 333–7.

[72]   On normative constitutional pluralism and conflict rules, see Chapter 1.3.1.

while still retaining heterarchy.[73] While this is certainly true, there are valid reasons for combining the practical and the theoretical in an assessment of the epistemic strand of constitutional pluralism.

First, since taking the normative claim seriously results in the need for epistemic pluralism[74] – as the normative claim questions the very nature of sovereignty, traditionally understood – therefore, it is difficult to fathom just one without the other. In other words, a credible argument revolving around the use of conflict rules as a means of reconciling constitutional conflicts should also say something about what ought the content of the normative theory of European constitutionalism look like. Furthermore, as the previous two chapters argued, and what is also the basis of the above-discussed criticism of uncertainty, using conflict rules results in relativising the whole conflict. This is an inadequate solution from the perspective of normative constitutional theory.

Second, such a practical perspective reveals the deficiency of purely meta-theoretical and epistemological argumentation. Take for example the epistemic strand of constitutional pluralism developed by Walker. Initially Walker maintained that constitutionalism 'posits a set of standards to which constitutional government should aspire, thereby contributing to the debate over how the European polity *ought* to operate and be justified'.[75] His later works, however, have not presented at the practical level answers to such normative ought questions. Instead, he took what could be called the epistemic turn: of trying to frame the discussion instead of actually having the discussion. Walker is correct in how 'political epistemology' is important because it can draw the lines for what is possible and desirable in practice, and because it can help to explain whether or not the EU has or can have a constitution.[76] However, as long as political decisions are not taken to fix the apparent prob-

---

[73] See e.g. M. P. Maduro, 'Contrapunctual Law: Europe's Constitutional Pluralism in Action', in N. Walker (ed.), *Sovereignty in Transition* (Hart Publishing 2003); M. Kumm, 'The Jurisprudence of Constitutional Conflict: Constitutional Supremacy in Europe before and After the Constitutional Treaty' (2005) *European Law Journal* 11(3), 262–307; L. Besselink, *A Composite European Constitution* (Europa Law Publishing 2007).

[74] Although see Walker (n 40), p. 338, for how 'epistemic pluralism does not itself necessarily follow from either of the other two claims [descriptive and explanatory pluralism]'.

[75] N. Walker, 'European Constitutionalism and European Integration' (1996) *Public Law*, 266–90, pp. 267–8.

[76] See N. Walker, 'European Constitutionalism in the State Constitutional Tradition' (2006) *Current Legal Problems* 59(1), 51–89, p. 52.

lems,[77] all that such epistemological ponderings can do is try to explain away the problems. In other words, meta-theoretical and epistemological aspirations have not proven to be useful when it comes to developing the constitutional constellation of the EU.

Furthermore, in a recent restatement of the theory, Walker seems to concede that amending the EU Treaties is the preferred solution to fixing the persistent problems in the current constitutional constellation. According to Walker, most accounts of constitutional pluralism focus too much on courts, whereas according to him constitutional pluralism should be about the EU as a polity; it should be about 'the generative forces of political community'.[78] Having stated this, Walker then outlines different approaches within European constitutionalism ('particularism', 'holism', 'federalism' and 'pluralism') and presents the argument for why his specific version of constitutional pluralism is superior to them.[79] Then, Walker discusses the EU as a polity and what constitutional pluralism could offer it.[80] Under his analysis, the EU as a polity has suffered from 'structural drift': there has been no grand vision on the development of the EU's constitution but rather it has been developed through individual instances.[81] This is connected, in Walker's view, to the epistemic problem of 'inadequate reflexivity': although many proposals have been put forth on the development of the EU, and while these might counter structural drift, the starting point of these proposal is too narrow and modest; what we are missing is a 'reflexive effort on the part of the constituencies making up the polity as a whole to (re)build a political project from first principles'.[82] The issue of 'frustrated initiative' has contributed to this problem: there is no agreement on the direction to which European integration should be developed. Lastly, Walker outlines what he calls 'speculative engagement': most academic proposals for the development of the Union seem to assume some sort of a constitution-making initiative upon which they are building, although that is not the case in practice.[83]

Having outlined the problems of the current constitutional constellation, Walker then presents his argument for what should be done about them under

---

[77]   Recall, how MacCormick stated that the solution should be found through political means. See N. MacCormick, 'The Maastricht-Urteil: Sovereignty Now' (1995) *European Law Journal* 1(3), 259–66, p. 265.

[78]   Walker (n 38), p. 336.

[79]   Ibid., pp. 337–47.

[80]   Ibid., pp. 347–52.

[81]   Here Walker mentions specifically the European Stability Mechanism and the Fiscal Compact, which are two of the case studies of this book.

[82]   Ibid., p. 350.

[83]   Ibid., pp. 350–52.

a pluralist framework.[84] Here, he seems to concede the point that courts are, after all, what pluralism is all about and the problem that we should try to fix.[85] Walker suggests that we draw from the experience of the failed Constitutional Treaty. In practice, to adopt a new EU Treaty, which would be essentially pluralist: 'a pluralist documentary initiative in the form of a constitution of the supranational level'.[86] According to Walker, this would carry two benefits. First, the EU's competences would be defined more clearly, which would reduce conflicts between national courts and the CJEU. Second, the adoption of this new Treaty would signal mutual acknowledgment on part of both systems.[87]

One can easily agree with the first point. In fact, amending the EU Treaties so as to make the division of competences more explicit and to outline the nature and effects of the principle of primacy of EU law would solve most of the problems described in the case studies and the two preceding chapters. However, Walker's second point is difficult to digest. The EU has no constitution-making capacity (*pouvoir constituant*). In practice, this is evident already from Article 48 TEU, which outlines the procedure for revising the EU Treaties: the European Parliament is only consulted in this procedure, whereas the decision is taken by the European Council (which is an institution that represents the Member States), and finally ratified by all Member States in accordance with their respective national constitutional requirements. Simply put, the EU has no constitutional capacity to signal 'acknowledgment' of the 'equal' constitutional authority of the Member States; the EU functions according to the system of conferred powers, as established in Article 5 TEU. Is Walker, thus, advocating to transform the Union from its current form into a federal state in the proper sense? How would that be pluralist, as opposed to the federalist vision that he first argued against at the beginning of the article?

To summarise, either the epistemic strand of constitutional pluralism is a theory *in abstracto*, in which case it is unable to solve the practical problems that we can observe taking place in Europe. Alternatively, if practical political solutions are suggested, they do not seem to be pluralist, but monist in the European or national sense.[88] Yet, it is still worthwhile to assess the epistemic strand of constitutional pluralism from a methodological perspective.

---

[84] Ibid., pp. 350–55.

[85] Ibid., p. 354: 'Finally, and coming full circle, we return to the judicial level at which the questions of CP [constitutional pluralism] first arose.'

[86] Ibid., p. 353.

[87] Ibid., p. 354: 'it would lend conviction and legitimacy to judicial perspectives on both sides which, in asserting the constitutional authority of their own system, were also prepared to acknowledge the equal constitutional authority of the other system'.

[88] See *supra* n 31.

8.4   EPISTEMES OF CONSTITUTIONAL PLURALISM

Even if constitutional pluralism cannot be the normative theory of European constitutionalism, could the various epistemic aspects of constitutional pluralism still be useful in some respect? Moreover, if so, what conclusions should be drawn from this regarding EU legal studies?

Epistemic constitutional pluralism flows from the observation that the EU as a constitutional polity is itself suffering from an epistemic problem. As Walker has explained: 'Epistemically, the EU is struggling to acquire a basic grammar for the new language of political authority it must speak.'[89] In essence, how would it be best to translate the national constitutional language for the post-national setting?[90] The necessity of acquiring such a new constitutional language follows from taking constitutional pluralism's normative claim seriously: truly appreciating the mutually existing and competing sovereignty claims of different constitutional sites in a heterarchical fashion requires acknowledging that 'there is no neutral perspective from which their distinct representational claims can be reconciled'.[91] Thus, various epistemic starting points need to be adopted.

This epistemic problem is heightened by persistently inadequate reflexivity on part of the different constitutional actors. In practice, the way in which the various proposals put forth for the development of the EU are presented from the presenters' respective viewpoints, the way they never truly engage with each other, and the way there is no reflexive effort by the national polities to '(re)build' the EU as a polity by starting from the principles.[92] Appraising constitutional pluralism, Walker argues, would enable to overcome this issue by offering the required and necessary epistemic basis for renewing the constitutional system,[93] for escaping the epistemic limits of state based conceptualisation.[94]

What is the role of legal scholarship in this process?[95] In addition to the political and the judicial, legal scholars can also be seen as actors and as sites of activity, who can contribute to the debate on solving the problem of

---

[89]   N. Walker, 'Europe's Constitutional Momentum and the Search for Polity Legitimacy' (2005) *International Journal of Constitutional Law* 3(2–3), 211–38, p. 221.

[90]   See Walker (n 57).

[91]   Walker (n 40), pp. 338–9.

[92]   Walker (n 38), p. 350.

[93]   See ibid., pp. 351–5.

[94]   See Walker (n 1).

[95]   On the relationship between the object- and the meta-languages of legal scholarship, see Tuori *European Constitutionalism* (n 3), p. 5.

contested authority; of essentially coming to terms with constitutional plurality and learning to embrace constitutional pluralism.[96] In comparison to the other actors, legal scholars have no institutional or given authority within this debate, but rather their possible authority stems from their capability to analyse the EU as a political and constitutional entity. According to Walker, legal scholars have resorted to the old state-based conception of authority while trying to explain the new post-Westphalian order, and while doing this, they have only been able to act reactively. Walker argues that due to the 'global legal configuration' lacking a hierarchical political or legal order, scholars are the best suited, out of the three groups of actors, to analysing it and perhaps thus also resolving the authority issue. As he explains it, due to the nature of the new entity no one is authorised to speak for it, but therefore no one else is better equipped to analyse it than legal scholars.[97]

If the Westphalian constitutional language can somehow be translated to the post-Westphalian, and if the accompanying epistemic grammar of constitutional pluralism can somehow aid in understanding and developing the EU as a constitutional polity, then Walker's aspirations are warmly welcomed. It seems, however, that this process suffers from, first, a too high degree of abstraction, and secondly, a thus ensuing lack of practical relevance.[98] Tuori has presented a more plausible approach in relation to developing constitutional language based on the double hermeneutics of social science: the constitutional theorist is to construct a constitutional meta-language that reflects the object-language used by the constitutional actors themselves.[99] Notwithstanding, Walker's 'translations' can be credited for being able to overcome an inbuilt and subconscious epistemic foundation based on a specific national legal order, a 'primary epistemology'; an issue which seems to plague most 'general' legal theories.[100]

The calls for acknowledging the various epistemic perspectives can also be of use when trying to, first, understand why national courts contest the primacy of EU law and the interpretive authority of the CJEU, and second, in trying to

---

[96]   This function is similar to what Tuori has called the dual citizenship of legal scholarship. See K. Tuori, *Critical Legal Positivism* (Ashgate 2002), p. 285, and passim; K. Tuori, *Ratio and Voluntas: The Tension Between Reason and Will in Law* (Ashgate 2010), p. 20, and passim.

[97]   N. Walker, 'Beyond Boundary Disputes and Basic Grids: Mapping the Global Disorder of Normative Orders' (2008) *International Journal of Constitutional Law* 6(3–4), 373–96, pp. 393–6.

[98]   See Krisch (n 66), pp. 324–7.

[99]   See Tuori, *European Constitutionalism* (n 3), pp. 5–6.

[100]   See J. Husa, 'Kaleidoscopic Cultural Views and Legal Theory–Dethroning the Objectivity?' in J. Husa and M. Van Hoecke (eds), *Objectivity in Law and Legal Reasoning* (Hart Publishing 2013), pp. 198–9. See also n 41.

find solutions to this.[101] Actually, this comes very close to what Husa has called epistemic universalism: the way comparative law scholars must abandon the nationally oriented, epistemically internal perspective if they are to truly understand the various legal orders or cultures they wish to study.[102] Due to various 'bridging mechanisms' between the EU Treaties and national constitutions,[103] the comparatist's approach based on epistemic universalism would suit that purpose well. However, invoking such epistemic universalism should not be interpreted as propagating the adoption of completely free-standing epistemic positions as that would lead to accepting the contending sovereignty claims. The point is, rather, that adopting such epistemic universalism might be of use for the CJEU when it is confronted with competing national constitutional claims, for example like that in *Gauweiler*, or, if having to interpret Article 4(2) TEU on national constitutional identity, like in *Sayn-Wittgenstein*.[104] Although from a normative perspective national courts are captive of their own constitutions,[105] they too might benefit from such epistemic universalism.[106]

The event-driven and reflexive characteristics of EU legal scholarship – instead of being imaginary and proactive – is a problem in its own right and not just in relation to constitutional pluralism. Thus, Walker's calls for developing EU legal scholarship in this sense can be welcomed, even though one would not endorse the normative claim of constitutional pluralism. In addition, the same applies to what types of proposals should be made for the future devel-

---

[101]   Cf. what Tuori calls 'legal perspectivism' and how he has taken the 'legal cultural' turn in assessing plurality and Article 4(2) TEU. See Tuori (n 3), *European Constitutionalism*, Chapter 3.

[102]   J. Husa, *A New Introduction to Comparative Law* (Hart Publishing 2015), pp. 20–22.

[103]   E.g. Arts 4(2), 6(3) and 48 TEU, but also the preliminary reference procedure of Art. 267 TFEU. The term is taken from Walker (n 1), p. 592.

[104]   C-62/14 *Gauweiler* EU:C:2015:400; C-208/09 *Ilonka Sayn-Wittgenstein* EU:C: 2010:806.

[105]   See Tuori *European Constitutionalism* (n 3), p. 103: 'EU law and national constitutional orders, both subject to their respective *Grundnorm* and both claiming interpretive autonomy, inevitably arrive at opposite positions in the *Kompetenz-Kompetenz* issue.' Further, see T. Tuominen, 'Reconceptualizing the Primacy–Supremacy Debate in EU Law' (2020) *Legal Issues of Economic Integration* 47(3), 245–65.

[106]   E.g. how the German Federal Constitutional Court, on the one hand, thinks that the German concept of national constitutional identity differs from that enshrined in Art. 4(2) TEU, while, on the other hand, it claims that its *ultra vires* and identity review is similar to the review conducted by other European constitutional courts. See M. Claes and J.-H. Reestman, 'The Protection of National Constitutional Identity and the Limits of European Integration at the Occasion of the Gauweiler Case' (2015) *German Law Journal* 16(4), 917–70.

opment of the EU and through which lenses or with what parameters those proposals should be assessed.

But how could EU legal scholarship escape this paradigm? As Tuori points out, modern culture is reflexive culture: it is able to reflect on itself and contest its own validity.[107] However, because of such reflexivity, just as modernism makes art out of art and literature out of literature, EU legal scholarship seems to make legal scholarship out of legal scholarship. This, it would seem, leads to legal scholarship assuming a path towards an ever-higher level of abstraction; or at least this is perhaps from where the reflexive characteristics of EU legal scholarship and the meta-theoretical nature of Walker's analysis stems and the reason also for some of the criticism presented towards constitutional pluralism.[108]

When it comes to the last point – that scholars are in a privileged position to explain the post-state polity since it has no order and thus no authority which could define it – Walker's general claim cannot be sustained. This is because, as was argued in the two preceding chapters, in the EU's legal order it is the CJEU that has, according to the EU Treaties, and should have, according to very practical reservations, interpretive authority (interpretive *Kompetenz-Kompetenz*); whereas constitution-making capacity (*pouvoir constituant* or legislative *Kompetenz-Kompetenz*) is vested in the Member States as 'masters of the Treaties'.[109] Thus, there is no need for the academic community to possess 'an agenda-setting initiative' in relation to the political and the judicial,[110] since in this respect the issue is already settled. In other words, if seen from the perspective adopted here, it can be said that the EU and EU law has already acquired its own constitutional vocabulary and grammar, which the CJEU now tries – to the best of its capabilities – to enforce against the defiant national courts. Notwithstanding, constitutional pluralism can be commended for raising awareness of the existing value plurality within the EU and the ensuing need for dialogue to respond to this.[111]

---

[107] Tuori, *Ratio and Voluntas*: (n 96), p. 20.

[108] Thus, Schütze has argued that the way forward is actually the way backwards in that the European experience should be appreciated in light of the American federal tradition. See Schütze, *From Dual to Cooperative Federalism:* (n 47); Schütze, 'Federalism as Constitutional Pluralism:' (n 47).

[109] Although their capacity as the 'masters of the Treaties' is somewhat limited. See K. Sowery, 'The Nature and Scope of the Primary Law-making Powers of the European Union: The Member States as the "Masters of the Treaties?"' (2018) *European Law Review* 43(2), 205–23.

[110] Walker (n 97), p. 396.

[111] See M. Claes, 'The Primacy of EU Law in European and National Law' in A. Arnull and D. Chalmers (eds), *The Oxford Handbook of European Union Law* (Oxford University Press 2015), p. 204.

To conclude, although some helpful aspects that stem from epistemic pluralism can be distinguished, as long as its basic idea is 'to instil an axiom of epistemic incommensurability into the highly disputed discourse about constitutionalism and constitutionality'[112] the EU's legal order will be at odds with it. This is so, because due to this underlying logic it is actually part of the tendency of perpetuation and thus just keeps on reproducing the problems that constitutional plurality creates instead of actually solving them. In other words, the epistemic grammar of constitutional pluralism aids the relativisation of the constitutional conflict but does not support providing an answer to the ensuing sovereignty-debate.

8.5   CONCLUSION: WHAT IS LEFT OF EUROPEAN CONSTITUTIONAL PLURALISM?

No one can deny the existence of constitutional plurality within the EU's legal domain. Furthermore, constitutional pluralism as an academic effort has formed somewhat of a hermeneutic circle in that it was born out of practice, was then developed by academics and has then be addressed by courts.[113] This can be seen in the German Federal Constitutional Court's ruling on the Treaty of Lisbon and also the CJEU's decision in *Kadi*.[114] However, should a conclusion be drawn that such plurality is desirable and that normative pluralism should be embraced? Can a move be made from observations of facts to judgments of value? That is to say, that can the ought be derived from the is? According to Hume's guillotine, there is no connection between facts and values. It needs to be acknowledged, of course, that various arguments have been presented in the favour of constitutional pluralism; arguments, which can be persuasive and which in themselves might not derive from the is – the fact of plurality. However, this in itself does not stop the guillotine from chopping off the premise of the pluralists' argument. This is especially so, as the various examples and theoretical and conceptual arguments that have been presented above speak against constitutional pluralism being the 'ought' of European constitutionalism.

Notwithstanding, Searle has argued for an understanding of institutional reality which bridges the gap between is and ought. According to him, institutional facts can create desire-independent reasons for action either explicitly or implicitly. Explicitly this takes place when an agent commits to a course

---

[112] Jaklič (n 31), p. 32.
[113] M. Avbelj and J. Komárek, 'Introduction' in Avbelj and Komárek (n 37), p. 7.
[114] See BVerfGE 123, 267 (*Lisbon*); C-402/05 P and C-415/05 P, *Kadi I* EU:C:2008: 461.

of action for example on the basis of an agreement and implicitly when an agent recognises the binding authority that someone has over them.[115] If constitutional pluralism in the EU were an institutional fact[116] – that it created desire-independent reasons for action for the various national and European constitutional actors, either explicitly or implicitly – then the disconnection between the is and the ought in the pluralists' argument would be surpassed. But as far as can be observed, and all of the above speaks in this direction, European constitutional pluralism is not an institutional fact. On the contrary, due to explicit contestation and the lack of implicit conformity on the part of the different constitutional sites, constitutional pluralism is not an institutional fact in this sense. What happened in the *Gauweiler saga* is the perfect example of this: in situations of open conflict, were courts are unwilling to express mutual deference, accommodation or restrain on part of their claims, the theory is put under acute pressure and no factual basis for its claims can be distinguished.[117] In the language used by Searle, constitutional pluralism simply lacks the required collective intentionality that is a prerequisite for the existence of institutional reality.

Thus, it appears that, within the context of the EU, constitutional pluralism's descriptive claim is true, but the normative claim needs to be abandoned. The epistemic claim is discouraged due to its perpetuative tendencies, although it can have some meaningful applications in the political, legal and academic domains. Constitutional pluralism as a theory – in its aspiration of being the normative theory of European constitutionalism – is to be discarded. Although it is able to offer insightful conversation openers and reflections on the state and future development of the EU as a polity, and it may well be 'the only party membership card which will guarantee a seat at the high tables of the public law professoriate',[118] it is ultimately unable to address the problems that its normative variance creates.

---

[115] See J. R. Searle, *Making the Social World: The Structure of Human Civilization* (Oxford University Press 2010), pp. 130–32.

[116] On how Walker has addressed sovereignty through Searle's conceptualisation, see N. Walker, 'Late Sovereignty in the European Union' in N. Walker (ed.), *Sovereignty in Transition* (Hart Publishing 2003), p. 7, fn. 12.

[117] See Fabbrini (n 58), pp. 1013–14.

[118] J. Weiler, 'Prologue: Global and Pluralist Constitutionalism – Some Doubts' in G. de Búrca and J. Weiler (eds), *The Worlds of European Constitutionalism* (Cambridge University Press 2012), p. 8. Weiler's view can be categorised as a moderate critique towards constitutional pluralism since he accepts both the pluralist and hierarchical tendencies of constitutional systems but highlights how 'constitutional pluralism privileges one pillar and thus misconstrues the very nature of the constitutional' (p. 17).

9.   Conclusion: equality instead of pluralism

The primary interest of this study focused on the constitutional practice that amounts to the phenomenon called constitutional pluralism. How did the national courts and the Court of Justice of the European Union (CJEU) participate in the European-level political process during the euro crisis? What effects did this have? On the basis of assessing such questions, it was argued that constitutional pluralism is not an adequate normative theory of European constitutionalism. This is, in essence, the inequality thesis.

While answering these questions, this study sought to assess the argument put forth by constitutional pluralists. This is, namely, that the eminent plurality is both inevitable and desirable and thus a version of European constitutionalism based on pluralism should be embraced. The primary thesis of this study was presented in direct opposition to such an argument and claimed that constitutional pluralism is not an adequate normative theory of European constitutionalism because of the problems that the eminent plurality creates. To substantiate this thesis this study sought to explore the effects of such plurality. Ultimately, the task was to describe how interaction between national constitutions and the EU's constitutional order has functioned during the euro crisis and to then assess these events from a constitutional perspective.

The results concerning the primary research questions of this study can be separated into the practical and the conceptual. In relation to the participation of national courts in the discourse on European constitutionalism during the euro crisis, Chapters 6 and 7 presented the inequality thesis and discussed its legal and political ramifications. A distinction was made, on the one hand, to those courts that are able to participate before the point of no return, and on the other hand, to those that are able to participate after the point of no return. The point of no return refers to the point of time in the process of enacting a legal mechanism at which it becomes effective or is accepted by the CJEU. After this moment individual national courts can no longer obstruct it from coming into force. From the *Gauweiler saga* also an argument concerning how national courts can interact with the CJEU was distinguished. As was explained in Chapter 5, the CJEU did not allow a direct challenge to the Outright Monetary Transactions (OMT) programme, but it did admit an abstract and hypothetical referral from the German Federal Constitutional Court. This shows how the German court has a special relationship with the CJEU.

These observations are the descriptive basis from where the inequality thesis stems. The starting point of the EU's constitutional order, based on the EU Treaties, is the equality of Member States before the Treaties – in addition to which, the Union shall respect the Member States' national identities inherent in their fundamental structures, both political and constitutional, as explicated in Article 4(2) TEU. Under the reading proposed here, Article 4(2) TEU is to be understood to have both a horizontal and a vertical relation: the equality clause is there to guarantee horizontally the equality of the Member States vis-à-vis each other in relation to the EU's constitutional order, whereas the national identity clause is there to vertically protect the Member States' from the EU breaching its competences.

On a literal reading, Article 4(2) TEU seems to prioritise equality as it is mentioned before national identity. A substantive systematisation would come to the same conclusion, as the whole point of the EU having its own legal order means that it is to be applied unilaterally – equally – to all of the Member States. The national identity clause should not be understood in a manner that accords Member States prerogatives towards the EU that end up privileging them vis-à-vis each other and thus breaching equality. To this end, political and legal problems were distinguished from the way that some national consti-tutions make possible the participation of national courts in the European-level political process and the way in which these national courts defiantly use these powers.

Courts that were able to participate before the point of no return, or in a manner that is clearly distinct from what would have been possible for other courts, were seen to have been able to hijack the European-level political process by defining terms to which the crisis response mechanisms must conform. Notwithstanding, courts acting after the point of no return also might have an influence, but only in a more restricted and indirect manner, as their decisions might need to be taken into consideration sometime in the future.

The inequality thesis coupled with the problem of hijacking creates at least five different legitimacy concerns when it comes to the participation of national courts. First, the fact that some national courts are already in a better position to affect the European-level political process than others questions the legitimacy of such interventions by courts. Second, Article 48(4) TEU specifies that amendments to the EU Treaties shall enter into force after being ratified by all the Member States in accordance with their respective constitutional requirements. In some Member States this means that ratifica-tion is subject to review by a court. The same is also true when international law-based treaties are used for the development of the EU, as was the case during the euro crisis. However, this is not to be read as giving national courts a role in the European-level political process as nowhere in the EU Treaties are national courts granted such a role. Third, the system established by the EU Treaties already contains many procedural and substantive mechanisms for taking national concerns into consideration. Furthermore, when such consideration is undertaken by the CJEU or some other EU institution the problems produced by the participation of national courts are avoided. Fourth, when it comes to allocating powers between different governmental institutions, courts might not be the correct institutions for making such decisions on economic policy related issues. This also questions the legitimacy of the participation of national courts in this specific case. Fifth, national courts can also, due to the way and point at which they participate in the European-level political process, be faced with a predicament that affects the outcome of their decisions. This too will reduce their claimed potential to induce legitimacy.

Together the inequality thesis and arguments of a legitimacy deficit create interesting scenarios. In the worst-case scenario, a national court might argue that its own constitution requires for EU law to superimpose on another Member States economic austerity policies; policies, which its own constitution would not allow to be imposed onto itself. The same is also true from a procedural perspective. If a court seeks to guarantee the relevance of its state's national democratic institutions, and thus affects the functioning of the European-level political process, it is effectively denying the equal importance of the democratic institutions of the other Member States that seek to participate to this process through the mechanisms prescribed in the EU Treaties. Thus, it is doing something that it would most likely not accept being done in relation to its own state's democratic institutions.

Next, the more conceptual arguments presented against constitutional pluralism in Chapter 8 are considered. Four critiques towards constitutional pluralism were distinguished: the historical critique, the criticism of uncertainty, the criticism of equality, and the criticism of legitimacy. Basing on the last critique, constitutional pluralism's credentials for being the normative theory of European constitutionalism were assessed. Here, too, the conclusion of the assessment was that the theory does not provide answers to questions or issues that would be most in need of them. Since the first three critiques all revolved around the same practical aspects that were already discussed above, it is not worth restating them here. However, the critique of legitimacy needs to be shortly restated as it relates to answering the primary research questions, through which the main argument of this study is substantiated.

The critique of legitimacy maintained that the theory of constitutional pluralism fails to address issues that would be crucial for it to become a viable normative theory of European constitutionalism. It was argued that as a theory constitutional pluralism tries to explain the functions of courts and how courts could express mutual deference towards each other in a polity beset with plurality, but that it does not address all issues which would be central for the polity to function legitimately; it does not provide answers to the difficult ought questions. Thus, constitutional pluralism fails to convince that it should be the normative theory of European constitutionalism.

These research outcomes – descriptions and assessment of the effects of plurality on the constitutional architecture of the EU – lead to the conclusion that constitutional pluralism is not a valid normative theory of European constitutionalism. Hovering somewhere in between nation-state constitutional monism and European constitutional monism, European constitutional pluralism is an admirable attempt to come to terms with the difficult political and legal concerns that affect the functioning of the Union. While such an attempt has its merits, it ultimately has to be discarded because it seems to create more problems than it is able to solve. This concludes the answer to the primary research questions.

The secondary interest of this study was in the asymmetrical structure of the Economic and Monetary Union (EMU) and the consequences it has for European constitutionalism. How did the asymmetrical structure of the EMU affect the formation and adoption of the crisis response measures? What consequences did this have on European constitutionalism? On the basis of assessing such questions, it was argued that the EMU's asymmetrical structure is unsustainable. The asymmetrical structure is the primary substantive reason for why national courts contested the crisis response measures and why the rulings of the CJEU in cases such as *Gauweiler* are open to criticism from a constitutional perspective. Furthermore, it was also argued that the asymmetry of the EMU can be seen to affect behind all of the crisis response measures in the sense that their adoption and use is interlinked, and they all aim to purport the financial stability of the euro area as a whole, despite the vagueness of that objective.

Answering the secondary research questions switches the perspective from the general to the specific; from the EU's constitutional order in general to the Economic and monetary Union in specific. Although intentional, the EMU's asymmetrical structure seems to be at the root of the criticism that was presented towards the crisis response mechanisms. This criticism contains two, somewhat contradictory tracts.

On the one hand, some of the measures were criticised for eradicating the demarcating line between economic and monetary policy; a line that from an economic perspective seems rather artificial but one that was nevertheless intentionally set up in Maastricht. Partly, this eradication was rather direct, as for example was evident in how the CJEU had to argue towards different ends although pursuing similar means in *Pringle* and *Gauweiler*. In the former the CJEU forcefully argued to establish how the instrument in question concerned economic policy, but almost before the ink had dried, in the latter, the CJEU sought to establish how in that case the instrument concerned monetary policy.

Ironically, both measures were aimed at safeguarding the financial stability of the euro area as a whole.

The more indirect ways of eradication are based on, for example, the interlinkages between the uptake and use of the different crisis response mechanisms. Due to the functioning of the Fiscal Compact, the European Stability Mechanism (ESM), the Banking Union and the OMT programme being interlinked, their uptake was also conditional on the other: the European Central Bank was willing to announce the OMT programme only after the Banking Union was announced, as centralising banking supervision created the necessary conditions for the European Central Bank to dare to buy government bonds through the OMT programme; OMT purchases could only be directed towards Member States that have accepted assistance from the ESM; ESM assistance can only be given to Member States that have implemented the Fiscal Compact.

On the other hand, the following argument can also be distinguished from the discussion in the case studies: the already mutualised monetary policy requires a centralised economic policy alongside in order to overcome both the original cause of the crisis, or at least the need for the crisis response mechanisms, and also to give a firmer footing to some of the new mechanisms created through the crisis response measures. In other words, how the lack of a centralised economic policy first resulted in there not being adequate legal frameworks to govern the EMU, which might have been one of the reasons for why there were not enough legal mechanisms in place to prevent the crisis. Second, following the crisis, how the lack of a proper economic policy competence also resulted in the criticism that some of the crisis response mechanisms did not have an adequate legal basis in the EU Treaties.

This study does not take a stance for either side and argue that the original decision taken in Maastricht needs to be respected and the strict demarcation upheld or that the EU Treaties should be amended and economic policy should be centralised to the EU. The above-mentioned findings do, however, substantiate the thesis that the EMU's asymmetrical structure is unsustainable. It is unsustainable because economists see it as artificial and politicians as something which restricts the decisions that they nevertheless want to take. Whether or not this asymmetrical structure should be changed and whether or not there would be enough political support for this is not a legal question and hence beyond the scope of this study. However, from the legal perspective of this study it has been established how this asymmetry has affected the formation of the crisis response measures and what consequences this has had for the EU. This further explains why such asymmetry is unsustainable. The secondary research questions have thus been answered.

A further point regarding constitutional pluralism still needs to be addressed as part of the overall conclusions of this study. This will lead towards more general self-reflections when it comes to this study and also reflections regarding the methodology of EU legal studies in general. In the introductory chapter constitutional pluralism was questioned by asking is it just too theoretical and thus, has theory building not met polity building. Perhaps initially constitutional pluralism connected theory building and polity building. However, its later, more metatheoretical and epistemological aspects seem to have developed it towards rather abstract constitutional theory. This move might be explained by the same answer that was given to the primary research questions: constitutional pluralism is just not practically feasible, thus as a theory it is somewhat naturally inclined to drift to such philosophical realms.

These metatheoretical and mostly epistemic aspects of constitutional pluralism were discussed in Chapter 8. There, it was concluded amongst other things, that constitutional pluralism can be used as a descriptive taxonomy, as was done through presenting the modalities of constitutional pluralism. Such categorisation, as a heuristic device, can be useful for understanding and analysing constitutional practice in composite polities, such as the EU. Furthermore, that as an academic effort, constitutional pluralism is of course welcome since it can draw and has drawn attention to the difficult political and legal problems that a composite polity such as the EU faces. Thus, it has been a fruitful conversation opener. However, since the meta-language of the scholar has perhaps drifted too far apart from the object-language of the constitutional actors, the practical usability of these conversations is easily lost.

Notwithstanding, the epistemological discussion that constitutional pluralism has started might be useful for the methodological development of EU constitutional scholarship more generally. This is because it establishes a connection with the theoretical discussion that has been vivid amongst comparative law scholars already for a while. The fact that there are several bridging mechanisms between the EU Treaties and national constitutions – such as Articles 4(2), 6(3) and 48 TEU, but also the preliminary reference procedure of Article 267 TFEU – makes the use of comparative (constitutional) law very relevant. Thus, EU constitutional law scholarship should become more associated with a comparative law approach rather than maintaining a strict EU law approach or trying to develop a specific EU constitutional law methodology. The acceptance of epistemic pluralism would actually force EU legal studies in this direction. This is because if the perspective of the CJEU or of EU law is not the only valid perspective, then EU constitutional scholarship cannot be the only valid approach.

Being led by epistemological pluralism towards comparative law methodology has its caveats though. On the one hand, it seems that there has been an increase in methodological self-reflection in EU legal studies during the past two decades; at least a lot has been written on the development of EU legal studies as an academic field and the methods used in EU law. However, there seems to be a gap in this discussion and the actual practice of EU legal studies. On the other hand, it can just as fairly be argued that EU legal studies is still underdeveloped when it comes to self-reflection and methodological debate. This seems to be the case especially when EU legal studies is compared to comparative law or international law. The answer to such methodological infancy could be sought by opening EU legal studies to the discussions flourishing in comparative law and international law. After all, is not EU law an offspring of international law and comparative law in some sense? This however would bring with it a new problem, or actually, the same problem as already confronted, but in a different guise. It has been argued that the methodological discussion within comparative law is mostly metatheoretical and thus of no progressive value to the actual feat of comparison. This is quite similar to the argument presented here; namely, that constitutional pluralism loses the value it might have by extrapolating itself to the metatheoretical level.

To conclude, the original input and added value of this study came from the way that the two most topical themes in European constitutionalism were connected; a feat which has not yet been done in the literature to the same extent as here. Combining these two themes enabled the enrichment of the discussion within both of them respectively by bridging the gaps between them. If read individually, the conclusions of Chapters 6–8 might not seem especially noteworthy. However, it is their joint effort of trying to bridge the practical and the theoretical that makes this research important. This concluding chapter has sought to demonstrate this.

It could still be asked, whether some of the views presented in the literature on constitutional pluralism are actually versions of nation-state constitutional monism disguised as European constitutional pluralism. Although it was stressed throughout this study that the Member States have more to gain from constitutional pluralism than the EU, and thus, how pluralists seem to favour the national on the expense of the European, an answer has not yet been provided to this question.

It would be easy to label some of the pluralists' viewpoints as versions of nation-state constitutional monism. This is so because any normative form of pluralism that acknowledges the possibility for national constitutions of having the final say in European matters invariably denies this from the EU's legal order. This might, however, be too hasty a conclusion. This is only the case if an undivided view on sovereignty is adopted, but as we know, the pluralists' aspirations are different. Thus, classifying some viewpoint as pluralist necessarily entails adopting such a post-sovereigntist view as well. Conceptually speaking, maintaining this is of course possible, but practically speaking it seems to inevitably result in those problems that have been described in this study.

Classifying the pluralists' viewpoints as disguised versions of nation-state constitutional monism would, thus, be discrediting them and dismissing their argument on false grounds as their whole premise is that sovereignty can be divided. On the other hand, if those aspiring for pluralism want their theory to become the 'is' of European constitutionalism, they should reformulate it in a manner that would answer the problems presented in this study. Answering this question, then, seems to be contingent upon the epistemic starting point one adopts on constitutionalism, specifically sovereignty, and therefore this question will remain without a definitive answer.

While the fact that this study moved at a general level leaves room for criticism, there was a good reason for this: constitutional pluralism, the defining feature of European constitutionalism, is a general phenomenon. Thus, it cannot be discussed in a meaningful manner through too specific of a viewpoint. The substance of this study, the euro crisis, has already been addressed at length in the literature. Thus, it is difficult to say anything new on that topic. As stated in Chapter 1, the niche of this study was the combination of the two central themes relating to European constitutionalism: constitutional pluralism and the euro crisis. Doing this would not have been possible without a certain level of generality. By connecting these themes, this study was able to contribute new knowledge to a field of scholarship that is constantly evolving and expanding. In this regard it was argued that the asymmetry of the EMU and constitutional pluralism are linked since contestation towards the crisis response measures by national courts, which is an expression of constitutional plurality, stems from the EMU lacking a proper economic policy competence.

While this study was conducted from the perspective of EU law – since the main issues that were addressed focused on the functioning of the EU, although they stemmed from the Member States' constitutional orders – the same phenomenon could have been studied from the perspective of the Member States and their respective constitutions. The above discussion on methodology and comparative law indicates the fruitfulness of such an approach for the study of the European constitutionalism. Such a comparative (national) constitutional law perspective on European constitutionalism could operate at a more abstract and conceptual level. Or it could be based on specific case studies. Further still, such case studies could also be used to substantiate the more general questions. A further investigation of the inequality thesis should look into the competences and jurisdiction of national courts and other institutions with constitutional review functions in detail. In this study it was only possible to schematise this aspect at a very general level.

Finally, the answers to the primary and secondary research questions lead, only naturally, to asking the following question: What then? Three simple suggestions can be derived from the findings of this study. These answers are here provided only in the most general terms, as the purpose of this study is not to engage with the discussion on the future constitutional and political nature of the European Union. First, international law-based measures should not be used for developing the EU and for furthering integration as they are the most apparent instance of when inequality surfaces. Second, if the desired political goals are not attainable within the confines of the EU Treaties, politicians should not venture outside the scope of the EU Treaties but amend them to make possible pursuing these policy goals through the EU's own legal order. From the perspective of how to address the inequality thesis, this is the best alternative. Third, amending the EU Treaties so as to make the primacy of EU law more explicit and the position of the CJEU as the final arbiter unequivocal would put an end to such actions by national courts. This would most likely require amending the national constitution in most Member States, which would not be an easy task to accomplish. After this, European constitutional monism would prevail over national constitutional monism or European constitutional pluralism. It needs to be conceded that the second and third suggestions are not easy to attain. This is one of the reasons for why there are confrontations within the plurality of constitutions in the EU and for why constitutional pluralism as an academic effort has surfaced. It remains to be seen whether the horizontal equality aspect of Article 4(2) TEU can in the future provide a meaningful and practically applicable basis for the CJEU to address the inequality between the Member States in some fashion.

Bibliography

Adams, M., F. Fabbrini and P. Larouche (eds), *The Constitutionalization of European Budgetary Constraints* (Hart Publishing 2014).

Adamski, D., 'National Power Games and Structural Failures in the European Macroeconomic Governance' (2012) *Common Market Law Review* 49(4), 1319–1364.

Adamski, D., 'Europe's (Misguided) Constitution of Economic Prosperity' (2013) *Common Market Law Review* 50(6), 47–86.

Adamski, D., 'Economic Constitution of the Euro Area After the Gauweiler Preliminary Ruling' (2015) *Common Market Law Review* 52(6), 1451–1490.

Adamski, D., *Redefining European Economic Integration* (Cambridge University Press 2018).

Alexander, K., 'European Banking Union: A Legal and Institutional Analysis of the Single Supervisory Mechanism and the Single Resolution Mechanism' (2015) *European Law Review* 40(2), 154–187.

Alter, K. J., *Establishing the Supremacy of European Law: The Making of an International Law Rule of Law in Europe* (Oxford University Press 2001).

Amtenbrink, F., 'New Economic Governance in the European Union: Another Constitutional Battleground?' in K. Purnhagen and P. Rott (eds), *Varieties of European Economic Law and Regulation: Liber Amicorum for Hans Micklitz* (Springer 2014).

Amtenbrink, F., 'The Metamorphosis of European Economic and Monetary Union' in A. Arnull and D. Chalmers (eds), *The Oxford Handbook of European Union Law* (Oxford University Press 2015).

Andenas, M. and C. Hadjiemmanuil, 'Banking Supervision, the Internal Market and European Monetary Union' in M. Andenas, L. Gormley and C. Hadjiemmanuil (eds), *European Economic and Monetary Union: The Institutional Framework* (Kluwer Law International 1997).

Armstrong, K. A., 'The New Governance of EU Fiscal Discipline' (2013) *European Law Review* 38(5), 601–617.

Arnaiz, A. S. and C. A. Llivina (eds), *National Constitutional Identity and European Integration* (Intersentia 2013).

Athanassiou, P., 'Of Past Measures and Future Plans for Europe's Exit from the Sovereign Debt Crisis: What is Legally Possible (and What is Not)' (2011) *European Law Review* 36(4), 558–575.

Avbelj, M., *The European Union under Transnational Law: A Pluralist Appraisal* (Hart Publishing 2018).

Avbelj, M. and J. Komárek (eds), *Constitutional Pluralism in the European Union and Beyond* (Hart Publishing 2012).

Avbelj, M. and J. Komárek, 'Introduction' in M. Avbelj and J. Komárek (eds), *Constitutional Pluralism in the European Union and Beyond* (Hart Publishing 2012).

Babis, V., 'The Single Rulebook and the European Banking Authority' in F. Fabbrini and M. Ventoruzzo (eds), *Research Handbook on EU Economic Law* (Edward Elgar Publishing 2019).

Baglioni, A., *The European Banking Union: A Critical Assessment* (Palgrave Macmillan 2016).

Bándi, G., P. Darák, A. Halustyik and P. L. Láncos (eds), *European Banking Union. Congress Proceedings Vol. 1. The XXVII FIDE Congress in Budapest, 2016* (Wolters Kluwer 2016).

Baquero Cruz, J., 'The Legacy of the Maastricht-Urteil and the Pluralist Movement' (2008) *European Law Journal* 14(4), 389–422.

Baquero Cruz, J., 'Another Look at Constitutional Pluralism in the European Union' (2016) *European Law Journal* 22(3), 356–374.

Baquero Cruz, J., *What's Left of the Law of Integration? Decay and Resistance in European Union Law* (Oxford University Press 2018).

Barrett, G., 'First Amendment? The Treaty Change to Facilitate the European Stability Mechanism' (2011) *The Institute of International and European Affairs*, 1–27.

Barrios, S. et al, 'Determinants of Intra-euro Area Government Bond Spreads during the Financial Crisis' (2009) *European Commission, DG Economic and Social Affairs*.

Bast, J. and L. Orgad (eds), 'Constitutional Identity in the Age of Global Migration' (2017) *German Law Journal* [special issue] 18(7).

Beck, G., 'The Legal Reasoning of the Court of Justice and the Euro Crisis – The Flexibility of the Court's Cumulative Approach and the Pringle Case' (2013) *Maastricht Journal of European and Comparative Law* 20(4), 635–648.

Bellamy, R., *Political Constitutionalism: A Republican Defence of the Constitutionality of Democracy* (Cambridge University Press 2007).

Besselink, L., *A Composite European Constitution* (Europa Law Publishing 2007).

Besselink, L., 'National and Constitutional Identity Before and After Lisbon' (2010) *Utrecht Law Review* 6(3), 36–49.

Besselink, L., 'Respecting Constitutional Identity in the EU. A Case Note on C-208/09 Ilonka Sayn-Wittgenstein' (2012) *Common Market Law Review* 49(2), 671–694.

Besselink, L., 'The Proliferation of Constitutional Law and Constitutional Adjudication, or How American Judicial Review Came to Europe After All' (2013) *Utrecht Law Review* 9(2), 19–35.

Besselink, L., 'Parameters of Constitutional Development: The Fiscal Compact In Between EU and Member State Constitutions' in L. Serena Rossi and F. Casolari (eds), *The EU After Lisbon: Amending or Coping with the Existing Treaties?* (Springer 2014).

Besselink, L., 'The Parameters of Constitutional Conflict after Melloni' (2014) *European Law Review* 39(4), 531–552.

Besselink, L., 'The Bite, the Bark and the Howl: Article 7 TEU and the Rule of Law Initiatives' in A. Jakab and D. Kochenov (eds), *The Enforcement of EU Law and Values: Ensuring Member States' Compliance* (Oxford University Press 2017).

Besselink, L. and J.-H. Reestman, 'The Fiscal Compact and the European Constitutions: "Europe Speaking German"' (2012) *European Constitutional Law Review* 8(1), 1–7.

Besselink, L., M. Claes, Š. Imamović and J.-H. Reestman, *National Constitutional Avenues for Further EU Integration* (European Parliament, Directorate General for Internal Policies, Policy Department C, 2014).

Beukers, T., 'The New ECB and its Relationship with the Eurozone Member States: Between Central Bank Independence and Central Bank Intervention' (2013) *Common Market Law Review* 50(6), 1579–1620.

Beukers, T., B. de Witte and C. Kilpatrick (eds), *Constitutional Change through Euro-Crisis Law* (Cambridge University Press 2017).

Bieber, R., 'The Allocation of Economic Policy Competences in the European Union' in L. Azoulai (ed.), *The Question of Competence in the European Union* (Oxford University Press 2014).

Bobić, A., 'Constitutional Pluralism Is Not Dead: An Analysis of Interactions Between Constitutional Courts of Member States and the European Court of Justice' (2017) *German Law Journal* 18(6), 1395–1428.

Bodellini, M., 'To Bail-In, or to Bail-Out, that is the Question' (2018) *European Business Organization Law Review* 19(2), 365–392.

Boer, N. de, 'The False Promise of Constitutional Pluralism' in G. Davies and M. Avbelj (eds), *Research Handbook on Legal Pluralism and EU Law* (Edward Elgar Publishing 2018).

Bogdandy, A. von, 'Common Principles for a Plurality of Orders: A Study on Public Authority in the European Legal Area' (2014) *International Journal of Constitutional Law* 12(4), 980–1007.

Bogdandy, A. von. and S. Schill, 'Overcoming Absolute Primacy: Respect for National Identity under the Lisbon Treaty' (2011) *Common Market Law Review* 48(5), 1417–1454.

Borger, V., 'The ESM and the European Court's Predicament in Pringle' (2013) *German Law Journal* 14(1), 113–140.

Borger, V., 'The European Stability Mechanism: A Crisis Tool Operating at Two Junctures' in M. Haentjens and B. Wessels (eds), *Research Handbook on Crisis Management in the Banking Sector* (Edward Elgar Publishing 2015).

Borger, V., *The Currency of Solidarity: Constitutional Transformation during the Euro Crisis* (Cambridge University Press 2020).

Broin, P. ó, 'The Euro Crisis: The Fiscal Treaty – An Institutional Analysis' (2012) *Institute of International and European Affairs Working Paper Series* 5.

Brunnermeier, M. K., H. James and J.-P. Landau, *The Euro and the Battle of Ideas* (Princeton University Press 2016).

Burgess, M., *Federalism and European Union: The Building of Europe, 1950–2000* (Routledge 2000).

Calliess, C. and A. Schnettger, 'The Protection of Constitutional Identity in a Europe of Multilevel Constitutionalism' in C. Calliess and G. van der Schyff (eds), *Constitutional Identity in a Europe of Multilevel Constitutionalism* (Cambridge University Press 2019).

Calliess, C. and G. van der Schyff (eds), *Constitutional Identity in a Europe of Multilevel Constitutionalism* (Cambridge University Press 2019).

Canotilho, M., T. Violante and R. Lanceiro, 'Austerity Measures Under Judicial Scrutiny: the Portuguese Constitutional Case-Law' (2015) *European Constitutional Law Review* 11(1), 155–183.

Capolino, O., 'The Single Resolution Mechanism: Authorities and Proceedings' in M. P. Chiti and V. Santoro (eds), *The Palgrave Handbook of European Banking Union Law* (Palgrave Macmillan 2019).

Chiti, E. and P. G. Teixeira, 'The Constitutional Implications of the European Responses to the Financial and Public Debt Crisis' (2013) *Common Market Law Review* 50(3), 683–708.

Claes, M., 'Negotiating Constitutional Identity or Whose Identity is it Anyway?' in M. Claes, M. de Visser, P. Popelier and C. Van de Heyning (eds), *Constitutional*

Conversations in Europe: Actors, Topics and Procedures (Intersentia Publishing 2012).

Claes, M., 'The Primacy of EU Law in European and National Law' in A. Arnull and D. Chalmers (eds), *The Oxford Handbook of European Union Law* (Oxford University Press 2015).

Claes, M. and J.-H. Reestman, 'The Protection of National Constitutional Identity and the Limits of European Integration at the Occasion of the Gauweiler Case' (2015) *German Law Journal* 16(4), 917–970.

Cloots, E., *National Identity in EU Law* (Oxford University Press 2015).

Cloots, E., 'National Identity, Constitutional Identity, and Sovereignty in the EU' (2016) *Netherlands Journal of Legal Philosophy* 45(2), 82–98.

Cour-Thimann, P. and B. Winkler, 'The ECB's Non-Standard Monetary Policy Measures: The Role of Institutional Factors and Financial Structure' (2013) *European Central Bank Working Paper Series*, (1528), 1–44.

Craig, P., 'The Stability, Coordination and Governance Treaty: Principle, Politics and Pragmatism' (2012) *European Law Review* 37(3), 231–248.

Craig, P., 'Pringle and Use of EU Institutions outside the EU Legal Framework: Foundations, Procedure and Substance' (2013) *European Constitutional Law Review* 9(2), 263–284.

Craig, P., *The Lisbon Treaty: Law, Politics, and Treaty Reform* (Oxford University Press 2013).

Craig, P., 'Economic Governance and the Euro Crisis: Constitutional Architecture and Constitutional Implications' in M. Adams, F. Fabbrini and P. Larouche (eds), *The Constitutionalization of European Budgetary Constraints* (Hart Publishing 2014).

Craig, P., 'Pringle and the Nature of Legal Reasoning' (2014) *Maastricht Journal of European and Comparative Law* 21(1), 205–220.

Craig, P. and G. de Búrca, *EU Law: Text, Cases, and Materials. Fifth Edition* (Oxford University Press 2011).

Craig, P. and M. Markakis, 'Gauweiler and the Legality of Outright Monetary Transactions' (2016) *European Law Review* 41(1), 4–24.

Curtin, D., 'The Constitutional Structure of the Union: A Europe of Bits and Pieces' (1993) *Common Market Law Review* 30(1), 17–69.

Curtin, D., *Executive Power of the European Union: Law, Practices, and the Living Constitution* (Oxford University Press 2009).

Dahan, S., O. Fuchs and M.-L. Layus, 'Whatever It Takes? Regarding the OMT Ruling of the German Federal Constitutional Court' (2015) *Journal of International Economic Law* 18(1), 137–151.

Davies, G. and M. Avbelj (eds), *Research Handbook on Legal Pluralism and EU Law* (Edward Elgar Publishing 2018).

Dawson, M. and A. Bobić, 'Quantitative Easing at the Court of Justice – Doing Whatever it Takes to Save the Euro: Weiss and Others' (2019) *Common Market Law Review* 56(4), 1005–1040.

Dehousse, R. and J. Weiler, 'The Legal Dimension' in W. Wallace (ed.), *The Dynamics of European Integration* (Pinter Publishers 1990).

Dermine, P., 'The Ruling of the Bundesverfassungsgericht in PSPP – An Inquiry into its Repercussions on the Economic and Monetary Union' (2020) *European Constitutional Law Review*, FirstView article published online 19 November 2020.

Donnelly, S., 'Expert Advice and Political Choice in Constructing European Banking Union' (2016) *Journal of Banking Regulation* 17, 104–118.

Donnelly, S., 'Advocacy Coalitions and the Lack of Deposit Insurance in Banking Union' (2018) *Journal of Economic Policy Reform* 21(3), 210–223.

Douglas-Scott, S., *Constitutional Law of the European Union* (Longman 2002).

Dragomir, L., *European Prudential Banking Regulation and Supervision: The Legal Dimension* (Routledge 2010).

Dyson, K., 'Fifty Years of Economic and Monetary Union: A Hard and Thorny Journey' in D. Phinnemore and A. Warleigh-Lack (eds), *Reflections on European Integration: 50 Years of the Treaty of Rome* (Palgrave Macmillan 2009).

Eichengreen, B., 'European Monetary Integration with Benefit of Hindsight' (2012) *Journal of Common Market Studies* 50 (Supplement 1), 123–136.

Epstein, R. and M. Rhodes, 'From Governance to Government: Banking Union, Capital Markets Union and the New EU' (2018) *Competition & Change* 22(2), 205–224.

Fabbrini, F., 'The Euro-Crisis and the Courts: Judicial Review and the Political Process in Comparative Perspective' (2014) *Berkeley Journal of International Law* 31(1), 64–123.

Fabbrini, F., 'After the OMT Case: The Supremacy of EU Law as the Guarantee of the Equality of the Member States' (2015) *German Law Journal* 16(4), 1003–1024.

Fabbrini, F., *Economic Governance in Europe: Comparative Paradoxes and Constitutional Challenges* (Oxford University Press 2016).

Fabbrini, F., 'Fiscal Capacity' in F. Fabbrini and M. Ventoruzzo (eds), *Research Handbook on EU Economic Law* (Edward Elgar Publishing 2019).

Fabbrini, F. and A. Sajó, 'The Dangers of Constitutional Identity' (2019) *European Law Journal* 25(4), 457–473.

Fabbrini, S., 'Intergovernmentalism and Its Limits: Assessing the European Union's Answer to the Euro Crisis' (2013) *Comparative Political Studies* 46(9), 1003–1029.

Fabbrini, S., *Which European Union? Europe After the Euro Crisis* (Cambridge University Press 2015).

Faraguna, P., 'Taking Constitutional Identities Away from the Courts' (2016) *Brooklyn Journal of International Law* 41(2), 491–578.

Faraguna, P. and D. Messineo, 'Light and Shadows in the Bundesverfassungsgericht's Decision Upholding the European Banking Union' (2020) *Common Market Law Review* 57(5), 1629–1646.

Ferran, E., 'European Banking Union. Imperfect, But It Can Work' in D. Busch and G. Ferrarini (eds), *European Banking Union* (Oxford University Press 2015).

Fichera, M., *The Foundations of the EU as a Polity* (Edward Elgar Publishing 2018).

Fioretos, O., 'Historical Institutionalism in International Relations' (2011) *International Organization* 65(2), 367–399.

Garrett, G., 'The Politics of Maastricht' in B. Eichengreen and J. Frieden (eds), *The Political Economy of European Monetary Unification. Second Edition* (Westview Press 2001).

Geeroms, H., S. Ide and F. Naert, *The European Union and the Euro: How to Deal with a Currency Built on Dreams* (Intersentia 2014).

Gérard, P. and W. Verrijdt, 'Belgian Constitutional Court Adopts National Identity Discourse: Belgian Constitutional Court No. 62/2016, 28 April 2016' (2017) *European Constitutional Law Review* 13(1), 182–205.

Gerards, J., 'Pluralism, Deference and the Margin of Appreciation Doctrine' (2011) *European Law Journal* 17(1), 80–120.

Gerards, J., 'Margin of Appreciation and Incrementalism in the Case Law of the European Court of Human Rights' (2018) *Human Rights Law Review* 18(3), 495–515.

Gestel, R. van and H.-W. Micklitz, 'Why Methods Matter in European Legal Scholarship' (2014) *European Law Journal* 20(3), 292–316.

Ginsborg, L., 'The Impact of the Economic Crisis on Human Rights in Europe and the Accountability of International Institutions' (2017) *Global Campus Human Rights Journal* 1, 97–117.

Gocaj, L. and S. Meunier, 'Time Will Tell: The EFSF, the ESM, and the Euro Crisis' (2013) *Journal of European Integration* 35(3), 239–253.

Goldmann, M., 'Constitutional Pluralism as Mutually Assured Discretion: The Court of Justice, the German Federal Constitutional Court, and the ECB' (2016) *Maastricht Journal of European and Comparative Law* 23(1), 119–135.

Goldmann, M., 'Discretion, Not Rules: Postunitary Constitutional Pluralism in the Economic and Monetary Union' in G. Davies and M. Avbelj (eds), *Research Handbook on Legal Pluralism and EU Law* (Edward Elgar Publishing 2018).

Gortsos, C. V., 'The European Deposit Insurance Scheme' in F. Fabbrini and M. Ventoruzzo (eds), *Research Handbook on EU Economic Law* (Edward Elgar Publishing 2019).

Gortsos, C. V., 'The Single Resolution Mechanism' in F. Fabbrini and M. Ventoruzzo (eds), *Research Handbook on EU Economic Law* (Edward Elgar Publishing 2019).

Grabenwarter, C., 'National Constitutional Law Relating to the European Union' in A. von Bogdandy and J. Bast (eds), *Principles of European Constitutional Law* (2nd edn revised, Hart Publishing 2009).

Grauwe, P. de, *The Limits of the Market: The Pendulum Between Government and Market* (Oxford University Press 2017).

Gregorio Merino, A. de, 'Legal Developments in the Economic and Monetary Union During the Debt Crisis: the Mechanisms of Financial Assistance' (2012) *Common Market Law Review* 49(5), 1613–1646.

Gregorio Merino, A. de, 'Institutional Report' in G. Bándi, P. Darák, A. Halustyik and P. L. Láncos (eds), *European Banking Union. Congress Proceedings Vol. 1. The XXVII FIDE Congress in Budapest, 2016* (Wolters Kluwer 2016).

Grimm, D., 'The Democratic Costs of Constitutionalisation: The European Case' (2015) *European Law Journal* 21(4), 460–473.

Grimm, D., 'A Long Time Coming' (2020) *German Law Journal* 21(5), 944–949.

Gros, D., 'On the Stability of Public Debt in a Monetary Union' (2012) *Journal of Common Market Studies* 50 (Supplement 2), 36–48.

Grote, R., 'Judicial Review' in *Max Planck Encyclopedia of Comparative Constitutional Law* (Oxford University Press Online).

Gustaferro, B., 'Beyond the *Exceptionalism* of Constitutional Conflicts: The *Ordinary* Functions of the Identity Clause' (2012) *Yearbook of European Law* 31, 263–318.

Habermas, J., 'Remarks on Dieter Grimm's "Does Europe Need a Constitution?"' (1995) *European Law Journal* 1(3), 303–307.

Habermas, J., *The Crisis of the European Union: A Response* (Polity 2012).

Habermas, J., *The Lure of Technocracy* (Polity Press 2015).

Halberstam, D., 'Constitutional Heterarchy: The Centrality of Conflict in the European Union and the United States' in J. L. Dunoff and J. P. Trachtman (eds), *Ruling the World? Constitutionalism, International Law, and Global Governance* (Cambridge University Press 2009).

Halmai, G., 'The Hungarian Approach of Constitutional Review' in W. Sadurski (ed.), *Constitutional Justice, East and West, Democratic Legitimacy and Constitutional Courts in Post-Communist Europe in a Comparative Perspective* (Kluwer International 2002).

Halmai, G., 'The Fundamental Law of Hungary and the European Constitutional Values' (2019) *DPCE Online* 39(2), 1503–1524.

Harden, I., 'The Fiscal Constitution of the EMU' in P. Beaumont and N. Walker (eds), *Legal Framework of the Single European Currency* (Hart Publishing 1999).

Heipertz, M. and A. Verdun, *Ruling Europe: The Politics of the Stability and Growth Pact* (Cambridge University Press 2010).

Heisenberg, D., 'The Institution of "Consensus" in the European Union: Formal versus Informal Decision-making in the Council' (2005) *European Journal of Political Research* 44(1), 65–90.

Hinarejos, A., *The Euro Area Crisis in Constitutional Perspective* (Oxford University Press 2015).

Howarth, D. and L. Quaglia, 'Banking on Stability: The Political Economy of New Capital Requirements in the European Union' (2013) *Journal of European Integration* 35(3), 333–346.

Howarth, D. and L. Quaglia, *The Political Economy of European Banking Union* (Oxford University Press 2016).

Howarth, D. and L. Quaglia, 'The Difficult Construction of a European Deposit Insurance Scheme: A Step Too Far in Banking Union?' (2018) *Journal of Economic Policy Reform* 21(3), 190–209.

Huber, P. M., 'The Federal Constitutional Court and European Integration' (2015) *European Public Law* 21(1), 83–108.

Husa, J., *The Constitution of Finland: A Contextual Analysis* (Hart Publishing 2011).

Husa, J., 'Kaleidoscopic Cultural Views and Legal Theory–Dethroning the Objectivity?' in J. Husa and M. Van Hoecke (eds), *Objectivity in Law and Legal Reasoning* (Hart Publishing 2013).

Husa, J., *A New Introduction to Comparative Law* (Hart Publishing 2015).

Ioannou, D., P. Leblond and A. Niemann (eds), '*European Integration in Times of Crisis: Theoretical Perspectives*' (2015) *Journal of European Integration* [special issue] 22(2).

Jaklič, K., *Constitutional Pluralism in the EU* (Oxford University Press 2014).

James, H., *Making the European Monetary Union: The Role of the Committee of Central Bank Governors and the Origins of the European Central Bank* (Belknap Press of Harvard University Press 2012).

Joerges, C., 'Constitutionalism and the Law of the European Economy' in M. Dawson, H. Enderlein and C. Joerges (eds), *Beyond the Crisis: The Governance of Europe's Economic, Political and Legal Transformation* (Oxford University Press 2015).

Joyce, M., D. Miles, A. Scott and D. Vayanos, 'Quantitative Easing and Unconventional Monetary Policy – An Introduction' (2012) *The Economic Journal* 122(564), 271–288.

Kaupa, C., *The Pluralist Character of the European Economic Constitution* (Hart Publishing 2016).

Kelemen, R. D., 'On the Unsustainability of Constitutional Pluralism: European Supremacy and the Survival of the Eurozone' (2016) *Maastricht Journal of European and Comparative Law* 23(1), 136–150.

Kelemen, R. D., 'The Dangers of Constitutional Pluralism' in G. Davies and M. Avbelj (eds), *Research Handbook on Legal Pluralism and EU Law* (Edward Elgar Publishing 2018).

Kelemen, R. D. and L. Pech, 'Why Autocrats Love Constitutional Identity and Constitutional Pluralism: Lessons from Hungary and Poland' (2018) *Reconnect-Europe Working Paper* No. 2.

Keppenne, J.-P., 'Fiscal Rules' in F. Fabbrini and M. Ventoruzzo (eds), *Research Handbook on EU Economic Law* (Edward Elgar Publishing 2019).

Kilpatrick, C. and B. de Witte (eds), *Social Rights in Crisis in the Eurozone: The Role of Fundamental Rights' Challenges* (EUI Depart of Law Research Paper No. 2014/05).

Kommers, D. P. and R. A. Miller, *The Constitutional Jurisprudence of the Federal Republic of Germany.* (3rd edn, revised and expanded, Duke University Press 2012).

Krisch, N., 'Europe's Constitutional Monstrosity' (2005) *Oxford Journal of Legal Studies* 25(2), 321–334.

Krisch, N., *Beyond Constitutionalism: The Pluralist Structure of Postnational Law* (Oxford University Press 2010).

Kukovec, D., 'Hierarchies as Law' (2014) *Columbia Journal of European Law* 21(1), 131–194.

Kukovec, D., 'Law and the Periphery' (2015) *European Law Journal* 21(3), 406–428.

Kumm, M., 'The Jurisprudence of Constitutional Conflict: Constitutional Supremacy in Europe Before and After the Constitutional Treaty' (2005) *European Law Journal* 11(3), 262–307.

Kumm, M., 'Rethinking Constitutional Authority: On the Structure and Limits of Constitutional Pluralism' in M. Avbelj and J. Komárek (eds), *Constitutional Pluralism in the European Union and Beyond* (Hart Publishing 2012).

Kumm, M., 'Rebel Without a Good Cause: Karlsruhe's Misguided Attempt to Draw the CJEU into a Game of "Chicken" and What the CJEU Might do About It' (2014) *German Law Journal* 15(2), 203–216.

Lang, A., 'Ultra Vires Review of the ECB's Policy of Quantitative Easing: An Analysis of the German Constitutional Court's Preliminary Reference Order in the PSPP Case' (2018) *Common Market Law Review* 55(3), 923–952.

Laprévote, F.-C. and F. de Cecco (eds), *Research Handbook on State Aid in the Banking Sector* (Edward Elgar Publishing 2017).

Lastra, R. M., *Legal Foundations of International Monetary Stability* (Oxford University Press 2006).

Lastra, R. M., *International Financial and Monetary Law. Second Edition* (Oxford University Press 2015).

Lastra, R. M. and J.-V. Louis, 'European Economic and Monetary Union: History, Trends, and Prospects' (2013) *Yearbook of European Law* 32(1), 57–206.

Lavapuro, J., T. Ojanen and M. Scheinin, 'Rights-Based Constitutionalism in Finland and the Development of Pluralist Constitutional Review' (2011) *International Journal of Constitutional Law* 9(2), 503–531.

Leino, P. and J. Salminen, 'The Euro Crisis and Its Constitutional Consequences for Finland: Is There Room for National Politics in EU Decision-Making?' (2013) *European Constitutional Law Review* 9(3), 451–479.

Leino-Sandberg, P. and J. Salminen, 'A Multi-Level Playing Field for Economic Policy-Making: Does EU Economic Governance Have Impact?' in T. Beukers, B. de Witte, and C. Kilpatrick (eds), *Constitutional Change through Euro-Crisis Law* (Cambridge University Press 2017).

Lenaerts, K., 'EMU and the EU's Constitutional Framework' (2014) *European Law Review* 39(6), 753–769.

Lenaerts, K., 'The Principle of Democracy in the Case Law of the European Court of Justice' (2014) *International and Comparative Law Quarterly* 62(2), 271–315.

Lenaerts, K. and J. A. Gutiérrez-Fons, 'To Say What the Law of the EU Is: Methods of Interpretation and the European Court of Justice' (2014) *The Columbia Journal of European Law* 20(2), 3–61.

Lenaerts, K. and P. van Nuffel, *European Union Law* (3rd edn, Sweet & Maxwell 2011).

Lenaerts, K., I. Maselis and K. Gutman, *EU Procedural Law* (Oxford University Press 2014).

Letsas, G., 'Two Concepts of the Margin of Appreciation' (2006) *Oxford Journal of Legal Studies* 26(4), 705–732.

Lionello, L., *The Pursuit of Stability of the Euro Area as a Whole: The Reform of the European Economic Union and Perspectives of Fiscal Integration* (Springer 2020).

Loughlin, M., 'Constitutional Pluralism: An Oxymoron?' (2014) *Global Constitutionalism* 3(1), 9–33.

MacCormick, N., 'The Maastricht-Urteil: Sovereignty Now' (1995) *European Law Journal* 1(3), 259–266.

MacCormick, N., *Questioning Sovereignty: Law, State, and Nation in the European Commonwealth* (Oxford University Press 1999).

Mader, O., 'Enforcement of EU Values as a Political Endeavour: Constitutional Pluralism and Value Homogeneity in Times of Persistent Challenges to the Rule of Law' (2019) *Hague Journal on the Rule Law* 11, 133–170.

Maduro, M. P., 'Contrapunctual Law: Europe's Constitutional Pluralism in Action', in N. Walker (ed.), *Sovereignty in Transition* (Hart Publishing 2003).

Maduro, M. P., 'Europe and the Constitution: What if This is as Good as it Gets?' in J. H. H. Weiler and M. Wind (eds), *European Constitutionalism beyond the State* (Cambridge University Press 2003).

Maduro, M. P., 'Three Claims of Constitutional Pluralism', in M. Avbelj and J. Komárek (eds), *Constitutional Pluralism in the European Union and Beyond* (Hart Publishing 2012).

Markakis, M., *Accountability in the Economic and Monetary Union: Foundations, Policy, and Governance* (Oxford University Press 2020).

Mayer, F., 'Rebels Without a Cause? A Critical Analysis of the German Constitutional Court's OMT Reference' (2014) *German Law Journal* 15(2), 111–146.

McNamara, K., 'Economic Governance, Ideas and EMU: What Currency Does Policy Consensus Have Today?' (2006) *Journal of Common Market Studies* 44(4), 803–821.

Menéndez, A. J., 'The Existential Crisis of the European Union' (2013) *German Law Journal* 14(5), 453–526.

Miettinen, S. and M. Kettunen, 'Travaux to the EU Treaties: Preparatory Work as Source of EU Law' (2015) *Cambridge Yearbook of European Legal Studies* 17(1), 145–167.

Miller, V., 'The Treaty on Stability, Coordination and Governance in the Economic and Monetary Union: Political Issues' (2012) *House of Commons Research Paper* 12/14, 1–58.

Möllers, C., 'German Federal Constitutional Court: Constitutional Ultra Vires Review of European Acts Only Under Exceptional Circumstances; Decision of 6 July 2010, 2 BvR 2661/06, Honeywell' (2011) *European Constitutional Law Review* 7(1), 161–167.

Moloney, N., 'European Banking Union: Assessing its Risks and Resilience' (2014) *Common Market Law Review* 51(6), 1609–1670.

Mooij, A., 'The Weiss Judgment: The Court's Further Clarification of the ECB's Legal Framework' (2019) *Maastricht Journal of European and Comparative Law* 26(3), 449–465.

Morra, C. B., 'The Third Pillar of the Banking Union and Its Troubled Implementation' in M. P. Chiti and V. Santoro (eds), *The Palgrave Handbook of European Banking Union Law* (Palgrave Macmillan 2019).

Mundell, R., 'Theory of Optimum Currency Areas' (1961) *American Economic Review* 51(4), 657–666.

Neergaard, U., C. Jacqueson and J. Hartig Danielsen (eds), *The Economic and Monetary Union: Constitutional and Institutional Aspects of the Economic Governance within the EU. The XXVI FIDE Congress in Copenhagen, 2014* (DJOF Publishing 2014).

Nicolaidis, K. and R. Howse (eds), *The Federal Vision: Legitimacy and Levels of Governance in the United States and the European Union* (Oxford University Press 2001).

Ohler, C., 'The European Stability Mechanism: The Long Road to Financial Stability in the Euro Area' (2011) *German Yearbook of International Law* 54, 47–74.

Padoa-Schioppa, T., *The Road to Monetary Union in Europe: The Emperor, the Kings, and the Genies* (Oxford University Press 2000).

Padoa-Schioppa, T., *The Euro and Its Central Bank: Getting United After the Union* (MIT Press 2004).

Patrignani, E., 'Complex Legal Pluralism' (2015) *Retfaerd* 38(4), 19–33.

Peers, S., 'The Stability Treaty: Permanent Austerity or Gesture Politics?' (2012) *European Constitutional Law Review* 8(3), 404–441.

Peers, S., 'Towards a New Form of EU Law?: The Use of EU Institutions outside the EU Legal Framework' (2013) *European Constitutional Law Review* 9(1), 37–72.

Pernice, I., 'A Difficult Partnership Between Courts: The First Preliminary Reference by the German Federal Constitutional Court to the CJEU' (2014) *Maastricht Journal of European and Comparative Law* 21(1), 3–13.

Piqani, D., 'The *Simmenthal* Revolution Revisited: What Role for Constitutional Courts?' in B. de Witte, J. A. Mayoral, U. Jaremba, M. Wind and K. Podstawa (eds), *National Courts and EU Law: New Issues, Theories and Methods* (Edward Elgar Publishing 2016).

Piqani, D., 'In Search of Limits for the Protection of National Identities as a Member State Interest' in M. Varju (ed.), *Between Compliance and Particularism* (Springer 2019).

Pisani-Ferry, J., *The Euro Crisis and Its Aftermath* (Oxford University Press 2014).

Pliakos, A. and G. Anagnostaras, 'Fundamental Rights and the New Battle over Legal and Judicial Supremacy: Lessons from Melloni' (2015) *Yearbook of European Law* 34, 97–126.

Pliakos, A. and G. Anagnostaras, 'Adjudicating Economics II: The Quantitative Easing Programme Declared Valid' (2020) *European Law Review* 45(1), 128–146.

Pollack, M. A., 'The New Institutionalisms and European Integration' in A. Wiener and T. Diez (eds), *European Integration Theory* (Oxford University Press 2004).

Rask Madsen, M., H. Palmer Olsen and U. Šadl, 'Competing Supremacies and Clashing Institutional Rationalities: the Danish Supreme Court's Decision in the *Ajos* Case and the National Limits of Judicial Cooperation' (2017) *European Law Journal* 23(1–2), 140–150.

Reestman, J.-H., 'The Fiscal Compact: Europe's not always able to speak German: On the Dutch' (2013) *European Constitutional Law Review* 9(3), 480–500.

Reestman, J.-H., 'Legitimacy Through Adjudication: the ESM Treaty and the Fiscal Compact before the National Courts' in T. Beukers, B. de Witte and C. Kilpatrick (eds), *Constitutional Change through Euro-Crisis Law* (Cambridge University Press 2017).

Reh, C., A. Héritier, E. Bressanelli, and C. Koop, 'The Informal Politics of Legislation: Explaining Secluded Decision- Making in the European Union' (2013) *Comparative Political Studies* 46(9), 1112–1142.

Rijpma. J. J., 'You Gotta Let Love Move: ECJ 5 June 2018, C-673/16, Coman, Hamilton, Accept v Inspectoratul General pentru Imigrări' (2019) *European Constitutional Law Review* 15(2), 324–339.

Rodrik, D., *The Globalization Paradox: Democracy and the Future of the World Economy* (W. W. Norton & Company 2011).

Rosas, A. and L. Armati, *EU Constitutional Law: An Introduction* (3rd edn, Hart Publishing 2018).

Rynck, S. de, 'Banking on a Union: The Politics of Changing Eurozone Banking Supervision' (2016) *Journal of European Public Policy* 23(1), 119–135.

Sadeleer, N. de, 'The New Architecture of the European Economic Governance: A Leviathan or a Flat-Footed Colossus?' (2012) *Maastricht Journal of European and Comparative Law* 19(2), 354–382.

Saurugger, S., A. Hofmann and T. Warren, 'National Constitutional Courts As Veto Players in the EMU Crisis' (January 7, 2020). Available at SSRN: https://ssrn.com/abstract=3599037 or http://dx.doi.org/10.2139/ssrn.3599037.

Scherer, P., 'European Monetary Policy – What Works Legally and What Doesn't? The ECJ's Judgment Regarding the OMT Programme' (2015) *European Law Reporter* (4), 106–112.

Schiavo, G. Lo, *The Role of Financial Stability in EU Law and Policy* (Wolters Kluwer 2017).

Schiavo, G. Lo (ed.), *The European Banking Union and the Role of Law* (Edward Elgar Publishing 2019).

Schimmelfennig, F., 'Efficient Process Tracing: Analyzing the Causal Mechanisms of European Integration' in A. Bennett and J. T. Checkel (eds), *Process Tracing: From Metaphor to Analytical Tool* (Cambridge University Press 2015).

Schütze, R., *European Constitutional Law* (Cambridge University Press 2012).

Schütze, R., 'Federalism as Constitutional Pluralism: "Letter from America"' in M. Avbelj and J. Komárek (eds), *Constitutional Pluralism in the European Union and Beyond* (Hart Publishing 2012).

Schütze, R., *From Dual to Cooperative Federalism: The Changing Structure of European Law* (Oxford University Press 2013).

Schütze, R., 'Constitutionalism and the European Union' in C. Barnard and S. Peers (eds), *European Union Law* (Oxford University Press 2014).

Schütze, R., *European Union Law* (Cambridge University Press 2015).

Scott, J. and D. M. Trubek, 'Mind the Gap: Law and New Approaches to Governance in the European Union' (2002) *European Law Journal* 8(1), 1–18.

Searle, J. R., *Making the Social World: The Structure of Human Civilization* (Oxford University Press 2010).

Shapiro, M. and A. Stone Sweet (eds), *On Law, Politics, and Judicialization* (Oxford University Press 2002).

Shaw, J., 'The European Union – Discipline Building Meets Polity Building' in P. Cane and M. Tushnet (eds), *The Oxford Handbook of Legal Studies* (Oxford University Press 2003).

Slaughter, A.-M., A. Stone Sweet and J. Weiler (eds), *The European Court and National Courts: Doctrine and Jurisprudence: Legal Change in its Social Context* (Hart Publishing 1998).

Sluis, M. van der, 'Similar, Therefore Different: Judicial Review of Another Unconventional Monetary Policy in Weiss (C-493/17)' (2019) *Legal Issues of Economic Integration* 46(3), 263–284.

Smits, R., *The European Central Bank: Institutional Aspects* (Kluwer Law International 1997).

Smits, R., 'The European Central Banks Independence and its Relations with Economic Policy Makers' (2007) *Fordham International Law Journal* 31(6), 1614–1636.

Smits, R., 'The Crisis Response in Europe's Economic and Monetary Union: Overview of Legal Developments' (2015) *Fordham International Law Journal* 38(4), 1135–1191.

Snell, J., 'Gauweiler: Some Institutional Aspects' (2015) *European Law Review* 40(2), 133–134.

Snell, J., 'The Trilemma of European Economic and Monetary Integration, and Its Consequences' (2016) *European Law Journal* 22(2), 157–179.

Snell, J., 'The Internal Market and the Philosophies of Market Integration' in C. Barnard and S. Peers (eds), *European Union Law* (3rd edn, Oxford University Press 2020).

Sowery, K., 'The Nature and Scope of the Primary Law-making Powers of the European Union: The Member States as the "Masters of the Treaties?"' (2018) *European Law Review* 43(2), 205–223.

Spuller, G., 'Transformation of the Hungarian Constitutional Court: Tradition, Revolution, and (European) Prospects' (2014) *German Law Journal* 15(4), 637–692.

Stone Sweet, A., *Governing with Judges. Constitutional Politics in Europe* (Oxford University Press 2000).

Stone Sweet, A., 'Constitutional Courts' in M. Rosenfeld and A. Sajó (eds), *The Oxford Handbook of Comparative Constitutional Law* (Oxford University Press 2012).

Teixeira, P. G., 'The Legal History of the Banking Union' (2017) *European Business Organization Law Review* 18(3), 535–565.

Teixeira, P. G., 'The Future of the European Banking Union: Risk-Sharing and Democratic Legitimacy' in M. P. Chiti and V. Santoro (eds), *The Palgrave Handbook of European Banking Union Law* (Palgrave Macmillan 2019).

Thelen, K., 'Historical Institutionalism in Comparative Politics' (1999) *Annual Review of Political Science* 2(1), 369–404.

Thiele, A., 'The "German Way" of Curbing Public Debt' (2015) *European Constitutional Law Review* 11(1), 30–54.

Timmermans, C., 'The Magic World of Constitutional Pluralism' (2014) *European Constitutional Law Review* 10(2), 349–358.

Tridimas, T., 'Constitutional Review of Member State Action: The Virtues and Vices of an Incomplete Jurisdiction' (2011) *International Journal of Constitutional Law* 9(3–4), 737–756.

Tridimas, T., 'The ECJ and the National Courts: Dialogue, Cooperation, and Instability' in A. Arnull and D. Chalmers (eds), *The Oxford Handbook of European Union Law* (Oxford University Press 2015).

Tridimas, T., 'General Report' in G. Bándi, P. Darák, A. Halustyik and P. L. Láncos (eds), *European Banking Union. Congress Proceedings Vol. 1. The XXVII FIDE Congress in Budapest, 2016* (Wolters Kluwer 2016).

Tridimas, T., 'The Constitutional Dimension of Banking Union' in S. Grundmann and H. W. Micklitz (eds), *The European Banking Union and Constitution: Beacon for Advanced Integration or Death-Knell for Democracy?* (Hart Publishing 2019).

Tridimas, T. and N. Xanthoulis, 'A Legal Analysis of the Gauweiler Case: Between Monetary Policy and Constitutional Conflict' (2016) *Maastricht Journal of European and Comparative Law* 23(1), 17–39.

Tröger, T. H., 'The Single Supervisory Mechanism' in F. Fabbrini and M. Ventoruzzo (eds), *Research Handbook on EU Economic Law* (Edward Elgar Publishing 2019).

Tsebelis, G. and H. Hahm, 'Suspending Vetoes: How the Euro Countries Achieved Unanimity in the Fiscal Compact' (2014) *Journal of European Public Policy* 21(10), 1388–1411.

Tuominen, T., 'The European Banking Union: A Shift in the Internal Market Paradigm?' (2017) *Common Market Law Review* 54(5), 1359–1380.

Tuominen, T., 'Aspects of Constitutional Pluralism in Light of the *Gauweiler* Saga' (2018) *European Law Review* 43(2), 186–204.

Tuominen, T., 'Mechanisms of Financial Stabilisation' in F. Fabbrini and M. Ventoruzzo (eds), *Research Handbook on EU Economic Law* (Edward Elgar Publishing 2019).

Tuominen, T., 'The "Financial Stability of the Euro Area as a Whole": Between Jurisdiction and Veridiction' (2019) *No Foundations: An Interdisciplinary Journal of Law and Justice* 17, 161–182.

Tuominen, T., 'Reconceptualizing the Primacy–Supremacy Debate in EU Law' (2020) *Legal Issues of Economic Integration* 47(3), 245–265.

Tuori, K., *Critical Legal Positivism* (Ashgate 2002).

Tuori, K., *Ratio and Voluntas: The Tension Between Reason and Will in Law* (Ashgate 2010).

Tuori, K., 'The Many Constitutions of Europe' in K. Tuori and S. Sankari (eds), *The Many Constitutions of Europe* (Ashgate 2010).

Tuori, K., *European Constitutionalism* (Cambridge University Press 2015).

Tuori, K. and K. Tuori, *The Eurozone Crisis: A Constitutional Analysis* (Cambridge University Press 2014).

Underhill, G., 'The Political Economy of (eventual) Banking Union' in T. Beck (ed.), *Banking Union for Europe: Risks and Challenges* (Centre for Economic Policy Research (CEPR) 2012).

Ungern-Sternberg, A. von, 'German Federal Constitutional Court Parliaments — fig leaf or heartbeat of democracy? Judgment of 7 September 2011, Euro rescue package 1' (2012) *European Constitutional Law Review* 8(2), 304–322.

Vandamme, T., 'EU Directives and Multi-Level Governance: Can Lessons Be Drawn from Cooperative Federalism?' (2014) *Maastricht Journal of European and Comparative Law* 21(2), 341–358.

Varoufakis, Y., *Austerity* (Random House 2018).

Verdun, A., 'A Historical Institutionalist Explanation of the EU's Responses to the Euro Area Financial Crisis' (2015) *Journal of European Public Policy* 22(2), 219–237.

Véron, N., *Europe's Radical Banking Union* (Bruegel 2015).

Vilpišauskas, R., 'Eurozone Crisis and European Integration: Functional Spillover, Political Spillback?' (2013) *Journal of European Integration* 35(3), 361–373.

Visser, M. de, *Constitutional Review in Europe: A Comparative Analysis* (Hart Publishing 2014).

Waldron, J., 'The Core of the Case Against Judicial Review' (2006) *The Yale Law Journal* 115(6), 1346–1406.

Walker, N., 'European Constitutionalism and European Integration' (1996) *Public Law*, 266–290.

Walker, N., 'Flexibility within a Metaconstitutional Frame: Reflections on the Future of Legal Authority in Europe' in G. de Búrca and J. Scott (eds), *Constitutional Change in the EU: From Uniformity to Flexibility?* (Hart Publishing 2000).

Walker, N., 'The Idea of Constitutional Pluralism' (2002) *Modern Law Review* 65(3), 317–359.

Walker, N. (ed.), *Sovereignty in Transition* (Hart Publishing 2003).

Walker, N., 'Late Sovereignty in the European Union' in N. Walker (ed.), *Sovereignty in Transition* (Hart Publishing 2003).

Walker, N., 'Postnational Constitutionalism and the Problem of Translation' in J. Weiler and M. Wind (eds), *European Constitutionalism Beyond the State* (Cambridge University Press 2003).

Walker, N., 'Europe's Constitutional Momentum and the Search for Polity Legitimacy' (2005) *International Journal of Constitutional Law* 3(2–3), 211–238.

Walker, N., 'Legal Theory and the European Union: A 25th Anniversary Essay' (2005) *Oxford Journal of Legal Studies* 25(4), 581–601.

Walker, N., 'European Constitutionalism in the State Constitutional Tradition' (2006) *Current Legal Problems* 59(1), 51–89.

Walker, N., 'Beyond Boundary Disputes and Basic Grids: Mapping the Global Disorder of Normative Orders' (2008) *International Journal of Constitutional Law* 6(3–4), 373–396.

Walker, N., 'Taking Constitutionalism Beyond the State' (2008) *Political Studies* 56(3), 519–543.

Walker, N., 'Constitutionalism and Pluralism in Global Context' in M. Avbelj and J. Komárek (eds), *Constitutional Pluralism in the European Union and Beyond* (Hart Publishing 2012).

Walker, N., 'The Philosophy of European Union Law' in A. Arnull and D. Chalmers (eds), *The Oxford Handbook of European Union Law* (Oxford University Press 2015).

Walker, N., 'Constitutional Pluralism Revisited' (2016) *European Law Journal* 22(3), 333–355.

Weiler, J., 'The Community System: The Dual Character of Supranationalism' (1981) *Yearbook of European Law* 1(1), 267–306.

Weiler, J., 'The Transformation of Europe' (1991) *Yale Law Journal* 100(8), 2403–2483.

Weiler, J., *The Constitution of Europe: 'Do the new clothes have an emperor?' and other essays on European integration* (Cambridge University Press 1999).

Weiler, J., 'Prologue: Global and Pluralist Constitutionalism – Some Doubts' in G. de Búrca and J. Weiler (eds), *The Worlds of European Constitutionalism* (Cambridge University Press 2012).

Wendel, M., 'Judicial Restraint and the Return to Openness: The Decision of the German Federal Constitutional Court on the ESM and the Fiscal Treaty of 12 September 2012' (2013) *German Law Journal* 14(1), 21–52.

Wendel, M., 'Exceeding Judicial Competence in the Name of Democracy: The German Federal Constitutional Court's OMT Reference' (2014) *European Constitutional Law Review* 10(2), 263–307.

Wilkinson, M., 'Economic Messianism and Constitutional Power in a "German Europe": All Courts are Equal, but Some Courts are More Equal than Others', *LSE Law, Society and Economy Working Papers* 26/2014 (2014).

Witte, B. de, 'Direct Effect, Primacy, and the Nature of the Legal Order' in P. Craig and G. de Búrca (eds), *The Evolution of EU Law* (2nd edn, Oxford University Press 2011).

Witte, B. de, 'Using International Law in the Euro Crisis: Causes and Consequences' (2013) *ARENA Working Paper* 4, 1–23.

Witte, B. de, 'Euro-Crisis Responses and the EU Legal Order: Increased Institutional Variation or Constitutional Mutation?' (2015) *European Constitutional Law Review* 11(3), 434–457.

Witte, B. de, 'The Preliminary Ruling Dialogue: Three Types of Questions Posed by National Courts' in B. de Witte et al (eds), *National Courts and EU Law: New Issues, Theories and Methods* (Edward Elgar Publishing 2016).

Witte, B. de and T. Beukers, 'The Court of Justice Approves the Creation of the European Stability Mechanism outside the EU Legal Order: Pringle' (2013) *Common Market Law Review* 50(3), 805–848.

Zavvos, G. S. and S. Kaltsouni, 'The Single Resolution Mechanism in the European Banking Union: Legal Foundation, Governance Structure and Financing' in M. Haentjens and B. Wessels (eds), *Research Handbook on Crisis Management in the Banking Sector* (Edward Elgar Publishing 2015).

Zbíral, R., 'A Legal Revolution or Negligible Episode? Court of Justice Decision Proclaimed Ultra Vires' (2012) *Common Market Law Review* 49(4), 1475–1491.

Index